ALSO BY NICHOLAS D. KRISTOF

With Sheryl WuDunn

Tightrope:
Americans Reaching for Hope

A Path Appears:
Transforming Lives, Creating Opportunity

Half the Sky:
Turning Oppression into Opportunity
for Women Worldwide

Thunder from the East:
Portrait of a Rising Asia

China Wakes:
The Struggle for the Soul of a Rising China

Chasing Hope

Chasing Hope

A Reporter's Life

Nicholas D. Kristof

ALFRED A. KNOPF
New York
2024

Grateful acknowledgment is made to the following for permission
to reprint previously published material:

Ralph Blumenthal: "Editing a Story."
Reprinted by permission of Ralph Blumenthal.
The New York Times Company: Excerpts from "The Day After"
by Nicholas Kristof, copyright © 2002 by The New York Times Company;
"An Open Letter From Dylan Farrow" by Dylan Farrow, copyright © 2014
by The New York Times Company; and "Is Donald Trump a Racist?"
by Nicholas Kristof, copyright © 2016 by The New York Times Company.
Reprinted by permission of The New York Times Company.

Photos are from the author's collection unless otherwise noted.

Library of Congress Cataloging-in-Publication Data
Names: Kristof, Nicholas D., [date] author.
Title: Chasing hope : a reporter's life / Nicholas D. Kristof.
Description: New York : Alfred A. Knopf, 2024. |
"This is a Borzoi Book published by Alfred A. Knopf."
Identifiers: LCCN 2023012344 (print) | LCCN 2023012345 (ebook) |
ISBN 9780593536568 (hardcover) | ISBN 9780593536575 (ebook)
Subjects: LCSH: Kristof, Nicholas D., [date] | Journalists—
United States—Biography. | Journalism—United States.
Classification: LCC PN4874.K727 A3 2024 (print) |
LCC PN4874.K727 (ebook) | DDC 071.3092 [B]—dc23/eng/20230830
LC record available at https://lccn.loc.gov/2023012344
LC ebook record available at https://lccn.loc.gov/2023012345

Jacket photograph of the author on the Pacific Crest Trail
in northern Washington State by Caroline Kristof
Jacket design by Chip Kidd

Manufactured in the United States of America
First Edition

For my wife, Sheryl WuDunn,
and for our children—
Gregory, Geoffrey and Caroline—
because the burden falls hardest on family
when a journalist covers wars, riots and epidemics,
sneaks past checkpoints to cover genocide
or crashes in a plane in Congo.
When it came to getting in trouble,
I was an incorrigible recidivist,
but Sheryl's love always shone through her exasperation.
My previous books were written by the two of us together,
so I finally have the chance to show appreciation
and dedicate a book to her.

Journalism is the graduate school from which you never graduate.

—PETE HAMILL

Journalism will kill you, but it will keep you alive while you're at it.

—HORACE GREELEY

Hope is being able to see that there is light despite all of the darkness.

—DESMOND TUTU

Do not go where the path may lead; go instead where there is no path and leave a trail.

—ATTRIBUTED TO RALPH WALDO EMERSON

Contents

Author's Note

Any full name in this book is a real one. In some cases, I use a first name alone to protect a person's privacy; most are real, but a few are pseudonyms.

Sometimes I quote dialogue from decades ago. Occasionally I had contemporaneous notes or writings that provided precise words quoted, but in most cases I had to re-create conversations from my memory and the memory of others involved. In such cases, I hope the thrust of the dialogue is correct, but the quotations are unlikely to be exact. I also know well from my own reporting career how memory plays tricks on us, and I expect mistakes have crept into this memoir. I am solely responsible for any errors, and this account is, like my life, incomplete and imperfect.

Chasing Hope

1

A Plane Crash

Journalism is an act of hope. What impels reporters forward is our faith that if we get the story and shine a light in the darkness, the public will respond and change will come. That's why reporters rush toward gunfire, talk their way into drug dens, scramble toward riots and, in my case right now, take a small plane into the heart of the Congo civil war.

Our adventures are not always well executed, however, and at the moment, I'm not brimming with hope. The plane is in trouble, and I'm petrified, thinking: *So this is how I die.* Not in old age, inconsolable grandchildren at my bedside on the family farm in Oregon, with the farm dogs giving up gopher-hunting to come inside and nuzzle their goodbyes. No, my end is looming far from family in a fiery plane crash in the vast Congo rainforest.

I'm in a chartered plane with other journalists. Our small plane is sputtering, the pilot steadily losing control. It looks as if my ashes won't be scattered on the farm and on the Pacific Crest Trail, as I had hoped, but rather my remains will mingle with termite mounds in a jungle on the other side of the world. A baboon or okapi may notice, but no one else will.

Sheryl WuDunn, my wife, will get a call from Bill Keller, the *New York Times* foreign editor, saying that my plane is missing in a rebel-held part of Zaire and that everything is being done to locate the plane:

It's probably just a forced landing on a remote airstrip, or maybe the rebel army has kidnapped the plane and passengers for ransom. Then there will be air searches that prove unsuccessful, for it's easier to find a flea in a baobab tree than a downed plane in the endless Congo basin.

This is not what I want to be worrying about. I'm a perpetual optimist, so I conjure ways in which I won't perish. Maybe the plane will reach a road or airstrip to land on. Or maybe a meadow will abruptly appear in the jungle and the pilot will somehow bring the plane down even without its landing gear.

I know I'm kidding myself. I've seen the terrain: an endless expanse of forest. There's no place to land. The plane is damaged and coming down. Time is almost up.

It's 1997, I'm the absentee Tokyo bureau chief of *The New York Times*, and I've spent more than a decade as a *Times* foreign correspondent, in Hong Kong, China and Japan. But now, as I huddle over my knees in the "brace position," staring down at my white sneakers with my clammy hands clasped on the back of my head, as our propeller plane wobbles downward toward a crash, as the pilot struggles with the instruments of a plane that has lost its hydraulic lines so that he can't even dump fuel, as I prepare for the impact and wonder if I will be torn apart by the crash or incinerated in the subsequent fire, or both, I keep thinking: It was not supposed to end this way.

The idea had been to cover other people's tragedies, not to become one. The plan had been to write a series of articles that might move hearts and policymakers. But we already have killed an innocent man, and his body is dangling from our plane as an emblem of shame. Somehow I've not only wandered into a Graham Greene novel, but I've become the well-meaning Quiet American who makes everything worse. I'm mortified as well as terrified.

I can feel us descending, but since I can't see anything more than my sneakers, I have no idea when the last moment will come. Will we hit in a second or a minute or ten minutes? Will I survive in good enough condition to wrestle the door open and help the injured out before the plane bursts into flames?

The rainforest below is vast. The Congo basin is Africa's largest rainforest, four times the size of California, Oregon and Washington combined. Its vastness turns humans into specks, a tiny part of a complex natural order. The basin is home to gorillas, elephants, bonobos, okapi, chimpanzees, crocodiles and twenty-foot pythons. The rainforest stretches into the horizon, largely unbroken by roads or signs of habitation. You look down through the airplane window and for long periods see no sign of humans, just an endless landscape of trees, hills and an occasional blue creek or river. It's mesmerizing and humbling to see so vast an expanse in which humans have left so little mark.

My satellite phone! It's in my pack. Maybe I could use it to go online and hurriedly buy more life insurance? No. I dismiss the thought. The plane windows are too thick to allow a signal. My last purchase will not be life insurance.

MY DREAM SINCE I was a kid was to be a journalist flying into civil wars, covering humanitarian catastrophes, mobilizing a response. It had seemed so glamorous. In high school in rural Oregon, I had read about foreign correspondents with awe, and seen journalists on television shows like *Washington Week in Review*. I read globe-trotting correspondents in the *Times*, and in university I invited dates to watch movies about foreign correspondents like *The Killing Fields* and *The Year of Living Dangerously*. (My dates weren't always impressed by my movie choices.)

I had wanted that life quite fiercely, and I had toiled and sacrificed to achieve my journalistic dreams. I had spent thirteen years at *The New York Times*, mostly in the rarified world of the overseas bureau chief. I had won a Pulitzer and other prizes. And although it seemed too earnest to talk about in the cynical world of a newsroom, I was also engaged in another life task that remained incomplete: I hoped to pay forward the debt my family owed to the diplomats and journalists who rescued my dad in the aftermath of World War II. They took risks. They breached convention. They skirted boundaries. I owe them my existence.

Over the years I had become aware of the downsides of the career of a foreign correspondent. This was a life that split up marriages. It could be unfair to kids and sometimes orphaned them. I had lost a good friend, a *Times* colleague named Nathaniel Nash, to a plane crash in the aftermath of the Bosnian war, and he had left behind his wife and an eight-year-old son and twin five-year-old daughters. Nathaniel loved his family and was prudent, but he boarded a government plane carrying Secretary of Commerce Ron Brown and died along with everyone else aboard when their plane slammed into a hillside in Croatia.

How does a journalist balance the imperative of covering global crises with the imperative to be there for family members? Sheryl didn't think I appreciated the risks, and now she was proven right.

MY OFFICE IS in Tokyo, one of the most comfortable *Times* bureaus, located in Tsukiji, right next to the fish market and some of the freshest sushi in the world. I should be there with Sheryl now, ordering a *negitoro don* and bathing it in so much soy sauce that our Japanese colleagues grimace. This should be my year of living luxuriously, not dangerously. But my whole career has been a restless one, steering clear of the White House and prestigious assignments in Europe, while gravitating to conflict and crises—just like the one my father had survived. I want to be in the thick of it. So *Times* editors let me escape the safety and comfort of Japan to fly into mass starvation and a civil war in Zaire, the tottering nation soon to recover its earlier name of Democratic Republic of Congo.

I chose a different branch of journalism from the pack. Some reporters love roving the halls of Congress and asking pointed questions at press conferences. That's important, but it's not me. I'm impatient with journalism as stenography, and I don't want to spend my life scribbling notes at news conferences. I'm pursuing change. I want to get on scene and figure out for myself what is happening. I want to invest journalism with purpose and harness it to a cause larger than ourselves. I envision journalism not just as a technical craft but as one with an ethical mission: a better world.

That's risky, I know. It can backfire and undermine journalistic credibility, for one journalist's moral purpose is another's megalomaniacal crusade. There's an arrogance in assuming any journalist has the answers or can help point to a solution. But kids are starving to death here in Congo; if telling those stories forcefully can summon aid to save children's lives, is that so awful?

Probably it was in China that I left the straight-and-narrow journalistic path and took the road less traveled. One milestone came when I saw the government there crush the Tiananmen democracy movement, massacre its people and arrest my friends. Another came when a Chinese dissident asked me to help him escape to America. More broadly, I came to see how writing about humanitarian crises could make lives better on a grand scale. Once I was aware of the power of that spotlight, it was difficult not to use it. But now, as I crouch in a propeller plane staring at my shoes, my mission-driven journalism isn't working out so well, and my stomach clenches at the thought of the effect of the plane crash on Sheryl and the kids.

Colleagues have always teased me about my luck in journalism: "You go somewhere, and a crisis breaks out before you leave the airport." Reporters said that with a touch of envy, for we dine uncomfortably on the misfortunes of humanity. Catastrophes had propelled my career forward in ways that felt unsettling: The world suffered, and I thrived. True to form, on this trip I had traveled somewhere and a crisis had arisen, but my luck seems to have disappeared. The basic rule of foreign correspondence is not only to get to the crisis but also to get back and file. Can I meet that test?

I'm on this airplane because the *Times* wanted to call attention to the rebellion and war in Congo, and so did I. But let's be honest: I was also drawn to a project with the allure of front-page stories. The United Nations Refugee Agency was a partner in this aim, for it wanted to call attention to a deadly refugee crisis in the center of the country. A young United Nations official, Filippo Grandi, was in charge and thought more news coverage would help galvanize resources to ease the refugee crisis. So Filippo, who would later head the refugee agency, chartered a Grumman G-159 Gulfstream plane to take reporters from Nairobi, Kenya, to Kisangani, in central Congo.

I was one of sixteen reporters who turned up at Nairobi's Wilson Airport on April 6, 1997, to board the twin-engine plane, which was thirty-two years old, more aged than some of the passengers. Dale, the pilot, was a good old boy from Oklahoma. He was a legend in East Africa: a superb pilot but also a cowboy. He had flown missions for the contras in Nicaragua and flown cargo into South Sudan for rebels there. Now he made a living flying people in and out of war zones.

Dale was a burly man and a big personality who filled a room and a cockpit. Old-timers said he had a big heart that led him to fly humanitarian missions, but he camouflaged it with swagger, cynicism and loud wisecracks, often inappropriate. He stood by the plane steps as we boarded in Nairobi, flirting with the women and cracking off-color jokes.

Beside me as we boarded was Steve Crowley, a *Times* photographer who was the opposite of a cowboy. Clean-cut, polite and charming, Steve was based in Washington, D.C., and normally wore suits to cover the president and Congress; he was more comfortable in the White House than in a war zone. Steve had asked for a field assignment abroad to broaden his experience, so the photo editor suggested he travel with me to cover the war in Congo.

After boarding, we rolled down the runway in Nairobi with complete inattention to seat belts, took off and flew uneventfully toward our first stop, Goma in eastern Congo. The cockpit doors were open, and as we descended toward the Goma landing strip, I saw something disconcerting: a crowd of perhaps five hundred people gathered directly in front of us on the runway.

"You can't land in that crowd!" someone yelled to Dale as the plane rushed toward the ground.

"Oh, they do this all the time," he shouted back. "Last minute, they'll move out of the way."

I held my breath as the plane descended, but Dale was right—the crowd parted like the Red Sea, as people laughingly ran aside at the last possible moment, waving joyfully. Dale seemed to know what he was doing after all.

After we disembarked in Goma, the rebels who occupied the airport seized our passports. After some negotiation, they agreed to return them upon payment of a $100-a-person "fee"—which immediately disappeared into the rebel leader's pocket.

"I need a receipt," I told him in French. "Anything more than $25, I need a receipt to get reimbursed."

"A receipt?" He looked blank.

"Wait a moment." I scribbled on a page in my reporter's notebook: *Received $100 from Nicholas Kristof for passport processing in Congo.* "Just sign below," I said. He squinted at it, not understanding the English but not concerned either, and he signed it. That would keep the *Times* accountants happy.

In Goma, we visited the rebel headquarters and tried unsuccessfully to get a laissez-passer document that would get us through rebel checkpoints. The rebels were set up to fire grenades at government trucks but not to deal with journalists. After a few hours, we reboarded the plane and Dale took it to the end of the runway, turned around and paused for a few minutes while preparing to take off. Steve Crowley stood up and walked over to the cockpit to look at the mass of people in front of the plane and take a few photos. He returned, shaken.

"Oh, my God," Steve told me as he plunked down in the seat next to me. "The crowd has gathered again. They're playing chicken with the aircraft."

I got up and walked a few feet forward to the cockpit. "You sure they'll move out of the way when we take off?" I asked Dale. "There are more by the moment."

"No problem," Dale shouted over his shoulder to us. "They'll run to the side at the last minute." He revved the engines.

I took my seat again, too acquiescent, and Dale sent the plane charging forward at the crowd. I looked ahead through the cockpit window, and again, incredibly, Dale was right—the crowd parted, laughing and waving—and then he wasn't. One man remained standing still as the rest of the crowd ran aside. He was in his fifties, lean and frail, bald, with a long face, and he was staring in puzzlement at us. I'll never forget that look. He evidently had joined the crowd but had no idea

A crowd begins to gather on the airstrip in Goma in front of our plane, a few minutes before we take off. Dale is on the left, and his co-pilot is on the right.

what was going on. The man didn't realize that this was a game of chicken, or maybe he was blind from cataracts or trachoma, glaucoma or river blindness; there are so many ways to become blind in central Africa. The man stood, stolid, a calm pillar in a sea of movement as our plane hurtled toward him.

I dug my hands into my thighs. Dale pulled the nose of the plane up, trying to get over the man, but there wasn't time. He got the plane three feet off the ground and then we all felt the collision as the right wheel assembly slammed into the man at ninety miles per hour, killing him instantly and collapsing the landing gear. The plane shuddered, and in the hands of a less skilled pilot we would have crashed at that moment. But Dale managed to steady the plane and gain altitude.

Steve, who was sitting next to me by the window, pointed wordlessly. There was the man's body six feet away through the window, wrapped around the right landing gear. He was motionless and obviously dead.

Inside the plane, we were stunned into silence.

"Can you land again?" someone finally asked Dale.

"I can't land here," Dale replied, his bluster gone, his Oklahoma accent thicker. "We just killed a man here. If we landed here, they might beat us all to death. I've got to find another place to land."

Dale turned around and stood up, framed in the cockpit door, as his Kenyan co-pilot stayed at the controls. Dale's face was drained of color as he explained that the hydraulic lines had snapped, and without hydraulic fluid he couldn't move flaps or other crucial controls.

"We're going to have to crash-land," Dale bellowed, now with urgency. "The right landing gear is smashed. Get your seat belts on. You know the brace position?"

He looked around at us. We nodded, but someone must have looked uncertain, because he explained: "Bend over with your head between your knees and your hands over your head. You want to make sure you protect your head, and you don't want to slam into the seat in front of you."

We nodded again. Aside from Steve and me, our group included a camerawoman from CNN, a reporter from Agence France-Presse and a handful of well-established freelancers. Nobody managed to say anything. We were afraid to ask what we were really thinking: *What happens when you try to land in a forest? What are our chances? Will we make it?*

"Get in the brace position when I tell you to," Dale added curtly. "I'm going to see what I can do." He turned and assumed his captain's seat in the cockpit. The Kenyan was silent and concentrating on the controls. Steve was cursing himself under his breath. "What a stupid way to die," he muttered. "I'm not afraid of dying, but I can't believe I'm going to put my family through this."

I was feigning calm, as if I'd been in dozens of plane crashes. I scribbled notes in my reporter's notebook about the unfolding catastrophe, to give myself something to do and to follow the perpetual journalistic instinct to bear witness to death and destruction. Even my own.

For me, taking notes was calming. I thought of Sheryl and my boys. Gregory had just turned five, so he would remember me. But Geoffrey? His third birthday would be next month. Would his earliest memory be his dad's funeral?

Quick—should I write Sheryl and the boys a farewell note? Perhaps a note would comfort Sheryl, or soothe her distress over my finally managing to kill myself despite all her warnings. Or perhaps I should write a note to my unborn daughter, a self-introduction to the father she would never know. I turned to a blank page and thought for a few moments, my pen poised over my notebook. My fingers didn't move. It was proving difficult to think of something suitably loving, witty and pithy when I was hurtling toward my death. I was thinking: *What am I doing here?*

WE'RE RACONTEURS, journalists are, so when we get together at a hotel bar, idly wondering what we can plausibly expense, we share stories. That's what any memoir does, and it's what I'm doing here, but this is also the tale of how journalism has been transformed over the last half century—ever since *The Carlton-Yamhill Review* published my first article when I was in eighth grade in 1973.

When I joined the *Times* in 1984, it wasn't all that different from the *Times* of the 1940s. But on my watch, journalism changed more than in any period since, well, perhaps since Gutenberg. I now sometimes file by satellite phone and contribute not just articles but also videos, podcasts, newsletters, Facebook posts. Public attitudes toward journalists have changed, too. I now have a drawer for death threats, so the police can sort through them if I'm found with a knife in my back. I see people cheerfully wearing T-shirts reading "Rope. Tree. Journalist. Some Assembly Required."

I try to smile at those shirts, but my heart breaks. When you've lost colleagues to violence and feared death yourself at the hands of mobs, your sense of humor about lynching is strained.

We in the news business have made countless mistakes and too often been lapdogs rather than watchdogs, but this memoir is still a love letter to journalism. We are sometimes cynical, but journalism itself should never be. Its fuel is a sense of mission, a feeling of responsibility to record history on the run, a determination to get out and talk to people and uncover the truth. Even, as I said, to bring about change. That's what drew Steve Crowley and me to Congo in 1997.

The country was unraveling into a civil war and mass atrocities that would ultimately claim 5 million lives, according to mortality studies sponsored by the International Rescue Committee. That's more than three times the number of lives lost in all the wars in American history, going back to the Revolutionary War. It's the most lethal conflict since World War II. The Congo deaths, in a much smaller country than America, were mostly of civilians, often of children dying of hunger or disease as collateral damage, but also included massacres, mutilation and pillage. Women were raped, and men were castrated. Those Congolese, some of them my friends, are courageous people whose suffering too often went unnoticed—and precisely because the suffering went unnoticed, it was allowed to persist. As journalists, we don't pack guns but we do fight back at mass murder with our own weapon, the craft of storytelling. And while journalism has changed so much over the last few decades, storytelling is fundamentally the same today as in the time of the Bible. Maybe it seems a lopsided battle, taking on gunmen with keyboards, but words can have impact. That's why dictators and warlords murder dozens of journalists each year: They fear us, and they're right to do so.

A central job of a journalist is to get people to care about some problem that may seem remote. How do we engage readers so that a crisis in Congo or Yemen feels tangible enough to inspire them to write to a member of Congress? How do we make palpable the climate change that threatens the planet?

A first step is getting there: boarding dubious planes, talking one's way through checkpoints, fighting off bedbugs, shaking hands with gunmen so they'll be less likely to shoot you. Reporting rests on this faith that truthfully capturing the reality on the ground makes a difference and serves a higher purpose. Scratch a cynical journalist and an idealist bleeds. What draws us into this business certainly isn't money or family-friendly hours but in part some notion that journalism upholds the public interest.

So I'm writing this book not so much because of *my* stories but because I believe in *our* journalism. I hope to remind people of the power—and responsibility—that news organizations have not just to produce quarterly earnings but also to shine a light on what can be changed in the world, even as some people profit from the darkness.

Sure, I cringe when I turn on the television and see commentators pontificate or manipulate the public. Our ranks have encompassed charlatans and hate-mongers, including Father Coughlin, Rush Limbaugh, Bill O'Reilly, Sean Hannity and Tucker Carlson. All this is amplified today: Good journalism has never been so outstanding as it is today, and yellow journalism has rarely been so vile. Yet for all journalism's faults, for all the disrespect directed at it these days, I'd still argue that journalism is a calling with purpose and meaning. We tilt at windmills for a reason, and occasionally we hit something.

Journalism is an act of hope. It rests on the conviction that excavating the truth makes a difference, that sunlight is a disinfectant for government, that reporting can be a battering ram on behalf of people suffering injustice. I've lost friends because they stood up to dictators and fought to uncover wrenching truths—in Syria, Iraq, Turkey, Somalia and elsewhere. Other friends have been imprisoned or tortured. A Kurdish journalist I know has still not recovered after he was imprisoned for his writing and his wife was brought in and raped in front of him. I honor these journalists, and I know their work made a difference. I've seen how accountability journalism can get officials jailed while extricating innocent people from prison. The spotlight of journalism can raise the cost of torture, war and genocide and save vast numbers of lives. Since my late friends can't tell their stories, let me try to share something of this crazy life, where we hear gunfire and sometimes rush toward it.

It may seem strange that a journalist should emerge from a career covering war, genocide, sex trafficking and addiction talking brightly about hope. But the truth is that while my reporting has shown me the human capacity for evil, it has underscored even more the human potential to intercede, to solve our problems and to bend that arc of the moral universe toward justice. It has also been a privilege to get to know extraordinary figures who make me feel better about humanity. I've interviewed warlords and terrorists, but the people who have left the deepest impression are the saints who give their all to make this a better world. They remind us that when we are tested, humans are capable of unimaginable courage, strength, resilience and goodness. Archbishop Desmond Tutu's ability to laugh, in the face of all the evil he confronted, lives in my heart; it is a wild, infectious, glorious cackle, often self-mocking, and it both warms me and reminds me that we humans, at our best, constitute a work of art.

When a columnist interviews such heroes, or when a local reporter covers a city council meeting for a weekly newspaper, we mostly take notes in a reporter's notebook. You've probably seen these notebooks. Journalists all across America use them: They're four inches by eight inches, half the size of a stenographer's pad. They fit into a back pocket or a jacket pocket; mine lives in my left hip pocket. Reporter's notebooks are convenient because they have plenty of room for notes but

Sharing a joke with Desmond Tutu during a panel discussion.
Credit: American Academy of Achievement.

are unobtrusive and can be hidden quickly if you run into an angry mob. It was such a notebook that was in my hands in the plane over Congo.

These notebooks date to the reporter Claude Sitton, a son of the South who covered the civil rights movement for the *Times*. Brave, pathbreaking reporters like Sitton and many others, white and Black alike, risked their lives to convey the reality of Jim Crow to the public, and their work had a far-reaching impact. "The civil rights movement would have been like a bird without wings if it hadn't been for the news media," said Representative John Lewis, the civil rights leader whose skull was fractured while leading the march in Selma in 1965. One way of judging the importance of news coverage, Lewis noted, was that white racists first beat and incapacitated the reporters and only then attacked Black leaders.

Sitton wasn't partisan and he wasn't a crusader. He was utterly committed to accuracy and never toned down a story because it was inconvenient or didn't mesh with his larger narrative. Yet he did have a larger concern for justice and refused to be a loudspeaker for southern politicians seeking to mislead the American public.

As the civil rights movement began, journalists typically carried stenographer notebooks. White racists would club those carrying such notebooks. So Sitton cut stenographer notebooks in half the long way, so that he could hide one in his pocket. Later he found a stationery company in Richmond, Virginia, willing to make these narrow notebooks, and he bought a case of them and shared them with friends on the front lines. Their use gradually spread through the journalist ranks. For a time they were called Claude Sitton Notebooks. When we use them, we honor Sitton's commitment to go to hell and back to get the truth. Because that is what we do.

A FRENCH JOURNALIST behind me in the plane suddenly howled in alarm. "My seat doesn't have a seat belt," he shouted.

"Then lock yourself in the toilet in back," Dale yelled back through the open cockpit door. "That way you won't be thrown around."

The reporter started to walk back to the toilet but then stopped.

"No!" he wailed. "I don't want my body found with my head in the toilet. That would be too undignified!" There was a ripple of nervous laughter. It was a release—we were all eager for distraction—and the Frenchman tried wedging himself on the floor in front of his seat.

"Look at the plane door and the lever to pull to open it," I said to Steve. "Study how it opens. There could be a fire. We may have to get out quick."

Steve nodded. He looked stricken.

"Look," Steve said, pointing out the window at the body. "Something's gone."

The lower half of the dead man's body, which had been swinging in the air, had dropped off.

In the cockpit, Dale was wrestling with the plane, trying to direct it even as the controls didn't work properly.

"It's time," Dale shouted over his shoulder. "We're coming down. Get in the brace position."

I tucked my reporter's notebook in my hip pocket so it wouldn't fly around. "You okay?" I asked Steve.

He nodded and managed a weak smile. He had adjusted a film camera and a digital camera, and both were sitting on his lap. You could almost see him thinking: *What's the appropriate exposure for a fireball?*

"You?" he asked.

I shrugged and pretended that this was just a typical day in the life of a foreign correspondent. We tightened our seat belts and leaned forward in the brace position. And waited.

A nanosecond later I feel gossamer threads lifting my hopes again. It's the irrepressible optimism of a family of survivors who work to maximize odds. I know that I'm lucky to be in an aisle seat near the door, and I'm ready to lunge toward it. I've studied the door release so closely that I could manage it in the dark if needed. My dad survived against all odds, and he and my mom raised me to surmount barriers.

So, somehow, as the small plane is plummeting into the central African jungle, I still am chasing hope.

2

Overthrowing the Patriarchy,
in Eighth Grade

My journalism career was born at the west end of Yamhill Grade School, where the big kids ruled. The school was a long, one-story, red-brick building with first grade at the east end and rowdy seventh- and eighth-graders at the west end. At the beginning of my eighth-grade year, some of my classmates decided that Yamhill Grade School should have a school newspaper, and they held an organizational meeting after school. I didn't go, because at that point I wasn't so interested in newspaper work. The next morning my friend Brad Larsen hailed me in the hallway.

"We formed a newspaper," he said. "We all wanted to write for it, but no one wanted to be editor."

I shrugged, not particularly interested, and asked: "So who will be editor?"

Brad smiled craftily.

"You," he said. "We chose you as editor, because you weren't there to say no."

I suspect the English teacher, Michael McDonald, suggested the arrangement. He taught vocabulary and was extremely impressed that I knew the word "archipelago"; that seems to have been my qualification for editing a newspaper.

Actually, although McDonald and my classmates didn't know it, I did have experience in the newspaper world. When I was in kindergar-

ten, a family friend gave me a John Bull Printing Outfit, a toy printing system with movable type. My mother showed me how it worked:
You inserted the rubber capital letters on a block so as to spell words,
rolled it on an ink pad, then pressed it on paper. My first "newspaper"
covered an incident involving my best friend, Thomas, and his sister,
Margarita:

RECENTLY THOMAS GANN WENT TO SEE HIS
GRANDMOTHER. MAGARITA RODE A STINGRAY

BIKE SHE RODE THOMAS AND WHEN MARGARIT
STOPPED SHE SAID THOMAS JUMP OFF. THOMAS
DID AND FELL ON HIS NOZE.

My first journalism effort. Unfortunately, I neglected to recruit a copy editor.

That was the entirety of the newspaper, and Thomas and I went
door to door selling copies for two cents each. We were indignant that
when we showed our newspaper to potential customers, some would
read the entire newspaper and then refuse to buy it.

The injustice perhaps soured me on journalism until I got to Yamhill Grade School. My childhood before that was a bit of a blur, for my
parents were academics—my father a political scientist, my mother

I was a handful for my mom.

an art historian—and we bounced around when I was young from Chicago to New York City to Palo Alto to Waterloo, Canada. I didn't know where I was from.

My mother grew up around Chicago, where her family had lived for generations, while my father was Armenian. He was Polish. He was Romanian. I'll explain shortly, but suffice it to say that while his identity was complicated, this much was clear: He was a refugee. In 1952, my dad had been sponsored to come to the United States by a group in Oregon, and he fell in love with the state. While he left Oregon for graduate school, he was always plotting to return. In 1971, we made it. He took a pay cut to leave Waterloo and take a job at Portland State University, and my mom soon landed a professorship there as well. For $65,000 we purchased the world's most beautiful farm. It was nestled in the hills above Yamhill, where the Willamette Valley melts into the Coast Range. The farm had seventy-three acres of forest, cherry orchard, hay field and cattle pasture, plus a couple of ponds and a spring.

I was thrilled. After so much wandering—I had lived in nine homes my first twelve years—I loved the farm and felt a deep yearning to put down roots and find my community. Yamhill itself was then home to 540 people, with a single flashing red light, a general store, an agriculture feed store, a phone booth and four churches.

On my first full day at Yamhill Grade School, in seventh grade, I walked down the gravel road from our farm to the school bus stop two-thirds of a mile away. It was a blustery November day: dark, chilly and drizzling slightly but also achingly beautiful with shades of green so rich that Oregon should trademark them. I did not of course take an umbrella, because Oregonians scoff at umbrellas. We believe it only encourages rain.

It felt spooky walking down the hill through the forest, especially the lonely section that passed a spring and an abandoned homestead shack. Trees and dense foliage lined the narrow driveway, and I tried not to imagine cougars lying in the bushes, tails slowly waving, ready to pounce on their breakfast.

At the bottom of the hill I met my neighbors, also waiting for the No. 6 school bus.

"I'm Bobby," said a solid fifteen-year-old, three years older than me. "And this is Mike, my younger brother." Mike, who was nine, made a face, and Bobby pretended to swing at him.

"What's school like?" I asked after introducing myself.

Bobby shook his head dismissively. "I'm going to quit as soon as I turn sixteen," he said. "Then I'll join the marines like my dad did. He lied about his age to join the marines at sixteen during the Korean War and got shot twenty-two times!" He paused and we all nodded solemnly to acknowledge the magnificence of being so thoroughly perforated.

"He's okay now?" I asked.

"He's strong," Bobby said. "He works at the mill."

"You'll meet him," Mike burst in. "He can show you how to shoot like they do in the marines."

"We can go shooting," Bobby added enthusiastically. "I'll show you my guns. Much more fun than school. You're going deer hunting, right?"

"I don't know," I said.

Mike started jumping up and down, miming that he had a rifle. "Bam, bam, bam!" he said, firing wildly.

"Lots of deer around," Bobby said. "And some elk and bear. Sometimes a cougar."

"Umm, do the cougars ever bother humans?"

"I'll protect you," Mike shouted, pointing his imaginary rifle around. "Bam! Bam! Bam!"

"And I've just started a trapline that I'll show you," Bobby added. "I'm going to catch raccoons and other animals, skin them and sell the pelts. Some of the trapline is actually on your property."

"That might be a problem," I said hesitantly. "We have a dog. Wouldn't want her to get caught in a trap."

(I was actually thinking: *You put out steel leg traps for animals to get caught in! Is there anything more cruel?* One of my favorite books was *Rascal*, about a boy and his pet raccoon.)

"I'm going to get a trapline, too," Mike interjected with typical exuberance. "Then I'll have enough money to buy my own guns."

I needn't have worried much about Bobby's trapline, or Mike's ambitions to start one. Bobby moved his traps off our property so the dog wouldn't get caught, but he wasn't industrious about setting or checking the traps and soon grew bored of them. Mike never started a trapline. Bobby and Mike were always better at talking about how to make money than at earning it.

School Bus No. 6 arrived, we boarded, and as a new student I found myself a celebrity. Many of the kids at Yamhill Grade School had been there since first grade, making any new kid a curiosity. Questions were fired at me in a friendly way:

"You living up on the cherry orchard place?"

"What grade are you in?"

"You play football?"

"Or baseball?"

"How are you at basketball?"

"How are the deer up there? You seen bucks up there?"

"I heard there's a three-legged deer up there somewhere. Runs perfectly fine. Not sure what happened to it. Maybe someone shot its leg off."

"Can I go hunting in the woods there?"

"You seen Bigfoot yet? Billy Beard says Bigfoot lives up in those woods."

"I *know* Bigfoot is up there," the boy named Billy Beard interjected. "It's a fact."

"You're at the end of the road, right? Be careful when you go by

Collecting hay bales with my dad on the family farm. The farmhouse is in the background. The cherry orchard is below the house.

the McKoon place. Mrs. McKoon's crazy. She shot one of the Harringtons' cows."

"Where are you moving from?"

"How's fishing in your big pond? That great blue heron eating all the fish?"

Mike and Bobby helped answer the questions. Bobby was a bit shy, but Mike took pleasure in showing off his new neighbor. Once we got to Yamhill Grade School and walked inside, the seventh-grade boys took over the hospitality committee and were very welcoming—and very focused on how I would contribute as an athlete. Billy Beard took charge of me at recess and warned me about Bigfoot, the legendary ape-man of the Pacific Northwest, as he had me shoot baskets. He was appalled that I couldn't shoot a jump shot.

"Just like this," he said, and the ball would go swish. Then I'd try a jump shot and would miss by a mile. I felt my popularity crumbling.

Seventh grade had sixty students and two teachers. Math and science for seventh and eighth grade were taught by Richard Newby, a genial man who was very religious, very kind and deeply rooted in the community. Trying to teach science to seventh- and eighth-graders would test Job, but Newby never got angry or upset.

For a science teacher, his views of science were idiosyncratic. He

That's me as a student
at Yamhill Grade School,
victim of a dubious haircut
at home.

regularly showed us "science films" that came from a Bible supply house and taught us that Darwin was wrong and Creationism was right. One film argued that the story of the Creation propounded in Genesis was literally true, suggesting that the Earth was only thousands of years old, not 4.5 billion years old.

TO MY SURPRISE, I loved editing the new Yamhill Grade School newspaper. We put out issues on our own schedule, covering school news and including an editorial by me thundering against the Vietnam War. I was largely reflecting my parents' views, for they were liberals who closely followed the news. NPR was always playing in our house, and we were the only household in Yamhill that subscribed to *The New York Times*. It arrived by mail, a week late. I began reading the *Times* myself—gravitating to the features and to the columnists.

The school newspaper gig afforded me the opportunity to write for the local newspaper, *The Carlton-Yamhill Review*. I wasn't paid but was happy to be exploited. At fourteen, I gained my first professional byline, writing a story on deadline about the Yamhill sixth-grade class making a day trip to Seattle. And I experienced what most journalists know in our hearts is an attraction of the profession: the ego thrill of the byline.

To the discomfort of our principal, whose mild manner was belied by the paddle he kept in his office for disciplining students, I used the school newspaper as an instrument for editorial crusades. This also fit well with another new interest: girls. I thought maybe my newspaper role could help me win their hearts. And thus was my first journalism campaign born.

Yamhill Grade School had a rule that girls couldn't wear blue jeans, and this deeply annoyed them. No blue jeans to school in a farming community?

I penned a mocking editorial asking what Yamhill Grade School was afraid of. Was it something to do with the denim fabric? No, because girls were allowed to wear jeans so long as they weren't blue. Something with the blue dye in blue jeans? No, because girls were allowed to wear blue pants as long as they weren't denim. Aha, I concluded: The Yamhill Grade School administration must have engaged in research in chemistry to show that the combination of denim, blue dye and female flesh is toxic. I asked the administration to lay out this evidence—or let girls wear blue jeans like the rest of us.

Girls loved the editorial. The principal didn't like the snark but quietly tweaked the dress code to allow girls to wear blue jeans. Half the student body enjoyed a better quality of life as a result. The power of the press! My campaign had succeeded in its three aims: 1. Impress girls. 2. Give me something to talk about with girls. 3. Overthrow the patriarchy.

3

A Family of Spies

A tortuous family history helped turn me into the kind of reporter I became. We Kristofs were spies, prisoners and refugees, and we were rescued by strangers. All this shaped me, so my story begins before I did.

My father grew up in a noble Armenian family in eastern Europe, in an area called Northern Bukovina, where the flag kept changing. It was successively overseen in the last few hundred years by the Ottoman Empire, Russia, Galicia, Austria-Hungary, Romania and the Soviet Union, and since 1991 it has been part of Ukraine. It was Austria-Hungary when my dad was born and Romania when he was growing up, and his was an idyllic childhood, with thousands of acres to roam—my father loved to hunt wild boar—and in place of school a team of French and German governesses, plus a Romanian tutor.

Our family is a reminder that identity can be complicated. When people heard my dad's accent and asked about his origins, he would say he was Romanian. To the same question, my father's sister would say she was Armenian. And my father's brother would say he was Polish. My uncle would phone and speak to my father in Polish; my aunt would call and speak to him in Romanian.

Although my grandfather was fully Armenian, no one in the family still spoke Armenian when my dad arrived on the scene. The main language in the house was Polish (my father's mother was a Pole from Lviv). Meanwhile, the language of the village was Ukrainian, the government language was Romanian and the cultural languages were French and German. Our family was Armenian Catholic, and my grandmother went to a Catholic girls school in Lviv so strict that girls weren't allowed to bathe naked; they had to wear a nightdress to protect themselves from themselves.

Even names were malleable: The Armenian family name was Khatchikian, the Polish version was Krzysztofowicz and the variant used in Romania was Kristofovici. There was a "Von" before it during Austria-Hungarian times to signify nobility, but much of the time, my dad went by his Polish name: Władysław Krzysztofowicz.

World War II interrupted the idyll and left the family heartsick. Nazi Germany and the Soviet Union were fighting each other in Northern Bukovina, and both sides slaughtered civilians. My family regarded both the Nazis and the Soviets as barbarians. One of my relatives was a Polish army officer who was among some 22,000 Poles murdered by the Soviets in the Katyn Forest massacre in 1940. It was clear that if the Allies triumphed, the Soviets would seize our properties and perhaps wipe out our family. Yet our family had deep ties to Poland, and it was equally clear that if the Nazis won, much of Poland would be swallowed up and a long night would fall over Europe. My father's village, Karapchiv, had a large Jewish minority that would be at enormous risk if the Nazis prevailed.

Romania initially sided with the Nazis to fight off the Soviets, and my dad was drafted into the Romanian army. He was an interpreter and courier, and one day in 1942 he was housed near Stalingrad in the home of a Russian woman, an enemy. He saw that there was an empty bedroom but didn't want to impose on her—plus he was full of lice—so he rolled his sleeping bag out on the kitchen floor. "No, don't sleep here," she told him. "Come with me." She led him to the room of her absent son, and then she cooked dinner for my father.

"Why are you doing all this for me, when you're on the other side of this war?" my dad asked her.

"My son is fighting with the Soviet army," she replied. "I don't know where he is. But I hope that if he needs a bed, someone will be decent to him even though he is the enemy. I'm treating you as I would want my son to be treated." My father often spoke of that moment of humanity in a war mostly devoid of it. The Romanian army was poorly provisioned and suffered huge losses; one of my father's best friends was run over by a Soviet tank, and many others perished in other ways. In early 1943 he became very sick, was demobilized and returned home.

When I was growing up and other kids talked about their dads heroically battling the Nazis, I kept quiet. I didn't want to admit that my father had actually fought for a year on the same side as the Nazis. Then Romania switched sides in the war in 1944 to join the Allies, so my father had the distinction of being the only parent around who had been on both sides of World War II. But that didn't seem a good thing to brag about.

There was more to the story, though. The Krzysztofowicz family, facing the choice of supporting either the Nazis or the Soviets, chose neither and instead spied against the Nazis for the West. The family participated in the Bolek II Polish resistance network, which carried intelligence on the Nazis through Poland, into Romania and on to a secret radio transmitter in Bucharest run by a family member. The information was then broadcast to Ankara, which relayed it to the Polish government-in-exile in London.

Looking back, this was an extraordinary action by my family members. By helping to defeat the Nazis, they were increasing the likelihood that the Soviets would seize our family properties and perhaps send family members to Siberia. By spying on the Nazis, they were working against their interests as well as risking their lives. One of the heroes of the family was my cousin twice removed, Izabela Krzysztofowicz Jaruzelska, a sworn member of the Polish resistance. With her daughter and son-in-law she dared challenge the Nazis on their own turf in Nazi-occupied Poland. It was her son-in-law who ran the secret radio transmitter in Bucharest that the Bolek II network depended on.

The couriers working for the Bolek II network used our family properties as safehouses, and my grandfather supported one particularly brave courier, Aleksander Rybicki, who for years had been running perilous missions across borders from Poland. Rybicki was wounded several times and once escaped arrest by the Gestapo only by jumping off a moving train. His wife, Kazimieri, was arrested by the Nazis in 1942 and refused to disclose Aleksander's whereabouts; she was sent to Auschwitz and died in the gas chambers there. After Kazimieri's arrest, Aleksander Rybicki continued his courier missions, and my grandfather supported his work financially. Our family also told him that if he was ever arrested while crossing into Romania, he should claim to be a relative of ours.

That's what happened: In February 1943, Romanian border guards captured Rybicki as he crossed from Poland at night. He said he was fleeing Poland and was a relative of ours, and my aunt Litka went to the police station to see him. "I saw the terror in his eyes," she said, and she vouched for him, saying he was a cousin.

I was able to obtain from Romanian security archives the files on my family, including those from this incident. "Brave, admirable woman, Litka!" my translator, Gelu Trandafir, emailed me after going through the documents. "She must have been beautiful and influential, because she completely stunned the soldiers." I remember Aunt Litka as a somewhat reserved, even stodgy elderly woman, but the archives show that she buffaloed the soldiers into allowing her to speak privately with Rybicki and then walk out with his suitcase, which had a false bottom. In it were three important papers with intelligence eagerly sought by the Allies about the Nazi military in Poland and the Nazi concentration camps. Litka passed them along to her contacts in the resistance, and they were forwarded to the Allies in London.

The next day, however, the captain in charge of the border post sent troops to the area where Rybicki had been arrested. There was snow on the ground, so trampled snow showed the location—and in the daylight the guards found a flashlight with microfilms that Rybicki had thrown away when he was detained. This changed everything. It was now obvious that Rybicki was not a simple refugee but a spy supported by our family. Litka hurried off to the border post to negotiate with the captain, who laid the microfilms in front of her. She lit a cigarette. Her confession in the security archives records her next step: "I also lit him a cigarette, and seeking to take advantage of the captain's carelessness I set fire to the film."

That was Aunt Litka? I would never have imagined this from the elderly woman I remembered, who stood out mostly for her love of her dog and her horses. The archives record that the captain frantically extinguished the fire and then angrily demanded a large bribe. After extensive negotiations, my grandfather gave Aunt Litka $1,050 to bribe the captain, who burned the microfilms himself. The espionage seemed to have been hushed up. But the bribe was equivalent to many years' salary for the captain, who promptly quit and married—and it was too much money to conceal. People talked, and the Gestapo got wind that something was afoot.

In June 1943, two cars showed up at our family home and arrested Aunt Litka and my grandfather; two weeks later the authorities also arrested my father and uncle. They were all taken to Bucharest for interrogation, but Romanian officials had some wiggle room under the Germans and tried to protect my family. The Romanians let my family members get together to concoct alibis. Most important, the Romanians did not allow the Gestapo to interrogate and torture my father or other family members. Aunt Litka's statements in the security files are fascinating: At first, she says almost nothing, and then she steadily amends them as others in the spy ring make confessions that she must respond to. In the end, Aunt Litka was sent to a concentration camp in Romania, along with Rybicki, but she insisted (falsely) that no one else in the family was involved, so my father and grandfather and the others were released.

It was far worse for those arrested on the Polish side of the border, for the Germans were in direct control there. Cousin Izabela and her daughter, Teresa, were arrested and brutally tortured by the Gestapo, and then transported to Auschwitz, where Teresa was subjected to medical experiments. Izabela died in Auschwitz on December 9, 1943, but Teresa survived. (Teresa spoke of this period only once that I know of, saying that the Auschwitz doctors' experiments had left her feeling like minced meat.) Izabela's son-in-law, Boguslaw Horodynski, who ran the underground radio station in Romania, was imprisoned by the Romanians and the radio station shut down. Petru Groza, a future leader of Romania, was in the same prison as Horodynski and described him as "this wonderful man" who "calmly runs the entire collective establishment [of Polish prisoners], smoothes out internal divisions, presents the prison administration with their grievances; in brief, with fatherly care and authority, he steers the boat on which these shipwrecked sons of yesterday's Poland seek to reach the shore of their once homeland and happiness."

When Romania switched sides in the war in 1944, Aunt Litka was released along with Rybicki and Horodynski. But it was only a temporary reprieve. After the war ended, Rybicki was arrested by the Soviets in 1946 and sent to Siberian prison camps for the next decade, mostly toiling in mines. He finally made his way back to Poland, moved in with his mother and eked out an existence working for a museum until his death in 1983.

In the immediate postwar period, Horodynski lived in Romania and was recognized as a hero—too publicly. He attended a joyous celebration on Romania's National Day, December 1, 1945, to mark the end of the war, with most of the diplomatic corps attending. There the British ambassador made a catastrophic error. In the presence of the Soviet ambassador, he hailed Horodynski for his cooperation with the Allied forces and contributions to winning the war. The Soviets arrested Horodynski the next day, apparently distrusting anyone who had worked with the West.

Horodynski was sent to a labor camp in Kolyma, Siberia—which Solzhenitsyn described as the "pole of cold and cruelty" in the Soviet Gulag. Horodynski reportedly was forced to toil in a mercury mine. American and British officials asked Russia for mercy, and Romanian prime minister Petru Groza personally asked Stalin to intercede—to no avail. Horodynski's fate is uncertain. One version is that he died in the Gulag in 1952. The other is that he was released in 1956, probably in an amnesty by Premier Nikita Khrushchev, and died while trying to walk back to Poland.

So much heroism, so much tragedy. My father told me stories about these people as I was growing up, and how could I not be inspired by the courage of these relatives of mine confronting the Nazis and Soviets alike and struggling against impossible odds to keep the candle of freedom burning?

As a journalist, I've heard countless people apologize for autocrats. The left was soft on Mao, and the right has been soft on Putin. I hear: *You can't apply Western standards to other countries. Sure, mistakes have been made, but economic growth has been strong. This is a fractious country that needed a strong hand. What about Guantánamo and Abu Ghraib—the United States violates human rights, too. To make an omelet, you need to break some eggs.*

I hear those arguments, and I flinch—for Izabela was one of those broken eggs. Horodynski was sacrificed for the Soviet omelet. My father almost was shattered as well.

THE SOVIETS SEIZED Northern Bukovina in 1944, appropriating my family's lands and wealth. My dad fled south on horseback to Romania, taking back roads to evade capture by the Soviets or murder by Ukrainian nationalists. A xenophobic Ukrainian militia had already massacred thirty-four Jews in the village and attacked Armenians along with other landowners. They had buried alive my great-aunt and great-uncle, and now they killed our farm manager and his wife.

As my dad fled to southern Romania, the iron curtain was falling across Europe. Soviet soldiers were de facto kings, and one night in the Romanian town of Craiova, several drunken Russian soldiers amused themselves by clubbing my father and nearly killing him, leaving him bloodied in the street. For decades afterward, he would have nightmares about that beating, and as a child I would regularly wake in the dark to hear his screams and then my mother's frantic efforts to wake him.

"It's just a dream, it's just a dream," she would say.

The screams would fade, and he would sit up. "It was so real," he'd say. "I'm sorry."

In my eyes as a little boy, my father was strong and capable of anything, and it was difficult to imagine what could spark such terror in him. As I grew older I understood that my father's loathing of every form of despotism came from his family history, losing multiple relatives to German Nazis and also to Soviet Communists. If my columns show a passion for human rights, it's inherited as a Lamarckian trait.

My dad desperately wanted to escape the Communist bloc. It wasn't that he was particularly repressed, for he had a decent job in a forestry company. But he had nothing to look forward to. "I was ready to risk my life," he wrote in an essay. "I could not resign myself to live the rest of my life without any hope."

In September 1948, he swam the Danube River in the dead of night to escape Romania and landed, breathless and exhausted, on the Yugoslav side of the river. Yugoslavian police promptly arrested him and sent him to a concentration camp and later to an asbestos mine and finally to a forest logging camp. But he was the only educated person at the logging camp and soon was entrusted with helping run it. As a result, he was allowed to make a trip to Belgrade, where he slipped into the French Embassy.

My father met a newly arrived French diplomat, Robert Morisset. In diplomatic terms, my dad's imprisonment was none of France's business or Morisset's, for my father wasn't a French national or even a Yugoslav national. But Morisset saw a chance to do good: After listening to my dad's story, Morisset wrote to the Yugoslav authorities inquiring about my father's case. It was a short, simple inquiry, but it was enough to force some official to look up my father's file and add a notation that there was foreign government interest.

Morisset also gave my father a laissez-passer document with instructions to hide it while in Yugoslavia; it could antagonize local officials but would help him get a French visa if he ever managed to leave Yugoslavia. My dad sewed the document inside the lining of his jacket. Morisset also added my father's name to a French Foreign Ministry list of people who should get a French visa if they managed to escape Yugoslavia. I've long wondered why a French diplomat was so helpful to a refugee on leave from a prison camp who simply wandered in one day, although it couldn't have hurt that my father spoke beautiful French.

It turns out that Morisset helped many Romanian refugees in Yugoslavia. This was not his job, and indeed Morisset may have gone rogue to some extent. After the collapse of Communism, a Romanian publication called *Revista Memoria* ran a tribute to Morisset and noted:

> His diplomatic task was not to help such fugitives. On the contrary, the instructions of the French government were categorical, calling on him to refrain from getting involved in such issues, for that could strain diplomatic relations. Yet he didn't hesitate to do so, assuming a responsibility that far exceeded his mandate. He considered it a human obligation, one that transcended his temporary diplomatic responsibilities.

It seems that Morisset was able to save Romanian lives because on his own initiative he had obtained tuberculosis medicine to save the life of the eight-year-old daughter of a top security official in Yugoslavia. The official asked Morisset how he could repay him. Instead of asking for something personal or for some benefit for France, Morisset asked the official to free Romanian refugees from prison camps and allow them to travel to the West. The official asked for names. I'm guessing that my father's name was among those that Morisset provided.

So often since then I've heard Western diplomats say that they are distressed by human rights abuses but can't do much in a foreign country—and I think of Robert Morisset. He saw that France had values as well as interests, so he used his influence to protect helpless Romanian refugees. Morisset never became ambassador to a country—I wonder if his rule-bending held back his career—but he achieved something grander: He was a lifesaver, and his impact is etched in our family history. Morisset and his wife died childless, he in 1990 and she in 2000, and despite the help of the French diplomatic service I have been unable to find any relatives. But his life's work continues in mine, for I'm still trying to pay forward that debt we Kristofs owe to him and to France.

By January 1950, Yugoslavia was tired of its Romanian refugees. It let some go to the West, and it shot others. My dad was afraid that he was so useful to the logging camp as its prisoner/manager that he would be kept there forever. So he rolled the dice. He insisted on leaving the logging camp and returning to the concentration camp for Romanian refugees and taking his chances.

Probably because of Robert Morisset, his gamble paid off. After a few weeks in the camp, he was put in a closed boxcar with other refugees. They knew that if the train went east, they would probably be executed. If it went west, they might make it. The train finally jerked and began moving, and those aboard waited to see the next station to know in what direction they were moving. A boy looking through a crack in the wall finally saw the next station and shouted, "Going west!"

I still struggle to understand where my father's determination came from—to escape from Romania, to sneak into the French Embassy, to defy the Yugoslav authorities by leaving the logging camp and risking execution. My father was not by temperament a gambling man or risk-taker, yet he repeatedly risked his life. He framed it as an unwillingness to live a life that was not free, but I think another factor was his preternatural optimism that he could live by his wits, navigate an inhospitable terrain and manage to survive. My guess is that this confidence originated with a sense of agency that came with his early life of privilege, and he in turn transmitted to me that sense of self-efficacy and the optimism that goes with it.

My dad's refugee document, given to him after he escaped Yugoslavia.

My father made his way to Italy and then to France, but he couldn't get a work permit in Paris. He worried that neither he nor his yet unborn children would ever be fully accepted in France, and he began to search for a way to get to America. He attempted a sham marriage to an American woman, but that fell apart at the last moment. Then another path opened. Even without a permit, he had found unofficial work in Paris cleaning hotel rooms, and one of these belonged to Marge Cameron, a young woman from Portland, Oregon, who was working for the Marshall Plan. They grew friendly, and she convinced her parents and her parents' church, the First Presbyterian Church of Portland, to sponsor my father through Church World Service.

Getting an American visa was a challenge, but my father had a friend who knew two brothers who were prominent French journalists. Those two journalists were friends with the United States ambassador and harangued him into giving my father a visa. When I've tried to sort out what is appropriate for me to do as a journalist, I've thought of those two brothers. Helping my father get a visa wasn't part of their job and journalists should avoid asking for favors from official contacts—but it's also true that their kindness transformed our family's life.

So in September 1952 my father found himself on the *Marseille* as it entered New York Harbor. The weather was foul, but my father stood on deck to celebrate the beginning of his new life. An elderly lady from Boston was on deck as well and chatted with him.

"You see?" she asked, pointing to the Statue of Liberty. She tried to explain the poem on the base: "Give me your tired, your poor, your huddled masses yearning to breathe free . . ." My father shook his head. He didn't understand, but she wrote the words on a piece of paper and gave it to him.

"Keep it as a souvenir, young man," she said.

Then she corrected herself: "Young *American*!"

My father caught that—"Young American!"—and was astonished. He was a stateless refugee who could not speak English and had not yet set foot in the United States, yet he was already being called an American. My dad was not particularly sentimental, but he carried that piece of paper in his wallet for years. And although I'm not sentimental either, if it hadn't crumbled to dust, I'd be carrying it today.*

Upon my dad's arrival in Oregon, his sponsors couldn't really communicate with him, so that first afternoon they took him to a baseball game—permanently souring him on baseball. A few days later, they placed him in a job at a logging camp in Valsetz, miles from nowhere in the Oregon Coast Range. But it was a good union job that paid well, and loggers ate steak in the dining hall. Steak! America truly was a land of miracles!

With union wages and parsimonious spending, my father was able to save enough to attend Reed College. He rented a small room in a house near the campus, but after a time the landlady refunded the rent he had paid.

"I'm not going to charge a refugee," she said. "You need the money more than I do."

Meanwhile, my dad's English was improving and his name was shortening: He decided that Władysław Krzysztofowicz wasn't a name that worked well in the United States. He experimented with the Romanian version, Ladislas Kristofovici, but that still wasn't well

---

* During the 2016 presidential campaign, as the Syrian civil war was raging and Donald Trump was calling for a ban on Muslim immigrants, the First Presbyterian Church in Portland was locked in an internal debate about whether to sponsor a Syrian refugee family. The church invited me to speak, and when I did I thanked the church for taking a chance on my dad. It didn't solve the global refugee problem, I said, but it was transformative for the Kristofs. Afterward, the church decided to sponsor a Syrian refugee family.

suited for American tongues. So he shortened it still further to Ladis Kristof and mostly went by Kris Kristof.

As I was growing up, my dad's family history gave me some sense of the world, of foreign languages, of the malleability of countries, borders and names. It also was a lesson in impermanence and fragility. In America, we are confident in our borders and assured that our homes, wealth and titles will not be seized; my grandfather took it hard that on his watch he had lost the family estates—and the "Von" in his name, signifying nobility—so that he was forced to spend his final years in poverty in Poland. As a little boy, I remember how we sent him boxes of dried soups to help him get by. Yet the family story also taught me as a boy to appreciate the ironies of history. While I thought it would have been rather nice to have a mansion to live in and a large estate to roam, my dad told me that he was grateful to have been displaced. The life of a nobleman in an Eastern European village would have been confining, and he relished the intellectual adventure of American university life. He felt liberated and decided he wanted to be an academic.

After Reed, my dad went to the University of Chicago to complete a PhD in political science, and there he became entranced by an art history graduate student named Jane McWilliams. She was the opposite of a newly arrived refugee: Her Quaker ancestors came to the United States in 1686 to flee religious persecution. Jane grew up in the Chicago area and was blessed with a prodigious mind, entering the University of Chicago at sixteen and graduating at eighteen. Although she was a Presbyterian from the Chicago establishment, she was untroubled by going out with a Catholic Armenian refugee. She had previously dated a Black man, which was highly unusual in the mid-1950s.

While Jane McWilliams's roots in America went way back on her father's side, her mother, Mary Shakespeare, was English. Very English. The Shakespeares were proud to be distantly related to the Bard, and Jane's first cousin in England was in fact named William Shakespeare. That helped him get restaurant reservations but sometimes caused confusion. When he was in a car crash and woke up in the hospital, a nurse asked his name. He told her, and she looked concerned.

"There, there," she said. "Just get some rest."

Jane's family included strong women, suffragettes and feminists. Her great-grandfather Hugh McWilliams was a tailor and supposedly the first person to make pants for women in America, in the 1840s. It's said that a friend of his, Elizabeth Smith Miller, complained that she couldn't hold a lamp while walking upstairs at night because she had to use one hand to hold her baby and the other to lift her skirts. Hugh McWilliams solved her problem.

Jane's grandmother Amy Goodman Shakespeare was a formidable character who a century ago would bicycle through London, grabbing the backs of public buses to tow her through traffic. Jane's mother, Mary Shakespeare, wrote for magazines including *Punch* and *The Atlantic* at a time when few women wrote professionally. Jane herself showed the same strength. One evening she was walking near the University of Chicago when a man grabbed her and held a gun to her head. Evidently by prearrangement, a car careened up to the curb, and someone inside pushed open the back door.

"Get in the car," the man with the gun told her.

Instead, she screamed and grabbed the gun, and they fought over it. "Get in the car," the man kept ordering, but she fought and shouted, and her screams brought someone running over, frightening the gunman. He jumped in the car himself, abandoning the gun in her hands.

Jane McWilliams, in short, was a match for Kris Kristof, and they married in 1956 at the University of Chicago. I arrived on the scene in 1959, putty in the hands of two deeply moral parents.

4

A Glimpse of Journalism

Our family stood out in a conservative working-class area like Yam-hill, and as an adolescent I was sometimes embarrassed by this. The principal sent a note to parents asking if any of them didn't want their child paddled for misbehavior; my parents were the only ones who responded. For me, that was about as bad as getting paddled!

I yearned for a family like everyone else's, bonding over fixing carburetors and arguments about the Trail Blazers, Portland's pro basketball team. Our household was oblivious to sports and pop culture, and we didn't have a television for most of my childhood.

My dad stuck out by speaking with a strong accent. In retrospect, most people in Yamhill found that endearing and liked to talk to him. But while I was proud that he spoke seven languages, I would have preferred that he simply spoke unaccented English like everyone else. I loved him, admired him and was a bit embarrassed by him.

We once joined a softball game with several other families in a park. My dad played right field and in the first inning expertly fielded a ground ball. A runner on first base was heading for second base and could easily have been out if my dad had thrown the ball to the second baseman. Instead, my dad threw the ball at the runner as he was halfway between first and second, and drilled him in the back. My father was proud of his aim and couldn't understand why the runner wasn't out; he protested that it was much more difficult to hit a fast-moving runner than somebody standing on second base. We all laughed, but I was mortified.

Our approach to farming likewise raised eyebrows. Most local farmers ran cattle on their pastures, but we determined what kind of livestock to raise in our own way: We checked out books on animal husbandry from the university library. The books recommended sheep, because they graze very efficiently, extracting more grass per acre and doing less damage with their hooves—plus they produce wool as well as meat.

That made sense. So we checked out another book on breeds of sheep and decided to get Corriedales, a variety mostly found in Australia and New Zealand and known for its fine wool as well as its tasty meat. A dual-purpose sheep! We would have an edge over other sheep breeders!

We bought a herd of Corriedale sheep and unleashed them on our pasture—and immediately realized why our neighbors in the hills didn't often raise sheep. Coyotes were everywhere, and they loved lamb even more than consumers did.

So we went back to the library to research the most evidence-based approaches to protecting sheep from coyotes. The optimal solution

I got my passion for the outdoors from my dad.

from our book learning was an obscure Hungarian breed of dog called the Kuvasz, used in central Europe to protect herds of sheep. The Kuvasz is a magnificent dog, white and strong like a Great Pyrenees but with a softer face. We were hooked. We managed to find a Kuvasz puppy for sale and bought her for what was then the extravagant price of $300. We named the puppy Tisza, after a river in Hungary, and we were initially impressed: Tisza spent the night outside barking, keeping us awake but presumably fending off packs of coyotes. What a conscientious guard dog.

Then on Tisza's fourth day as savior of our sheep, she decided to play with the lambs and got carried away. She killed one and badly mauled another. This was a catastrophe, for the rule in our area was that any dog that kills a sheep must be shot. The assumption was that if a dog develops a taste for killing sheep, it will never stop—and while a coyote or cougar might kill one sheep for food, a dog could quickly kill an entire flock for sport.

Yet how could we execute Tisza? She was a beautiful, loving ball of white fur who waited at the top of the hill for me to come home from school each afternoon. As soon as she spotted me, she would bark in excitement and race down to greet me. For an only child alone on the farm each afternoon until my parents came home at night, she was a loving companion.

What's more, admitting to Tisza's felonious behavior would be humiliating. The neighbors had snickered as the Kristofs bought sheep to graze in a coyote killing ground, and snickered more when we bought Corriedales. The neighbors knew what we did not: Corriedales and other white-faced breeds sold at the weekly auction for a considerable discount compared to local black-faced sheep. And while Corriedales did produce good wool, there wasn't a market for high-end wool in Oregon, so our farm was likely to be subsidizing our sheep rather than the other way around.

There was only one realistic option: We engaged in a cover-up. I buried the dead lamb, and we covered the wounded lamb with Blu-Kote veterinary wound dressing. This meant that for the next month we had a bright blue lamb, which visitors noticed. We answered questions artfully.

"What's the matter with that lamb?"

"Which one?

"Why, the bright blue one."

"Oh, the blue one? He's a fine ram lamb. Two months old. His mom is Tenney, that ewe over there."

"But why is he bright blue?"

"Oh, he was injured. No big deal. He's fine now."

"Injured how? He must have been all mangled."

"Oh, some predator. We weren't home when it happened."

To her credit, Tisza was contrite after a furious scolding and never hurt a sheep again. Ever since we have always had a Kuvasz on the farm, guarding the property.

I took on sheep as my 4-H project and continued it in FFA—Future Farmers of America—when I reached high school in ninth grade. The high school in Yamhill felt grand and grown-up, for it encompassed students from the nearby town of Carlton as well and was called Yamhill Carlton High School. It had been built in 1935 as a New Deal project to employ ninety unemployed workers. The result was a solid red-brick school building that ever since has served as the core of the community and has educated generations of local students.

I loved Yamhill Carlton High School. It was a big deal in the area,

Showing my Corriedale sheep with the FFA at the Oregon State Fair.

FFA was a big deal in the school—and it became a path for me to blend in. I was a flop in vocational agriculture classes, for I could scarcely arc-weld a simple bead across an iron plate. But while my welding skills were pathetic, I held my own in FFA public speaking and leadership contests. We wore our blue FFA ties, white shirts, and blue and gold FFA jackets, and we felt very grown-up.

My parents commuted to work in Portland but were otherwise occupied with the farm, which was more work than we had anticipated. During lambing season in the winter, I would get up at 3 a.m., put on rubber boots, grab a jacket to wear over my pajamas, and trudge through the mud to check for newborn lambs. If a ewe had a new lamb, I'd put them in a stall in the barn, connect a heat lamp to keep the lamb warm, and see if I could help the lamb start suckling its mother's milk. This might be a long task on a cold night.

In English, it's striking that the words for animals are from Anglo-Saxon, while the terms for food are from French. That's because Anglo-Saxons were raising *pigs*, *sheep* and *cows*, while the Norman conquerors were dining on the resulting *pork*, *mutton*, *beef* and *veal*. When I got up at 3 a.m. to tend to a ewe that was lambing, I felt like an Anglo-Saxon peasant.

One day when I was thirteen my dad taught me how to drive our tractor. It seemed to go well. So after the driving lesson, I headed the tractor into the barn to park it.

How could I have known a tractor would take so long to brake?

By the time the tractor had come to a stop, it had hurtled through the back wall of the sheep shed; if it had gone another few feet I would have been badly injured. Even today, I see my old repair patch in the wall.

From tractor driving, I soon graduated to car driving—and for a farm boy, that was liberating. Without a driver's license, work opportunities were limited. During the previous summers, I picked strawberries, because the berry farms rented school buses to pick kids up each morning at 7 a.m. and return us at about 2 p.m. There would be more than a hundred of us out on a berry farm, typically ages ten through fifteen, hunched over and picking berries, sometimes eating them, some of us periodically getting into berry fights, listening to Jim Croce or Kenny Rogers blaring from someone's radio. The term "child labor" wasn't in our lexicon.

What troubled me wasn't children in the fields but rather my dismal picking ability. I was a lousy berry picker, earning maybe $7 for a full day's work; some kids managed to pick about twice as fast as I did. "You're a good kid and don't throw berries," one manager said in puzzlement, "so how can you be so slow?" At that time, strawberry picking seemed to us a proxy for life skills and capacity for income generation, so my future did not look promising. I was a good reader and a bad strawberry picker, and we understood that for most of history the former was an irrelevant pastime while the latter reflected practical skills that would matter much more to a kid in a farming town; it just turned out that I happened to grow up in a period when returns to good reading would be enormous and returns to manual labor would collapse.

With a car, we could graduate from strawberry picking and drive ourselves to more lucrative jobs hauling hay or irrigation pipes, earning perhaps $2 an hour. Most important, with a car we could ask girls out.

"A car, man, that's what girls want in a guy," my neighbor Bobby Stepp assured me. "You get your license, and girls will be all over you. They just want to get in the back seat and make out with you."

"Even if it's an old car?" I asked doubtfully. "I'll be driving our old Ford station wagon. It's my parents' backup car."

"Doesn't matter," Bobby said confidently. "If it's got a back seat, girls will be after you."

I wasn't sure whether to believe him, partly because I'd never seen any girl show an interest in Bobby. His brother, Mike, said Bobby was always lying, but that didn't extinguish my hope of leveraging a car to improve my love life. I wasn't entirely sure about the distinction between the front seat and the back seat but was embarrassed to ask Bobby. So I nodded in a worldly way and wondered if I should check out a book from the library about techniques for making out.

I will spare you my stumbling, clumsy acts of discovery in this domain.

Turning sixteen and getting a driver's license also allowed me the chance to work in professional journalism. After my eighth-grade experience as a crusading newspaper editor, I had nurtured my interest in journalism by reading *The New York Times* and other papers. I took journalism classes in high school and worked my way up the school paper. But more important, as soon as I had my driver's license, I wrote to the editor of the county newspaper, the *News-Register*, in nearby McMinnville, and asked for a job. The editor, Jeb Bladine, was in his late twenties, and perhaps that's why he was willing to hire a sixteen-year-old. Jeb also knew that the county had lots of farmers and that he didn't know much about agriculture, so he saw me as a way to fill the gap.

"You live on a farm, right?" Jeb asked. "You understand farming?"

"Sure," I said, exhibiting my dad's kind of self-confidence, not acknowledging that I couldn't have told the difference between a field of wheat and a field of oats.

"So write a few stories for me," Jeb suggested. "I'll pay twenty-five cents a column inch, plus something for photos. Let's see how it goes."

I threw myself into the job. I stockpiled dimes and would excuse myself from class to use the coin telephone in the high school to phone people I needed to interview, like agricultural experts. But mostly I just drove around and dropped in on farms and started talking to people. When I said I was writing something for the *News-Register*, they were friendly, and I always asked who else I should talk to. Instead of working my way through my "Story Ideas" list, I found it grew longer and longer.

In the evening I would drive to the *News-Register* building and let myself in with the key Jeb gave me. The newsroom—three or four desks, plus Jeb's—awed me. It was cluttered and dingy, with old copy and photos scattered around, and I looked at the old Royal manual typewriters and realized that all the copy in the newspaper would pass through them. In the evening, the newsroom would be mostly empty, so I'd sit down at one of the typewriters and begin hammering out a story triple-spaced, so Jeb could edit it. Often I'd work until midnight, and then leave the pages on Jeb's desk for him to edit and pass on to the typesetter.

It was exhilarating. Sometimes when school ended at 3:15 p.m. I'd have no idea what I would write, but by midnight I would have filed a long feature and left two rolls of film for the photo lab to process. Seeing my byline on the front page was thrilling, and simply the process of crafting an article was gratifying. I've never tried my hand at sculpture, but it seems a parallel task.

I sometimes covered sports and found it great training. There's a reason sports reporters are some of the most vivid journalistic stylists:

Foreign correspondents or columnists can get away with turgid prose and the excuse "Damn it, this is important!" Sports reporters rarely have that excuse, and readers often know how the story ends, so the writers are forced to enliven every paragraph. Football and basketball games also meant tight deadlines, and I liked the pressure. I'd scrawl an article on a pad of paper, barely able to read my own writing, knowing that it was due in thirty minutes—and at the last minute I'd finish and call it in.

Journalism wasn't more lucrative than haying, but it was more fun. I was astonished that I could spend time talking to interesting people and get paid for it. I worried that Jeb might figure out how much I enjoyed this work and freeze my pay forever, but instead he upped me to thirty cents a column inch—and gave me invaluable editing and tutoring.

The *News-Register* used photos extremely well, sometimes running large stand-alone pictures to tell a story. The paper's superb photographer, Tom Ballard, took me under his wing and coached me, and I fell so in love with photography that I was in danger of choosing photojournalism over writing. I built a darkroom in our basement and spent many happy hours shooting—Tisza was a regular subject, as were my parents and friends—and studying contact sheets to figure out which prints to blow up afterward.

At Powell's Books in Portland, I bought a used copy of *The Best of Life*, a collection of photographs that had appeared in *Life* magazine. I pored over the photos, trying to understand the photographer's choice of angles, of lenses, of lighting, of aperture, of shutter speed. Sometimes I stole techniques. Tom Ballard took photos of my buddy Bob Bansen's cow with her nose filling the foreground, distorted by a wide-angle lens. Every cow I've photographed since, I've used the same approach; I extended it to camels and even to a cooperative hippo in Mali. At Powell's I also found a textbook called *News Editing* that explained how to write tersely and vividly, with plenty of examples. I became a word nerd, reading William Safire's "On Language" column religiously and becoming sensitive to distinctions such as those between "uninterested" (not interested) and "disinterested" (no interest at stake). A judge in a case should never be uninterested but always disinterested.

I bought other books about journalism that gave me glimpses of a much loftier world than the one I knew at the *News-Register*. The books described reporters grilling the president at the White House or, better yet, gallivanting around the world to cover wars and earthquakes. There was a special reverence for the foreign correspondent and the way he (back then, it was always a "he") covered the world for the audience at home. Foreign correspondents have the trust of their editors and the authority and expense account to jump on a plane and go wherever they think best, the books said. One book noted that some of them are Rhodes Scholars; I decided I had better be a Rhodes Scholar.

The *News-Register* staff had a sense of mission, without overdoing it. On the way to lunch one day with Tom Ballard and a few others, we saw a woman park her car, dump fast-food wrappers and a pile of other trash out her car window, and then march off for some shopping. We were all indignant, and Tom snapped a photo of the car and the trash. The next day's newspaper ran the photo with a caption about litterers. We journalists were not just observing from the sidelines but leaping into the arena to hold bad actors accountable! Standing up for community norms! I loved this profession.

5

A Wimpy Kid

I was as narcissistic as any teenager, but in our household it was difficult to be entirely self-absorbed. In the 1970s, my parents co-founded
the Amnesty International chapter in Portland, and our dining table
became cluttered with appeals for political prisoners around the world.

When the Soviet Union sent a delegation of clergy to the United
States in 1979 to trumpet the USSR's supposed religious freedom, my
parents organized a petition that gathered hundreds of signatures on
behalf of religious prisoners of conscience there. The Oregon Council
of American-Soviet Friendship, which organized the visit, refused to
allow a meeting to present the petition, but my dad arranged to be the
interpreter for the Soviet delegates—and handed them the petition.

"You can't do that!" the organizer protested, outraged at the intru-
sion. But my dad continued in Russian, further enraging the sponsors.
The Oregon Council of American-Soviet Friendship sent a furious
two-page letter to my mother afterward. "The propaganda you dis-
seminate is clearly designed to deceive people, and to arouse their
hostility against the Soviet Union," the letter said. "It is one part of a
campaign to revive the cold war and the nuclear terror." For my part,
I was thrilled to have parents who were rule-breakers as well as human
rights champions.

My dad was very clear about how others had saved his life, and he
was exasperatingly attentive to paying it forward. We could never pass

hitchhikers on the road, even if they looked like potential murderers from the Manson family. Sometimes they ended up on our couch for a night or two. My home overflowed with empathy and the confidence that any of us could do something—write letters, sign petitions, call members of Congress—to make a difference.

This empathy and self-efficacy was not always present in neighbor homes. We had many fantastic and supportive neighbors who tutored us on farm techniques, but some of my friends' homes were toxic with violence and alcoholism. One evening I was hanging out with Bobby and Mike Stepp outside their house when a commotion erupted inside. We went to look and found their dad swinging a baseball bat around the living room.

"A bat!" Robert Stepp shouted. "There's a damn bat in the house." It took me a moment to realize that he was targeting a flying bat—with a baseball bat. Then he clubbed a stuffed chair, which shuddered under the assault, and a terrified brown bat flittered about and flew off into the kitchen. We all edged closer to the kitchen to monitor the battle.

Robert Stepp had a good union job at the sawmill that enabled the family to buy a home and live a comfortable life. But he and his wife were alcoholics, getting drunk most evenings, and Robert periodically became violent when he had been drinking. He beat his wife and beat the kids. I normally gave him a wide berth, especially in the evenings.

Crash! Robert Stepp whacked the wall where the bat had settled for a moment. A dent appeared in the wall, but the bat had darted to the side and was now flying over our heads.

"Robert!" shouted his wife, Lorena. "You idiot, you're breaking things!"

"Shut up!" he yelled back. "Or I'll break you."

I ducked as he waved his club and sent it whistling over our heads. A floor lamp shattered. I realized I was more in danger than the bat and retreated to the front door. I was no expert at drunkenness, but it was obvious that both Robert and Lorena were slurring their words.

"Maybe open the windows and doors?" Bobby suggested timidly, but his dad paid no attention. Robert was a tough old jarhead and thought his two sons were wimps; he rarely paid them much attention, except to scoff at them or beat them.

"I got the bat," Robert shouted, and there was another crash, with the sound of tinkling glass.

"Robert, you dolt!" It was Lorena's voice, and then there was a thwack that sounded like a punch, followed by a scream. The bat darted back into the living room, and I stepped outside so I could safely watch while also perhaps showing the bat an exit route.

Mike and Bobby joined me, both scared of their dad. The bat unfortunately didn't take our hint to head for the doorway, and the next few minutes involved Robert swinging his bat in increasing frustration at the furniture and walls of his own house, denting the walls and smashing everything in sight.

"I think I'd better go," I told Bobby softly.

He nodded.

Our area north of Yamhill struggled more than most with alcohol and, later, drugs, along with an overlay of domestic violence. The area included a hamlet, Cove Orchard, that for decades had been a trouble spot. At one time, Cove Orchard had a school, a post office, two churches and a store with two gas pumps. But the local well water turned out to be salty, and the ground was a clay not suitable for septic tanks, so waste from outhouses leached into the creek and water table. A place so undesirable offered homes with only one attraction: They were very cheap. The area struggled and lost its school and post office. At least two neighbors lived in shacks with no electricity or running water.

The cheap land and low rents attracted some dysfunctional families. It probably didn't help that many of the men worked in industries like logging where hard drinking was part of the culture, and that the Cove Orchard store sold alcohol to adults on credit—or to kids for cash.

The Yamhill area was overwhelmingly white, with just three Black kids in my school along with a couple of Asian Americans from a single family, a handful of Latinos and a somewhat larger share of Native Americans (some of whom didn't acknowledge it until years later). This wasn't an accident, for Oregon at its founding had barred Black people and had long borne hostility toward Asians, Native Americans and others, including Catholics, partly through an active Ku Klux Klan. Yamhill had had a Chinese resident for decades at the beginning of the twentieth century, and in the complex way of small towns he seems to have been simultaneously much loved, much mocked and much condescended to.

Many people openly expressed bigoted attitudes or used racial epithets toward Blacks, Latinos and Asians, but minorities weren't enough of a presence in the area to stimulate substantial resentment. People were more likely to mock Mormons, because they were a large and growing presence, and hence were perceived as a threat. Interracial dating didn't cause problems, and when I ran for student body president, it initially looked as if the only Black student in my grade might run and beat me (in the end, he didn't run). That said, the community was utterly white in its ethos, and it was common for white people in Yamhill in the 1970s and 1980s to make harsh comments about the struggles of African Americans in particular. Folks said the problem was "deadbeat dads," "junkies," "lack of personal responsibility" and "bad choices," all of which were sometimes assumed to be reflective of Black culture, and the presumptive policy lesson was the need for law-and-order policies, a war on drugs and a crackdown on social welfare benefits. People didn't mean for bigoted stereotypes to apply to their Black friends but to the generalized mass of African Americans elsewhere. None of us knew it then, of course, but a generation later many of the pathologies that had afflicted urban Black America swept through rural white America and devastated communities like Cove Orchard that had previously been smug about personal responsibility.

My neighbors in Cove Orchard included the five Knapp kids, who boarded the No. 6 school bus each morning right after I did: Farlan, Zealan, Nathan, Rogina and Keylan. Farlan, tall and thin with a mop of dark hair, was in my grade at school. He was quiet and intelligent, but he didn't like school and showed no interest in schoolwork. He had already been held back one year, which embarrassed him and made him dislike school even more. He might have been able to excel at sports, but he was always working to earn money.

Farlan's dad, Gary Knapp, a scary drunk, had a job laying sewer pipes, and his mom worked on a nearby filbert farm. The family was industrious, and Farlan and his mom had a side business refurbishing cars to earn extra money. Farlan and his younger siblings also took jobs a few nights a week catching chickens on chicken farms and loading them on trucks. They would come home at 3 a.m. and then get up a few hours later to do chores and go to school, where they would fall asleep in class. If the Knapp kids found no joy in school, they found trauma at home. When drunk, which was every night, Gary Knapp beat the kids and his wife and menaced them with his gun.

"I just want to kill my dad," Farlan once confided to a group of us. We shuffled awkwardly.

"You don't mean it," one of us replied. "He's your dad."

"Yes, I do mean it," Farlan said with vehemence. "I want to kill him. And I'm going to do it, too."

Gary drank himself to death before Farlan could get around to killing him, but I wondered at Farlan's fervor. The loathing in his voice was almost as frightening as the slurring in Gary's voice when he shouted at his family. What does that do to a boy to make him want to want to murder his father? Does that hatred gnaw at his mental health? How can it not?

Among some of my Cove Orchard friends, including Farlan, there was an ethos that approved of violence as a useful tool, believing that those who use it are to be admired, and concluding that men and boys must never show weakness. Another good friend on my No. 6 bus, Kevin Green, often told me with pride about the time his dad had chopped off part of his brother's finger. Kevin was a sweet, good-natured kid, but he seemed to dream of a chance to display a similar toughness. He thought it was masculine to fight, shove a teacher, cut off a man's finger. Walking away was sissy. Standing up to your abusive dad and killing him would have been the epitome of toughness.

I was nonconfrontational, so I rarely found my manliness tested. But on at least one occasion, I was put to the test.

One of the mischief makers on my No. 6 bus was Chris Lawson, a tough kid a couple of years behind me in school. Chris wasn't big but he was solid and muscular, with plenty of practice using his fists. He was mercurial—funny when he was in a good mood, a truculent bully on a bad day. I was friendly with Chris and his brothers and sister. One day we were riding home on the school bus and horsing around in a friendly way, but I apparently hurt Chris's finger. The next thing I knew he was standing up and furiously punching my head and shoulders. Chris was both younger than me and smaller than me, so the code of honor stipulated that I was obliged to turn around and deck him. Optimally, I'd leave him unconscious or in tears.

Instead, I jumped out of his range and turned to face him.

"What are you doing, Chris?" I asked lamely. "What on earth are you doing?"

We stood there glaring at each other, Chris's fists ready for a fight, my arms at my side. The other kids watched as I shook my head and moved up a few seats, wondering if he was going to march up the aisle and assault me again. Instead, Chris's best friend, Mike, came up and tried to negotiate between me and Chris.

"You want to fight Chris?" Mike asked. "You want to come by his place and fight him?"

"I've got to go home and do chores," I said.

"Come by when you're done."

"Okay, maybe I will. It'll take me about an hour to do chores."

But I could tell from the amused glint in Mike's eye that he knew I wouldn't show. I wish I could say that this was an early sign of a deep commitment to pacifism. But mostly I was afraid that Chris would beat the hell out of me.

Nowadays one might say that exposure to violence and drunkenness in Cove Orchard might be traumatizing, but I wasn't marked by it the way my friends were. The difference is that this was directed at them, in their homes, while I saw it mostly indirectly as it was refracted through them. My exposures were also buffered by my nurturing family. Scientists measure stress in children by testing saliva for levels of the stress hormone cortisol, and unsurprisingly they find that a young child's cortisol level soars upon receiving a shot at the doctor's office. But if a parent is holding the child, then cortisol levels rise much more modestly. That sense of parental embrace, protection and comfort buffers the pain of the outside world—and that was my experience.

It was always evident that my family circumstances were a world apart from those of the Knapps or the Stepps. It wasn't that the Kristofs were materially much better off, since my parents had overextended themselves in buying our farm and we were pinching pennies. We didn't heat our house all winter, except with firewood in the living room fireplace; my bedroom was icy at night. For the first few months, we couldn't afford a chainsaw, so I'd come home from school and spend an hour or two with the handsaw or axe, cutting firewood to keep us warm for the evening.

When I lettered in cross-country during my freshman year in high school, I didn't get a letterman's jacket—the sign of a big man on campus—because it was $35 and seemed extravagant. But when I realized that girls thought guys with letterman's jackets were hot, it became an indispensable investment, and I did get one sophomore year. Meanwhile, the Knapps bought Farlan a Ford Mustang for his sixteenth birthday, which left me jealous because that would have been unimaginable in our household.

I never got braces as a kid, even though my teeth were very crooked (I got braces as an adult). Very few of my schoolmates in Yamhill ever got braces, probably because they were expensive and perfect teeth seemed a luxury. In our family, we never sat around and discussed "Is it worth $1,000 to fix these crooked teeth?" It was more that crooked teeth were an accepted part of life and didn't matter much, while fixing them was expensive. My dad had crooked teeth, I had crooked teeth, my classmates had crooked teeth. Yamhill had a democracy of crooked teeth encompassing the professors' kid and the farmers' kids.

To some degree this reflected national trends at the time. In post–World War II America, there was often a shared sense of community across class lines, at least within any ethnic group (building solidarity across racial lines proved more difficult, although Robert Kennedy worked at it). Blue-collar and professional households lived side by side and had far more in common than today. True, the General Motors lawyer lived in a nicer house than the General Motors assembly-line worker, but they sometimes lived in the same neighborhoods and their kids often attended the same schools and played together. Now the income and educational gap has widened, and the GM lawyer is more likely to live in a gated neighborhood and dispatch children to private schools. The working-class family is more likely to wrestle with divorce, single parenting, poverty and substance abuse, while the professional family's complaints will be more about Tesla repairs and the cost of SAT tutoring.

Yet although my friends and I were integrated by class in the 1970s and the economic differences were not striking, we were different in every important noneconomic way. The Knapps and Stepps had no books in their houses, while in my home we had thousands of books in multiple languages. I was always read to when I was young; they never were. And as education became the single greatest predictor of success, exposure to books and development of verbal skills became a factor in the chasm emerging in America.

Yet it wasn't just books that surrounded me, it was also love. My parents didn't beat me; they embraced me. They modeled respect, civility and compassion, not violence. If I had returned bloody from a fistfight, the first question would have been a distressed "What happened?"—not "Does the other guy look worse?" My mom and dad didn't ask about my homework or pressure me to excel, but they were proud when I did and we always assumed that I would graduate from high school and college.

We measure poverty with metrics of income and wealth, but that doesn't get at the real gaps. Looking back, the kind of poverty that mattered most had to do with how infrequently children were read to, or hugged, or told they were loved, how often they were beaten or saw their mom beaten, how often they were afraid, how often they were told that a boy should fight or that the measure of a man is the ability to beat up someone else. I intuitively understood that my family was nurturing in a way that was not true of many other households. I thought of Farlan Knapp, tormented by his yearning to murder his dad, and I decided I was fortunate to have a loving, brilliant and optimistic dad even though he had an accent and no idea how to play baseball.

6

High School Rabble-Rouser

My political career began by accident when we held elections for sophomore class president. The freshman class president had been nominated to serve again, but he had carelessly neglected to pay the required class dues and so wasn't eligible. A top athlete was nominated, but he hadn't paid his dues either. Our best basketball player? No.

"Who has paid dues?" our class advisor asked. Records showed I was just about the only boy. A few girls had also paid dues, but sexism made it difficult for kids to perceive a girl as class president. So, benefiting from chauvinism, I was elected class president. Momentum carried me forward until by senior year I served as student body president and district FFA president as well as newspaper editor.

That's one of the advantages of a small school—it's easy to become involved in all kinds of areas. The cross-country coach was desperate to have enough students to constitute a team, so he flattered and cajoled me and my buddy Brad Larsen to try out, and it turned out that if you could breathe you made the team. Running became a major part of my life.

Bill Drayton, the godfather of social entrepreneurship, argues that the key to building successful citizens is to nurture in adolescents a confidence that they can tackle problems and make a difference. My parents had always cultivated that in me, and I felt particularly empowered in a small school. Our problems were small enough that we could resolve them together. Farming taught me the same lesson: If I had a ewe who was lame, I could trim her hooves or treat her for foot rot, and she would recover. Problems felt manageable rather than vast and hopeless.

At Yamhill Carlton High School, teachers cared for us and supported us, and so did the community. Friday night football games brought Yamhill and Carlton together, and so did FFA and other school activities. My friend Brett Peloquin and I grew irritated at school fees, like the mandatory $9 "book fee," so as sophomores we drafted a bill for the state legislature to ban school fees for low-income students. Our state senator sponsored it unchanged, and it passed. Governor Bob Straub signed it into law and gave me the pen. Wow, I thought, citizens truly can have an impact!

The Carlton-Yamhill Review, the local weekly newspaper, went bust, so my classmates and I converted the school newspaper into a community newspaper and sent it by mail to every home in the area. More impact. I was full of high-minded principles. We would use our school newspaper to knit together the community and provide accountability. Yet after hubris comes the fall.

Sure enough, I went astray. A Yamhill man, Roger, was a member of an extremist right-wing group called the Posse Comitatus that was a precursor of today's militias. Roger was thirty years old, living with his wife, Karen, and their one-year-old son. Small and lean, Roger was balding prematurely in front with his remaining black hair combed to the side. He wore a suit when I interviewed him. His house was neat, but the gate was a giveaway: A sign warned that anyone entering without permission risked "forfeiting his life." He was a conspiracy theorist who believed that America's leaders were communists, and he said he was ready to "arrest" any government official who came onto his property.

"I'm the master here," he told me. "I've been waiting for the tax assessor this year. I had everything necessary for placing him under citizen's arrest if he passed that sign. I've had enough of government."

Above all, Roger was determined to stand up to anyone who tried to register his guns.

"I made that promise years ago, and there's hundreds of thousands of people just like me," he said. "The day they come after the guns is the day we turn those guns on the people who come after them."

Karen was sweet and didn't want her husband to give an interview, for fear of the neighbors' reactions. But Roger wanted to make waves and thought people would welcome what he had to say. He was too eager for an article to listen to Karen. So I proceeded to write about him for the school paper and for the *News-Register.*

I thought that if Yamhill had an extremist in town who was threatening violence, we should all know about it. Journalism as a public service. But down deep at some level, I knew Roger was harmless. He talked a good game and had wild views, but he didn't seem at all likely to act on them. Meanwhile, Karen's premonition was right. After my article, he was pretty much drummed out of Yamhill and ended up as a custodian at a government office in Salem. Roger didn't blame me, but he was chastened and hurt. I remained in touch with him for a couple of years and saw that I had harmed his entire family, including innocents like Karen and their son, and it was hard to see that the public was safer.*

Perhaps that's a benefit of starting in journalism in a small town: You see the pain you are capable of inflicting. Good journalism is always going to embarrass people, wound their pride and in some cases set back their careers and harm family members. That's often necessary. But in a large, anonymous city, it is easy to whack people—maybe too easy—even when it's not entirely necessary. In Yamhill, where you would run into the people you wrote about at the T&E General Store, you were always aware of the impact on them and their families. Sometimes that led to an unfortunate pulling of punches and to coverage that wasn't as aggressive as it should have been—but it also made it harder to be gratuitously cruel. I've tried ever since, not always successfully, to remember that those I write about are complicated people, and that in journalism "humane" and "tough" need not be antonyms.

My article in the school paper about Roger didn't go over well with the school board, and it came on top of other tensions. My friend Brett Peloquin had written something mildly critical of President Jimmy Carter, and the school had censored it on the theory that a school paper shouldn't criticize the leader of the free world. I wrote an editorial denouncing censorship. That was censored. Then to fill the space where the editorial would have gone, I submitted quotations from

---

* That's why I'm not using Roger's last name here. I've lost track of him, and a search online didn't turn up any recent activity. But if he has calmed down and is living quietly with Karen somewhere, I don't want his statements to me in the 1970s to cause him new embarrassment.

Thomas Jefferson and John Stuart Mill hailing freedom of expression; they were censored.

It didn't help that I was taking on the school administration on other fronts. The principal, short of funds for a project that he thought would benefit students, quietly drained the student council's account. As student body president, I discovered this and forced him to restore the money. I also managed the campaign of a cross-country running buddy, Loren Collins, for the school board. Loren had just graduated from the high school and as a college freshman was running for the board and promising to shake things up. All this irritated some board members.

"Some people are getting too big for their britches," one board member said somberly at one board meeting, staring at me. In the end, the board suspended our role as a community newspaper for a month, though we could still circulate in the school.

We staff members were horrified. I quickly drafted a protest editorial that the others signed. It was censored, of course, but it was published in a national education magazine and thus received far more notice. We ended:

> Perhaps in publishing this editorial we are further jeopardizing the future of this newspaper. Maybe so, but there is more to life than tact and diplomacy. There comes that time when you have to say what you think and think what you say. For us, that time has come.
>
> We are told that we are too big for our britches. If being too big for our britches means hoping and dreaming of great things, if it means setting high goals, if it means taking an interest in the life around us, then we plead guilty. Under these circumstances, we hope our pants never fit.
>
> We are not angry, but we are saddened and dismayed that termination of the paper should be the price for covering a controversy. To borrow a phrase from Adlai Stevenson, we feel like the little boy who stubbed his toe in the dark. He was too old to cry, but it hurt too much to laugh.

The most difficult part of this furor was coming to terms with how many good friends thought I was in the wrong. These included teachers, parents and students whom I admired.

"This is a school newspaper," one of my teachers told me gently. "It's not *The Washington Post*. The local taxpayers are paying for this paper. They want some control over what's in it. Is that so wrong?"

"But we should be encouraging students to get engaged, to speak out," I protested.

"Really?" she asked. "This is a school. Teachers are here to guide students. So why not let teachers guide student editors? Why the need to be so edgy? Why keep testing the limits?"

Each side stepped back. The school board reinstated the newspaper, and Gene Belt, a hog farmer whom I particularly respected on the board, worked with me to smooth the troubled waters. We all loved the community, we all wanted the school paper to serve Yamhill and Carlton, and we were all willing to compromise to get there.

More than two decades later, when I was editor of the Sunday *New York Times*, I was surprised to discover that the politics of that job were somewhat easier to navigate than those of the editorship of a small-town paper where everyone knew each other.

I HAD ALWAYS KNOWN I would go to college, but hadn't given much thought to where. In the fall of my senior year, I took the SATs, did well, and applied to the University of Oregon and Stanford University. On a whim I applied to three more colleges I had heard of: Harvard, Princeton and Swarthmore. I hadn't visited any of them and didn't know much about them. No one from Yamhill had ever gone to colleges like that, and my grades were good but not spectacular. I was first in my class, but that was only because my rival for valedictorian, a truck driver's daughter, first lost her mother to cancer and then became pregnant and had a baby.

All in all, I didn't feel like Harvard material. But the Harvard admissions committee included a member from rural Oregon, and elite universities were looking to diversify their student bodies by recruiting farm kids, so I was a beneficiary of affirmative action—and most of all, of course, I was a beneficiary of the extraordinary privilege of growing up with every advantage in a loving family that lived and breathed education. In the spring of 1977 I was accepted everywhere I applied. Because Harvard seemed particularly renowned, I decided I would be a Harvard man.

I graduated from high school that June: We graduates unabashedly displayed our crooked teeth to the world as we cheered and celebrated. About one-third of those who entered with my class had dropped out by graduation, and few of us went on to a four-year college. Farlan Knapp and his four siblings all dropped out. Neither Bobby Stepp nor Mike Stepp graduated. Billy Beard did, even though he hadn't passed enough classes to qualify, because the school wanted to be sure he didn't return next year. Clayton Green had been kicked out of school in ninth grade for fighting.

We didn't know it then, but an era was ending in America. For three decades after World War II, the economic pie had been growing and inequality had also declined. But now well-paying union jobs were beginning to disappear all over the country, partly because union membership was collapsing and partly because manufacturing jobs were migrating abroad. Soon it would no longer be possible for a high school dropout or someone with only a high school diploma to get a union job at the sawmill or steel factory and step on an escalator to a middle-class life. We were oblivious enough to remain full of naïve hope. We celebrated our high school graduation and wrote sweet messages in each other's yearbooks, but when I look back now, I perceive an elegy for an era of opportunity in working-class America.

7

Faking It at Harvard

I emerged from the Harvard Square subway station, lugging an aging yellow suitcase. At the gate to the university, I paused and gazed at Harvard Yard beyond. I was excited but intimidated, for the campus up close looked even more imposing and regal than it had in photos. I, on the other hand, did not look imposing.

I had deferred admission for a year to travel around Oregon as a state FFA officer and then had spent the summer working on a farm in France. The gap year gave me time to work, travel and gain maturity, and I've recommended it to others as well; a generation later, each of my kids took a gap year and worked or studied or both. In my case, to save money and time, I came directly from France with just my farm work clothes. After spending several months picking peaches, cherries and pears, my clothes and I smelled like a fruit salad—one that had been left out in the sun for a week. My parents had mailed a box of my clothing to Harvard, but it would take a week or two to arrive.

Slowly I lugged my suitcase through the gate. Harvard Yard was full of families unloading cars and carrying boxes up to the new students' dorm rooms. Somewhere in there were my classmates, but they were outnumbered by parents and siblings. I was just about the only one who came by subway without an escort.

I was nervous, but slightly fortified by advanced placement scores. Yamhill Carlton didn't offer advanced placement courses, but a teacher had helped me sign up for the tests without benefit of the courses. I earned top scores, qualifying me to start at Harvard as a sophomore. From France, I wrote my parents about how thrilled I was and why: "They alleviate some of my fears about competing at Harvard with all of those Einsteins."

In the first week of Harvard, during which I had to decide whether to begin as a freshman or sophomore, I asked a sophomore out to a movie. Over ice cream afterward, my date confessed that her roommates had teased her about robbing the cradle and dating a "little freshman." That decided it: I became a sophomore.

Harvard was a different world for me. Yamhill had been nearly exclusively white and Christian, while Harvard was more diverse. The student body included a modest number of African Americans and Latinos, along with a large population of Asian American and Jewish kids. My mother's family probably had some Jewish roots, but I hadn't known any Jewish kids in Yamhill. Suddenly at Harvard half my friends were Jews, and I had to master a new vocabulary of Yiddish insults. Yet in other ways, Harvard was a monoculture: Students were overwhelmingly affluent, liberal and from well-educated families. They believed in helping struggling Americans but didn't know many.

My Harvard classmates often seemed much more sophisticated and better prepared than I was. While flirting with a classmate during my first week, I boasted about spending the summer in France. The girl smiled delightedly and replied in rapid-fire French with slang that left me desperately nodding, repeating "*Oui, oui*," and hoping she wasn't asking me a question. How could I have known that she attended a French lycée in New York City?

A few weeks into the term, a few dozen of us streamed into a squat brick building just off Harvard Yard to participate in the competition—or "comp"—for students wanting to join the most famous student newspaper in the world, *The Harvard Crimson. The Crimson* was a daily newspaper and, for the staff, a gateway to *The New York Times, The Washington Post, Newsweek* and *Time*, the leading news publications of the day. But to get on the staff, students had to survive the grueling eight-week comp. Supposedly Ben Bradlee, the *Washington Post* editor, had had to drop from the comp, while Walter Lippmann, the legendary columnist, failed the comp as many as three times, depending on whose version of history you listened to.

Our group included a student from my introductory writing class, Bill McKibben, along with David Sanger, Jeff Toobin, Nell Scovell and dozens of others who went on to great things journalistically. The *Crimson* president, a burly senior with chaotic hair named Francis J. Connolly, explained how the comp would work: We would come in at least two afternoons a week and be assigned stories to report and write that day on deadline. After four weeks, editors would "cut" those of us who weren't producing great articles. After eight weeks, some more would be cut, but at that time a number of us would then be anointed as editors of *The Crimson*.

Connolly told us that the newspaper had strict standards. We would have to memorize the stylebook and its oddities: spell out cardinal and ordinal numbers from one through ten, use numerals for 11 and higher, write "per cent" with a space but "percentage" without, and capitalize the "The" in *The Crimson* when it is a noun but not as an adjective: "They entered the *Crimson* building to comp for *The Crimson*." Our bylines and the names of everybody we interviewed had to consist of first full name, middle initial and last name: Not Billy Smith, but William L. Smith III. (That's why my name on the spine of this book isn't Nick Kristof but Nicholas D. Kristof.)

I was still trying to figure out the difference between ordinal and cardinal numbers when Connolly moved on to integrity. We must never slant stories to help friends, and we must resist seduction by the rich, the powerful and the famous. We would be ruthlessly edited, and we should understand that *The Crimson* took priority. He and other top editors worked seventy hours a week at the paper, in addition to taking classes and meeting other academic requirements. It was an important responsibility, he growled, and we had to accept the counsel of editors. For example, if we weren't rigorously edited, we might libel someone and cost *The Crimson* tens of thousands of dollars.

"Anybody here who claims to know what libel is?" Connolly barked. It was clear that he was ready to pounce on anyone who tried to answer, so we kept quiet. Then David Sanger, a nerdy-looking kid from White Plains, New York, raised his hand.

We all rubbernecked.

"Oh, you think you know what libel is?" Connolly asked, the way a cat might address the mouse in its paws. "What do you think libel is?"

Sanger didn't seem to notice the danger. "Well, it's a false statement about a person that when published injures that person's reputation and causes damage," he said.

There was a silence. Connolly evidently found the answer disappointingly good. You could see him trying to find a way to poke a hole in it.

"No," he said finally, "that's not right!" He gained enthusiasm. "That's why you've got to listen to editors, because that's just not right. You see, a libel doesn't have to be about a person. It can be about a corporation. So I hope you'll listen . . ."

David Sanger's hand shot up again. "Excuse me," he said forcefully.

There was stunned silence. Connolly stared grimly at Sanger, and there was menace in the stillness.

"Yes," Connolly finally responded.

"A corporation is a legal person," Sanger offered helpfully. "So when I say libel is a false statement of fact that injures a person's reputation, that can be either an individual or a corporation."

I sought out Sanger that evening and chatted with him about journalism. He was intriguing, and I thought I should meet him while he was still alive. Much later, he was best man at my wedding and a longtime colleague and close friend at the *Times*.

Eight weeks later, Sanger and I survived the comp and joined the *Crimson* staff. I loved *The Crimson* and by spring was working thirty or forty hours a week in the building. It was full of smart people, and we furiously debated policy in editorial meetings. I had felt far to the left in Yamhill, but suddenly at Harvard I felt like a conservative. Young liberals at Harvard were convinced that sex differences were the result of a social construct, and that if we socialized boys and girls similarly, they would emerge alike. As a farm boy, I rolled my eyes at that. We didn't give dolls to our ewe lambs and trucks to our ram lambs, but they ended up very different: You didn't have to worry about ewes, but turn your back on a ram and he might butt you. Our cattle and chickens taught me the same lesson, for it was blindingly obvious why Spain didn't try cow fights and why there was no tradition in the South of hen fights. I tried to make this point to a date but retreated when she accused me of comparing her to a sheep.

In 1980, *The Crimson* endorsed the far-left candidate Barry Commoner for president, so David Sanger and I and an ally wrote a dissent supporting Jimmy Carter for reelection. We likewise debated Middle

East policy with a gravity that suggested that the world hung in the balance, and we wrote critiques of each other's work in a volume called the "Open Book," knowing that these would be stored in the Harvard library for historians to pore over. In the men's room at *The Crimson*, someone had inscribed: "For historical purposes, please date your graffiti."

While I took to journalism, I also embraced academics. I majored in government but loved my economics and data science classes as well as intellectual history, philosophy, physics and literature. And while I understood that I had been admitted to Harvard as an affirmative action student from farm country, I discovered that I had a knack for academic work. I was a fast and competent writer, so I could compose papers quickly on the typewriter and required only a single draft.

My epiphany that a Yamhill farm kid could succeed at Harvard came at the end of my first semester, when I got all A's and picked up my comparative government term paper from the professor, Jorge Domínguez. "This is an extraordinarily well-written, well-researched and thoughtful paper," Domínguez wrote on the last page. "It is the kind of paper whose quality we expect only from grad students (but they, of course, don't write so well)." Domínguez invited me to his

As an editor of *The Harvard Crimson*, in the newspaper's newsroom.
Photo courtesy of Harvard University.

office, asked about my classes and told me that I could be at the top of my graduating class. With that encouragement, I threw myself into academic work and spent enormous amounts of time in the library until it closed at 1 a.m.

Harvard was intellectually exciting, but also anthropologically fascinating. Just as former Andover and Exeter students studied me as an example of *Homo oregonus*, I scrutinized my peers. In particular, until I arrived at Harvard I had never really met someone who was neurotic or admitted to it. And now I was surrounded by friends who boasted about how neurotic they were.

I had of course grown up with people who had mental health issues or unusual obsessions—Farlan Knapp, remember, wanted to murder his dad—but the term "neurotic" wasn't in the Oregon lexicon. Nor had I ever met anyone in therapy: Apparently, once you got an orthodontist, the next step was a therapist.

There were a dozen of us from Oregon in my year at Harvard, and we dined together monthly at a roving "Oregon Table." In hushed voices, we would compare notes. "Are we the weird ones?" someone asked. "Or are we normal, and they're weird?" At the time, we Oregonians felt a certain superiority over the East Coasters for avoiding neuroses, but in retrospect I think we were wrong. We just covered it up. If our crooked teeth weren't a topic, our crooked psyches were even less so. Mental health services weren't readily available, and anxiety and insecurity weren't issues people felt comfortable talking about. In later years, as growing numbers of my Oregon friends died by suicide, I wished that we had been more open about neuroses. We could have saved lives.

For my part, I engaged in introspection during my daily run. I'd take a break from the books each evening, sometime between 8 p.m. and midnight, and run a fast six miles along the Charles River. The nights were cool, the streetlights were adequate, the cars were few, the smell of the Charles filled my nostrils, and the lactic acid in my tiring legs felt refreshing. In those days before cell phones and personal music players, that was my chance to review the day, think about the next one and sort out my life.

After a shower, I'd return to the library. When my assigned reading became too tedious, I would stroll about, browsing the library stacks. One night while grazing on the shelves, I came upon *Who's Who*, the two-volume book listing prominent people, and I searched for my dad's name. Yes, there he was: *Kristof, Ladis Kris Donabed, political scientist, author* . . .

Who's Who entrants are invited to submit brief notes about the values that inspire them, and my father's followed his entry:

> War, want and concentration camps, exile from home and homeland, these have made me hate strife among men, but they have not made me lose faith in the future of mankind. Personal experience, including my own unsteady progress through life, has taught me to beware of man's capacity for plain stupid, irrational, as well as consciously evil, behavior, but it also taught me that man has an even greater capacity for recovery from lapses . . . In short, I remain a rationalist and an optimist at a time when the prophets of doom have the floor. My query is, if man has been able to create the arts, the sciences and the material civilization we know in America, why should he be judged powerless to create justice, fraternity and peace?

I read it again, then a third time. I had sometimes cringed when my dad spoke with an accent or muddled sports figures with rock stars, and I had a young person's impatience to move on and find new role models. But this brief essay spoke to me deeply, perhaps because I felt that I had inherited that optimism. I lugged the book to a photocopier and copied the page, then cut out that entry. I taped it to the wall above my desk—without telling my dad I had done so.

INCREASINGLY I THOUGHT I might end up as a writer. Every morning I read the *Times*, *The Crimson* and *The Boston Globe*, with a particular focus on the columnists. Anthony Lewis was my role model. He elevated a moral and worldly voice, about apartheid in South Africa and hunger at home, without ever shouting or speaking down to me. He was a journalist who observed, but his observation was harnessed to a sense of mission, and he was intellectually brilliant. Because he taught part-time at Harvard Law School, I was able to talk with him a couple of times when I was a student. He was thoughtful and nuanced in a way that I desperately wanted to be.

The summer after my first year at Harvard, I worked at the *Statesman Journal* in Salem, Oregon, and loved it. I happened to be working one weekend when forty-one sperm whales beached themselves near the town of Florence. I drove there with a photographer, Bob DeGiulio. It was a mesmerizing scene. The whales were still alive: thirty-five and forty feet long, caught in the sand, with huge eyes that watched us helplessly as we approached. They struggled in the sand or in pools of bloody water, their sides heaving, their tails thrashing, their blowholes spouting trickles of water. Local fishing crews tried vainly to use boats to pull them out. But the whales weighed up to 50,000 pounds each, and they were immovable. Some gentle souls poured buckets of water on them to relieve their distress, while heartless souvenir-hunters tried to carve out their teeth when no one was looking. Hundreds of sightseers flocked to the beach, and their dogs barked at the whales—and the whales looked back sadly and reproachfully.

A veterinarian was there and was trying to euthanize the whales, but didn't know how.

"I can put a fifty-pound dog to sleep," the vet told me. "But a fifty-thousand-pound whale? Where do I inject a whale? And what's the dose? They didn't teach this in vet school. I have no idea what to do."

As I watched and reported, the tide came in, half covering some of

Some of the forty-one sperm whales stranded on an Oregon beach.
Photo by Robert DeGiulio.

the whales. That gave them new hope, and two whales in particular thrashed about and seemed close to freeing themselves. The tide grew red with their blood, but then the high tide peaked and the waves slowly retreated. The whales gave up, exhausted, their mouths and blowholes half covered by wet sand.

It was heartbreaking to witness the whales' struggles but also in some sense thrilling. I felt guilty about the adrenaline rush while such suffering was unfolding before me. The torment of the whales sickened me, yet I couldn't turn away. They looked at me, and I looked at them. I hated being there, but I also wanted to stay longer and document the death throes—and I couldn't reconcile those conflicting impulses in myself.

So many times since then I have looked into despairing eyes like those—in scenes of genocide, war, natural disaster and epidemics—and I have felt a similar clash of emotions. The suffering tears my guts out, but I'm simultaneously traumatized by what I see and also determined to chronicle every last bit of it. At some level, a journalist bears witness to tragedies on behalf of all society, with a responsibility to call attention to them. The whale beaching was an indelible memory, and the experience confirmed my yearning to become a journalist and make effable the ineffable.

Yet how to get there? The *Statesman Journal* editors said they would like to hire me if they had an opening, but I dreamed of something at the national level. The *Statesman* was full of outstanding, hardworking reporters, yet almost none of them made it to *The Oregonian*, the next newspaper up in the hierarchy. And *Oregonian* reporters almost never made it one notch even higher, to *The Seattle Times*, let alone to the *Los Angeles Times* or to the national newspapers of the East Coast. I could imagine for myself a successful career as a *Statesman* reporter, perhaps winding up at *The Oregonian* if I worked hard and was lucky, but I didn't see any path at all to becoming Tony Lewis.

Walter Mears, a legendary political writer from the Associated Press, happened to visit the *Statesman Journal* while I was there. Mears was one of the most-read journalists in America, one who helped shape the narrative of the presidential campaigns he covered. Mears was a journalistic god, but what I remember best was what a *Statesman Journal* editor said about him.

"You know how he became No. 1 at the AP?" the editor asked me.

"He was exceptionally good and wrote like the wind?" I suggested.

"Yes, that too," the editor said. "But there were lots of reporters like that. Then one Christmas Eve early in his career, there was a fire at his home, and his wife and their two children were burned to death. Mears overcame that by escaping into his work. He distracted himself by working all the time. Fourteen hours a day, seven days a week. That's what set him apart. That's why he's so successful. That's what you do to get to the top."

That weighed on me. Is that what it took to make it to the premier echelon in journalism? Losing one's family and fighting the pain by working every waking hour? The price didn't seem worth it.

My backup plan was to become a lawyer or an academic, or perhaps work in government, but none of that captivated me as much as being paid to cover whale beachings. So I did my best with newspaper internships, trying to learn as much as I could. The following summer *The Boston Globe* rejected me for a summer internship, but I did get one at *The Oregonian*, covering the police but also writing editorials. And I learned from my plentiful mistakes. In one feature, I wrote about crime victims and mentioned a man who had been shot, Jack Pray. Publication of the story was delayed, and when it was about to run I called up the hospital to make sure that he was still alive. I asked to be connected to the nurses' station to check on the status of Jack Pray. Someone answered the phone, in a faint voice.

"This is Nick Kristof from *The Oregonian*," I said. "I just wanted to make sure that Jack Pray was still kicking. What's his condition?"

There was a long pause. "I think I'm alive," the voice replied. "This is Jack."

The Oregonian editors were open to hiring me, and that was encouraging. Given my reservations, I continued to work for *The Crimson*, focused on academics and prepared to apply to law school. I also applied for a Rhodes Scholarship. My Christmas present came early during my senior year: On December 21, 1980, after grueling state and regional interviews, I was named one of America's thirty-two Rhodes Scholars. Instead of going to law school in the fall, I would go to Oxford.

I SAW THAT LUCK, both bad and good, is cumulative and self-reinforcing. I had plenty of friends in Yamhill whose misfortunes multiplied: Their factories closed, they lost good union jobs, they self-medicated, they were arrested for possession of controlled substances, they couldn't find good new jobs because of their arrest records, they quarreled with their partners over money, they broke up, their kids struggled and they blamed themselves. Conversely, I seemed to keep winning the lottery precisely because I had previously won. I had hit the jackpot with my parents, and then I had been exceptionally lucky to be admitted to Harvard. That made it easier to win the Rhodes Scholarship, and winning that caught the eye of editors.

At the time, I saw my success through the prism of luck because I didn't have the vocabulary of privilege, but of course that's what it was. Good fortune isn't randomly distributed, except in the sense that we're all subject to the lottery of birth, but it is closely linked to race, class and the country one is born in. One advantage leads to another, and I was experiencing that now. My parents had also nurtured in me the confidence to try to bring about change, and that had led me to run for student body president in high school, propose that the school paper become a community paper, and draft the state law on school fees. In the Kristof household, anything felt possible, and that was one of the greatest gifts my parents gave me—it was another kind of privilege, and it too built on itself.

Among the editors impressed by my Rhodes Scholarship were those at *The Washington Post*. So the summer after I graduated I won a coveted internship there on the national desk.

Giants roamed the *Post*'s newsroom. David Broder, the legendary political reporter, advised me on how to cover senators: *Don't just interview them in their offices. Follow them around. Go see them in their home states.* Don Oberdorfer, the diplomatic correspondent, taught me about China—as well as how to cook Korean food. Don Graham, the publisher, was a regular presence in the newsroom, always humble and enthusiastic—and telling great stories about his time as a Washington police officer. Jim Hoagland, Peter Osnos and William Greider were superb editors who always had time for an intern and would throw stories my way. Bob Woodward answered questions about how to manage confidential sources: *Nurture them. Treat them with respect. Check in with them even when you're not on a specific story.* I liked to write science stories, so the science reporter Phil Hilts told me about a puzzling new report by the Centers for Disease Control of five cases of illness among gay men in San Francisco; Phil wrote about that CDC account, which would eventually be remembered as the first report of AIDS.

The titan overseeing these giants was Ben Bradlee, the executive editor: profane, decisive, charismatic, irreverent and brilliant. He had been a confidant of John Kennedy's and recounted how he had spent the evening of the crucial 1960 West Virginia primary waiting for the results with Kennedy at an X-rated movie theater, watching a porn film about a lustful housewife. Later Bradlee built the *Post* into a top-notch national newspaper and always had fun doing so. Editors told worshipful stories about Bradlee behind his back. My favorite concerned the time Secretary of State Alexander Haig briefed the press but insisted on being referred to only as "a senior official." Don Oberdorfer wrote the story about the "senior official," and Bradlee ran a photo beside the article showing Haig, with a caption explaining it was of "a senior official."

I loved Bradlee's willingness to go after politicians and hold them accountable, but sometimes there was a "gotcha" quality to *Post* reporting that left me uncomfortable (it's a strain of reporting that I think has grown over the decades, especially on social media). It may have been a by-product of reporters and editors trying too hard to please him. Once I was assigned to write about a Reagan administration official, J. Donald Millar, who had been appointed to run an occupational safety agency—which he then tried to move to Atlanta, his hometown. My editor wanted a snarky piece about him, a government official who wanted to move the agency for the sake of personal convenience. As I dug into the facts, it became clear that the move to Atlanta had been discussed before Millar was picked and had nothing to do with him. I told my editor, but he didn't want to give up a delicious gotcha narrative. We argued over it and finally published a toned-down piece that pleased neither of us.

Bradlee wasn't an efficient manager but he was an exceptional leader. Whenever editors have asked my advice about running a newsroom, I've told them how I'd watch Bradlee rally the troops. He would walk through the newsroom and, barely pausing, clap a reporter on the back and say something like *Great piece today. Nailed it. Go get 'em!* This would slow Bradlee by three seconds but result in that reporter working harder for months to come. Bradlee's approval was what we all sought.

Working for the *Post*'s national desk was intoxicating. Senators fell over themselves to be quoted by me. House members sought me out. Everyone took my calls. When a young socialist was elected mayor of Burlington, Vermont, I thought that might make a story, so I called his office one afternoon to figure out if I should make a trip there. I spoke to some man who answered the phone in the mayor's office and for thirty minutes we discussed the new mayor, Bernie Sanders, and the significance of the election of a socialist. Whenever I inquired about Sanders's plans, the aide answered with "we," which I thought a cute example of the staff fervor for the new mayor. Before hanging up, I asked the assistant's name. "Oh," he said, a bit sheepishly, "actually, I'm Bernie Sanders."

At first, I thought the willingness of politicians to talk to me arose from their erroneous belief that I was a full-fledged *Post* reporter, but it turned out that they didn't care that I was an intern. They just cared about being quoted. Some members of Congress were in what I thought of as the 5 p.m. gang: You could call their offices at 5 p.m. and get a quote within an hour, in time for an evening story on deadline. A young New York congressman named Chuck Schumer was in the group and very effective with a quote.

All this was a bit disillusioning about politicians. I had thought that House members and senators spent their time wrestling with policy and discussing issues with administration officials, but I saw that they calculated that they could most influence the White House by being quoted in the *Post*—even if by an intern. Anyone with a *Post* byline, however temporary, was courted. One day I was interviewing a staff member for Representative Ed Markey, and another man kept trying to intrude on our conversation in an ingratiating way. It took me a while to figure out that this was Markey himself.

My interest in journalism grew steadily: If I wanted a path to have impact, journalism offered it. But while politics reporting made the front page, it was also often reactive and formulaic. I enjoyed it, but perhaps even more I admired foreign and science coverage, as well as investigative projects. I wanted to find a niche to report for the *Post* or a paper like it, but in a way that would give me space to craft my work and leave an imprint on my stories.

At the end of the summer, editors said they wanted to hire me for the Metro section. I was headed for Oxford and wasn't in the job market, but I felt I was finally on the cusp of the big leagues.

8

From Oxford to the Khyber Pass

My new home as a Rhodes Scholar at Oxford was Magdalen College, perhaps the most beautiful of Oxford's colleges. Dating from the 1400s, it has a medieval bell tower, chapel and cloisters, a "deer park" with stags, and a walking trail through the woods. A river runs through it, with boats for students to borrow. It has hosted some of the world's leading scholars, including C. S. Lewis and Seamus Heaney, and I was amused that its "New Building" was constructed in the eighteenth century.

I settled in at Magdalen to study law, and I enjoyed both the rigor of the law and the brilliance of Magdalen's dons. But while I loved Oxford's studies, I loved Oxford's schedule even more: For every eight weeks of term, we had six weeks of vacation. In theory, we were supposed to spend the vacations reading and studying, but this was also an incredible chance to travel the world—and report. I began to cold-call news organizations to see if I could drum up interest in freelance pieces on my travels, and *The Wall Street Journal*, *The Oregonian* and *The Observer* were all interested.

On my first Oxford vacation, I traveled with a Rhodes Scholar from Washington State, Chris Suits, through Poland. Our trip coincided with the high point of Poland's Solidarity movement against the Communist government. We visited the shipyards in Gdansk, the center of the labor movement, where workers were full of confidence that they could overturn Communism and turn Poland into a free country.

"Poland is coming alive," one man told us. The world was closely following events in Poland in hopes that the Communist dictatorships in Eastern Europe might collapse, and I began to think how I might write something for one paper or another.

On December 13, 1981, Chris and I were on a train from Warsaw to Krakow when the train halted on the tracks in the middle of the night for two hours. It was a cold, crowded train and Chris and I didn't have seats. As we stood, exhausted, near the end of a railcar, a wave of incredulous chatter swept through the train.

"The government going crazy," someone told us in broken English.

"It's emergency," said another.

"War!" said one. "State of war!"

Chris, who spoke Russian, finally figured out that the Polish president had imposed martial law, arrested Solidarity leaders, closed the borders and cut off phone, telex and telegram service. This, of course, was long before the Internet, so Poland was sealed off. Overnight it became a black box. All the world was focused on events there, but outsiders had little idea of what was actually going on. Journalists couldn't get in, and those in the country—most of them in Warsaw—couldn't file their stories or talk to anyone outside the country.

Chris and I stayed with my Polish cousins and uncle, and I spent every moment in Krakow interviewing underground labor leaders, evading checkpoints and climbing over fences to talk to striking workers. The big challenge was filing my stories, but I learned that tourists were being allowed to leave the country by train and began to track down American tourists, hoping they might help me out.

"I'm a journalist," I explained each time. "Would you be willing to carry out an article of mine? When you're in Vienna, you can call *The Washington Post* collect, using my name—I'll give you the phone number—and then read it over the phone to them. Okay?"

"That sounds dangerous," one traveler said skeptically.

"How much will you pay me?" another asked.

But several did agree to carry out my articles. While the *Post* had no idea I was in Poland, I hoped that it would accept the charges if it received a collect call purportedly from me.

I handwrote each story and tried to find two people to carry out each one, as a backup. It may seem a bit extreme to go to such trouble to file stories on vacation for a newspaper that wasn't expecting them, but I saw an opportunity and wanted to get the word out about the repression in Poland. I couldn't fight the dreaded riot police directly, but I could hold them accountable in my articles—if I could just get the stories out of the country.

Two Middlebury students on Christmas vacation were eager to help, so they smuggled out my first story. The *Post* was confused to get the call but accepted the charges. Editors were thrilled when they realized they had an exclusive dispatch from inside Poland. The article ran as the lead story on top of the front page. I continued to find people to carry stories out, even as the *Times* and other news organizations gnashed their teeth in frustration at being unable to get coverage.

The tale of a former summer intern smuggling out news stories from Poland to *The Washington Post* generated its own interest. In Oregon, a Portland television station sent a crew to the Yamhill farm to do a story along the lines of "Local Parents Terrified for Son in Poland." The interview didn't go as planned:

> BREATHLESS INTERVIEWER: You must be so worried about your son in Poland under martial law!
>
> LADIS KRISTOF: Oh, no, he'll be fine. He'll take care of himself.
>
> BREATHLESS INTERVIEWER: But they're arresting people there! They're shooting people!
>
> LADIS KRISTOF: Nicholas will be careful. And it's actually a very good opportunity for him. He wants to be a journalist, and this is very big news.
>
> BREATHLESS INTERVIEWER: But what if he can't get out? What if he's stuck in Poland under martial law?
>
> LADIS KRISTOF: That would be lucky for him, because then he can keep reporting.

I had no idea that my stories were reaching the *Post* and causing a stir, and I didn't fully appreciate the world's fascination with the mystery of what was going on in Poland. Chris and I finally took a train out of Poland, and at the border with Czechoslovakia, Polish soldiers searched our bags and found my Solidarity materials. They pulled me off the train and threatened to imprison me. "This is war!" one said. But they didn't really know what to do with me, so they eventually returned me to the train without the contraband.

"You are banned from Poland for life!" one said firmly. (Over the decades, I've been banned from several countries "for life." But in each case it has turned out not to be my life but that of some bureaucrat or autocrat.)

We rolled on through Czechoslovakia in an empty, unheated train, bundled in sleeping bags, and when we pulled into Vienna, suddenly there were cameras in our faces. Dozens of camera crews met each train coming from Poland in hopes of getting information.

"We've got a couple of English-speakers here!" one cameraman bellowed joyfully. And the mob of reporters charged us. It's useful— and sobering—for a journalist to occasionally see journalism from the other end.

WHEN I RETURNED to Oxford, I pored over contracts, torts, international law and more, but also spent plenty of time socializing with exceptionally smart people. I regularly found myself tossing ideas around with a gifted philosophy student who had become a vegetarian in the course of studying animal rights. His arguments made me think of the personalities of the sheep we raised, and I began to have my first doubts about meat-eating.

Outside Magdalen, I hung out with a range of other brilliant scholars. I met Tony Abbott, an Australian full of charm and considerable ability as a boxer. He thought he was headed for a political career, but all my Australian friends said he was too conservative to get anywhere in politics. (They kept saying that until he became prime minister of Australia in 2013.) Another friend was a Princeton graduate named Elena Kagan, who shared my interest in both law and journalism. We occasionally had meals or caught a play together.*

I had brought a football and a Frisbee to Oxford, so we often had football or Ultimate Frisbee games on the lawns of Magdalen's New Building. One of the gang was my pal George Brandis, an Australian

---

* When Elena was nominated for the Supreme Court by President Obama in 2010, there were rumors that she was gay and that Republicans would make this an issue. The *Times* decided to prepare an article in case the topic came up, and, according to the version I heard, someone in the Washington bureau delicately raised the issue with Elena. I soon received a call from a colleague in the bureau. He was chortling but managed to get this out: "Elena Kagan said: 'I'm not gay. Just go ask Nick Kristof.'" I suspect she meant that I could confirm that she had no history of lesbian partners. But that's not how it was perceived by my colleagues.

who played Frisbee with more gusto than skill but taught me to become a word collector. He and I would exchange words.

I would come across a delightful word like "Pecksniffian," meaning someone who is hypocritical and proclaims fake moral principles (after the Dickens character Mr. Pecksniff), and throw it into a conversation with George. He would seize it and might toss back "gambrinous" (full of beer) or "roorback" (a dirty rumor used against a political opponent). This pretentious logophilia (love of words) occasionally found its way into my prose, as when I sneaked "pullulate" into a column about Afghanistan: "The crisp mountain air pullulated with hope."

George also introduced me to the work of Sir Isaiah Berlin, the Oxford philosopher and historian of ideas who became my intellectual hero. Berlin was a small man, and a giant. Graying, with angular features and bushy eyebrows overshadowing his black horn-rimmed glasses, he was a formal man who strolled around Oxford in a suit with a dark hat. A Russian Jew from Latvia, Berlin spoke eight languages and was a brilliant conversationalist and scholar. I felt my IQ rising just by being in the same room with him.

Berlin believed in what he termed the "pluralism of values." He argued that there may be a deep human yearning to find the One True Answer, the single most important goal, the paramount value, but that in fact there are many things we consider important and must juggle: freedom, dignity, equality, health, opportunity. These values are sometimes in conflict, and there is no single yardstick by which to compare them; they are incommensurate. So our job is to advance clumsily, doing what we can to achieve multiple and competing goals while recognizing that the outcome will be an imperfect, muddled compromise. That has always resonated with me, for it fits the complicated world I've reported on.

It's okay to acknowledge that our moral judgments may be flawed, Berlin argued, even as we act on them. We're humans; we get things wrong. We should have the humility to accept that our "truths" may not be eternal—yet if they reflect our best judgment, we should act on them unflinchingly. We can be intellectually humble without necessarily being paralyzed by uncertainty and handwringing.

"Principles are not less sacred because their duration cannot be guaranteed," Berlin wrote. "Indeed, the very desire for guarantees that our values are eternal and secure in some objective heaven is perhaps only a craving for the certainties of childhood."

I reached out to Sir Isaiah and he graciously agreed to meet me and my friends. We peppered him with questions, and in his answers he epitomized a French word he liked, *épater:* to dazzle, to astonish, to amaze. What struck me most was his intellectual humility. He said he had moved away from philosophy and toward the history of ideas because he didn't think that he was adding much to the field.

"It doesn't seem cumulative," he said of philosophy. "We're still arguing about some of the same things we were debating two thousand years ago. I didn't see that I had much to offer."

Above all, Berlin was deeply suspicious of any political or economic system that seemed too perfect, too neat or too confident in its answers. This made him hostile to Communism but also opposed to the free-market fundamentalism of Margaret Thatcher and Ronald Reagan. He was skeptical of dogmatism and ideologues and taught me to prefer complexity and nuance, which all in all is a healthy mindset for a journalist.

WHILE I ENJOYED OXFORD, Ultimate Frisbee and word-trading, I relished travel and journalism more. I wrote occasionally for *The Washington Post* and *The Oregonian*, often on subjects I knew little about. I managed to win a prize for *The Oregonian* for Africa coverage, which was amusing since I was simply a law student writing articles while on vacation about a continent I was curious about.

Journalism is a perfect occupation for the curious: It pays you to venture into new areas and try new things, and wide-ranging questions produce good quotes and better stories. A burden of a journalistic career is that you usually never become truly expert in anything, in the way a scholar masters a small slice of some discipline, but the upside is that a reporter has license to follow whims and dive into new areas and call the leading experts to sup their hard-earned knowledge.

In England, I was curious about the intersection of sports and the British upper class, so I covered the Henley Royal Regatta for *The Washington Post*. The regatta is one of the world's premier rowing events, but I had no idea what I was doing. I kept hearing terms like eights, scullers, stroke side, rigger jigger, blade spoon, feathering and crabbing, and I needed a translator. My heart sank when I met my competition in covering Henley: The *Times* had sent its "rowing correspondent," Norman Hildes-Heim, to cover the regatta. "Hey, Norman!" the Georgetown coach shouted at him. "How are you, old buddy?" Hildes-Heim, a middle-aged man in a jacket and tie who exuded confidence, knew rowing, knew the coaches and knew the regatta. This could have been humiliating for me. Fortunately, for all the rivalry among newspapers, journalists sometimes look out for each other.

"You want a little introduction to rowing?" Norman asked gently, after it became clear that I was clueless. Instead of lording it over me, he gave me a crash course so I could cover the regatta. He explained which races my readers would be interested in and why, while also showing me the process for boarding a motorboat to follow the race. Afterward, we interviewed the coaches together, and he asked all the smart questions as I wrote down the responses.

Norman rescued his competitor, and I resolved that if I ever became a professional journalist, I would pay it forward by helping other young reporters.

I continued to travel during each Oxford vacation, financing my trips by writing articles for *The Wall Street Journal* and *The Observer*. The problem was that while they would pay for articles, they wouldn't cover my expenses—and ever since then I've had a deep sympathy for freelance journalists who must cover their own travel costs.

On a trip to Pakistan and India, I traveled to the tribal areas on the Pakistan-Afghan border to report on heroin production. These areas were closed to foreigners, and if I had hired a car and driver like any sensible correspondent, I would have been stopped at a checkpoint and turned back. But I couldn't afford a car and driver, so I bought a ticket for a few cents and jammed myself deep inside standing-room-only space in the back of a local bus. Soldiers at checkpoints don't bother looking for foreigners in the middle of local buses. I was traveling with a fellow Rhodes Scholar and law student, Tom Patterson, and Tom was amazingly compliant about being dragged into no-go areas to interview gunmen about their heroin sales.

Darra Adam Khel was our first stop. It was a village with scores of gunsmiths making AK-47s, handguns and even heavy weapons. Every few minutes in Darra, a gunsmith would step out of his shop with a weapon and test it by firing a burst into the air. The gunsmiths were Pashtuns with long beards; they looked like Hebrew Bible prophets who happened to be equipped with automatic weapons. Many shops also sold hashish or heroin, and one gunsmith showed me a remarkable gun disguised as a pen.

"It can write just like any other pen," he said, showing me. "But you take out the ink nib like this"—he showed me—"and put in a .20-caliber bullet. Then you cock it like this. Then push the pocket clip, and it fires out the writing end."

I wanted a pen-gun! And it was only $5!

"I've got to get it," I told Tom.

"Is that a good idea?" Tom asked. "What are you going to tell customs officials at Heathrow when they find you bringing a disguised gun into England?"

"You think they'd find it?"

"Hmm. I wonder if you'll be able to continue your Rhodes after you've completed your prison sentence."

"Okay, okay," I said. "But that's the coolest pen I've ever seen."

The next day, I dropped by the U.S. Consulate in Peshawar to find out what the diplomats there knew about the heroin trade. I said I was writing an article for *The Wall Street Journal,* which was strictly true, and I didn't correct their misimpression that I was a *Journal* foreign correspondent. The press officer was delighted to see an American journalist and brought in the consul general, and we spent a wonderful hour chatting. As I excused myself, the consul general asked where I was staying, in case they wanted to get ahold of me.

"Oh, it's a small hotel," I said. "I'll drop by again in a couple of days." I didn't want to tell them that Tom and I were staying at a $2-a-night dive whose other guests were shooting heroin.

"Which hotel?" the consul general persisted.

"Er, the Khyber Hotel," I said.

"Oh, you mean the Khyber Intercontinental?"

"No, it's just called the Khyber Hotel."

"Hmm." The consul general was perplexed. "I know all the hotels in town. You don't mean Green's Hotel?"

"No, it's just the Khyber Hotel. A couple of blocks past Green's Hotel. It's a small place."

"The Khyber Hotel." The consul general was mystified.

"Ohhhh, I know!" the press officer said, turning to the consul general. "Remember, it's the place where that addict died this spring? We had to ship the body home."

I sensed my credibility plummeting.

9

"I Will Shoot You"

One of my most useful learning experiences in journalism came when I was almost shot in Ghana.

In early 1982 I was scheming with my Rhodes friend Dan Esty to use an Oxford vacation to travel across West Africa so I could write for *The Wall Street Journal.* We planned to travel overland through ten countries from Nigeria to Gambia. A Harvard classmate from Ghana had invited us to stay with him, and Ghana had just experienced a military coup d'état, creating interest among editors.

A few days before we were to leave, Dan dropped by my room. "We've got a big problem," he said.

"I just got a letter from our host in Ghana," Dan explained. "Except he's not in Ghana. His family has fled the country, they were almost shot, and he says the country is in chaos. Soldiers are out of control. He emphasizes that it's too dangerous and we should absolutely cancel plans to visit Ghana."

"But we've paid for tickets," I protested. "And Ghana is in the middle of our trip."

"Yeah, I know."

"We should be fine," I suggested. "Look, let's go to the border and learn what we can. If it seems too dangerous then we'll have to go around or figure out another way."

As often happens with journalists, I was not dispassionate in evaluating the risk. I wanted to go to Ghana to write stories, so I discounted the danger signs.

We flew to Nigeria and set out. We traveled by shared "bush taxi"— a crowded car or minibus—through Benin to Togo, which neighbors Ghana, and then paused for reconnaissance. Togo was full of refugees from Ghana who warned that the army was broadcasting warnings: *Every loyal Ghanaian should be alert for counterrevolutionaries from abroad.* They also warned that the official exchange rate was extortionate— 2.7 Ghanaian cedi to the dollar, while unofficially the rate was about 40 to a dollar. If we changed money at the official rate, Ghana would be prohibitively expensive. But if we changed money at the more reasonable black market rate, we could face "unprecedented revolutionary justice." It wasn't clear just what that meant, but a man in the city of Tema had just been shot for going outside after curfew to urinate.

So I pulled my Frisbee from my pack, and Dan and I tossed it to each other on a Togo beach as we weighed our lives against the potential black market savings. The Frisbee went back and forth, and so did we, but finally we figured out how to commit the perfect crime. Ghanaian refugees were selling their cedi, so it was easy to buy from them in

Taking a break on my cross-Africa trip. *Photo by Dan Esty.*

Togo. We then put the bills in plastic bags and inserted the baggies in a bottle of Nivea body lotion that we bought in the market.

"This is masterful," I told Dan. "Even if a soldier picked up the Nivea bottle and unscrewed the top, he would see only lotion."

As we prepared to cross into Ghana, I told Dan that he had to be the one carrying the Nivea bottle.

"Why should I be the one risking execution?" Dan asked.

"Well, I'll be a journalist in Ghana, and journalists shouldn't break the law."

"So you're okay with using smuggled currency," Dan said, "but journalistic principles prevent you from actually carrying the contraband?"

"Yeah, it would look bad if a journalist were shot for currency smuggling," I told him. "Plus, this way I can always write your obituary."

Dan reluctantly agreed to carry the Nivea bottle in his pack as we crossed the border. Ghanaian soldiers examined our bags, but not closely, and we boarded a bus for Accra, the capital. There were several military checkpoints along the way where we all had to get off the bus and be screened. At one, a soldier with an AK-47 took me aside. I had my single-lens reflex camera on a strap around my neck, and that was probably why.

Everybody else returned to the bus and looked through the window as the soldier pointed his rifle at my chest.

"I will shoot you," he said, speaking English with a strong accent. That seemed an unusual thing to say, so I thought maybe I had misunderstood.

"What did you say?" I asked.

"I will shoot you!" He gestured with his gun at my chest. "I will shoot you ten times."

I waited for him to explain. But he just looked at me expectantly. There was silence for a moment.

"I will shoot you," he repeated, a bit impatiently. "I will shoot you ten times."

"Ten times?" Then I realized that was perhaps the wrong part of his statement to question.

"Yes, yes," he said eagerly, thinking he was getting through to me. "I will shoot you. Ten times."

In retrospect, I think he wanted my camera, or hoped that I would offer him a bribe to save my life. But I was too thick to understand.

Finally, disgusted by my obtuseness, he shrugged and stepped aside so I could board the bus. The passengers beamed at me and a few shook hands with me. I think they were congratulating me on my integrity for refusing to pay a bribe.

We rolled into Accra and found a dilapidated $5-a-night hotel in the center of town (it would have been $74 at the official rate). With the curtains drawn we carved open our Nivea bottle and extracted our currency. We felt triumphant, but we were now concerned by the presence of the cut-up plastic bottle. Surely anyone would look at it and conclude, *Currency smugglers who deserve unprecedented revolutionary justice!*

"Dan," I suggested, "I think you should throw the Nivea bottle away somewhere outside. We shouldn't leave it in the room."

"Why me?"

"It wouldn't really be appropriate for a journalist . . . ," I began.

"Oh, right." He rolled his eyes. "Those ethics again."

Dan set out with the telltale carcass of a Nivea bottle. After a few blocks, he threw it in a trash can and started to walk away. But then he worried that some government agent might be tailing him and recover it. So he retraced his steps and picked the bottle out of the trash to search for some place to discard it where it couldn't be recovered. Now, Dan is a brilliant guy. Today he's a professor at Yale Law School and a leading expert on climate policy. But international smuggling can cause lapses even in geniuses.

When Dan returned to the hotel room, he looked crestfallen and a bit scared.

"I did something really stupid," he told me. "You may want to kill me now."

"Oh, no. What did you do?"

"That Nivea bottle? I threw it on the roof of the National Museum of Ghana."

"*What?*"

"Well, I didn't want anybody to find it."

"So you threw it on a national monument?"

"Yes, right afterward I thought: Why did I do that?"

I opened the room door and peeked out in each direction.

"The SWAT team isn't here yet," I said. "Seriously, Dan, did anyone see you?"

"Well, there were some people around. Not many. But I do stand out in Ghana."

"So much for our perfect crime. If they execute you first, I'll still try to do that obituary of you. But it's going to be a mean one."

We got away with it. After Accra, we set out by bush taxi and a couple of days later were approaching the Ivory Coast. I was feeling pretty cocky. I had good material for a *Journal* article and my head swelled as I contemplated the beginning of an illustrious career as a dashing foreign correspondent, going where others dared not go. A fearless writer! A second Hemingway!

About ten miles from the Ivory Coast border, we were on a dirt road going through the jungle in an old Peugeot station wagon jammed with nine people, our luggage on the roof. The road was a rusty red, and dense green vegetation pressed in from both sides of the road, with palms presiding from above. The red clay and green foliage made a beautiful scene. There was no village nearby, no huts—and then all of a sudden we encountered a military checkpoint, which consisted of two armed soldiers, both of them drunk.

They ran at our bush taxi, raising their weapons and pointing them at us as the vehicle braked. The soldiers seemed enraged. The friendly chatter in the car stopped. The soldiers shouted at us in the Fante language, apparently ordering us out of the car. We all hurriedly obeyed. The African passengers began grabbing their bundles and untying them, so we assumed that the soldiers had demanded that we show them our bags. We opened our backpacks.

Up until this point, we had largely benefited from racial discrimination in Africa. Whether because local people had absorbed colonial attitudes or because they wanted to be hospitable to foreigners, they often tried to put us at the head of lines, or give us the best rooms in a hotel, or place us in the front seats of bush taxis (part of the reasoning seemed to be that police were less likely to demand bribes if two white guys were in front). In any case, our period of privilege had abruptly ended.

The two soldiers yelled at Dan and me and motioned for us to step aside with our bags, and they seemed thrilled to detect our fear. Then they went through everyone else's luggage, seizing some of it. There wasn't much worth stealing, but they took whatever appealed to them, including a bottle of liquor that they sampled and that left them even more drunk. I wasn't sure if they were going to pass out first or shoot us first, but they finally worked their way through the other passengers and let them get back in the vehicle with their bags—and then they turned to us. I was afraid that our vehicle would drive off, but it stayed.

One soldier was perhaps twenty and of medium height, and particularly animated and ferocious. He regularly pointed his AK-47 at our chests and shouted. He had a round face and might have looked pleasant in another context, but now his eyes were bloodshot and his features distorted by anger. The other soldier was in his mid-twenties and also of medium height. Neither had shaved for a month. The older one was slightly less drunk and spoke a bit of English. Perhaps he was an officer, because he carried only a pistol. He interpreted when necessary but let the younger one take charge.

The young one shouted at us unintelligibly.

"Where you come from?" the older one translated for us.

I paused, wondering whether to say Canada, because nobody hates Canadians. For this reason, to be able to pass myself off as Canadian if necessary, I had memorized the Canadian national anthem, "O Canada." However, if they asked for documents, I wasn't sure I could convince them that my American passport was actually a Canadian passport. I was too indecisive, and Dan piped up, "America."

The younger soldier started shouting again, with a mention of "CIA."

"You are with CIA?" the older soldier asked.

"No, no!" Dan said. "Students. We are students. We have come to help Ghana. We love Ghanaians."

The younger soldier wasn't paying attention. Muttering something about CIA, he dumped my backpack out on the dirt, and then Dan's beside mine. He started to kick things around with his toe but then knelt down and used his hands to examine our belongings. I had three books on West Africa that he studied but gave up on. My socks and underwear weren't interesting. But then he saw something white and grabbed it and waved it triumphantly, with more shouting.

"This is radar?" the older soldier asked, pointing to it. "CIA radar?"

The young soldier was triumphantly grasping my Frisbee.

"No, no," I said. "It's for playing. It's a game."

"You throw it," Dan explained. "I'll show you."

As he reached for the Frisbee, the young soldier leaped back and pointed the gun right at Dan's chest, and for one terrible moment I thought he was going to shoot.

"No, no," Dan said. "It's a toy. It's called a Frisbee." He slowly mimicked throwing it. "I can show you."

The soldiers spoke a bit and closely examined the Frisbee. They didn't let Dan hold it, apparently for fear it could be a weapon, but they put it on the ground, quite delicately, and then went through the rest of our gear.

"Your money?" the older soldier asked. "You do black market?"

"No black market," I assured him, trying to look appalled at the suggestion.

"How much you pay to taxi?" he asked. That felt like a trick question, because there was an official price that was ridiculously low, so everybody paid a higher black market price—and that was illegal.

"We haven't settled on that," Dan said quickly.

"You pay with dollars?"

"Oh, no," I said. "We're in Ghana. We pay with cedi." I wasn't sure that it was illegal to pay in dollars, but it sounded as if it was the kind of thing that led to unprecedented revolutionary justice.

"Show me."

We pulled out our wallets and showed him our Ghanaian currency. We each had about $15 worth of the local currency. The young soldier grabbed all my Ghanaian cedi, and the older one grabbed Dan's. The soldiers looked at our empty wallets and then told us to remove our shoes and socks in case we had secreted money there.

What they didn't realize was that we were showing them decoy wallets that we carried, so that if we were robbed we could hand over a wallet and a respectable amount of money—you never want to disappoint a gunman—while our U.S. dollars and credit cards were stashed in pouches tucked inside our pants.

The soldiers spoke between themselves, with our stuff still scattered on the road, and then the older one told us to turn around. We did so.

"Put hands on head," the older soldier told us, and we followed his orders, as the young soldier resumed shouting.

"Walk away to edge of road," the older soldier said. Suddenly I was convinced they were going to shoot us in the back, dump our bodies in the jungle, and take our belongings.

Would our bodies ever be found? Would my parents ever know what had happened to me? I felt a great heaviness. My journalistic career was ending before it began. My grand dreams were collapsing. I would never be a foreign correspondent, just a decaying corpse in the jungle.

Dan read the situation exactly the same way. He slowly turned around to face the soldiers, and I did the same.

"I'd just like to pick up my things off the ground," Dan said soothingly, and he slowly stooped to pack things. When he wasn't shot, I followed.

"I'm not sure what you're planning, but the American Embassy is going to be looking for us," Dan added.

At that moment we benefited from a helpful diversion: An overcrowded bus came rumbling down the road. There were dozens of people on it. Plenty of people to rob.

The younger soldier ran toward the bus, shouting wildly, and as he lifted his rifle I thought he was going to rake it with bullets. But the bus stopped in time and he began to shout at the passengers and order them out with their bags. The older soldier sensed the opportunity, and he followed the younger soldier toward the bus.

"Hey!" It was the driver of our bush taxi, whispering urgently. He motioned to our bags and gestured for us to load them quickly. We did so and jumped in the vehicle, and our taxi took off. I crouched down, in case the soldiers shot after us, but I don't think they even noticed.

Terror was seared into me that afternoon. On that road I felt that I might die, and I had no control over the outcome. We were extraordinarily lucky that our car had waited for us, that the bus had rolled along right when it seemed we might be shot, and that the driver had been willing to rush off with us when the soldiers were distracted.

It had seemed valiant and heroic to venture into western Ghana in the middle of a revolution—just what a brave correspondent should do to get the story!—but now it seemed idiotic. The job of a journalist, I realized, isn't just to get the story; it's to get the story and then get out to file it safely. And I had risked not just my life but Dan's as well.

I've been held at gunpoint many times since, more times than I can count, but that early encounter will forever be imprinted on my soul. In retrospect, it was useful to get a good scare early in my journalistic career. Ever since, when I've pondered whether to go down a dubious road in some conflict area, I've tried to remember that everything is always going fine until it isn't—and at that point, there's no way out. Those minutes of terror on that red road in the green jungle may have helped keep me alive in the decades since by knocking some sense into me.

Yet the tenuousness of life that I came to understand on that road also provided a larger framework for my journalism: If I'm going to take risks on occasion, I want to do it for a purpose larger than a page one byline or my news organization's quarterly profits.

10

Making Mistakes in Arabic

War-torn Beirut is not an obvious tourist destination, but in 1982 I convinced a couple of Oxford friends, one from Canada and the other from Australia, to come with me on a journey through the Middle East. Israel had recently invaded Lebanon, and I thought I would have good writing opportunities. We stayed on a floor in mostly Christian East Beirut but crossed the no-man's-land into Muslim West Beirut for a day. We stopped by the Commodore Hotel, where many Western journalists lived as they covered the civil war, and we hung out with Loren Jenkins from *The Washington Post*. He didn't know me from Adam, but I said I had interned at the *Post*, so he invited us to his room for a long conversation about the mess in Lebanon.

The Commodore was something of a safe haven, partly because it was surrounded by taller buildings that absorbed gunfire, and partly because the owner was a brilliant businessman who negotiated with militias to keep his guests safe—and well connected to phone and telex lines. The Commodore was also remarkable for its African parrot, Coco, who did a perfect imitation of an incoming shell. Coco would perform, and everyone in the bar would dive for cover.

My friends and I visited Sabra and Shatila, two Palestinian refugee camps. Afterward, it was evening and we needed to get back to East Beirut. We quickly became lost and were afraid to ask people the way to East Beirut. Finally we found the last checkpoint on the West

Beirut side, and the Muslim gunmen there said that the East Beirut checkpoint was a few hundred meters ahead on a winding path through bombed-out buildings. They warned us that we shouldn't go through at night, but we had no place to stay in West Beirut, and it seemed a short distance. We had been warned that extremist Shia militias sometimes roamed the no-man's-land, stopping and executing people, but I discounted that as rumor or exaggeration. So we set out.

It was dark and spooky, for we were walking through the ruins of buildings that had been destroyed by years of shelling. We walked fast—until suddenly a group of gunmen materialized around us. They pointed their weapons at us, and we paused and raised our hands.

"*Marhaba*," I said, greeting them warmly in Arabic, or as warmly as possible when your voice is shaking. "*As-salamu alaykum.*"

"Who are you?" the lead gunman asked in English, for it must have been obvious we were Westerners.

"We're visitors," I said. "Tourists. We're just trying to cross back to where we're staying."

"You're tourists?" The gunman sounded very skeptical. "Here?"

"Yes! Tourists!"

"Where are you from?"

"Canada," my friend said. I wondered about saying Canada as well, but I was afraid they were going to ask for our passports next.

"America," I said, and they didn't shoot me.

"Australia," said my other buddy, Peter W. Collinson, in a thick Australian accent, and the gunmen got very excited.

"Israel? Did you say Israel?"

"No, no!" Peter said, panicked. "Australia! Australia!"

"Israel?" The gunman was confused and didn't understand Peter's accent.

"Australia," I said, afraid that this Shia militia was going to kill us immediately in retribution for Israel's invasion. "He's saying 'Australia.'"

The gunman understood now. "Okay, Australia," said the leader, deflating. "I understand. We are from Israel, and we thought you were, too."

It turned out that this wasn't a Shia militia but a group of invading Israeli troops patrolling the no-man's-land. They were happy to see an American and very friendly to us, directing us on our way to East Beirut and suggesting that Jerusalem made a better tourist destination than a Beirut no-man's-land in the middle of a war.

A few days later, Christian militias invaded the Sabra and Shatila camps and slaughtered many hundreds of civilians, perhaps thousands. Many of the people I had seen were now dead. I was still scared by events in Beirut but determined to cover stories like the massacres in the camps.

On the same trip, we also traveled through Syria and visited the city of Hama, where the government had recently crushed a rebellion by sending in the army and mowing down thousands of civilians. For weeks, the army had used artillery, tanks and bombs to destroy the center of Hama. What was left was a vast field of rubble, perhaps a few hundred acres. Credible estimates of the death toll ranged from about 10,000 to 40,000.

I wanted to write about the massacre, but I needed witnesses. Most people were too terrified to talk to me, but I found an old man on the fringe of the destroyed area who was looking for anything he could salvage in the remnants of his home. Perhaps because of his age, he was

Following Oxford custom, friends doused me with champagne after I finished my final exams.

less afraid and wanted to tell me what had happened. He pantomimed aircraft attacking the city, then soldiers shooting machine guns, and I think he tried to tell me that several of his children or grandchildren had been slaughtered. But he spoke only Arabic, and he and I were deeply frustrated by each other's linguistic limitations.

It was that day in Hama that I began to think about learning Arabic. I wanted to be able to cover stories like this massacre, and I realized that Arabic would be an enormous help. So as I was finishing up at Oxford, I applied to the intensive Arabic program at the American University of Cairo. I was offered a scholarship to study Arabic for a year.

Some Rhodes friends were moving into finance, and a contingent was heading for Harvard Law School. I had also applied to Harvard Law School to continue my legal studies, and there came a week in the spring of 1983 when I had to choose between Harvard and the American University. In a larger sense, it was a choice between a secure career as a lawyer or an insecure career as a journalist.

I felt a certain tug toward the more conventional choice. I had won academic prizes at Oxford and was gliding toward first-class honors in law; in one law subject, I earned a mark that supposedly was the highest ever awarded. I could imagine life as a senior partner at some prestigious law firm with a corner office and a luxury weekend house to drive to in my Mercedes, or as a distinguished law professor like Ronald Dworkin. Yet I kept thinking about that scene of the whales on the beach, or the day trying to report on the massacre at Hama, or the people I'd seen in the Sabra and Shatila camps who died so soon afterward, or those I'd seen in villages in Mali and Niger, or in Pakistan and India—villages a bit like Yamhill, where people had few opportunities and rarely received attention. I thought of my father and his journey, and the people who had helped him along the way, and of people in the extended family who had died or been sent to Auschwitz or Siberia because no one was there to bear witness. This was a fork in the road for me, and I thought of Robert Frost's poem about taking the road "less traveled by, / and that has made all the difference."

At the end of the week I told Harvard Law School no, and sent an acceptance to Cairo. I preferred to be a journalist, even if that meant giving up the Mercedes for a beat-up Chevy. And that has made all the difference.

I ARRIVED IN CAIRO in the middle of the night. I smiled as I wended my way in a shared taxi through the darkened city. Its complicated odors filled my nose and lungs: sweat, coffee, urine, jasmine and the Nile, all to the background music of Umm Kulthum, the legendary Egyptian singer, dubbed "Egypt's fourth pyramid." By the time I reached the American University in Cairo near Tahrir Square, the muezzin's call to prayer was echoing through the city.

My first conversation in Arabic was cautionary. *"Ismak eh?"* the doorman to my building asked me. He was a nice Sudanese man who slept in the building entrance. I was thrilled because I understood what he was asking: *What is your name?* So I beamed and answered.

"Ismi Nick." My name is Nick. I thought "Nick" would be easy for him to pronounce and simpler than "Nicholas Kristof." But he gasped and took a step backward.

"Ismak eh?" he repeated.

I knew something had gone wrong, but I had no idea what. Beaming, I strode toward him. We Americans have long adhered to the principle that anybody can understand English if it's spoken loudly enough, so I raised my voice:

"Ismi NICK!"

He just looked at me in horror and hurried off.

I asked my Arabic teacher about that. He laughed and laughed.

"You know what 'Nick' means in Arabic?" he asked.

"If I knew, I wouldn't be asking," I said grumpily.

"It means 'fuck,'" he explained. What was worse was the conjugation: *Nick* was the familiar form, like *tu* in Spanish or French, so I was not only vulgar but also condescending. Worst of all, it was the imperative. American friends would see me across the Bab el-Luq market and shout "Hey, Nick," and we would almost start a riot.

Arabic is a poetic language but also very difficult, with complex grammar and sounds that didn't exist in my mouth or brain when I began my studies. It's strange to measure a language by size, but Arabic is also a *big* language. It has a special word for losing one's children or for a chariot used to carry a virgin into battle, and an Arabic-speaker must master in effect two languages: the casual Arabic spoken among friends and family, and the formal Arabic used on the television news or on public occasions. Then there are regional differences—for Egyptian Arabic is different from Saudi Arabic or Tunisian Arabic, for example.

I developed new respect for Arabs for managing to master this difficult language. I worked hard but felt like a bumbling fool every time I opened my mouth.

Over the New Year's break I traveled to Sudan with three friends so I could report on the divisions then splintering the country into a Muslim north and a Christian south. We took a ferry from Aswan, with six of us thrown together in the cabin. That night I put my food on the table beside my lower bunk and promptly went to sleep. Something woke me in the night. I turned on my flashlight and saw three rats chewing on my food on my nightstand, eight inches from my nose. I sat up and shouted at them, and someone turned on the overhead light. The rats continued eating. There were other rats on other nightstands, and several more on the floor. Everybody yelled at them, and they rather leisurely sauntered off, looking over their shoulders as if to say *See you in a bit.*

The two of us on the bottom bunks strongly believed we should leave the light on to discourage the rats from returning. Those on the top bunks, out of range, thought that was ridiculous. Fortunately, we prevailed on those in the middle bunks to understand that the rats just might be able to jump onto their bunks as well and crawl over their faces, so we left one light on. Sure enough, whenever we were quiet for fifteen minutes or so, a rat would reappear. I didn't sleep.

The boat took us to the Sudanese town of Wadi Halfa, where we went through immigration. Most of us had international certificates showing we had had yellow fever vaccinations, but a few didn't. The Sudanese health inspectors told those who lacked certificates to roll up their sleeves and gave them yellow fever shots right then and there—without changing needles. I've wondered how many cases of HIV and hepatitis were transmitted by those public health officials, and ever since then I've always carried a second copy of my vaccination certificate in case my original gets lost or confiscated.

I looked at the Sudanese train that was supposed to take us south to the country's capital, Khartoum, with deep suspicion. There were no lights inside, and what if it was full of rats? My travel mates took their seats inside the train, but I was still traumatized by the encounter the previous night. So when I saw a few Sudanese climbing on top of the train to ride on the roof, I thought that made sense.

"No tunnels?" I asked a Sudanese man who spoke some English.

"Tunnels?" he asked. I figured that if he didn't know the word, that probably meant there weren't any. I climbed on top of the train. It was slightly rounded rather than flat, but wide enough that it didn't feel precarious.

To ride on top of a Sudanese train may be the best rail experience there is. It's not luxurious, but the wind keeps you pleasantly cool and the air is fresh. You get a lovely view of the surrounding scenery, occasionally passing a village where the children wave frantically and run alongside for a hundred yards. The train goes slowly, especially when it strains uphill. Occasionally, there is a carcass of a train car that derailed and was abandoned, and it's best not to reflect on the fate of those who were riding on top.

One of my friends, a young woman from Arizona who lived in Cairo, got off the train at Atbara to hitchhike east to Port Sudan. We said our goodbyes and agreed to meet up in Khartoum, but that evening her vehicle slammed into a truck that had stopped in the middle of the road. Her vehicle had no seat belts and didn't have good lights.

The best seat on a train in Sudan isn't a seat; it's the roof.

She would have survived the crash if a hospital had been nearby. But it took more than twenty-four hours to get her to a hospital, and she was dead on arrival. I wrote her parents and I've thought about her so many times since. She loved her freedom and adventure, and she didn't take greater risks than others, but her luck ran out.

I was fortunate early in my career to learn the hard way that invulnerability is a myth; one feels safe until one is dead. That's what I learned on that road in Ghana and again when my friend died in Sudan. Those experiences helped balance my confidence and sense of agency against an understanding of how things can suddenly go terribly wrong.

I WROTE ABOUT Sudan for *The Washington Post*, and editors there told me again how much they wanted to hire me. So after my year in Egypt and two years at Oxford, I figured it was time to end my studies and get to work. I flew to the United States in August 1984 to begin a full-time career in journalism.

Alan Otten, the London bureau chief of *The Wall Street Journal*, had repeatedly given me freelance assignments and now tried to get me a job as a foreign correspondent for the *Journal*, but two successive foreign editors, Seth Lipsky and Karen Elliott House, not unreasonably thought I was too green to be a foreign correspondent. I wasn't concerned, though, because the *Post* had always said that it would hire me when I was ready.

When I showed up at the *Post*, the national and foreign editors were enthusiastic, and so were my friends on the staff. The *Post*'s newsroom felt like home to me, after two summer internships on the national desk, alongside fellow interns who included David Remnick and Ruth Marcus. I wanted it to be my permanent home.

My love, alas, was unrequited.

I sat in the glass office of the metro editor, Larry S. Kramer, and all his body language suggested wariness, even hostility. While the national and foreign desks wanted me on staff, the desk that actually hired young reporters was the metro desk, covering the D.C. area, and Kramer didn't want other editors telling him who to hire. He wanted to bring on his own people, not protégés of other editors. He didn't want metro used as a waypoint by ambitious journalists on their way to becoming national or foreign correspondents.

"Are you sure you really want to cover cops in D.C. or Bethesda?" he asked, rightly skeptical. "You don't just want to use it as a stepping stone to a foreign bureau?"

I dissembled and claimed enormous interest in spending the rest of my life in Bethesda.

"You're up for spending three years in Maryland?" Kramer asked me. "And then three years in Virginia, working for metro?"

"I'd be delighted to work for metro," I said, trying to dodge the question. "It's one of the sections readers care about the most."

But of course Kramer was right: I did want to use metro as a stepping stone. The upshot was that he never refused to hire me, but neither did he actually take any steps to hire me. Other editors spoke up for me, but they didn't push him.

So I decided to head to Tunisia. The *Post*'s stringer there, Jim Rupert, was leaving, and I figured that I could improve my French and Arabic and enjoy a great adventure. I arranged to contribute on a freelance basis—or "string"—for the *Post*, NPR, *The Observer* and a couple of other publications. I booked a flight for Tunis, with a stopover in New York to see David Sanger and other friends there. After graduation, David had taken a job as a copy boy at the *Times*, rapidly graduated to clerk and then became a reporter on the business section. I was envious of him.

11

Abe Rosenthal Makes an Offer

In New York, David Sanger offered me his couch, along with exciting job intelligence. The *Times* business editor, John Lee, was looking to hire some people. "I mentioned you to him," David said. "He said he'd be happy to look at your résumé."

So I gave David both a résumé and a cover letter to hand-deliver to Lee, and I frantically began to develop an enthusiasm for business news. I started reading the *Times* business section cover to cover, along with *The Wall Street Journal*, even reading articles on the day's bond trading. John Lee's secretary contacted me to set up an appointment, and I showed up for it brimming with the kind of reverence a priest might feel on making a pilgrimage to the Vatican.

I arrived early, so I stood outside the *Times* building entrance for a few minutes, watching people stream in and march past the guards. The staff members, nonchalant and chatting, seemed oblivious to their exalted status. I surely knew some of their bylines even if I didn't know their faces. When it was time, I took the elevator up to the third-floor newsroom and was escorted by Lee's secretary past messy desks and bustling reporters to the business section; I tried to sneak looks at the names on the desks as I went by to see who these divinities were.

John Lee turned out to be a big, warm man of about sixty with graying hair and horn-rimmed glasses resting on a prominent nose. Gracious and courtly, he came from Virginia, spoke slowly and exuded a southern formality and charm. He had been a foreign correspondent in London and Tokyo, so we spent much of our conversation in his office discussing Oxford, Evelyn Waugh and British society.

"I'm an Anglophile," John told me, and we traded enthusiasms about Rupert Brooke and Auden and Shakespeare, and then about climbing Mount Fuji, about traveling around South Korea. I told him about my English cousin Dr. William Shakespeare and we drifted on to compare notes on *Hamlet* and *Macbeth*. Somehow we never got around to talking about my (lack of) knowledge about business. At the time, I thought I had managed to distract John from the central part of the interview, but in retrospect I think John simply believed in hiring smart young people who could write about anything. He had brought on David Sanger, who was doing a stellar job writing about technology, and he would later bring on a string of other outstanding young journalists including Todd Purdum, Elizabeth Kolbert and Dick Stevenson.

I was charmed by John and eager to work for him, but not excited about the usual route for a recent graduate—serving as a news clerk for a year before becoming a reporter.

"I think we may be able to get around that," John told me. "Let me see what I can do. I don't think we can settle things before you go to Tunisia, but could you stick around a few more days to talk to our personnel people?"

"Sure," I said. "I'll delay my trip."

A few days later I met with Bill Stockton, the deputy personnel boss for the newsroom. Bill made it clear that the *Times* didn't take on reporters without full-time experience but thought I'd be an interesting prospect in a couple of years. He, too, had people to introduce me to.

"Can you postpone your move to Tunisia a few more days?" he asked. "It'd be good for you to meet Jimmy Greenfield," the newsroom's hiring boss.

"That's a good reason to postpone it," I said, "if Sanger doesn't mind me staying on his couch a little longer."

Greenfield, when I met him, was warm and friendly but very vague about job possibilities. We had an amiable discussion about international reporting, and I realized that the editors all figured that John Lee had already vetted me for knowledge of business.

"Say, when are you leaving for Tunisia?" Greenfield asked me as our time ran out.

"Tomorrow evening," I told him.

"Hmm, too bad," he said. "If you were staying just a bit longer, I'd have loved for you to meet Abe Rosenthal. That way, if a job becomes available in the next year or two, he'll have seen you and will know who you are."

"I can delay my trip, if that helps."

"That'd be perfect. Wait just a minute."

He disappeared, and I sat in his office waiting for him to return. A minute stretched to five. Ten minutes passed. I wondered if he had forgotten me. Then after fifteen minutes he returned and handed me a slip of paper. "Here's your appointment with Abe," he said.

Abe Rosenthal was at the time the executive editor of the *Times* and a legend in journalism. Formally, he was A. M. Rosenthal, because when he had been a young reporter he realized that an overtly Jewish name like Abraham Rosenthal would be less likely to get a byline. Some other Jewish reporters at the paper, like Abraham H. Raskin, used their initials: A. H. Raskin. But Abe Rosenthal didn't have a middle name and didn't want to be just A. Rosenthal. So he went to his "A. Rosenthal" newsroom mailbox and penciled in an "M" to give himself a middle initial. An editor took note and his byline became A. M. Rosenthal. Abe sometimes claimed a middle name of Michael, but his son, Andy, told me that was invented to match his adopted middle initial.

A. M. Rosenthal's career soared, for his writing sparkled like no one else's. He could be effervescent and poetic at a time when most coverage was stodgy and wooden, and he later became an equally creative and brilliant editor—but a tempestuous one. Reporters admired Abe but were also scared of him. He demanded complete devotion from his staff and periodically fired those who didn't meet his standards.

David Sanger filled me in on the latest display of Abe's tyrannical side. An outstanding young reporter in the *Times*'s Washington bureau, David Shribman, was covering national politics and had caught Abe's eye with beautiful writing, hard work and a knack for creative stories; he reminded Abe of his younger self. Abe wanted to nurture Shribman's career and, earlier that year, had offered him a plum job as a foreign correspondent in Nairobi or Hong Kong. This was the path of foreign correspondent that Abe himself had taken to journalistic greatness, but Shribman politely declined. David explained that his love was American politics and noted that his wife, Cindy Skrzycki, had a job in Washington at *U.S. News & World Report* and could not simply move locations.

Abe was appalled that David didn't embrace the opportunity. His anger became clear some weeks later when David, while in Omaha covering the 1984 presidential campaign, received a call from Bill Kovach, his Washington bureau chief. According to David's contemporaneous notes (reporters take notes as a reflex), the conversation went like this:

> KOVACH: Abe's thought it over and decided that you are the one to take over the U.N. bureau . . .
> SHRIBMAN: Am I allowed to say no?
> KOVACH: It would be a mistake.
> SHRIBMAN: You know, I've got a wife who works. We just can't pick up and move off.

Kovach said he needed an answer that afternoon; David said he didn't buy a suit that quickly. After consulting with Cindy, David called Kovach back and said he couldn't ask his wife to sacrifice her career and therefore told Kovach no. Kovach told him he was making a big mistake and that Abe would object violently. The next day, Kovach called. From David's notes at the time:

> KOVACH: I am taking you off the campaign. Come back home. You have been reassigned to the metropolitan staff effective in sixty days.
> SHRIBMAN: Is there anything else, Bill?
> KOVACH: No.

The reassignment to the metro desk in New York was an insult and a step down. Metro was often where junior reporters started at the paper, or where reporters were sent if they committed a journalistic crime. And of course it was still impossible to reconcile with Cindy's career. Abe was punishing David to send a warning to the entire staff to obey his will and whims.

While Abe's mistreatment of Shribman was known within the *Times*, there was another part of the story that most were unaware of. David had also had a call with Seymour Topping, then the managing editor, who often worked behind the scenes to try to restrain Abe. Topping wasn't as brilliant or creative a journalist as Abe but was steady, universally admired, utterly decent and an excellent newsroom manager. David's notes show that Topping said he was "horrified" by Abe's actions and added: "The whole thing is just mad . . . If I knew a way to undo this, I would. I don't." Topping offered to help Shribman find a new job at any newspaper in the country. Topping was devoted to his own wife, Audrey, and his emphasis on family shines through in his comments to David at the time: "Your first priority is your family. That should be management's point of view. Unless a person does that, he will not be well balanced. One's family should take first priority, and I admire you for your strength of character. I'll watch you at a distance and see that your service is not forgotten." I wonder if Topping's comments on the importance of family were casting shade on Abe himself, for Abe had not prioritized his family and had divorced his wife, later taking up with a newsroom secretary in a flamboyant way that scandalized the newsroom.

In retrospect, David Shribman acted heroically and made it easier for those of us who followed him. He challenged the tradition that wives would be sacrificed for their husbands' careers, then true at the *Times* and in many other fields. American diplomats as well were then overwhelmingly men who brought their wives with them to foreign posts, where the women were expected to accept either being housewives or serving as poorly paid secretaries at the embassy. This system was insulting to women and made it impossible for them to pursue their own careers, and it was of course also an obstacle for those of us men who wanted to marry strong, independent women. By refusing to go along with that tradition and standing up for Cindy, David signaled that young journalists would no longer tolerate such a sexist system.

Three days after David was pulled from the campaign, Abe met him in the Washington bureau. Abe said he was baffled at David's rigidity; he insisted that Cindy could find a new job in New York City. "It's just a job," Abe said dismissively of Cindy's position at *U.S. News & World Report*. Abe hugged David but said he had been a disappointment and that he wouldn't have hired David if he had realized he was unwilling to show commitment to the *Times*. David refused to budge and declined to take the New York job.

"Then you must leave," Abe told him, adding that he could not write for the *Times* again. Kovach told David that he should come in over the weekend, when no one would be around, to clear out his desk.

Word of David's ouster reverberated through the journalism world, and by week's end both *The Washington Post* and *The Wall Street Journal* were scrambling to hire him. In the end, he moved to the *Journal* and later became Washington bureau chief of *The Boston Globe*, lauded as one of the top journalists in Washington.* That was still to come when my appointment was made with Abe, but Shribman's downfall was on my mind. I had tremendous admiration for Abe as a journalist but feared him as a potential boss.

When the day of my appointment came, Abe's secretary met me at the elevator and walked me over to the great man's office. It was elegant and palatial, the biggest office I'd ever seen. The main room had a vast conference table for twenty people filling the front end. I was expecting someone hard-bitten, aloof and perhaps seven feet tall, but Abe turned out to be rumpled, medium height and full of warmth. He had a full head of modishly long hair, fleshy cheeks and intense eyes, even through his eyeglasses. He gripped my hand and told me how much he had admired my Poland coverage in the *Post*, how he wished it had been in the *Times*. Abe was himself a former correspondent in Poland and had intently followed the coverage of martial law there, including, it turned out, mine. This was a stroke of luck for me. He then led me to a cozy inner office with a three-part Japanese screen and a small table where we sat and chatted.

Abe had spent some of his happiest years as a foreign correspondent in Poland, India and Tokyo, so he asked about my time in Poland and my travels in India. I related some of my adventures and asked him about his favorite postings. Instead of a grueling interrogation, it was like a chat at the bar comparing war stories.

"I loved India," he said. "I loved the excitement, the drama, the stakes of the country. I felt the stories truly needed to be covered. In Japan—well, it was comfortable, it was lovely"—he gestured to the screen—"but it lacked passion. I knew Japan would be just fine without me."

Abe reacted well to me for some of the same reasons that he had

---

* In 2022, I checked with David Shribman to see if what I was writing about Abe Rosenthal's treatment of him was correct. He said it was, and we joked about "AMR"—as Abe was known in the newsroom. "The other day I saw a New York license plate beginning 'AMR' and it gave me the shivers," he told me. "Forty years later, the guy still haunts me."

responded badly to David Shribman: I loved foreign reporting, lacked a family to slow me down, was eager to fly off on a moment's notice to cover some distant crisis, and didn't mind miserable working conditions. We chatted more about India, and I told him about sleeping on the floor at the Golden Temple in Amritsar and staying at a fifty-cent-a-night "hotel" in Uttar Pradesh. His eyes lit up. We talked about the gritty awe inspired by holy men wading into the Ganges River at Varanasi as bodies were cremated on funeral pyres on the shore. We both remembered the periodic popping sound from human skulls exploding in the flames.

I also mentioned that I worried that India's leaders controlled the economy too tightly, in ways that held the country back and magnified suffering. Dirigiste management meant that India's economy was stagnating, I said. That left hundreds of millions of people in poverty and missing the chance for education and better nutrition and health.

Abe looked uncomfortable at that. "But Indian leaders want to lift up the whole country," he protested. "They don't just want a free market that creates tycoons and mansions in the cities, while leaving most of the population behind in the countryside. Isn't it better for India to develop more gradually and bring the whole country along at once?"

"No, I don't think so," I said. "Indians are dying in the meantime. South Korea and India had similar per capita income levels in 1950, yet South Koreans are thriving today. And hundreds of thousands of Indian children die each year of something as basic as diarrhea."

"That's a little harsh, isn't it?" he said, and he was frowning. "It's a lot harder to move a giant country like India than a small place like South Korea. And I always thought South Korea was a little soulless."

I paused. Did I really want to challenge A. M. Rosenthal, at a hiring interview, no less? Did I want to be Shribman'd before I was even hired? His face was clouded as he awaited my answer. He clearly felt a warmth and nostalgia for India and didn't care for my analysis. Yet I couldn't agree with him.

"Hmm," I started carefully. "I think India would do much better for its own people if it unleashed its economy. Yes, some tycoons might get rich. But 70 percent of India's children are stunted from malnutrition. A third of kids aren't even in primary school. You've seen the leprosy, the beggars, the hand-pulled rickshaws in Calcutta."

Abe nodded.

"If the economy grows a bit faster," I suggested, "that gives parents more resources to feed children or send them to school or get them vaccinated. Other countries in Asia are doing it, and India can, too."

He was glowering skeptically at me, and I felt a job receding. I had hoped that the interview might lead to a job in a year or two, but now it felt as if it might never happen. So I was taken aback when Abe suddenly smiled and stuck out his hand.

"Congratulations!" he said. "You're a reporter for *The New York Times*."

I gaped at him. He looked concerned. "If you want the job."

"Of course I want it!" I said. "I'm thrilled. Truly thrilled. This is a dream come true."

"So who are you going to call first?" Abe was beaming, and his tone was avuncular. "Your parents? A girlfriend?"

"My parents. My dad came to the U.S. as a refugee in 1952, and his first purchase in America—to teach himself English—was a Sunday *New York Times*."

"That's perfect," Abe said, and he seemed genuinely moved. "We're so glad to have you."

The terrifying stories about Abe were true, but he was simultaneously tough, emotional and sentimental, qualities not ordinarily found in the same person; he also had a great heart and could be a nurturing mentor. To me, he showed only kindness. I think that was partly because of our shared interest in the world and fondness for human stories, and also because he saw something of himself in me. All that explains why Abe hired me directly as a reporter rather than making me work first as a clerk for a year.

Abe and I spoke for another five minutes, but I have no memory of what we discussed. I kept thinking: *I've done it! I'm a reporter at* The New York Times! *And I thought something else:* I'm twenty-five years old, and I've achieved my career dream. This is the job that I will retire from many years from now when I'm old and gray.

12

Cub Reporter

Goddammit, Carl, you fucked me! You fucked me!"
Bob Cole, the *Times* mergers and acquisitions reporter, a sturdy, blustery man in his shirtsleeves who made me think of an army drill sergeant, was shouting into the telephone a few desks away from mine. "Carl" seemed to have difficulty getting a word in edgewise, but from the context of the dressing-down I figured out it was Carl Icahn, the famous financier. Cole was yelling at Icahn and instructing him next time to leak only to the *Times*. And, specifically, only to Bob Cole.

I was a brand-new business reporter. My first day was October 1, 1984, and I wished I had a tycoon to curse. Instead, it became obvious to me almost immediately that there had been a vetting failure: I had no idea what I was doing. John Lee gave me some "easy" assignments at the beginning, but nothing is easy when you don't know anything about the business world you're supposed to be covering.

"What's the difference between the New York Stock Exchange and the American Stock Exchange?" I asked a colleague. "And what's this Nasdaq thing?"

The reporter's eyes widened. You could almost see his thought bubble: *Who hired this guy?*

Bob Bennett, the banking reporter, coached me through a finance story and tried to educate me about accounting for loan loss reserves. I looked blank. "Before we get to loan write-offs," I said, "what's this bit about commercial banks and investment banks? What's the difference?"

Other reporters in the business section knew what they were doing. One had a PhD in economics, and several had been through business school. All had good networks. On the phones around me, I heard some reporters sweet-talking CEOs, and others, like Bob Cole, raking them over the coals.

Everybody around me was plugged in; I didn't even have a plug.

John Lee assigned me to cover international trade and economics. At the time, that meant the international debt crisis, sanctions on South Africa, oil prices, the surging dollar and more. The major figure in the international debt crisis was Bill Rhodes at Citibank, and I couldn't even get him on the phone. Meanwhile, my counterpart at the *Journal*, S. K. Witcher, had been covering the debt crisis for years and seemed to know everybody. I imagined her on the phone shouting "Goddammit, Bill, you fucked me!"

It took time for me to decode the *Times*. Shortly after I arrived, there was a farewell toast in a conference room for the stock market reporter, Alexander R. Hammer, who was retiring after a career in the business section spanning more than four decades. Alex had taken me to lunch my first week on the job, and he consumed enough martinis that I was in awe of both his expense account and his capacity to weave his way back to the office and write. At the farewell toast, Lee spoke movingly of Hammer's peerless intuition about markets, his profound knowledge of the players, his extraordinary understanding of why stock prices rise and fall. Michael Quint, the bond reporter, rolled his eyes at that one. "If stocks rise, Hammer says it's optimism about corporate profits," Quint whispered to me. "If stocks fall, he says it's profit-taking. No one has any idea."

That seemed too cynical, and I absorbed John Lee's tribute to Hammer as one of the business section's greatest journalists, a renowned figure on Wall Street, somebody who would be succeeded but never fully replaced. "Alex has been working here at the *Times* since 1939," Lee said. "He is our institutional memory. He's the person we all turn to for an understanding of leading companies."

"Wow," I said to David Sanger as we walked out of the conference room. "I guess Hammer was really a pillar of this section? How can they ever replace someone like that?"

David laughed. "Oh, that was John being diplomatic," he explained. "He's been trying to get rid of Hammer for years. John finally managed to nudge him out the door."

As part of my orientation, I spent brief periods in other departments at the *Times* to learn their mysteries, and one evening I hung out at the foreign desk. I was awed to see an article come in from Henry Kamm, whom I revered. Born in Germany to a Jewish father who was sent to the Buchenwald concentration camp, Kamm fled to the United States as a teenager, studied at Columbia and became a distinguished foreign correspondent for the *Times*. After the fall of South Vietnam in 1975, when large numbers of Vietnamese "boat people" fled to other countries in Southeast Asia, it was Kamm who indefatigably chronicled their suffering: attacked by pirates, dying of hunger and thirst, refused permission to land. It was because of Kamm's work that the United States was shamed into accepting large numbers of Vietnamese refugees who have since greatly enriched America. One of those Vietnamese families had settled near Yamhill, and I had helped the family move in. As the son of a refugee myself, I admired the way Henry had paid it forward—and I also admired the Pulitzer Prize he won in 1978 for his coverage of the refugees. Henry Kamm had changed the world, and I wanted to be him.

"I see Kamm filed a piece," I noted to a copy editor. "He's pretty amazing, right?"

"Amazingly incoherent," the editor scoffed. "His copy is a nightmare. He can't write his way out of a paper bag."

"But his Pulitzer!"

"Oh, you should have seen his copy when he filed it. The editors won that for him. They translated his copy into English."

That was disillusioning, or at least complicating. In defense of Kamm, the editor was exaggerating. It was true, though, that up close, some of my journalistic heroes looked a little less heroic. Some filed copy that was greatly improved by editors, but I still was awed by correspondents like Kamm. Instead of hanging out with diplomats in Bangkok, he had traveled to remote corners of Southeast Asia and elevated the voices of women who had been raped by pirates or parents whose children had been thrown overboard by captains of leaky vessels trying to reduce weight. Kamm had a heart, and he made suffering impossible to turn away from: That's what I wanted to do in my reporting. I knew that I wasn't a beautiful writer either, but maybe I could compensate like Kamm with hard work that shone a spotlight on dark corners of the globe.

To compensate for not knowing anything about business, I tried to be the first one in each morning and the last one out in the evening. I read every word in every business publication I could find. At night I read books on business and economics.

Gradually, I grew more comfortable writing about business and more familiar with the players. In journalism, one sometimes can compensate for a lack of knowledge by adopting a tone of utter authority. After I wrote pieces about the international debt crisis that moved prices of bank stocks, Bill Rhodes began returning my calls—possibly even before S. K. Witcher's. Soon I was regularly generating page one stories. At that time, reporters were allowed only one byline a day. Even so, we sometimes competed to have two or even three or four stories appear on the same day, because the cognoscenti would guess from the topic who had written them and the lack of a byline was a badge of honor signifying that the writer had multiple pieces in the paper on the same day. Sanger and I had a friendly competition to see who could have the most articles in the same day's paper. I think the winner had five, but I forget which of us it was. (I finally surrendered in the byline competition when Sanger was covering an overseas trip by President Bill Clinton and managed to have two front-page stories in the same day's paper, from different continents.)

After I'd been at the *Times* a few months, I had a call from Jim Hoagland, an assistant managing editor at *The Washington Post*, asking me to lunch in Manhattan—at a spot well away from the *Times* building. Jim was the kind of journalist I wanted to become: widely recognized as a master of foreign policy and the Middle East in particular. As soon as we were seated, he got down to business.

"There's a lot of consternation at the *Post* that we let you slip through our fingers," Jim said. "We thought we were going to hire you, and then we thought you were going to be our stringer in Tunisia, and somehow it didn't happen, and everybody's blaming everybody else. Metro blew it. Anyway, we'd like to bring you back to the *Post*. So I wanted to see if you would like to be our next India correspondent."

"Wow!" I said. I was overwhelmed. "Wow! That would be a dream."

"You'd be based in Delhi but covering Bangladesh, Nepal, Sri Lanka, Pakistan and Afghanistan."

"You know that I desperately want to be a foreign correspondent," I said.

"And you'd want to go to Afghanistan, right?" Hoagland asked. "Sneak in from Pakistan with the mujahideen?" I had the sense that the Afghan story was a priority for him, and I wondered if the outgoing India correspondent had not been enthusiastic about hiking across the mountains to cover the war in Afghanistan.

"I'd love to cover the Afghan story! Right now I'm covering bankers. I'd much rather cover the mujahideen, or unrest in Punjab or Sri Lanka. Those are the stories I care about. But . . ."

I paused. "But I've got to think this through. I do owe the *Times*. Give me a few days to think about it."

"Of course," Hoagland said. "But remember: Every reporter at the *Times* wants to go abroad. You're surrounded by people whose dream is to become a foreign correspondent, but there are only a few spots and most of those are filled by veterans who rotate from one bureau to another. Here's a chance for you to fill one of the most exciting foreign bureaus and make of it what you will."

The one thing I don't believe we discussed was pay. The *Times* paid new reporters a starting salary of a bit more than $50,000, equivalent to $140,000 in today's dollars, and presumably the *Post* would pay a foreign correspondent significantly more. But for young reporters like me with no family responsibilities, the attraction was all about the work, not the compensation.

"It's very tempting," I told Hoagland. "I'll get back to you."

I practically floated back to the *Times* office. This is what I had wanted since high school. Yet as I worked on stories over the next couple of days, as John Lee came by to chat with me about article topics, I felt like a traitor. I didn't know how I could possibly tell him I was leaving. Finally, I called up Hoagland.

"Jim, I really appreciate your offer, and I can't believe I'm saying no to something I want to do so much," I told him. "But John Lee and the *Times* took a chance on me when no one else would. I was a lost puppy, and they gave me a home. I owe them my loyalty. I just can't leave."

"Are you sure?" Hoagland asked. "This is an incredible opportunity for you. Do you have any assurances that you'll ever get a foreign post at the *Times*?"

"No assurances whatsoever," I told him. "And I haven't told them about your offer. I thought about trying to parlay it into a foreign assignment here, but I'm too new to even raise that. I'd be embarrassed to ask. So I know this may never happen. I worry I'm throwing away my chance to be a foreign correspondent. But I just can't do it."

Hoagland sighed, and there was quiet on the line for a moment. But he didn't try to change my mind. "I understand," he said. "Good luck at the *Times*. I hope you do get abroad."

I never told John Lee that I had returned his loyalty in this way. I should have, and now it's too late: He passed away in 2009.

AS A REPORTER at the *Times* in the 1980s, I had a freedom that journalists today could barely fathom. Much of the time, editors had little idea what I was working on: I would simply report a piece and file it when it was done. Even when editors assigned articles there was little hand-holding, and nobody offered much guidance on how to report a story.

In my first few months, the dollar was soaring on currency markets, making life difficult for exporters and for domestic manufacturers. I had written several pieces about this as the dollar daily rose to new heights but was working on another topic one day in February 1985 when, at about 6 p.m., the assignment editor, Allan Gold, came by my desk looking pleased.

"You're on page one, above the fold," he told me. "Abe really likes it."

"What story?" I was puzzled. I recognized that the page one meeting, in which Abe and other editors planned the front page, had just concluded, but I couldn't think of any piece I had written that was ready to go.

"Your currency piece," Allan said.

"Currency piece?"

"The exchange rate story. The big picture piece about the strong dollar."

"What currency piece? I don't have any currency piece."

Allan looked at me, thunderstruck.

"Didn't anyone talk to you?" he asked incredulously. "You're on page one with it."

"I don't know anything about this."

"Oh, shit!" Horror was spreading across Allan's face. "Oh, shit!" He covered his face with his hands for a moment, then stalked back to the editing desks and there was an angry conversation that I couldn't quite overhear. Then the economics editor, the brilliant Karen Arenson, walked over to my desk.

"Nick, there was a bit of a communication mix-up," she began delicately. "We proposed a big piece for the front page about the rising dollar and its impact on the American and global economies. You know, highest dollar rates in many years, impact on exporters and tourism, and so on. Someone was supposed to tell you, and we thought you were working on it."

I shook my head. "Nobody mentioned it."

"I know it's late," Karen said, "but any chance you can still do it? Er, for tonight?"

It was obvious that no editor wanted to confess to Abe that the story he admired didn't exist.

"When's the deadline? I'd have another hour and a half?"

"Yeah. Maybe I could get you a little more."

"Let me try. Some Japanese traders will still be in their offices. I can get quotes from them."

I reached a few people, jotted down quotes and started pecking away. I started with a lead paragraph about the dollar surging to record highs and then scribbled:

Currency traders at their computer screens expressed astonishment as light, nervous trading propelled the dollar to levels never before seen. Many said they had no relevant experience to judge what might happen next.

"We're in uncharted waters, and it's anybody's guess where the dollar is going to stop," said Lawrence L. Kreicher, an economist at the Irving Trust Company . . .

Our conspiracy of silence succeeded. The story appeared that night on the top of the front page, and Abe never learned the truth. That could not happen today, for reporters now complain about too many editors looking over their shoulders to check on how an article is progressing.

I felt some exhilaration at having pulled this off, but also a wisp of shame. Here was the story at the top of page one of the most important newspaper in the world, adding to the pressure on the White House to force down the dollar (which it did a few days later), and I hadn't invested the time or thought into it that the topic deserved. It was a little too easy, a bit too formulaic, a bit too glib. I wanted to provide rich, smart reporting that would make a difference, not just meet a deadline. I wanted page one stories, yes, but I wanted to earn them.

A dozen of us were the Young Turks of the *Times*, and we formed close bonds. We were all in our twenties, mostly from Ivy League institutions and quite full of ourselves. These friends made a wonderful network but I was awed and intimidated by their talent. David Sanger had the best nose for a page one story of anyone I knew: He could write a sensational "nut graf," explaining the significance of even an obscure story and vaulting it onto page one. Lisa Belkin was a beautiful writer, drawing me into topics that I had no interest in. Phil Shenon was a relentless reporter, digging up facts that others tried to hide. Esther Fein was a poet; I would read her features and think, How did she come up with that word choice? Todd Purdum, Willy Greer, Dick Stevenson, Elizabeth Kolbert, Lisa Wolfe and so many other friends dazzled me with their talents and perseverance, and collectively they forced me to recognize that I was far from the best writer or best reporter around. Others wrote in lapidary prose; I joked that as a farm kid, I wrote dirt clod prose.

I had always read newspaper articles as a technician might take apart an antique clock, from the perspective of *How was this put together?* In high school, I would read a great feature in the *News-Register*, *The Oregonian* or *The New York Times* and think as I did so: How would I have written this? Would I have thought to talk to that person? Would I have dared to write in this unconventional way? I tried to educate myself about techniques of writers I admired, like R. W. Apple Jr., Russell Baker or Anthony Lewis at the *Times*. Another model came in the form of *Times* editorials, for the editorial board was then led by two of the best writers on the paper, Max Frankel and Jack Rosenthal. A byline in the *Times* metro section, Maureen Dowd, also caught my notice for her bold and beautiful articles.

Now I turned this method of study on my fellow Young Turks. It felt a little weird to be employing my friends' work as teaching materials, but it was useful. I hadn't taken a journalism class since sophomore year of high school, so I dissected their writing and tried to understand their secrets. I also worked harder to master my beat of international business, and to make sure I never made mistakes.

I hated corrections. We all read them in the printed paper and thought, how did so-and-so get that wrong? One article even misspelled the name of the Sulzberger family that owned the *Times*, calling them the Sulzburgers. We all slipped up from time to time, and the paper required us to fix even innocuous errors. If we got a middle initial wrong, or an age, we ran a correction. If we said someone was affiliated with Baylor University when it was actually Baylor College of Medicine, we ran a correction. And of course if we referred to a Sulzburger, there was a correction. One day, I commiserated with David Sanger when he was fixing an error, and he shrugged.

"Actually, I kind of like running corrections," he said. "It shows how serious I am about fixing mistakes, even tiny ones."

I looked at David and tried to roll my eyes. I believe in eye-rolling, but I'm not very good at it.

"Look at *The Wall Street Journal*," he said. "They barely correct anything, while we run a correction if we said someone graduated from high school in 1970 and it was actually 1971. I'm kind of proud of that."

That made some sense to me. I never became exactly proud of my corrections, but I came to see them as an essential part of journalism. Soon after, I absentmindedly wrote "million" instead of "billion" in an article about the debt crisis; I kicked myself but wrote a correction.

One of the miseries for us Young Turks was the paper's insistence on honorifics, and its refusal to allow "Ms." When I interviewed a woman, I'd have to pry and ask if she was a "Mrs." or "Miss."

"None of your damn business," some would say.

"I'm sorry," I'd respond. "But for a second reference, we use honorifics. We say 'Mr.' for men, and either 'Miss' or 'Mrs.' for women. That's why I'm asking. So are you a Miss?"

"Call me 'Ms.'"

"I'm afraid the *Times* doesn't allow 'Ms.' Just 'Miss' or 'Mrs.'"

The upshot would often be a ten-minute harangue, with which I agreed, on the sexism of my employer.

It was particularly humiliating to work on a triumphal article about women making gains in a particular field, talk to leading feminists for comments, and then have to ask each one if they'd rather be Miss or Mrs. Lisa Belkin once had to ask Eleanor Smeal, head of the National Organization for Women, that question. I deeply admired Gloria Steinem, who became a friend as well as an inspiration, but I was never going to insult her by quoting her in any way that required a second reference to "Miss Steinem"—the way she was insultingly quoted in the *Times*. Gloria had founded *Ms.* magazine in 1971, and it had become a major national magazine that influenced my thinking and that of millions of Americans. She was also an old friend of Abe Rosenthal's from the time they had both lived in India in the late 1950s. But while we young reporters chafed at the paper's stodginess, Abe was adamant that "Ms." was a passing fad. He convinced the publisher, Arthur O. "Punch" Sulzberger, to hold the line and resist a change. It wasn't until 1986 that we were liberated and allowed to use "Ms." in articles. On the evening of the announcement, Ms. Steinem and several dozen feminists visited our newsroom with roses to applaud the change. The staff in the newsroom, overwhelmingly on Gloria's side, gave her a standing ovation.

"If I'd known it was so important to you, I'd have made the change earlier," Abe grumpily told Gloria.

In truth, the resistance to "Ms." was reflective of a broader boys' club attitude at the *Times* in those years. The senior editors were all men, and young women were judged by their bodies as well as by their copy. One female reporter's official personnel file at the paper in the mid-1980s had "Great tits!" scrawled on top. When Lisa Belkin first had a page one story, an editor told her that "now no one can say that the only reason you were hired" is that the editors like "looking at your legs." A couple of young reporters held a party on the Upper West Side a few months after I joined the paper and I was impressed to see Abe and Jimmy Greenfield show up. But everyone was drinking too much, and soon a couple of women reporters ended up on Abe's lap.

Ugh. This felt wrong to me, and it was infinitely more painful for ambitious women. They wanted to be great journalists, and it was demoralizing to be regarded as ornaments to be salivated over. Lisa Belkin was pained by the comment about her legs because it came from an editor who was comparatively young and genuinely helpful.

"He was one of the good guys," Lisa told me. "He was trying to compliment me. He thought he was saying something funny, or matter-of-fact, or both. But until that moment I didn't know that anyone was saying or thinking anything about my legs." As was tradition at the time, Lisa was presented with a metal plate of her first front page. "I put it in a closet," she said.

I had never met Punch Sulzberger or any member of his family, but I'd interacted with most of the senior editors at the paper, and I had some hope of advancement. Then after I'd been at the *Times* about nine months, John Lee called me into his office and asked me to be a national correspondent covering business and economics out of Los Angeles. I was a little wary of giving up a beat that I had turned into a regular feeder for page one stories, but I knew that succeeding as a national correspondent would help me achieve my aim of becoming a foreign correspondent. And in any case, I would have done anything John asked me to do. I took a couple of days and told him yes.

Shortly before leaving New York for Los Angeles, I was invited to join a page one meeting, where Abe and other editors made decisions about what to put on the front page. Senior editors sat at the conference table in Abe's office, while junior figures like myself sat in chairs along the wall. Abe introduced me at the meeting as the new hotshot Los Angeles correspondent, and several of those in the back with me turned out to be new hires. After the meeting, they gathered around me and asked me questions about adjusting to the *Times* newsroom. Proud to show off my vast(!) experience, I went on about the idiosyncrasies of the *Times* and offered suggestions for how to impress editors. One of the group was a middle-aged man who was quiet but listening intently, seemingly interested in my advice. He asked me about my plans for Los Angeles, and I was about to offer him some tips for succeeding at the paper when he spoke up.

"When you're in Los Angeles," he said, interrupting me gently, "be sure to look up my daughter, Karen *Sulzberger.*" He pronounced her last name carefully, to make sure I got it, and he had a wisp of a smile on his face.

I had just met Punch Sulzberger, and he had rescued me from myself. It was a typically gracious gesture from the patriarch of a family that made the *Times* the best newspaper in the world and then navigated it brilliantly into the digital age.

LOS ANGELES WAS a dazzling place to be a *New York Times* reporter. I was the youngest national correspondent at the paper and had the West Coast business world largely to myself, from the giant banks to the military contractors, from movie studios to mining companies. Someone in San Francisco covered technology—there were a couple of young tech companies called Apple and Microsoft that were said to be interesting—but everything else was mine. Because of the time zone, deadlines were mid-afternoon. A story would erupt midday, and I'd frantically make phone calls. It would be unclear if a story would come together in time. Often I'd get calls back at the last possible minute and I'd pound away on my keyboard, squeaking in right on deadline. It was nerve-racking and exhilarating.

The *Times* also gave me a portable computer for the first time. We didn't call it a laptop, but that's what it was. It was a Tandy 200, and it operated on four AA batteries and could file stories on a phone line at 300 baud—a painfully slow rate of several minutes to file a single, short story. I became expert at dismantling telephones in hotel rooms and phone booths so I could connect my Tandy and transmit articles. I loved it for its ability to do its job even on crackly lines; once I filed an article with it on a phone line in Mongolia that was so bad I couldn't have a conversation, but the Tandy 200 didn't let me down.

Phone lines were not the problem in Southern California. There I was stymied by uncommunicative executives. I tried to get to know CEOs there, but they presented a puzzle. I would work on a big-thought story for page one—about, for example, whether California was emerging as a financial capital for the country—and I would get great insights from scholars, economists and investment bankers. Within a company, the chief economist almost always had newsworthy thoughts. And then I'd sit down with the CEO, who would fill our allotted time with pablum and rah-rah sentiment.

This sometimes caused some friction. "I gave you an hour with our CEO," the public relations head of Security Pacific Bank once protested. "And you didn't quote him once."

"But he didn't say anything," I retorted. "You were there. What did he say that was interesting or quotable?"

"Well!" She paused and reflected. "Couldn't you have found something?"

At first I thought the CEOs were keeping their depths to themselves, trying to avoid saying anything controversial or provocative. After all, they had risen through huge organizations and elbowed aside thousands of rivals—they must be brilliant. Yet I gradually concluded that the distinguishing characteristic of a traditional Fortune 500 CEO was not intellect but rather an ability to manage people and bring out the best in a team, coupled with unwavering optimism. "They get up every day and are confident the company will soar," Michael Gisser, a mergers and acquisitions lawyer, told me. "Even when the company is sinking into the toilet."

One ethical issue arose almost immediately. Executives at Lockheed and other companies would periodically hold meetings with reporters in the Jonathan Club, an exclusive men's club in downtown Los Angeles. This was convenient, for my office was in the Hilton Hotel office tower nearby, but it troubled me because the Jonathan Club excluded women as members and had few, if any, Jewish, Black or Hispanic members.

I had no problem going into a racist or misogynist establishment to pursue a news story, but it felt inappropriate to do so for a social encounter or background briefing. I didn't consult with my editor, because he and other *Times* editors belonged to a club in New York that barred women—and the paper even paid the membership fees. I tried to organize an insurrection among business journalists in Los Angeles, drafting a joint protest letter asking Lockheed to move its briefings to a location that did not discriminate on the basis of race, religion or gender. Not a single reporter signed on.

"Look, I understand what you're saying," one fellow reporter told me. "But the Jonathan Club is convenient to everyone. It has great canapes. Plus, is it really our business how a private club manages its affairs?" In the end, I sent the letter out on my own. Nothing happened. (Years later, the Jonathan Club did open its membership and become more inclusive, as did the clubs in New York, and the *Times* stopped reimbursing executives for their club dues.)

In Los Angeles, I also learned the art of poking leaks in organizations. There's a misperception that reporters are simply the passive recipients of scoops. Not so. Mostly a good leak is the result of careful courtship of a source and an argument about why it's in the source's interest to leak, or why it's simply the right thing to do.

So I did what reporters do: I tried to build a rapport with my sources, in hopes I could use that relationship to extract information. Janet Malcolm of *The New Yorker* famously wrote: "Every journalist who is not too stupid or full of himself to notice what is going on knows that what he does is morally indefensible. He is a kind of confidence man, preying on people's vanity, ignorance, or loneliness, gaining their trust and betraying them without remorse."

Malcolm was ahead of her time: That put-down resonates with the current distaste for journalism and the decline in confidence in it as an American institution (along with other institutions). But not surprisingly, I disagree with her take. Yes, of course we court sources and try to insinuate ourselves into their hearts—but this mostly serves the public interest. That's how we learned about the Pentagon Papers, about the Watergate scandal, about human rights abuses in Iraq and Afghanistan, about sexual assaults that propelled the #MeToo movement and about so many of President Trump's abuses. We got people to talk to us, and that created accountability.

Journalists may sometimes trick or browbeat sources, but often they simply help sources find the courage to do the right thing, to get something off their chests. It becomes more dubious when journalists paint leakers in a kinder light than those who don't cooperate, or encourage policy leaks of trial balloons, or worse, of incorrect or misleading information. All that happens, and periodically we publish leaks that violate privacy or damage national security. So, yes, Malcolm was right that this courtship is fraught and sometimes abused, and of course she was right that we have ulterior motives as we try to charm our sources and build friendships. But ulterior motives? That's what salespeople have when they build relationships with customers. The difference here is that the outcome isn't higher quarterly profits for a company but a better-informed civil society. Our ulterior motives in journalism are typically aligned with the best interests of the public.

Southern California was a center for military contractors, and coverage of the industry relied upon leakers because much defense work was classified and not transparent. Leaks could help create accountability and protect taxpayers from being ripped off. I worked hard to penetrate the defense contractor world, following up every lead and informal contact I could. I once heard about a disgruntled employee—I'll call him Jason—at the General Dynamics subsidiary in San Diego that made cruise missiles. So I gave him a call and arranged to meet him. Jason said that General Dynamics routinely cheated the government by filling out time cards inaccurately, either exaggerating hours or misattributing hours to programs that had extra money available. He said he could introduce me to other employees who could confirm that.

While in San Diego, I dropped by to see the General Dynamics spokesman, and we chatted pleasantly in his office. I didn't mention that I was working on a piece about his company committing fraud.

Over the next few days, I spoke to many employees who acknowledged filing fraudulent hours. Jason connected me to some, while I met others at the factory gates. And whenever I talked to one employee, I would ask who else I could talk to. Some thought that the fraud was company-wide policy, while others believed it was simply low-level bosses acting on their own. The scale was difficult to gauge, but one of the employees I reached happened to work in computer systems.

"Do you want to see some internal documents?" he asked. He had access to all the corporate computers, so he printed out confidential memoranda from the top executives to each other. One was a memo from John McSweeny, the general manager of the subsidiary, disclosing that the government had found the company's security procedures "unsatisfactory" and would impose penalties.

By now it was Saturday morning, but I found McSweeny in the phone book and reached him at home.

"I understand that you've had some problems with handling classified materials and have been penalized by the government," I said.

"We're fine," he said. "Why would you say that?"

"Well, I have your memo here in front of me," I told him, and I read it back to him. He was furious that the company was not only caught out for bad security, but that its security was so weak it couldn't keep its most confidential memos out of *The New York Times*. I wrote about this on deadline for page one of the Sunday paper, and the company undertook a major search to find the leaker. It questioned everyone who had the memo but apparently never thought of the invisible IT people who could peer in and see everything.

13

Finding Sheryl ... and a Job Abroad

I'm setting you up," Eileen White told me. "Her name is Sheryl, and she's working with us at the *Journal* this summer. She's cute, funny and wicked smart."

"You're fixing me up with my competitor?" I asked teasingly.

"Anything to spy on you," Eileen replied, teasing back.

Eileen was an unlikely friend. We were ferocious competitors, for one of my goals in life was to embarrass the *Wall Street Journal* bureau in Los Angeles, where Eileen worked. She was one of nine reporters the *Journal* had covering business in Southern California, whereas the *Times* had me. I felt that I needed to beat them on stories if I was to distinguish myself as a correspondent, and they felt that it would be humiliating to be beaten by a sole rival. We were great friends and also bitter competitors. It helped that I could skip corporate earnings and other incremental pieces that swallowed most of the *Journal* reporters' time, and I tried to deliver scoops and deeply reported stories on page one that would make my *Journal* frenemies curse me over their morning coffee. One reason we remained good buddies was that Eileen and her colleagues reciprocated by regularly embarrassing me with their own scoops.

It was the beginning of the summer of 1986, and Eileen had invited me to a party—and then explained that she was fixing me up with her paper's new summer intern, Sheryl WuDunn. (Now I would have ten reporters in the *Journal* bureau working daily to embarrass me.)

"You'll really like her," Eileen continued. "She's from New York and just graduated from Harvard Business School. Very warm and friendly." Eileen paused, winked and added: "And cute!"

At the party, Sheryl indeed turned out to be all Eileen said, but she was also hanging out that evening with an investment banker whom Eileen had not mentioned, Jack. And Jack was cozying up to Sheryl.

Eileen had evidently forgotten that she was planning to set me up with Sheryl, for she had told Jack and Sheryl that she was setting them up with each other. "You've both graduated from Harvard Business School and have so much in common," she told Sheryl. Eileen hadn't said a word to Sheryl about me, although Sheryl had heard complaints in her bureau morning meetings about Kristof writing this or Kristof writing that. She thought it was some odious person's first name.

Jack and I chased after Sheryl at the party, getting her drinks, laughing at her jokes, asking her questions, and glaring at each other. I feared I was outgunned, for Jack was nine years older than I and a principal at Morgan Stanley. He was also good-looking, charming and witty, and my income was a rounding error of his. After a few hours of passive-aggressive dueling at the party, we prepared to decamp with the whole group to a new location.

"Hey, I'll give you a ride," Jack told Sheryl.

As I recall, Jack's car was a BMW. In contrast, my company-issued Chevrolet Celebrity, in a dull shade of blue, was the single least fashionable car in all of Los Angeles.

"I just put in a car phone," Jack added helpfully. "You can make a call while we drive there."

"Well, my car has a radio," I offered. It was a joke, but nobody laughed.

I no longer remember exactly what happened next, and Sheryl's memories of the day are even hazier, for she was used to being pursued. Did I invent some urgent reason why Sheryl had to ride in my car? Did I puncture one of Jack's tires? Did I club him over the head? I truly can't remember. But I do remember that when we left Eileen's place, Sheryl was riding shotgun in my Chevy.

Sheryl is a third-generation Chinese American who was born and raised in Manhattan. She was almost exactly my age and in her teenage years had been planning to become a doctor like practically everyone in her family. But at Cornell she took a course in intellectual history, abandoned pre-med and was planning to go to graduate school in literary theory when her mom told her to get some work experience first. Sheryl took an executive trainee job at Bankers Trust, then won a full scholarship to Harvard Business School. While there, she became interested in journalism. After beginning business school she spent the summer at the *Miami Herald,* and after graduating the following year came to Los Angeles to intern for *The Wall Street Journal.*

We dated all that summer, and Sheryl taught me about Chinese culture. One evening that involved ordering Chinese takeout, which Sheryl did laboriously in Chinese. This was not a great success. Sheryl spoke some Mandarin Chinese, the restaurant worker spoke Cantonese Chinese, and each thought the other would understand if they just raised the volume. I watched, amused.

"Just try English," I suggested. "This is L.A." Sheryl frowned at me, and the Tower of Babel order continued. While we waited for our food, I asked her, "So what did you order?"

"I'm not sure," she admitted. "We'll see."

Sheryl was staying in Los Angeles with her cousin, who was suspicious of me and protective of Sheryl. I got a lesson in Chinese family dynamics the first time Sheryl stayed over on a Saturday night. The phone rang at 3 a.m.

"Is Sheryl there?" a voice asked nervously. I handed the phone to Sheryl, who convinced her cousin that she wasn't bound hand and foot. The cousin had worried when Sheryl didn't return home by midnight and had found my phone number in Sheryl's writing by the house phone. But she felt awkward about calling me in the middle of the night, so instead she began calling other members of the extended family around the United States and Canada and getting their advice. Everybody weighed in: Some thought Sheryl was a big girl and could make her own decisions, while others thought it important to call in case she was locked in a dungeon by this white guy.

"It's kind of a Chinese thing," Sheryl explained wearily when she put down the phone.

We had a great time dating that summer of 1986, but it was hard to see how this would work out. Sheryl was leaving Los Angeles at the end of the summer to earn a graduate degree in public policy at Princeton University, and then she hoped to get a job in journalism in Hong Kong. Meanwhile, the *Times* didn't even have a Hong Kong

Cuddling with my then girlfriend, Sheryl WuDunn.

bureau and there were whispers that the paper was likely to dispatch me next to be a foreign correspondent in either West Africa or Japan. The national editor was also musing about making me Los Angeles bureau chief. Hong Kong wasn't even on the radar for me.

So at the end of the summer, Sheryl and I said goodbye. I called her regularly and we stayed in touch, but it wasn't clear we would even see each other again. Our romance seemed over.

Then in October, a colleague in the newsroom in New York called me. As a former clerk, he had master passwords that allowed him access to the newsroom's computer system in New York. At that time, work wasn't saved on individual personal computers but on a central system. Every six minutes, each person's work was logged automatically on that central computer. So my colleague was able to read a memo that Warren Hoge, the foreign editor, was drafting.

"You'll never guess what Warren Hoge is writing," my colleague told me. "A memo to Abe proposing a shuffle of foreign assignments. And one of the items? That the *Times* open a Hong Kong bureau with you as bureau chief."

"Hong Kong?" I couldn't believe it. "I haven't heard a peep about opening a Hong Kong bureau."

The Los Angeles bureau secretary came into my office to interrupt. "Nick," she said, "it's Lisa Belkin in New York on line two. She says you'll want to hear this."

I put my friend on hold and spoke to Lisa.

"Hey, Nick," Lisa told me. "Listen to this! Warren Hoge is writing a memo as we speak suggesting you for Hong Kong. For bureau chief there!"

The secretary appeared in my door again. "Sorry to bother you," she said, "but another call from New York. Todd Purdum on line three. Says it's urgent." I put Lisa on hold, and there was Todd, likewise telling me about Warren Hoge's confidential memorandum. Dozens of young reporters in New York seemed to be reading the memo as Warren wrote it. I juggled the three callers, and every six minutes, as the system saved a new rendition, they gave me an update. Then someone managed to print out the completed memo and faxed it to me. I read it before Abe did.

The next week, Warren Hoge called.

"This will be a bolt from the blue," he said, "but we're going to open a bureau in Hong Kong, and we'd like you to be the bureau chief."

"Hong Kong?" I repeated. "That is out of the blue! Yes, Warren, I'm in."

TO BECOME THE YOUNGEST foreign correspondent for *The New York Times*, after just two years at the paper, was like stepping on Aladdin's carpet. I was twenty-seven years old and accustomed to all-night buses and third-class trains. A few years earlier, after finishing at Oxford I had traveled through Asia and stayed in a cheap hostel in Hong Kong. Imagine how I felt when the *Times* now flew me business class to Hong Kong and then put me up at the Mandarin Hotel, one of the world's finest hotels, until I could rent an apartment. I had been equipped with a company credit card for airline tickets, a $10,000 cash advance for other expenses and intimations that expense accounts were not closely monitored. (The bean-counters who invaded newsrooms in the 1990s had not yet arrived, nor had the financial stressors that led to bean-counting.) One of my colleagues had just returned from a year in Africa and told me that the accountants had protested that his expense forms were incomplete.

"You're missing $70,000 in receipts," he was told. "You need to provide receipts for everything over $25."

"Well, I don't have any receipts," he replied. "And I don't remember how I spent the money. But I know I chartered a plane a few times, at $3,000 a pop. That adds up."

"You must have some receipts?"

"No. I travel light."

"Well, just write down what you remember, including big things like plane charters, and have it add up to $70,000."

Times lore recounted the time Johnny Apple, one of the greatest of foreign correspondents, with a gourmand's fondness for expensive food and wine (all of which he expensed), went to Russia in the winter. Supposedly he filed his lavish expense account for many thousands of dollars, listing dozens of meals and bottles of fine Burgundy, plus taxi rides and incidentals, and included the cost of an expensive fur coat from Finland that he felt he needed to fend off the cold. The accountant returned the expense form and explained that the *Times* had a policy of not paying for clothing. The story goes that Johnny resubmitted his expenses, without the coat, but with the exact same total. On top he had scrawled, "Find the fur coat!"

It was a great yarn, but the truth was more banal and also more revealing. Johnny had indeed expensed the fur coat, and the accountants simply accepted that expense the first time.

The *Times* provided bureau chiefs with cars, drivers here and there, and in a few cases palatial residences. There were other perks. After one foreign correspondent told Punch Sulzberger of the difficulties finding books abroad, Punch announced that any correspondent could send in lists of books, fiction or nonfiction, and they would be purchased in New York and sent out to us.

For a combined home and office, I rented (on the *Times* account) a beautiful six-bedroom apartment at 6 Po Shan Road with a view of the Hong Kong harbor so breathtaking that it sometimes made it difficult to concentrate on my work. Old-timers scoffed that I still wasn't spending enough, compared with bureau chiefs in the 1960s and 1970s, before editors had closed the bureau and moved the position to Beijing. "Joe Lelyveld had a spectacular house on the back side of the island," one veteran journalist told me. "And when Seymour Topping was here, he had a Chinese sailboat for picnics in the harbor. You can't lower *Times* standards!"

I loved the apartment view, but luxury is somewhat wasted on me. I don't typically eat fancy meals and I certainly don't buy fur coats.

Instead of hiring a car and driver in Hong Kong, I took the subway; it was usually faster. The lure of a foreign assignment wasn't the comforts but the chance for discomfort: the license to get out of my comfort zone and report on things that weren't getting adequate attention. I was also exhilarated by the intellectual challenge of wrapping my head around a foreign country, from its poetry to its history, and by the adventure of visiting parts of the world I wanted to understand better.

I wanted to leave my imprint on the coverage, and I wasn't sure what that would be. Maybe the extraordinary economic success of the region, and lessons for the United States? Maybe the ongoing political repression across the region, and the challenges for the West? Maybe some humanitarian or political crisis yet to unfold? Asia seemed the most fascinating place in the world, for many countries were growing economically at unprecedented rates, yet the continent was also home to some of the most repressive countries in the world, including North Korea and China. So much was happening, and I felt a bit like those nineteenth-century youths exhorted to *Go West, young man*, except that this was the East. Just as in the nineteenth century the western frontier captured the excitement and future of America, Asia's transformation made the Far East a place of global opportunity.

My second title, alongside Hong Kong bureau chief, was Asian economic correspondent, and I spent much of my time covering economic trends. This was a great education in how to nurture economic growth, but it didn't initially give me much of a chance to pay it forward and report on the human stories that I itched to cover, the way Henry Kamm had given voice to the Vietnamese boat people. But I was growing more confident that my time to cover such stories would come. In the meantime I wanted to cultivate my skills and learn the craft of landing in a country and filing a sophisticated story from outside the capital by the next evening. I treasured this journalistic opportunity, for it was the opposite of stenography; it was near-absolute freedom, for the 1980s truly constituted a golden era for foreign correspondents.

In those days before mobile phones and email, correspondents were only loosely monitored by editors, and I largely went as I pleased. I would buy a ticket, fly into a country and pursue the stories I was interested in, with little input from editors. Every evening I would file my whereabouts, usually by telex, so that the desk could reach me if necessary, but there wasn't the back-and-forth that exists today about where to travel and what stories to write.

This saved an immense amount of time that is now spent writing memos, but it did lead to a certain amount of abuse. Hawaii has always been well covered by correspondents in the winter, and Phuket and Bali perhaps get more attention than is their due. When I was single in Hong Kong, I went out briefly with a young woman in Perth, Australia—and made three reporting trips to Western Australia in as many months. I wondered what *Times* readers thought of this burst of intense coverage, since no other correspondent had visited Perth since the end of World War II.

Editors occasionally lost track of correspondents. Once, during a kidnapping crisis in Lebanon, the foreign editor asked the clerk to call the Beirut bureau chief and, when he was on the line, ordered him to leave at once for his own safety.

"I think it's fine here," the bureau chief retorted.

"We have intelligence that there's a kidnapping plot," the foreign editor said. "No more bravado. You've got to head for the airport and take the next plane out."

"I'm sure it's safe here. You see, I'm in Paris."

THE FIRST COUP D'ÉTAT I covered was in Fiji during a South Pacific swing from my Hong Kong base. My journey had started in Vanuatu, where I somewhat randomly booked a flight to the remote island of Tanna. "It's very traditional," someone told me. "It's the real Vanuatu."

It was. Tanna had a live volcano, and I climbed to the lip of it and saw red-hot magma churning and shooting boulders skyward. I wandered through traditional villages, and men invited me to join them in drinking coconut shells of kava, an intoxicating drink found across the South Pacific. I visited several villages where people were supposedly committed to wearing traditional garb: a penis sheath for men and a grass skirt for women, and nothing else. But I arrived unannounced, and the villagers were embarrassed when I caught them with their pants up. They sheepishly removed their shorts and T-shirts. Then we got high on kava and forgot about that awkwardness of me seeing them clothed.

Tanna was also my first experience with cargo cults. These are found throughout the South Pacific where American troops arrived with modern equipment on remote islands during World War II and were presumed to be gods. On Tanna, people worshipped a god named John Frum, who had come to Tanna once and would come again to reward those who followed him, or so the legend went. There are competing theories about the origins of this, but it may be that John Frum was a ship captain who said he was John from Chicago or Detroit or who knows where. The John Frum faith had its own church-like buildings and a strong community of faithful, and it was remarkable to me that this theology could have developed in less than half a century.

After Tanna, I flew to Tonga. While nosing around for stories, I discovered that the country was going through a fitness craze. Historically, Tongans had admired people with, er, heft, and the king weighed in at 462 pounds on the only scale in the country able to accommodate him—a luggage scale at the airport. But fondness for the Rubenesque had evaporated. I took Miss Tonga to dinner as part of my reporting, and she told me that she had once been pitied for being scrawny, with people continuously urging her to try to put on some weight (she was five feet ten inches tall and weighed 133 pounds). But fashion caught up with her and proclaimed her just right.

As for the king, she told me that he exercised on a particular street

The king of Tonga getting his exercise.

each evening, so I wandered over there and found the police putting up a "road closed" sign. Then along came the king, now a svelte 360 pounds, on a blue bicycle with an extra-wide seat, wearing plastic goggles, a polo shirt and king-sized shorts. A group of young male bodyguards jogged along with him as he rode for forty minutes; the king stared at me as I took photographs, and I stared back at him.

I was having a grand time in Tonga, but a telex from the foreign editor, Joe Lelyveld, interrupted: *There has been a coup in Fiji. Can you get there ASAP?*

I caught a flight to the Fijian capital and found the main hotel thronged with Australian reporters—who spent their days by the pool, their evenings drinking in the bar, and the time between writing far-fetched stories. I knew exactly what they were writing because the only way to file stories was telex, hence each reporter handed copy to the hotel's exhausted telex operator. In my travels I had picked up how to operate a telex machine, so I offered the telex operator a chance to nap while I transmitted my own articles, and that gave me a chance to read through the entire pile of work submitted by my competition. It tended to the sensational and managed to spell many names wrong. An exception was Keith Richburg, my *Washington Post* rival, a versatile journalist with long experience covering upheavals.

In 1986 Keith had been sent to cover the uprising in Haiti against President "Baby Doc" Duvalier. He had rented a car from Hertz at the airport and driven around for several weeks as the uprising gained ground and toppled the Duvalier regime. It was a huge story, and one day Keith was frustrated because he couldn't get a phone line out of the Hotel Castel Haiti to file his story. The *Times* reporter Joe Treaster had kept an open line to the head office in New York, so he fetched Keith and told him to dictate his story to the *Times* dictation room, which forwarded it to *The Washington Post*—a reminder that in crises, news organizations sometimes cooperate beautifully.

After Duvalier fled the country, Keith stayed for a couple of weeks to cover the new government and then went to the airport to return the car and fly back to Washington. The Hertz franchise in Haiti had been owned by a corrupt businessman close to Duvalier, so mobs had burned down the Hertz office. Keith parked his rental car beside the ashes and locked the keys inside. As he entered the terminal, he looked back and saw a crowd of people smashing the car to bits. The rental records were apparently burned, for Keith was never billed. "Cheapest car rental I ever had," he told me.

In Fiji as elsewhere, Keith was also impressive in his ability to party and (as I discovered when I spied on his copy) turn in first-rate articles. I felt guilty as I read his work, but not guilty enough to refrain, and I was confident that Keith would have returned the favor given the chance.

The next day Keith and I and a couple of others went out to cover protests against the coup, and we managed to get arrested. Troops took us to the local police station but didn't seem to know what to do with us. I was afraid they would take my notebook, so I frantically hid my real notes in my underwear and wrote fake notes for them to confiscate. Sure enough, while our fate was being decided, a police officer came into our room and said he'd have to take our notebooks.

"Oh, please don't," I told him. I thought I should purport to care about them, so I clutched the fake notes and pretended that they were important. "I need these for my article."

The police officer looked at me, then at my notes. "Well, okay then, you can keep them," he said.

Fijian police really were soft touches. The police chief came into the room and looked sternly at the group of us. There was silence. Then he broke into a smile. "Let's drink some kava," he suggested. A subordinate brought in a big jug of kava and some bowls, and we all got stoned on kava together. Eventually, the chief drove us back to the hotel, and it seemed the riskiest part of being arrested was the possibility of a crash because of his impaired driving.

I worried that the Fijian government might expel the entire foreign press corps. It would have been easy to round us all up because we were all staying at the same luxury hotel, the Suva Travelodge. So I had taken an additional room in a sleazy hotel a mile away in a gritty section of town, using a pseudonym and cash. I stayed there at night when I expected a roundup was most likely. That proved unnecessary for there never was an expulsion, but it did allow me to observe a brutal side of the coup that I would have missed in the high-rent district.

The fault line in Fiji was between indigenous ethnic Fijians and Indian immigrants who numbered almost half the population. Tensions were magnified by substantial differences in phenotype and occupation: The Fijians were mostly physically large and towered over me, while the Indians were typically small of stature. The Fijians dominated the military, while the Indians were active in business. The army had staged the coup to oust an Indian who had become prime minister, the first time a Fijian had not served in that position.

One morning, as I left my sleazy hotel to return to the Travelodge, I saw packs of young Fijian men hunting on the streets for Indians to beat. There was a menace in the air, so I decided to walk around and see what I could see.

We yearn to be heroes, to do the right thing, to stand for justice. But that morning I saw a big, drunk Fijian man grab a young Indian woman taxi driver and rip her shirt open. As I tried to summon the courage to pull him off, she managed to drive away and escape.

I walked on, wary of the roving mobs, though they weren't targeting me—they were too busy searching for Indians, who had mostly disappeared from the streets. Then I saw a group of three huge Fijian men catch an Indian man beside his car and toy with him as a cat toys with a mouse, throwing him around and smacking him.

Should a journalist intervene? Yes, I think so. We have human responsibilities as well as journalistic ones. I approached, very nervously. As I walked closer, wondering what to do, trying to summon the nerve to intervene, one of the Fijian men slammed the Indian man's head against the trunk of his car. The man's face bounced up, his nose streaming blood and possibly broken, and the Fijians laughed and slammed the man's head down again. One punched him. The Indian man was like a rag doll in the hands of men who weighed more than twice as much as he did, and it felt doubly outrageous because he was targeted only because of his race.

If I was going to act, this was the moment. If I believed that reporters should not just observe crimes but try to stop them, then I had to step up. I had good options. I could have shouted at them angrily. I could have said something milder, like "Hey, guys, that's enough, he's hurt." Or I could have walked over, introduced myself as a reporter and asked to interview the attackers; then they might have left the Indian alone. In all cases, the risk to me was manageable. Fijians weren't hostile to white Americans, and if they had menaced me I could probably have out-sprinted them to safety. But my nerve failed. I was fifteen feet away, but my mouth refused to open. I wanted to run over and pull the Indian man away, but my legs refused. I kept imagining those three big men putting the Indian man down and picking me up and slamming me into the car repeatedly. That thought paralyzed me. That scene of moral failure and personal paralysis remains vivid in my mind, yet I can't remember how the attack on the Indian man ended. Most likely, the three men tired of tormenting this man and wandered off to look for new Indians to abuse.

I found my way back to the Travelodge, afraid and shaken. I was horrified by the unraveling of the social fabric I had seen and still recovering from my own fear from walking through the mayhem, but most of all I was disturbed by my failure of nerve. I had expected better of myself. And I had learned that however heroically we may imagine ourselves acting, however nobly we may want to act in a crisis, our bodies sometimes balk. To be human, sometimes, is to set high standards for ourselves that we then fail to meet.

14

My Soulmate

I'm a romantic. So while it was fun to travel the world for *The New York Times*, it could also get lonely. It was amazing to stand at the lip of the volcano in Vanuatu, but it was a thrill that I wanted to share with a partner. I wanted to confide in a lover, share experiences, undertake the journey of life together. When a man seeks companionship, it can sometimes come across as a yearning for sex, and I believe in sex as much as the next person. But what we humans—men and women alike—yearn for isn't just money or sex or status, although all of those can help. What perhaps matters above all is a companion. I didn't know then how much research confirms that intuition, but I did feel lonely and unfulfilled. So I was thrilled when on one of my calls to Sheryl in the spring of 1987 to check in with her, she announced that she'd be coming to Hong Kong for the summer. "I have an internship with Reuters in Hong Kong," she told me.

I arrived early at Hong Kong's Kai Tak Airport to pick her up. As I waited for Sheryl, I clutched a bouquet of flowers in my right hand. Neither of us was entirely sure if our romance was still on. We had effectively broken up at the end of the previous summer, and I knew that Sheryl had previously had a very serious boyfriend for several years, a Chinese American businessman whom her parents adored. He had been a Harvard classmate of mine, and he checked all her family's boxes. Both boxes, that is:

Chinese? Yes.

Rich? Yes.

Sheryl had broken up with him before our dalliance the previous summer, but I was concerned they might have patched things up.

"Nick!"

I must have been catastrophizing about this threat because Sheryl was suddenly in front of me with her suitcase. She enveloped me in a hug.

We took a taxi to my place and caught up. Fortunately, the old boyfriend was still history. And while the previous summer's romance had been more like a summer fling, this updated version quickly did become serious. Sheryl was gorgeous, but she was also whip-smart and lots of fun. And from Sheryl's point of view, I wasn't some guy headed off to Africa but was now in the part of the world she wanted to work in. We spent all our time together, and I kept putting off trips so that I could stay in Hong Kong and be with her. But then pro-democracy protests spread across South Korea, the government there was imperiled, and I was dispatched to Seoul.

"You'll probably be there for a few weeks," Joe Lelyveld, the foreign editor, told me.

This was awkward. I spent a few days on my own in Seoul getting tear-gassed by the police as I covered the pro-democracy protests, burning up the phone lines with Sheryl as we tried to figure out how to wind up in the same place together. After one particularly debilitating day of tear gas, I found a dud tear gas grenade that hadn't gone off and picked it up as a souvenir. I carefully carried it back to the Westin Chosun Hotel, where most of us foreign correspondents were staying and where the government always put me in room 901, which was bugged. Almost immediately after bringing the dud to my room, I had to leave for a meeting with the national police chief.

"Your tear gas seems particularly brutal, worse than that in other countries," I said pointedly.

"Yes, it's the most potent anti-personnel gas in the world," he said proudly. "It's our special formula."

"But some of your tear gas grenades don't even go off," I said, trying to deflate his confidence. "I saw a dud today that didn't even explode."

He shrugged. "That may have been because it was cold today," he said. "When it warms up, it'll suddenly explode."

I thought of my hotel room thermostat and tried to remember what

I had set it at. I couldn't remember, but I knew it was much warmer than outside. I suddenly excused myself.

"I'm so sorry, but I have to go attend to something," I told him. I rushed back to the Chosun, afraid I'd find my floor sealed off by police and wondering whether I'd be imprisoned for harboring explosive materials or simply billed a few million dollars for rendering the ninth floor of the hotel unusable for a year. Would the *Times* let me expense that?

There was no sign of trouble, though, and I entered my room and found my grenade intact on the counter where I had left it. Very delicately, I carried it downstairs—that elevator ride was the longest of my life—and laid it to rest on the street, hoping that I wasn't under surveillance at that moment. I returned to my room and called Sheryl (although, since the phone was bugged, I couldn't share the story with her).

In South Korea I got to know Kim Dae-jung, then a dissident politician. The South Korean government had earlier sentenced Kim to death, and my parents among countless others had circulated Amnesty International petitions calling for his life to be spared. The Korean government had responded to the international pressure and freed Kim from prison, and when I met him he was living under house arrest in his home, where we would have lunch together. He pointed to nearby buildings and insisted that four of them had all been taken over by the government to spy on him. I was skeptical, but I admired Kim and his insistence on the universality of human rights. A top American official warned that Kim might be a Communist spy for North Korea, but that seemed to me ridiculous and a reflection of the American government's coziness with the dictatorship.*

Meanwhile, Sheryl, ever creative, had persuaded Reuters that the big Asia news was in South Korea and that she should move her intern-

---

* In 1997, after democracy came to South Korea, Kim Dae-jung was elected president. He limped across the stage to assume the presidency—his leg had been injured in an assassination attempt by the government—and showed great magnanimity in trying to heal divisions within his country and with both Japan and North Korea. This won him the Nobel Peace Prize in 2000. However, it turned out that he was wrong about the government occupying *four* nearby buildings; a former spy official told me it was actually *five*. One of this official's jobs was reading through Kim's garbage in case there was information that could be used to prosecute him, and as the official read drafts of Kim's speeches and letters he came to admire the man he was spying on, and he ended up voting for Kim. It was not for nothing that Kim was called "Asia's Mandela."

ship there. So she flew the next evening to Seoul and joined me at the Chosun. Now it must be said that foreign correspondents had a reputation, not entirely unearned, of being philanderers and raucous partygoers, regularly frequenting bars and brothels. The longtime foreign correspondent Edward Behr claimed that a well-known foreign correspondent was having sex in his Manila hotel room with a bar girl when she abruptly inquired, "Is it true that they're sending Tony from Hong Kong to Beirut?" I was teased by a few of my colleagues as a stick-in-the-mud. I didn't get drunk, didn't go to brothels; instead, I roamed villages, trying to understand Korean culture or language, or else I sat in my room writing essays for the Sunday Week in Review section.

Mark Fineman, a friend from the *Los Angeles Times*, was in the Westin Chosun coffee shop having breakfast and reading a newspaper the morning after Sheryl arrived. I had told Mark about Sheryl, but he had never met her. I'm not sure that he knew she was Chinese American. So when Mark saw me arrive for breakfast one morning with an Asian woman, he lit up.

"Kristof, you've finally found some action!" he shouted across the coffee shop. "Hope you didn't stay up past your bedtime!"

"Mark!" I tried to remonstrate, but he ignored me and appraised Sheryl as we approached his table.

"And a hot one, too!" he hooted. "Congratulations, my friend. Glad you took some time off."

Sheryl was looking at Mark as if he were a barbarian and was surprised when I sat down at his table. "Mark, this is Sheryl," I said mildly. "I've told you about her. She's transferred to work in Seoul for Reuters."

Mark deflated like a balloon.

"Ohhhhhh," he said. He paused and cringed. "Nice to meet you, Sheryl." He fumbled a bit. "I guess I misunderstood."

Sheryl smiled at him and nodded. "I think you did."

THE PHONE RANG and woke me up. It almost always did. A disadvantage of reporting in a time zone so far from New York was that any time editors wanted to talk to me, they were awake and I probably wasn't. That was fine for news stories, but it did get aggravating to be woken up at 3 a.m. by an editor in the travel section saying something like:

"Oh, hey, I'm glad you're up. I just wanted to chat about some possible ideas for travel stories over the next year . . ."

"Yeah, I'm up," I replied grumpily. "I had to get up to answer the phone."

"Oh, what time is it there, anyway?"

"A bit past 3 a.m."

"Oh, then I'm so glad you're up."

Joe Lelyveld tried to be reasonable about phone calls. He had been an outstanding correspondent in Hong Kong a decade earlier, and he knew the drill. So he tried to call during his morning before it got too late in Hong Kong or South Korea. Still, on this day, his call woke me up—he had an editing change on a story and wanted to make sure I saw it before deadline. I welcomed the call: On balance I preferred to be woken up than to be surprised with something under my byline. Then Joe made a specific offer.

"I'd like to make some changes in the bureaus," he said, "and I wondered if you'd like to move to China and take over as Beijing bureau chief."

"Wow!" I said. "I'm very interested."

"We'd give you a year of full-time language training," Joe continued. "So I'd like you to close down the Hong Kong bureau as soon as possible, begin the language training, and then start in China in a year."

I told Joe I'd think about it and get back to him in a few days, but I knew I would accept. China was the most populous country in the world, undergoing an economic transformation that would change the world, even as it brutalized dissidents along with minorities like Tibetans and Uyghurs. How could I say no to covering China?

The only thing that gave me pause was my personal life. I was twenty-eight years old, and a Beijing assignment would put me in China until I was well into my thirties. Sheryl could get a job easily in Hong Kong or Seoul, but China in the 1980s was more complicated. There was only a small foreign community in Beijing, and China controlled visas and residence permits tightly; there was no such thing as a girlfriend visa. I didn't know if Sheryl could figure out a way to go with me, and if she didn't, could we manage a long-distance relationship for years?

Should Sheryl and I get married? We were getting along wonderfully, but in this more serious iteration of our relationship, we'd only been together a few months. Wedding bells seemed premature. Sheryl and I were also different in many ways, with divergent priorities and styles. I'm not much interested in money, while Sheryl counts pennies and believes in building wealth. Neither of us cares much about material possessions, but Sheryl's idea of a vacation is a villa in Tuscany while mine is a sweaty backpacking trip. I'm not good at honoring birthdays, anniversaries and Mother's Day, perceiving them as overtaken by commercialism, while Sheryl sees them as part of the pulse of family life. We both work out every day, but I run while Sheryl prefers fitness classes (for a while she was a twice-a-week aerobics instructor). I have a thread of Oregon passive-aggressive mellowness in me, while Sheryl has a New York City assertiveness to her. I'm unperturbed when things go wrong, confident that they'll somehow work out; Sheryl knows that they periodically don't. We both acknowledged these differences and were sometimes frustrated by them, but we still found that we meshed beautifully. Without addressing our own future, we talked about the Beijing job during the next few days.

"You should definitely do it," Sheryl said. "It's China!"

"But it's quite a commitment. A year of language training. Then maybe five years in China. That's six years of my life."

"It's China!"

Normally, I was the optimist, confident that everything would work out. This time it was Sheryl who seemed unfazed by the challenges of China and enthusiastic about the opportunity presented to me.

"It's China!"

One obstacle if we did get married was the *Times*'s disdain for the careers of correspondents' wives, exemplified by Abe Rosenthal's mistreatment of David Shribman because Shribman didn't want to move and undermine his wife's career. It wasn't a single incident. Later, Abe sent a star reporter, Steve Weisman, to be Delhi bureau chief. Steve's wife, Elisabeth Bumiller, was a gifted reporter for *The Washington Post*, so it was natural for Elisabeth to write for the *Post* from Delhi as well. Abe tried to block that, arguing that one couple shouldn't represent the two most important American newspapers in a foreign capital. I understood his point, but the practical consequence of this policy would be to create one more obstacle for female journalists, since the ranks of foreign correspondents were overwhelmingly male. Fortunately, Ben

Bradlee paid no attention to Abe's protest, so Elisabeth was able to write for the *Post* and build her career.*

The chauvinism of the *Times* was obviously a catastrophe for young female journalists, but it also loomed large for many of us young male journalists. We wanted great foreign postings, but we also wanted to marry strong women who had opportunities to build their own careers and who were partners in every sense.

It wasn't then clear how feasible that was. If I was a correspondent for the *Times*, the newspaper would provide air tickets for Sheryl and an education allowance for any children, but it seemed unlikely that it would employ her and might even actively block her from getting a job at a rival publication. Still, there was a broad sense within the newspaper that Abe's policy had been unreasonable, and Abe had been succeeded as executive editor by Max Frankel, who was bringing a wave of changes and seemed intent on nurturing a kinder, gentler *Times*. There was hope that the newspaper would become more family-friendly, but little evidence of it so far.

A few days later I told Lelyveld I'd take the Beijing bureau chief role and began closing down the Hong Kong bureau and planning the move to China. This was awkward, for the current bureau chief in Beijing, Ed Gargan, had been there only a year. Gargan had been chosen by the previous foreign editor, Warren Hoge, and was clashing with Lelyveld. While Gargan was a beautiful writer and spoke decent Chinese, his interest was elegant features, while Lelyveld wanted someone more focused on hard news and government. This was a shrewd judgment in retrospect, given the cataclysm to come. Nonetheless, Lelyveld, who had a soft heart beneath a steely exterior, felt guilty about pushing Gargan out of Beijing so soon.

"He's in Tibet now, so I can't reach him," Lelyveld told me when I first accepted the posting. "I'll give him a call when he's back in Beijing to tell him that you'll succeed him."

"Okay."

I checked with Lelyveld again a week later when Gargan was back in Beijing. "I decided to tell him in a letter," Lelyveld told me. "This is just a normal rotation," he said, although of course it wasn't, "and I thought a phone call would make it seem more unusual than it is."

* Elisabeth was eventually hired by *The New York Times* and is now the paper's Washington bureau chief.

The *Times* had a woman in New York who organized moves by foreign correspondents, so when I decided that I would study Chinese in Taiwan she set in motion my move from Hong Kong to Taiwan. But she must have gotten her moves confused, for before Joe Lelyveld's letter arrived in Beijing, a telex arrived at the foreign desk from Gargan. It became legendary:

PRO LELYVELD

EX GARGAN

 JOE, I HAD A CALL TODAY FROM CROWN PACIFIC MOVERS TO PLAN MY MOVE FROM BEIJING. WHEN YOU GET A CHANCE, PLEASE ADVISE ME WHEN I'M MOVING. AND WHERE AM I GOING?

 CHEERS, GARGAN

BEFORE LEAVING HONG KONG and starting my language studies, I made a final reporting trip with Sheryl, traveling through southern China for a week and visiting her grandparents' villages in the Taishan area of Guangdong Province, near Macao. Taishan had been the home of many of the early Chinese migrants to America. The traditional language of Chinatowns across the United States was the Taishan dialect (a variant of Cantonese that they pronounced "Toysan"), and it was the Taishanese who came up with chop suey and started Chinese restaurants across the United States. Later waves of Chinese migrants brought other dialects, and the earliest waves assimilated (like Sheryl's family) and moved out of Chinatown.

We found what we believed was Sheryl's grandfather's village, so we asked if anyone there had Sheryl's Chinese surname. It's an unusual family name, 伍, pronounced "Wu" in Mandarin and "Ng" in Taishan dialect. (It's different from another much more common surname, 吴, also rendered as "Wu" in English.) We thought we just had to find the 伍 family in the village, and then we'd have located Sheryl's relatives.

Unfortunately, it turned out that everyone in the village had that exact rare surname. It was a clan village, in which all residents belonged to the same extended family. And while Sheryl knew her grandfather's full Chinese name was Ng Hokyik, she didn't know how to write it or how to pronounce it precisely in Taishanese. But a crowd gathered, and Sheryl explained through an interpreter.

There was puzzlement and much chatter. Sheryl tried several more times to pronounce Ng Hokyik. Finally, a woman lit up.

"That's my lineage!" she shouted. Her name was Wong Yugap, and she was Sheryl's second cousin. She was a fifty-six-year-old peasant who looked much older, and that was true of all the villagers. Sheryl and I towered over them, a tribute to our better nutrition, and they were weathered by years of stooping barefoot in the rice paddies. Few were educated, and they lived grueling, impoverished lives.

Wong Yugap was telling Sheryl about her grandfather and what a fine, tall man he was, and then interjected something that stopped us in our tracks: "He had two wives."

Sheryl had never heard this. But the villagers explained that her grandfather had taken his first wife to America and then some years later had brought her back, left her in the village, married again and taken the second wife—Sheryl's grandmother—with him back to America.

"His first wife didn't bear him a son," another woman explained. "She had two daughters, but he never got the son he wanted." The first wife had died in the village in the 1960s.

That was hard for Sheryl to accept. She checked later with her father, who vaguely knew of two other half sisters who had grown up in China, but it was something never discussed in the family. For a proud advocate of women's rights like Sheryl, it was wrenching to discover that she was a product of a legacy that discarded women who didn't bear sons. She wanted to be proud of her Chinese heritage, not embarrassed by its sexism. Sheryl was the firstborn in her father's family, and she wondered whether her grandpa had been disappointed when she arrived female.

Sheryl's relatives showed her an old, abandoned house that had been her grandfather's, and in a trunk there we found the papers he had used to gain admission to the United States. The Chinese Exclusion Act had barred most immigration from China, but there was a well-known trick in which Chinese shared identity documents to evade American bigotry: They pretended to be someone else who already was living in the United States, or the son of such a person.

Sheryl's grandfather had bought such papers from another villager and used them himself. We don't know if the papers represented a real person or a conjured one, but they were good enough to allow entry to the United States and a path to citizenship for Sheryl's family. We looked around the village and wondered who were the descendants of the man who had foolishly sold papers allowing admission to the United States. What had he used the money for? A new roof on his home? A plot of land? Food and drink? Was there any expense that would have justified losing access for family and heirs to grow up in the United States?

Both of our families embodied the transformative power of immigration to America. Chinese called America *Mei Guo*, meaning "the Beautiful Country," and at its best it truly could be a land of opportunity. It was sometimes easier to see that beauty from a distance, such as among the rice paddies of southern China.

While we were examining her grandfather's house, the crowd outside had been discussing something that we didn't quite understand, and now an elder introduced a peasant who was about thirty years old, short and lean with a month's stubble and what looked like a self-administered haircut.

"He's your relative," the elder told Sheryl, with a convoluted explanation of the relationship that probably meant he was a third cousin twice removed. "He's not married yet. He's a good young man. Hard worker. Quite tall. Very handsome."

This was aspirational marketing. He was tall for the village, but he looked more frail and wimpish than skinny, and he had a major overbite. He was as weathered as a piece of driftwood, while clad in a torn shirt and blue cotton trousers that Goodwill would have rejected.

"Nice to meet you," Sheryl said politely. The man looked terrified but said something terse in Taishanese.

"A good young man," the elder said. "He'll make an excellent husband."

I realized what was going on. "Sheryl, they're trying to marry you off to him," I whispered. "I think you should hold out for someone you can communicate with."

Sheryl tried to be gracious and move on, but the villagers were quite insistent in putting the man next to her and singing his praises. From the village's point of view, having a *rich* American—there was no other kind—marry into the village would bring wealth and benefits and perhaps American visas. It wasn't clear if the villagers understood that I was Sheryl's boyfriend, but I decided to stay close. I didn't want a large rock to fall on my head and remove me as an obstacle to this scheme.

In Taishan, Sheryl felt the weight of her ancestors on her shoulders. We went for a walk that evening, and she spoke about how she understood the enormous risks her grandfather had taken to move to America so that his progeny could enjoy greater opportunity.

"Am I living up to that?" she asked. "What am I doing with myself to build a future? What are we going to do, the two of us? What's going to happen when you move to China?"

I didn't know. Neither of us had good answers.

After the trip, Sheryl helped me move from Hong Kong to Taiwan for language study. She tried to coach me on learning the tones of Mandarin. "Repeat after me," she said. "*Ma, ma, ma, ma.*"

"*Ma, ma, ma, ma,*" I repeated dutifully.

"No, no," she said. "You just repeated '*ma*' four times."

"That's what you said to do!"

"No, no." She laughed. "I said '*ma*' in four different tones. Didn't you hear the difference?"

"Nope."

"'*Ma*' is a level tone. That's first tone. Then '*ma*' is a rising tone. You hear the difference? *Ma.* That's second tone. Then '*ma*' is a falling and rising tone. Third tone. And then '*ma*' goes down. '*Ma!*' That's fourth tone. *Ma.* You hear the difference?"

"They all sound exactly the same," I said. "*Ma.*"

Sheryl sighed. "We're going to have to work on you."

We took a vacation together in Indonesia over the Christmas holiday, traveling in remote parts of Java. We had been together for seven months in Hong Kong, but now she would leave me to finish her graduate degree in public policy at Princeton, so it felt as if we were coming to a juncture in our lives. I couldn't keep delaying choices. So I planned on staying in a nice hotel in the ancient city of Yogyakarta, taking Sheryl to a fine dinner and proposing to her. But to get to Yogyakarta, I had organized a winding fifteen-hour, third-class train ride through Java. Sheryl, not wanting to use the disgusting toilets, didn't drink much and suffered sunstroke and dehydration. That left her nauseated and throwing up. She suffered silently and didn't point out that traveling third class in remote parts of Java was not her optimal vacation, but I understood that myself. My love for her grew, but I wanted her

Moments after I proposed to Sheryl, we stood up as a newly engaged couple on the lip of Mount Bromo.

healthy when I proposed. A few days later, when she had recovered, we climbed an active volcano in East Java, Mount Bromo. We sat on the lip of volcano, staring down into the bowels of the earth as smoke enveloped us.

"Come sit over here," I urged Sheryl, for she was on a rock a couple of feet away with no room for me.

"This is fine," she said, looking nervously at the volcano. "We should leave in a moment. I don't want it to erupt while we're up here."

"Just come here for a moment."

"I don't want to fall into the volcano."

"I want you next to me!"

Sheryl smiled and came over to sit next to me. Once she had done so, I kneeled and looked in her eyes.

"Sorry to be so traditional," I said. "Will you marry me?"

Sheryl's mouth fell open and for a moment I wasn't sure how she might answer. But then she grabbed me. "Yes!" she said. "Yes!"

15

How Little We Knew

The *New York Times* bureau chief's apartment in Beijing was a large, well-bugged suite in Building Seven of a guarded government-run compound called Jianguomenwai, reserved for foreign diplomats and journalists. Jianguomenwai was the kind of soulless compound that Communist governments were good at erecting, but it was comfortable, quiet and air-conditioned. Within the paper, it was often said that the correspondent you wanted to follow in any bureau was John Burns. While John was a superb correspondent, the main reason was that he negotiated with New York to get lovely homes or refurbish old ones, acquire beautiful furniture and hire helpful staff. Wherever you were in the world—Kabul, Baghdad, Delhi—if you found particularly fine *Times* lodgings, you could guess that John had been there. Once when I visited John's bureau in Islamabad, I was very impressed by a local man he had hired; a few years later, he was Pakistan's ambassador to the United States and issued me a visa after the country's intelligence agency banned me.

Sheryl and I, newly married, fresh from language study in Taiwan, were fortunate that John had been in Beijing a couple of years before us, until he took a motorcycle trip through a remote area. The Chinese authorities arrested him, accused him of spying and after a brief imprisonment expelled him from the country. The Chinese government said that John had been reporting in a closed military area and was taking suspicious photos. This was monstrously unfair to John, who had informed the Foreign Ministry of his route in advance. Three years later, in 1989, a senior Chinese official gave John a formal apology and attributed his arrest to false charges concocted by "bad elements" in State Security. My understanding is that China had arrested John in retaliation for the defection of a senior State Security official to the United States.

China's unfair treatment of John Burns was compounded by the *Times*'s unfair treatment of him. At the time John was expelled, the United States was swooning over China, and there was a good deal of unfair tut-tutting about John provoking China by visiting a closed area. The *Times* didn't stand foursquare behind John as it should have, and it sentenced him to the Canada bureau—then the paper's equivalent of Siberia.

It was Joe Lelyveld who rehabilitated John and sent him to Bosnia, where he did heroic work covering the Balkan wars, won a Pulitzer and established his reputation as one of The Greats. One of the most memorable pieces of foreign reporting I know is a 1992 essay by John about the struggle of survivors to retain their humanity amid the destructiveness of war. Filed from Sarajevo, it began:

> As the 155-millimeter howitzer shells whistled down on this crumbling city today, exploding thunderously into buildings all around, a disheveled, stubble-bearded man in formal evening attire unfolded a plastic chair in the middle of Vase Miskina Street. He lifted his cello from its case and began playing Albinoni's Adagio.
>
> There were only two people to hear him, and both fled, dodging from doorway to doorway, before the performance ended.

Sheryl and I appreciated the work that John had done setting up the apartment in Beijing, by merging two smaller apartments, bringing in nice furniture and hiring a full-time live-in Filipina housekeeper—all paid for by the *Times*. But creature comforts couldn't insulate us from a dictatorial state. The People's Armed Police guarded the entrances to our compound and blocked Chinese citizens from entering. This became tricky with people like Sheryl who were of Chinese extraction but had foreign nationality. Sometimes the guards would try to block Sheryl from entering our compound, and sometimes they would look at her clothes and self-assuredness and judge that she was probably a foreigner. But Chinese citizens themselves were learning that if they showed enough self-confidence they could pretend to be foreigners and march by the guards as well—or, if challenged, could send the guards retreating by saying a few words in English or else in Chinese with a fake foreign accent.

We knew our apartment was bugged, partly because one of our Chinese friends worked part-time for State Security translating conversations in our building. Our building had a special floor where the State Security bugging teams worked; we could see them whenever shifts changed. During our brief overlap, our predecessor, Ed Gargan, pointed to an opening with wire mesh over it high in the entrance corridor of our new home.

"There's a camera in there," Gargan told us. "And some of the bugs are in there."

That wire mesh angered me; it felt like an insult whenever I passed it. It was an invasion of our privacy. A couple of weeks later I was on a ladder hanging posters nearby, and the irritation reached a breaking point.

"Sheryl, hand me a flashlight," I said. "Let's see if we can see through the mesh."

In my Beijing office at the *Times*. We could write on a computer, but all articles and messages were transmitted by a clunky telex in the corner.

Both of us perched precariously on the ladder as we tried to glimpse what was inside. It looked like a cubbyhole the size of a shoebox, with some suspicious gadgetry inside.

"What do you think?" I whispered in Sheryl's ear. "Should we knock out the mesh?"

Sheryl went to retrieve a hammer. I used it to smash the mesh, and we stared with wonder at the interior. There were no cameras, but the cubbyhole was indeed filled with electronics. We shone the light at one particularly suspicious object and I was thrilled that I could read and understand the Chinese characters for "electronic sound carrying device."

We had found a bug! Sheryl and I, having read spy novels, retreated to the bathroom, turned on the shower and faucets, and in whispers debated what we should do. Should we replace the mesh and ignore the bug? Should we smash it? Or should we leave it in place and use it as our private disinformation channel to the Chinese authorities? We settled on the third option and were discussing what kind of disinformation to transmit to State Security when a friend arrived at the front door. That's when we learned what an "electronic sound carrying device" actually is in Chinese.

It's a doorbell buzzer.

We were deflated, but it was a useful lesson in humility, a reminder that for all our presumption in explaining China to the world, we had little idea what was going on around us—and that any time we were too full of ourselves, too cocky about our analytical triumphs, we were probably about to learn that the world is more complicated than it seems. China is a vast country with multiple languages and dialects, in which people are reluctant to speak freely, and even the country's leaders seemed to have little idea what was going on in the provinces.

"When Dad goes on a provincial visit, he sends his drivers and guards out to talk to people, because he knows the officials will lie to him," the son of a Politburo member told us. We befriended a number of children of current or former Politburo members, partly because they felt protected: State Security was reluctant to tangle with a Politburo member's family. On at least one occasion, State Security detained the daughter of a senior official after she left our apartment, and it was the State Security officials who were chastised for overstepping their bounds. It helped that Sheryl was Chinese American, for the authorities were more tolerant about Chinese citizens socializing with an ethnic Chinese journalist who held a foreign passport.

IT WAS JOE LELYVELD who had offered me the China position, and our lives in China and beyond continued to be shaped by him in his role as foreign editor. He was an extraordinarily good journalist who excelled at bringing out the best in reporters.

A summa graduate of Harvard, Joe had spent his entire career at the *Times* and was widely regarded as one of its leading lights. When I was a new business reporter, an editor, Karen Arenson, told me: "You should get to know Joe Lelyveld. He's the smartest reporter at the paper, and he's now the London bureau chief." Joe wasn't into quick-hit "gotcha" stories, but he deeply believed in accountability journalism. He also was a master, as both reporter and editor, at conveying nuance in ways that readers would find interesting. And he had zero patience for journalistic tricks that attracted readers but felt like cheap shots or casual exaggerations. He accepted no compromises in accuracy.

Joe wasn't an ebullient cheerleader, the kind of back-slapper that Ben Bradlee had been at *The Washington Post*. He wasn't shy about expressing opinions, but he was personally reserved. The executive editor when we were in China, Max Frankel, was gregarious and affable, but newsroom reporters sometimes talked about being afraid to be caught in an elevator with Joe. The silence could be deafening.

The first time I met Joe I did sense that awkwardness. He was appointed foreign editor when I was in Hong Kong, and although we spoke regularly on the phone I hadn't encountered him in person when he offered me the Beijing job. After I had closed the Hong Kong bureau and was about to begin my Chinese-language studies, I visited New York and found Joe at his desk. I introduced myself and stuck out my hand. We shook hands firmly, and somehow his knuckle whacked his keyboard. He released my hand and clutched his right knuckle with his left hand. "It's okay," he said in a strained voice. When I saw him again a couple of hours later, he had a Band-Aid on his knuckle. I thought: How have I managed to injure my boss the first time I meet him, simply by shaking hands?

The awkwardness of that first encounter dissipated, however, and I admired Joe not only for his intellect and journalism, but also for his managerial skills. He managed to push his staff hard without losing any of his innate decency. I regularly received herograms from editors in New York, including Joe, and I relished them. But Joe was the only person I remember who once sent me a scolding note, and it left a deep impression (several years later, I asked him about it, and he couldn't recall it at all). I had spent a couple of days in Guangzhou and had written a piece about a huge flow of migrant laborers seeking jobs, but my permission from the government to stay in Guangzhou ran out before I could get more color and quotes from the migrants. Then I wrote it in grand style that levered it onto page one:

CANTON, China—A mass migration officially estimated at more than 2.5 million Chinese has flooded this city in the last few weeks, responding to the lure of southern China's prosperity.

"I'd heard that it was easy to make money here," Long Zaohong, a thirty-year-old peasant from neighboring Hunan Province, said as he sat on a bundle of his possessions in front of Canton's railway station. Mr. Long arrived Wednesday with four friends, part of a human wave that reached a peak of 100,000 arrivals a day and has since receded to about 6,000 daily.

If the reports are not exaggerated, the flow of people exceeds the entire emigration from the Chinese mainland to Taiwan at the end of China's civil war in 1949 . . .

A week later, Joe wrote me a letter complimenting me on the piece and on my work overall but adding:

I've been worried that we didn't ask you enough hard questions about the story and, more to the point, you didn't ask enough hard questions in reporting it.

You caught the significance of the influx—what it showed about Guangdong—but left us wondering how 100,000 people could travel into Canton every day (are there enough trains and buses?) and where the people went (were there squatter camps springing up?).

I mention this now not to chide you but to urge you to push yourself to be a little tougher, grittier and more persevering in your reporting . . .

I wanted to protest: *I wasn't allowed to stay in Canton to report more!* But Joe was fundamentally right. I shouldn't have left the reader with questions. When I couldn't get details, I should have written a more modest story instead of swinging for the fences with flamboyant page one language. Joe's pushback sometimes made reporters indignant, but our articles were better for it.

Joe was exceptionally good to Sheryl, taking her to lunch when she, then my fiancée, was at Princeton and I was studying in Taiwan, and nurturing her career for years thereafter. He hired Sheryl as a second correspondent in China, putting her on a contract to write from China—and marking a major step in the *Times*'s path toward more respectful treatment of spouses. Some other editors scoffed that now every wife would want to be a correspondent, and others complained that now a single couple would decide coverage of the world's most populous nation in their pillow talk. But skeptics were silenced when Sheryl proved a first-rate journalist who brought new depth to economic and business coverage of China. Initially, though, we had trouble getting Sheryl accredited by the Chinese authorities. The government didn't want any news organization to have more than one correspondent in Beijing, and it was Punch Sulzberger who solved that conundrum.

"Apply for Sheryl to represent not *The New York Times*, but a separate entity called *The New York Times* News Service," he suggested. "That way the Chinese get another news organization they can boast about, and it makes no difference to us whether she's accredited to the *Times* or to the news service." That worked perfectly.

In retrospect, it seems absurd to have only two people responsible for covering more than a billion people at a turning point in their history, not to mention responsibility for also covering Hong Kong, Macao and Taiwan, plus occasional duty farther afield if a crisis erupted in, say, Afghanistan or the Philippines. But at the time it was seen as a recognition of China's significance: Previously, the paper had had only a single correspondent in all China.

China was still perceived as a backwater. The *Times* sent its most experienced correspondents to London, Paris, Tokyo and a few other places deemed important, but it was willing to take a chance on a couple of twenty-somethings like ourselves to cover the world's most populous country. We threw ourselves into that absurdity. We lived,

The Beijing correspondents of the *Times* on the Great Wall, back when tourists were scarce.

breathed and dreamed in Chinese, and one high-level contact led to another. After a lunch with Wu Jinglian, a top government economist, I offered him a lift to wherever he was going next.

"Thanks," he said. "I'm going to Zhongnanhai."

So I drove him to Zhongnanhai, the walled Communist Party leadership compound, which foreigners were rarely allowed to enter. Neither of us knew what would happen when we got to the gate. But Wu showed his pass, and the flummoxed guards waved us in.

One of our dearest friends was Zhang Hanzhi, who had been Chairman Mao's English teacher, a senior Foreign Ministry official and the wife of the foreign minister. Zhang was extraordinarily charming, still beautiful in her late fifties, graying a bit, with perfect English, wry humor and a tremendous network that allowed her to pick up the most scandalous stories about Communist Party hardliners. She was quick with funny stories of Mao's sexual conquests and the soap opera of life in Zhongnanhai. She now lived in a beautiful imperial courtyard home, where we could visit her and leave State Security and the rest of Beijing on the other side of her high garden walls. I think we reminded her of her daughter, Hung Huang, who was our age and was then living in

New York (Huang later moved back to Beijing and became a cherished friend as well).

Zhang Hanzhi had enjoyed great privilege in China in the Mao period, but after his death she had spent two years under house arrest, encouraged to take her own life. Her guards brought her scissors one day, rope the next. But Zhang was a fighter, and her range of experience left her with a sense of nuance about China that few others had. I once asked Zhang about her late husband, Foreign Minister Qiao Guanhua, who had served in the 1970s. He was a Maoist who gave hardline speeches, and I couldn't understand how she had ever seen eye-to-eye with him.

"He didn't himself believe the things he said," she told us. "By the end of his life, he saw clearly that it wasn't working. But what could he do? Of course he couldn't admit it to anyone but me."

The gap between official rhetoric and reality was widening, largely because of corruption. One of our friends, a Politburo member's son, was paid $400,000 a year for serving on a corporate board, with no responsibilities. The company calculated that it could then bully local governments into handing over valuable land, which it would then develop at a huge profit. After all, no mayor or county executive wanted to risk antagonizing a Politburo member.

Because Sheryl was often mistaken for a local Chinese, we sometimes gained unexpected insights into what ordinary citizens had to put up with. Our friends once took us to a dance party for senior officials, with lots of alcohol. Wang Qishan, a future leader in his own right, was there along with many others. I was chatting with officials and didn't pay much attention as a cabinet minister, Lin Hanxiong, invited Sheryl to dance. He assumed she was local Chinese eye candy, for after leading her onto the dance floor he drew her into a tight embrace and wouldn't let her wriggle out. We knew that senior party officials sometimes assaulted Chinese women, but being groped by a cabinet minister was not an experience Sheryl had anticipated. I was oblivious to what was going on, but Sheryl, never a wallflower, was up to the challenge.

"Do you know who I am?" Sheryl asked Minister Lin in Chinese. "I'm an American." She paused and her voice rose: "AND I'M A REPORTER FOR *THE NEW YORK TIMES!*"

Minister Lin released her as if she were a red-hot poker. Afterward, we spread the word about what had happened, and he was soon fired for "society problems," often a euphemism for sexual misconduct.

For all the corruption, there was a great deal to admire both about China and about the Chinese. We became close to young reformers who had given up promising jobs in the West to return and build their country. They were so smart and so dedicated. I figured that once the dogmatic octogenarians died off, China would become more pragmatic, more capitalist and more democratic. Most of my friends thought so, too.

I took on a role as interviewer of Chinese high school students applying to Harvard, and I was dazzled by the caliber of the applicants. The SAT was not offered in China, so instead they took the GRE, intended for applicants to graduate school. And as seventeen-year-olds, in an unfamiliar language and without access to test tutoring, they routinely scored in the 98th or 99th percentile.

The conventional wisdom among China-watchers was that the population was too busy getting rich to worry about politics or to protest, but Sheryl and I weren't so sure about that. One activist I admired was Ren Wanding, an earnest accountant who was a pioneer of the human rights movement in China—and he ended up behind bars. After his release from four years in prison, an enterprising reporter from the *South China Morning Post* in Hong Kong found Ren, who agreed to give an interview but on condition that the interview also run in the *Times*. The *Post* reporter brought me in. I got credit for outstanding reporting when in fact I was simply riding the reputation of the *Times*.

Ren told us how in prison he had refused to write self-criticism. Instead, he wrote a four-volume treatise on human rights with the only materials he could find, toilet paper and the nib of a discarded pen. The warden responded by keeping him in prison for an extra year, after his sentence expired, because of his "bad attitude." But Ren continued to call for free elections and respect for human rights.

"I went through some very frightening experiences," he said, leaning forward in his chair and peering earnestly at me through his thick glasses. "But China has no democracy and no human rights, and its living standard is too low. These are even more frightening." I asked him what would happen to his wife and twelve-year-old daughter if he spoke up. "I already died once," he said, referring to his imprisonment. "So now there is nothing to fear."

16

Witness to a Massacre

Our first alert to the coming storm came when a Chinese journalist friend telephoned us on the early afternoon of April 15, 1989.

"Did you hear?" he asked as I picked up the landline. "Hu Yaobang has died." Hu was the former Communist Party leader who had been ousted two years earlier by hardliners. "I hear there may be something happening at Beijing University this evening," he added. "You might want to drop by."

Sheryl and I slipped into Beijing University that evening. The gates were guarded, but on earlier reporting forays we had figured out how to bypass the guards. The university had a dormitory for foreign students, who were assigned keys with strings to open their rooms. So we used a back gate near the foreign student dorm, looked young and confident, and waved a key on a string. We were in our late twenties, youthful enough that the guards thought we were students and let us through.

On the campus, students were putting up posters mourning Hu Yaobang and, in some cases, denouncing corruption and demanding democracy. The most incendiary poster declared "The wrong man died"—a suggestion that the person who belonged in a coffin was the country's supreme leader, Deng Xiaoping. Wang Dan, a scrawny democracy activist with owlish glasses whom Sheryl had befriended that spring, was in the thick of it; later he would become the No. 1 most wanted democracy leader in China.

"This could be a turning point," he told Sheryl. It was.

Over the next couple of weeks, the protests snowballed, but this led to a new crisis. Students had called for a major protest on April 27, 1989, but Deng Xiaoping resolved to crack down violently if it went ahead. The *People's Daily* and state television denounced the protest plans and issued brutal warnings. Everyone was terrified. Students knew that if they marched, they were risking expulsion and imprisonment. On the eve of the planned protest, some students spent the night writing their wills in case they were killed.

I drove out to the university district on the morning of April 27 with a heavy heart, ready to write an obituary for a brief student movement. The roads were lined with tens of thousands of People's Armed Police, and it was hard to imagine protesters managing to leave campus. I slipped onto the Beijing University campus the usual way, waving a fake key as I entered by the foreign student dorm, but there was no activity. Aside from secret police, the campus was dead. It was a glorious spring day, the sun shining after days of rain, so it seemed incongruous that this spectacular weather marked the apparent end of the democracy movement.

Then a bit after 9 a.m., Wang Dan and a band of a hundred students emerged from a dormitory waving banners and marching around campus. You could see other students wavering: They wanted to join but were scared. Gradually, they joined in until there were a thousand or more students protesting on the Beijing University campus, and then they marched toward the gates. Rows of armed police blocked their way, but the students jostled and pushed and finally forced their way through and onto the road. To everyone's surprise, the police didn't club the students or shoot them. Once the vanguard broke through, thousands more students materialized to join the march, as the police watched from the sides of the road.

Word spread rapidly. As the marchers passed other universities, tens of thousands more students joined the protest march, and so did ordinary citizens. A dam burst: Old people shouted encouragement from balconies, and shopkeepers rushed out to give drinks and snacks to protesters. The police tried many times to block the students, but each time a shoving match resulted in the huge throngs of young people forcing their way through. At one point, a group of police were surrounded by furious workers menacing them, and students had to rush over to insist that the police not be harmed.

Reporting on one of the early 1989 protests in which student pro-democracy protesters took over Beijing streets.

I walked alongside the students, deeply moved by what I saw, interviewing some participants all the way to Tiananmen Square, by which point the protesters pouring out on the streets numbered perhaps half a million. The students were giddy: Many of them were teenagers, and they appeared to have brought the dictatorship to its knees. They had risked everything out of a desperate yearning for a freer and more democratic China. As I walked with the students, I doubted that in their position I would have manifested such courage.

After reaching Tiananmen Square, the students marched back to their universities, cheered on all the way by the people of Beijing screaming support. This time at the gate of Beijing University, they were met not by phalanxes of armed police but by white-haired professors who were waiting for them, crying happy tears, cheering for them.

"You are heroes," one professor shouted. "You are sacrificing for all of us. You are braver than we are."

It was a privilege to witness the heroism of that day, and it was particularly memorable because it happened to be my thirtieth birthday. Sheryl and I didn't get a chance to celebrate, and we were up much of the night writing front-page articles about the demonstrations. But I didn't need cake: The protest was the most thrilling birthday present of my life. I had seen how a small number of committed people like Wang Dan, willing to take risks, could inspire a movement and gather hundreds of thousands to their cause—turning despair into hope. The United States prides itself on its democratic traditions, but we Americans could learn so much from the commitment to democracy shown that day by Chinese students.

After the student demonstrations on April 27, the protests surged. Government officials, workers, doctors, retirees, business owners and others joined in. Pickpockets announced that they would refrain from stealing from protesters. Students occupied Tiananmen Square and undertook a hunger strike: Whenever they fainted, ambulances rushed to rescue them and take them to hospitals; the haunting sound of the sirens blared around the clock, carrying students to hospitals.

"Our hearts bleed when we hear the sound of ambulances," said a gray-haired teacher who donated a week's wages to support the students. "I want to thank them. They represent our hearts. They represent our hopes."

Sheryl and I covering one of the early Tiananmen Square protests.

A professor we were friendly with, the son of a general and a distinguished Communist Party member in his own right, was inspired by his students and followed them to Tiananmen Square.

"How can I sit in the university, preparing research articles, when my students are risking their lives?" he asked. "If the tanks roll over them, the tanks will first have to roll over me."

Sheryl and I were reporting all day, writing all night and barely sleeping. In addition to our coverage of the crisis for the foreign section, the *Times Magazine* wanted a cover story, the Week in Review wanted a cover and so on. Rumors were flying, so the telex machine was constantly rattling with inquiries like this:

KRISTOF EX BACHELLER

BEIJING

MOST URGENT AND IMMEDIATE

    NICK, WIRES AND CNN REPORTING THAT CHINESE LANGUAGE PAPER IN HONG KONG IS REPORTING THAT AN ARMY OFFICER IN BEIJING ATTEMPTED TO ASSASSINATE LI PENG, WOUNDING HIM, AND WAS SHOT TO DEATH ON THE SPOT. REPORTS ARE UNCLEAR AS TO TIMING—COULD BE SEVERAL DAYS AGO OR JUST NOW. COULD YOU SEE IF THERE'S ANYTHING TO THIS AND CALL US OR TELEX? THANKS.

There was nothing to that report, or to most of these rumors, but they took time to chase down. Another urgent telex relayed to us from New York was that the American Embassy in Beijing was under attack. We drove over to the embassy and reported that it looked perfectly normal. Joe Lelyveld, to his credit, kept trying to slow this pace of demands on our time and in every conversation told us to report less and get more sleep. In one telex, he directed:

NICK AND SHERYL, EVERYONE HERE IS FILLED WITH ADMIRATION AND GRATITUDE FOR YET ANOTHER DAY OF REMARKABLE COVERAGE, YOUR BEST YET, AND THAT'S SAYING A LOT . . . NOW, PLEASE, EACH OF YOU IS ORDERED TO ENSURE THAT THE OTHER GETS SOME S-L-E-E-P, WHICH IS, IN CASE YOU'VE FORGOTTEN, "A NATURAL, REGULARLY RECURRING CONDITION OF REST FOR THE BODY AND MIND" (WEBSTER'S).

    ALLBEST, LELYVELD.

The telex machine churned out constant herograms for our reporting, from everyone from Abe Rosenthal to Henry Kissinger. But in
retrospect our journalism suffered from a profound selection bias: We
didn't have access to hardliners who favored a crackdown, and we didn't
try hard enough to reach them or reflect their views. Talking mostly to
supporters of the democracy movement, it was easy to think that the
movement would triumph. In retrospect, I don't think we adequately
conveyed to readers that many in the government were ready to massacre students if that's what it took to ensure their own continued rule.

Looking back, it's also fair to ask whether the pro-democracy protesters pushed too hard. If the students had demanded freedom of
speech but had not threatened Communist Party rule itself, might the
bloody crackdown have been averted? Could moderate Communists
like Zhao Ziyang, the reformist leader under Deng in the late 1980s,
have stayed in power and engineered continued reforms after the old
guard died? Might China then have evolved fitfully toward greater
democracy along the model of Taiwan or Mexico?

But that's not how democracy movements work. When people have
been repressed for decades and finally sense a chance at freedom, they
don't want to settle for a bit less repression. They push on and sometimes they win and sometimes—as in China in 1989, Iran in 2009,
Syria after 2011—they're brutally suppressed and life becomes even less
free. Mass movements for democracy are often unwieldy and leader-
less (because the government quickly imprisons leaders), which means
they aren't prone to make concessions. I also think that the discussion
of whether Chinese protesters pushed too hard risks veering into an
implication that the protesters brought the crackdown on themselves;
they didn't. Blame for the slaughter that ended the Tiananmen democracy movement lies with those who ordered the troops to open fire.

On the night of June 3, 1989, Chinese friends called with horrify-
ing news: Soldiers in trucks and armored vehicles were moving down
the Avenue of Eternal Peace from the west, mowing people down with
automatic weapons. They were headed for Tiananmen Square and the
student encampment there. Sheryl and I agreed that she would stay and
write, while I would rush to the scene. We embraced, and I ran for the
elevator. Then I thought of State Security and its camera in the elevator; I imagined someone locking me in the elevator between floors to

keep me from covering the story. I abandoned the elevator and raced down thirteen flights of stairs.

"Be careful!" Sheryl shouted after me.

"I will!" I shouted back, knowing that she wouldn't believe me.

Beijing citizens had set up barriers on the roads as tank traps to slow the soldiers, with only narrow passages for pedestrians and bicyclists to pass through. That meant I couldn't drive, so I jumped on my Chinese bicycle, a black single-speed Phoenix, and began pedaling down the avenue toward Tiananmen Square. I hunched over the handlebars, racing as fast as I could as crowds of people ran in the other direction. I swerved my way through the crowds and past the barriers, toward the gunfire ahead—and I kept thinking, *What kind of a crazy job is this that has me hurtling toward gunfire?*

I parked my bike on Tiananmen Square near the Mao portrait and frantically began to interview Chinese in the crowd around me. Soon afterward, the troops arrived. The soldiers assembled a hundred yards to the west and opened fire on us. At first the gunfire seemed to go over our heads, and I wasn't sure if the troops were shooting bullets or blanks. Then the troops lowered their aim. It wasn't continuous gunfire, but periodic bursts. When the first young man fell, I thought perhaps he had fainted, until I saw that half his head was blown away.

It was night, but Tiananmen Square was lit by overhead lights and by the glow of several army trucks and two armored personnel carriers that protesters had set on fire. There were thousands of people in the crowd, furious, chanting, waving fists. Some young men carried iron bars or hurled bricks or Molotov cocktails at the troops. But the bricks and fire bombs landed far short of the soldiers. In contrast, the army's automatic weapons were devastatingly effective.

I was now in the middle of a massacre. The People's Liberation Army was waging war on the people. Much of me wanted to run, run, run. I wanted to flee and grab Sheryl and head for the airport, then fly to a Thai beach and sit there for weeks staring at the turquoise sea. But journalistic discipline kicks in. Reporters are there to record what is happening. We're trained to suppress emotion and focus on the task of documenting news. It is an instinct that becomes ingrained in us, just as an emergency physician might rush to stop a geyser of blood rather than faint from it. As bullets whizzed around me, I knew this was history and I was conscious of the need to document it and also to survive, so I focused on taking notes and keeping a layer of protesters between me and the soldiers to absorb bullets. After ten minutes, I realized that because I'm a bit taller than most Chinese, there were several important inches of me that protruded above the crowd and were vulnerable. After that I hunched over as I ran around interviewing people. It was chaotic: I would ask people what they thought, what they planned to do, and they would call over friends who would all speak furiously as the massacre continued.

Soon I had trouble taking notes, for my pen did not work well. I switched pens, but the second one was no better. I realized that the problem was that my notebook pages were damp from the sweat on my palms: the sweat of fear. Some journalists show undaunted courage under fire; I was petrified.

Groups of young protesters twice commandeered city buses that they drove toward the troops. There were about a dozen people on each bus, clutching sticks or iron bars, somehow thinking that with the bus they could take the fight to the troops. They were scared, furious, desperate and valiant, and the crowds waved encouragement to them. Then the buses drove slowly toward the troops, who opened fire with hundreds of rounds, and I watched the protesters inside die. The shattered buses ground to a halt. One person fled from the first bus. The second bus caught fire and no one escaped the flames. In less than a minute, the students had gone from heroes to martyrs. I admired their courage but wished they hadn't been so brave or reckless, and I knew their families would never fully recover.

"General strike! General strike!" the crowd chanted. But as I ran from person to person, asking questions, many acknowledged that their ideals could not defeat machine guns, at least in the short run.

"Maybe we'll fail today," an art student told me, nearly incoherent with grief as he watched the body of another student being carted away, his head shattered by bullets. "Maybe we'll fail tomorrow. But someday we'll succeed. It's a historic inevitability."

The crowd fled east along the Avenue of Eternal Peace, and I ran with the throngs, always hunched over and trying to keep a layer of people in front of me. The gunfire paused, and the crowd regrouped when the bullets stopped. Some young men hurled bricks, none of which ever landed near the troops, and then the soldiers opened fire again. We ran back, the gunfire paused, and this grim cycle kept repeating.

The bravest people that day were the rickshaw drivers, pedaling small carts, and they taught me an indelible lesson. These were peasants from the countryside with little schooling, and my coverage had often been condescending toward people like them: *They say they want democracy, but they don't really know what it is. They can't define it. It's more that they're against corruption and inflation, and they don't necessarily want democracy for Tibetans and Uyghurs.*

Yes, there was something to all that. But that night, as the rest of us cowered, it was the rickshaw drivers who pedaled out toward the soldiers during each lull in the shooting and picked up the bodies of young people who had been shot. They placed the dead or injured on the backs of their rickshaws, and then turned and rushed back toward us and beyond to the hospitals.

I remember watching one husky rickshaw driver in a white tank top. He was in his late thirties with a round stubble-covered face, wearing flip-flops. As he drove out toward the soldiers, I held my breath, wondering if he would be shot. Then he picked up the motionless body of a young man and pedaled back frantically toward us, his legs pounding up and down like pistons, blood seeping out of the body onto his cart. Only then did I release my breath. The driver evidently recognized me as a foreign journalist, perhaps from my previous reporting in the square, for he swerved to pass by me and slowed so that I could document the scene.

"Tell the world!" he shouted at me. "Tell the world!" Tears were streaming down his cheeks.

This rickshaw driver might not have been able to define democracy—but he was risking his life for it. Hundreds were shot dead that night and thousands more were injured, yet so many ordinary Chinese like him stood fast. The heroism of these Chinese citizens has inspired me ever since. I still get emotional as I remember the courage I witnessed that terrible night. I would never again be condescending about uneducated people in poor countries aspiring for democracy. We have so much to learn from their commitment and valor.

On the old airport road, then a crucial artery into Beijing, a middle-aged bus driver tried to protect the students from attack. He saw a large army convoy approaching the city and hurriedly parked his public bus across the road, blocking it so that the army vehicles could not pass. The bus driver turned off the engine and stepped out on to the road as the army convoy braked to a stop. An officer stepped forward.

"Move the bus," the officer shouted.

The bus driver shook his head.

The officer pulled out his sidearm, pointed it at the driver and ordered him more urgently: "MOVE THE BUS!" The driver said nothing. Instead, he looked to the side of the road at the deep grass in the verge, barely visible in the darkness, and then he suddenly hurled the ignition key into that sea of high grass. I never found out what happened to the driver, but he inspires me to this day.

I wasn't sure that I would make it back to Sheryl that night, for bullets were flying all over. I remembered her admonition to "be careful," and I wanted to be. I kept thinking: *Maybe I should go now. It's time to go home and write.* But I was determined to record all that I could, and I knew the crowd was desperate to have me there as a witness. Staying was my way, perhaps a reckless one, of standing up to those who slaughtered students.

Finally, as my deadline approached, I knew I had to go home soon so I could file my story. There was no hope of recovering my bicycle, for the troops now occupied that area,* so I ran a mile and a half to the Peking Union Medical College Hospital to document the scene there and gather numbers killed and injured, and then ran a bit more than three miles back to our home. The distance from the hospital to home was roughly the same as I used to run in high school cross-country meets—five kilometers—and I ran with fury and intensity through empty streets, the gunfire now behind me. I kept thinking of the difference between the joy and exuberance of our high school meets and the murderous scenes that I was now running from.

This was long before cell phones in Beijing became common, so I had no way to call Sheryl or New York with an update, or just to let them know that I was safe. Everyone was anxious, and it didn't help that editors were constantly calling Sheryl to check if I was back.

"Don't worry," Joe Lelyveld told Sheryl. "He'll be back. He'll be

---

* It was weeks before the public was allowed access to Tiananmen Square again, and when I was able to return a tank was parked right where my bicycle had been. I expensed $89 for a new bicycle "to replace one run over by a tank." The accountants at the paper always said I had the most interesting expenses.

back. There's no point worrying." The worry in his voice made Sheryl fret all the more.

"There's one very important thing you need to do," Joe advised. "You need to keep track of the dead. We need to know how many have been killed."

"How do I do that?" Sheryl asked.

"Call the hospitals? You can figure it out. You have to keep track of the death toll. And call me the moment he's back." Being told to keep a tally of the corpses, as automatic gunfire rattled in the distance, didn't help Sheryl's peace of mind.

I reached Jianguomenwai and ran up the stairs—I certainly didn't want State Security to lock me in the elevator after all I'd witnessed— and turned the key in our apartment door. Sheryl raced forward at the sound, and I stood there panting, looking at her for a moment, and then we embraced. Neither of us could speak. Sheryl was beside herself, because I had made a grave mistake. In the chaos and my sleep-deprived state, I had forgotten that it was a Saturday night, which meant early deadlines for the Sunday paper. This meant that I arrived home long after Sheryl had been expecting me back, and because I was normally very respectful of deadlines she had imagined the worst. Never do that to your spouse.

With one arm still around Sheryl, I called the foreign desk, and a clerk answered.

"It's Nick Kristof," I said. "Can you put Joe on?"

"Thank God," the clerk said. "I'll get him. He'll be happy to hear from you." I heard her shout: "Joe, Kristof on line two."

Lelyveld came on and quickly verified that I was still in one piece. He said that we were almost at deadline and that the *Times* would run a wire story for the first edition and then plug my story in when it arrived.

"Just hold off, Joe," I urged. "I'll make the deadline. I want readers to get my story. I'll file in takes. It's all in my head. I wrote it in my head as I was running home." After getting shot at and witnessing the massacre, I wasn't going to have the *Times* use an AP story.

"We'll try to hold it for you," Joe said. "I can't promise."

I bent over the keyboard, my fingers flying as I wrote a story I hated to write. In two thousand words, rushed to New York by telex a few paragraphs at a time, I described the Chinese government using its army to wage war on its own citizens. My article led the front page the next morning under a six-column banner headline. Sheryl had filed her story earlier, about the scene on the streets in Beijing and the public rage at the soldiers. Together, Sheryl and I took up most of page one. Normally it's a journalist's dream to have a banner headline, but we were never so pained to lead the paper.

"Tell the world" was a mantra that we heard often from Chinese as the country lurched into a terrified post-Tiananmen silence. Citizens could not speak, so they wanted us to speak for them. They took great risks to help us do so. The army sealed off the hospitals to prevent further reporting on casualties, so a worker at the Peking Union Medical College smuggled us in by underground tunnels from a neighboring building. Not only were all the hospital rooms filled with patients shot in the protests, but the corridors were full of people lying on stretchers.

A thirty-one-year-old engineer with seven patents was fighting for his life after seven hours of surgery. His wife, exhausted and red-eyed, explained between tears that he had gone out when the shooting began. "The students are poor and weak," he had told her. "I've got to go and help them." She began weeping again. She loved her husband, she admired him, and she hated that he might leave her and their four-year-old daughter all alone.

Documenting the toll wasn't "work" but a mission, and Sheryl and I toiled almost around the clock to gather evidence and push back at the lies on Chinese state television. We were exhausted, but this was journalism with meaning; this is what I had yearned to do. In the midst of a massacre, I had found my place.

17

We Become "Hoodlums"

Deng Xiaoping was arguably the most important political figure of the last 150 years. Alternatively, you could make a case for Franklin Roosevelt or Winston Churchill, for Mao Zedong, or perhaps for Joseph Stalin. But I would vote for Deng, because it was he who set in motion the transformation of China and thus of the world economy, and who then by massacring protesters ensured that the economically burgeoning China would not liberalize as most other Communist countries had done. The most populous country in the world is an anomaly—a tangle of soaring living and education standards, a rising middle class, political and religious repression, menace against Taiwan—and Deng shaped it.

He was irrepressible. Three times the Communist Party purged him, and three times he fought his way back to power. From 1954, when Mao first appointed him general secretary of the Chinese Communist Party, until his death in 1997, Deng played a central role in his country's fortunes. He was an improbable leader, only about four feet eleven inches tall (some disputed that estimate, but he never stood still for my tape measure).

Lucian Pye, a veteran China scholar, described an audience with Deng:

As he settles into an overstuffed chair, his sandaled feet barely touch the floor, and indeed hang free every time he leans forward to use the spittoon. He has an atrocious Sichuan accent, which makes his words slur together like a gargle. There are few signs of liveliness of mind, of wit or humor, and no sustained, systematic pursuit of ideas.

Yet Deng could also be eloquent in his bluntness. On a visit to the United States, the actress Shirley MacLaine told Deng about her visit to China during the Cultural Revolution, when Deng himself had been purged. The actress waxed lyrical about how she had met a professor who had been sent out to the countryside to "learn from peasants" and how the professor had told her how grateful he was for the opportunity to work with his hands. She had been so impressed by his attitude and open-mindedness! Deng looked at her and there was a long pause.

"He lied," Deng said. "That was what he had to say."

Deng made brilliant use of aphorisms. The best known was his tribute to pragmatism over dogma: *It doesn't matter if a cat is black or white, but whether it catches mice.* My own favorite was his description of how policymaking is like crossing a stream by using bare feet to feel for the rocks, one by one: *mozhe shitou guohe,* literally "feel stones, cross river."

I admired Deng's pragmatism and his drive to unleash China's economy and the creativity of its own people. He lifted more people out of poverty more rapidly than had ever been accomplished in human history, and education and health outcomes surged. Deng's reforms nurtured a middle class that aspired to democratic rights, so that it looked for a time as if China would liberalize and become a more normal nation. Marx had said that capitalists were gravediggers of their own legacy because they were creating conditions for Communism, and it had seemed that by opening China and creating an educated middle class, Deng was a gravedigger for China's Communist Party. But he dispatched troops to kill students and prevent that outcome.

Deng was conditioned, like many in his generation, to prioritize order. His nightmare was *luan,* or chaos, which to him came from a lack of strong central authority. His father had been murdered by bandits in a period of weak government, and Deng experienced the brutality of out-of-control young people during the Cultural Revolution. Red Guards in that period drove his brother to suicide and terrorized his eldest son, Deng Pufang, into attempting suicide by jumping out of a fourth-floor window and breaking his back, leaving him permanently paralyzed. When Deng saw students protesting, he didn't envision democracy on the horizon but rather *luan*. So he ordered in the troops and sidelined leading reformers, and his legacy became a powerful nation that increasingly was prosperous, educated, authoritarian and backed by a military willing to throw its weight around the Pacific.

Although Chinese propaganda termed leaders like Deng "Marxist-Leninist," that was not quite accurate. They were Leninist in the sense that they believed in a centralized dictatorship and followed five-year plans, but Deng dismantled communes, empowered entrepreneurs and built up the private sector. What he nurtured was market-Leninism. The markets nurtured the gleaming high-rise office towers, and the Leninism spilled blood around them.

You never fully recover from watching an army turn weapons of war on its own people. Journalists long for a big story—but now that I had one I was heartbroken. The pain was amplified when the authorities began a nationwide sweep to arrest reformers, now often denounced as "hoodlums" who supposedly had planned a "counterrevolutionary riot."

Many of our friends disappeared into prisons and detention centers around the country. Ren Wanding, the brave accountant who in prison had written a four-volume treatise about human rights, phoned me and we discussed whether he would be jailed; a few days later, he was.

A few days after the Tiananmen massacre, we were sleeping one morning when deafening gunfire awakened us. We dived under the bed. It turned out that Chinese troops had decided to spray our compound with automatic weapons. A diplomat's child was by a window, but a Chinese nanny grabbed the boy and threw him to the floor, diving on top of him and saving his life.

We barely avoided a difficult ethical conflict a couple of days after the massacre. Our friend Fang Lizhi, a celebrated astrophysicist and dissident, was despised by hardliners, and he was concerned that he would be accused of fomenting the "counterrevolutionary riot" and executed. So he and his wife tried to reach us to ask if they could secretly stay in our apartment until the threat eased. We were away all that day in the university district, so we didn't have to make that decision. It would have been difficult to say no to a friend in danger, yet our apartment was insecure and bugged, and the government would have soon traced Fang and arrested him and us.

Unable to reach us, Fang instead hid on United States Embassy grounds. China erupted in fury at this, and Fang and his wife were stuck there for a year before Washington and Beijing agreed on a deal to release them to the United States.

FOREIGN CORRESPONDENTS LIKE to project toughness and confidence, and I certainly attempted to do so. I didn't acknowledge to Joe Lelyveld—or even to myself—how brokenhearted I was at the massacre and repression or how much I felt the strain. In part this was exhaustion from the pace of work, but mostly it was an emotional revulsion at what was unfolding. Sheryl and I had accepted an assignment to cover the rise of China, the emergence of a more open and capitalist system. We had expected stock exchanges, not massacres.

I have a vivid memory of collapsing on our bed, my veneer of toughness stripped off. I'm not sure if it was the night of the Tiananmen massacre, or the next day, when we visited the hospitals, or on the day troops fired on our compound. But I recall lying on the bed, utterly exhausted and finding tears trickling down my cheeks, weeping for a bleeding China, for my own shattered optimism about this country that I wanted to love.

The United States evacuated Americans from Beijing, and Sheryl's parents telephoned us to make sure we joined the exodus. "You've got to get out," Sheryl's mom warned. "They're shooting foreigners. You need to evacuate."

"But the news is here in Beijing," Sheryl explained. "We can't leave." She handed me the phone. Sheryl was raised with too much filial piety to tell her parents a flat "no."

"If everyone else is leaving," I said, "that's when journalists show up. We have to stay. Our job as correspondents is to go places that every sane person is leaving."

That seemed to add to Sheryl's parents' distress, so we tried a different tack. "It'll be perfectly fine," Sheryl said. "The worst is over."

It wasn't clear that this was true. The *People's Daily* and national television broadcasts denounced me by name. "This *New York Times* reporter named Kristof has in his reports boldly made false assumptions, played games with numbers, and spread new lies," the state media said, adding that I was "writing not news reports but fiction."

The next day I happened to have lunch at an empty Sichuan restaurant near Jianguomenwai. The staff were buzzing about something, and I was afraid they had recognized me and might poison my food. Then several waitresses approached. "Are you the one they mentioned on television last night," one asked. "The reporter who lies?"

"Yes," I said, sighing, and I began to explain that it was nonsense.

"Never mind," she interrupted, and the waitresses all beamed at me. "There's no need to pay your bill. We'll take care of it. We're all hoodlums here."

It became extraordinarily difficult to report in China, for we were poorly sourced in the hardline camp, and most people were too terrified to talk to us. Even those who had felt protected by their connections were now at risk. One of our friends, Wu Xiaoyong, the son of a Politburo member, was an executive for Radio Beijing. Smart, American-educated and fluent in English, Wu had the airy charm and self-confidence that came with his family rank—but also a strong moral compass. When the massacre was still underway, he hurriedly wrote a script in English and ordered it broadcast on Radio Beijing's English Service. At a time when Chinese state media were full of lies, the broadcast was stunning:

> Thousands of people, most of them innocent civilians, were killed by fully armed soldiers when they forced their way into the city. Among the killed are our colleagues at Radio Beijing. The soldiers were riding on armored vehicles and used machine guns against thousands of local residents and students who tried to block their way. . . . Radio Beijing English Department deeply mourns those [who] died in the tragic incident and appeals to all its listeners to join our protest for the gross violation of human rights and the most barbarous suppression of the people.

Soldiers were dispatched to Radio Beijing to arrest the news reader. Wu Xiaoyong stood up to the soldiers and said that he was responsible.

"I'm the one who wrote the script and gave it to him to read," he told them. "I take responsibility." Unwilling to arrest the son of a Politburo member, the troops retreated and consulted with the office of the prime minister. That office ordered them to go ahead and arrest Wu Xiaoyong, and they did so. He was detained for the next two years, although never formally charged.

Wu's journalistic integrity left a deep impression on me. I wondered what I would do if put to the test. Would I be willing to order such a broadcast? Then would I take responsibility when soldiers showed up? I had no idea, but the courage of Chinese like him inspired my sense of journalism as a public trust.

Even with the danger so great, some Chinese took enormous risks to help us. During the protests, Sheryl had met an idealistic twenty-three-year-old student leader named Liu Xiang who wanted to help us cover the democracy movement on the Tsinghua campus. We both liked him. Tall and gangly, with short hair framing a long face and a crooked smile, Liu was handsome and athletic, and full of self-assurance. His English was more enthusiastic than fluent, but he would telephone us and introduce himself in English: "Hello? Nikko? Sherry? This is Liu."

After the crackdown, the authorities interrogated Liu repeatedly. They knew he had registered us to get on campus, but they didn't know he had actively helped us. "Write down everything about the *New York Times* reporters," the interrogators instructed. "Write down where you met them—the date and time and the place—and what they asked you. Write what you told them, what secrets you gave out. You must tell everything."

Liu lied, claiming he had simply met Sheryl when she asked for directions once and had felt it was his duty to be nice to her since she is Overseas Chinese. He insisted that he had never spoken to us about politics. Incredibly, even as he was facing these interrogations, he continued to meet secretly with Sheryl to tell her about the crackdown on the campuses. Sheryl came back from these secret meetings moved by Liu's courage and by his commitment to getting the word out. He even dared meet her near Tiananmen Square. "It's where the police will least expect it," he explained with a laugh.

The courage and determination of friends like Liu reassured us. If they were willing to take enormous risks to help us cover the crackdown, we were willing to pour our souls into this effort. Our policy was never to ask Chinese friends for classified documents, but some brought us top secret documents of their own accord, and we published them. Some of these documents were extremely sensitive, including secret speeches of Deng Xiaoping. We were terrified of what would happen to the friends supplying the documents if caught, and we went to enormous lengths to protect our sources.

Then Liu abruptly disappeared. We didn't know if he had been arrested, fled to the countryside or simply decided to lie low. We couldn't contact him, so we waited and worried—and tried to find inspiration from the fortitude people like him had shown.

WHEN WE TRY to inject purpose into our journalism, however, it's easy for things to go wrong. It's difficult to write objectively about people who shoot at you and who outrage you, but taking sides can be like putting on blinders. One of the most important lessons I learned from my Tiananmen reporting is that victims lie, too.

When you see unarmed pro-democracy protesters being clubbed and shot, you side with them over soldiers and government thugs. We called out the government lies, for they were both obvious and odious: It was clear that the protests were not a "counterrevolutionary riot" led by "hoodlums" who instigated the violence. We were instinctively sympathetic to protesters, and this risked making us gullible when they lied.

Furious at the massacre, protesters and officials circulated rumors and exaggerated accounts, in particular that the death toll had been in the thousands. Sir Alan Donald, the British ambassador, sent a cable to London suggesting that 10,000 had been killed in the crackdown. At Lelyveld's urging, we had devoted enormous efforts to gather death totals at morgues all across Beijing, pulling strings and going through friends of friends. Eventually we got death totals at thirty different hospitals. Our best estimate was 400 to 800 people killed in Beijing and several thousand injured.

There were also lurid "eyewitness reports" that Tiananmen Square was knee-deep in blood, which I knew was wrong, or that China was descending into civil war with the 38th Group Army and the 27th Group Army shooting at each other. The *Times* even published an "eyewitness account" that had originally appeared in the *San Francisco Examiner* and *Wen Wei Po* newspapers, but I felt sick when I read it. It was a fraud. It described the army erecting machine gun nests on the roof of the History Museum overlooking Tiananmen Square, and it depicted soldiers setting up a row of ten machine guns and mowing down students who had gathered at the monument in the center of the square. "The gunners splayed on the ground were shooting right at the chests and heads of the students," the article declared.

I had been there, and I knew that was untrue. I wrote a corrective rebuttal to this "eyewitness account," and Lelyveld to his great credit published it.

So after Tiananmen, I found myself in the uncomfortable position of writing articles pushing back at the protesters' exaggerations. My view was that the Chinese government's brutality was awful enough that it shouldn't be embellished, but many reformers and survivors were furious at my fact-checks.

"Is that Nicholas Kristof?" a caller on the telephone asked me soon afterward. "This is the Hong Kong Journalist Association. We have just passed a resolution denouncing you for your lies in defense of the Chinese Communist Party." Even worse, the *People's Daily* quoted me approvingly.

I understood the reformers' indignation: I was discrediting some of the most sensational and effective attacks on the Communist Party. But a journalist's fidelity must be to the facts. The episode taught me a lesson that has been useful in my coverage of genocide, wars and atrocities: *Be as skeptical of victims as of perpetrators*. It's human nature that when people have suffered terribly, they exaggerate. They make things up. It's a way of fighting back. It may also be human nature for journalists to defer to victims of atrocities, but we do a disservice to our audience when we lose our skepticism.

18

The Prize

After Tiananmen, Sheryl and I were tailed by teams from State Security every time we left our apartment, apparently in an effort to learn who our sources were. I would go jogging, and State Security officers would follow me on motorcycles. Once I took a taxi and sent it through a series of turns to see if we were being tailed. We were, by multiple vehicles, and I pointed this out to the driver. He didn't believe it at first and executed a few more turns. Then he looked at me in puzzlement.

"What are you?" he asked. "A murderer?"

I hated being followed. We knew of reporters who had gotten sources in terrible trouble because of the surveillance. One of our friends, Lu Lin, a clothing trader who had previously been involved in the democracy movement, had spent six years in prison because a colleague of ours had once been searched and found with information incriminating Lu as a source. Lu bore no grudges—"It was nothing," he said of his imprisonment—but I couldn't imagine the guilt I would feel if I inflicted such suffering on a Chinese friend. Sometimes I would be driving on Beijing streets trying to shake a motorcycle tail and I would catch myself hoping that the motorcyclist would lose control on a fast turn and slide under a city bus. I wondered at the anger building in me.

In the spring of 1990, Sheryl and I won the Overseas Press Club and George Polk awards for international reporting the previous year, for coverage of Tiananmen. One evening in April as I was talking to the new foreign editor, Bernie Gwertzman, he said, "The Pulitzers will be announced today at 3 p.m. That's 3 a.m. your time, right? I hope we'll be able to call you and wake you up then."

We hoped so, too. I told Sheryl what Bernie had said and that made it hard to sleep that evening. But we did doze off fitfully, and then I happened to wake up and look at the clock: 3:10 a.m.

We didn't get it, I assumed. I felt a gust of sadness. I wondered if one of our competitors in Beijing had won. Dan Southerland from *The Washington Post*? David Holley from the *Los Angeles Times*? Both had done outstanding work. Were they dancing jigs nearby in their own apartments? Or perhaps Serge Schmemann had won for his extraordinary coverage of the collapse of Communism in Eastern Europe. It had been a historic year. I started to drift back to sleep when the phone rang. I sprang for it.

"This is Max." It was Max Frankel, the *Times* executive editor. "What time is it there?"

"It's . . . it's 3:18 in the morning," I said.

"Remember that time," Max said. "Because it's when you and Sheryl won the Pulitzer Prize for international reporting."

The telex machine didn't stop chattering for days. The press was attentive because we were the first married couple to win a Pulitzer for journalism, while Sheryl was the first Chinese American to win a Pulitzer. The Chinese-language press around the world was extremely proud of her award; our friend Dr. Leana Wen was then a young child who had just arrived in the United States from China, and her parents gave Leana a new English middle name, Sheryle (none of us can figure out where the second "e" came from).

Joe Lelyveld took advantage of our Pulitzer to push to elevate Sheryl from a contract writer to a full-fledged staff correspondent. That breached the *Times* tradition that staff correspondents first toil in the New York newsroom for a couple of years before being posted to a bureau (now it's routine for the *Times* to hire foreign correspondents directly, especially those with particular language skills). Other spouses had written for the paper on contracts, but none were on staff. Some editors complained that the implication of Sheryl's promotion was that "the way to become a foreign correspondent is to marry one." Some also raised concerns that Sheryl's hiring would set a precedent.

"Every other contract writer will want to be made a staff correspondent," Max Frankel warned, correctly. Lelyveld shrugged at that. "The precedent is that if you win a Pulitzer," he said, "you'll be considered for staff." Lelyveld's argument won the day.

Sheryl's hiring made her the first Chinese American reporter at the *Times*. More than that, it marked a milestone in the path away from the David Shribman epoch, in which spouses (which at the time meant wives) were told to sacrifice their careers so that a husband could advance at the *Times*. Now spouses would be judged by their abilities and would have a chance to contribute and climb the ladder as well. We were, I think, the first married couple to be staff foreign correspondents in a foreign bureau, but soon there were several other couples sent to overseas bureaus. More important, the hiring sent a signal that the paper would try to accommodate two-career couples, even if this sometimes required flexibility on all sides. I like to think that Sheryl's talent, coupled with her Pulitzer, blazed a pathway for other couples and Asian Americans in journalism.

While in the United States to receive the Pulitzer, we stopped in Oregon for vacation and more celebrations, including an assembly at my high school in Yamhill.

I had been largely away from Yamhill, mostly abroad as a student and reporter, for a dozen years, and it was evident that a shadow had fallen over the area. My old schoolmates who had gone to college were fine, but some others were struggling. My neighbors Bobby and Mike Stepp had dropped out of high school and were bouncing around from one low-paid job to the next, for they found it impossible to do what their dad had done and get high-paying union jobs at the sawmill. Mike and Bobby were both drinking too much and experimenting with drugs. We heard of a new drug called meth that was beginning to spread in the area. It was cheaper than cocaine and enlivened a dull and pointless life, people said.

The five Knapp kids who got on the school bus right after me had all dropped out of school as well. Farlan Knapp still dreamed of starting a wood furniture factory, but his focus was diverted by alcohol and drugs, and the same was true of his siblings. Chris Lawson, my nemesis who had punched me out on the school bus, was disappearing into an alcoholic haze. Billy Beard was often high on meth and getting into trouble with the law. When I got together with my friend Bob Bansen, who had become the local dairyman, we traded stories of old friends who had been arrested.

There was also a shadow over our Pulitzer Prize. We were feted as heroes, while our Chinese friends who had contributed so much to our reporting were jailed or in hiding or worse. One of our dearest friends and most important assistants, Xu Pei, had disappeared, and we had no idea where he was (he later reappeared from hiding, traveled to the United States and with our help began working for Voice of America). Wu Jiaxiang, Zhang Weiguo, Fang Lizhi, Liu Xiang—so many friends had disappeared. It felt as if an entire vast country had suffered a devastating blow, and we had somehow benefited. We couldn't even credit them by name at the time, for fear of adding to their troubles.

After we returned to China, it turned out that our winning the Pulitzer made the Chinese government target us even more. My relations with officials deteriorated further after I wrote a profile of the hardline prime minister, Li Peng, and noted how hated he was. Li presented himself as an orphan of the Communist struggle, and it was true that his father had been a revolutionary martyr. But Li never mentioned his mother, and Zhang Hanzhi relayed to me how much the mother had complained until her death about what an awful son he was. "Completely unfilial," his mother had protested. My article infuriated the prime minister, who tried to punish me by making me *chuan xiaoxie*— a Chinese saying meaning to make someone "wear small shoes."

The prime minister ordered the Foreign Ministry and State Security Ministry to lean on me, and I found myself regularly summoned to the Foreign Ministry to be scolded. Each time I would be ushered into a formal meeting room furnished with overstuffed chairs and antimacassars, and then our "handler," Zhao Xingmin, would rail at me in Chinese, and I would try to parry with my weak Chinese. A younger diplomat would always serve as notetaker. I once needled Zhao by citing a famous authority for journalists pursuing their mission despite criticism.

"As Chairman Mao said, 'We must persevere, whatever the risks,'" I said gravely. "How did he say it? 'No. 1, don't fear bitterness. No. 2, don't fear death.'" It was delicious to see Zhao sputter.

On a couple of occasions, the Foreign Ministry summoned me to protest articles that Sheryl had written, which seemed ridiculous. "You should talk to her directly," I suggested, trying to draw a smile. "She holds up half the sky!"*

Zhao was incapable of smiles. The next time I was called in over Sheryl's supposed sins, I grew exasperated. During the Cultural Revolution, the Communist Party had regularly ordered husbands to divorce wives who had made political mistakes (and vice versa), and this was known as *hua qing jie xian*, or making a clean break. So when Zhao finished his tirade about Sheryl, I nodded brightly and said in Chinese: "Very well, I'll *hua qing jie xian*."

Zhao stared at me, dumbfounded.

"Yes, I'll divorce her," I continued. "When a person makes a serious ideological mistake, we shouldn't make excuses. I must make a clean break. I should divorce her, right?"

Even the Chinese notetaker giggled at that. Zhao looked as if he would explode.

None of this was terribly professional, but I had calculated that Zhao had no influence within the Foreign Ministry. Sheryl and I had the respect of a top official and future foreign minister, Li Zhaoxing, so Zhao lacked the capacity to cause trouble. And, boy, it was satisfying to mock him.

It was a strange existence in China in those days: We were denounced by the government and, as I said, tailed every time we left our apartment. Yet even in this twilight zone, it was sometimes possible to connect with reality. I had cultivated editors of the *People's Daily*, feigning the professional bonhomie and courtesy that they craved, and at one point I interviewed several senior editors there. As I'd expected, they lied and claimed that everyone in the newspaper supported the current hard line.

A few days later, I received a phone call from a seventeen-year-old high school student who wanted to meet me. I was curious, and we had coffee together.

"My dad is an editor at *People's Daily*," she told me. "Dad brought your business card home and said you'd interviewed him. I copied down your number, but of course Dad doesn't know that I called you. He'd be

---

* Chinese officials often declared that "women hold up half the sky"—meaning that they contribute equally to society and should have equal rights. Sheryl and I entitled a 2009 book we wrote about empowering women *Half the Sky*.

horrified." She was delighted at her first chance to meet an American. We met a couple of times, including once at our home, and she told me about high school life and about the internal debates at the *People's Daily*. (Then, a decade later, she wrote a novel in which a Chinese girl, the protagonist, happens to visit an American reporter in his home in Beijing—it sounded very much like ours—and has wild sex with him on the carpet. I didn't know what to think of that, how to explain the book's scene to Sheryl, or what was going through the girl's mind when she visited.)

Sheryl was expecting our first child in 1992, and we decided to have the baby in Hong Kong in case of complications such as a C-section. Gregory arrived without incident at Hong Kong Island's lovely Matilda International Hospital. The Taiwan government sent a telegram of congratulations. The Hong Kong government sent flowers. And China refused to give Gregory a visa. Perhaps the Foreign Ministry officials thought that if they denied a visa to Gregory, Sheryl and I would cut our Beijing tour short.

I was, however, able to get Gregory a tourist visa through a cooperative travel agent, so we all returned to Beijing, but the Foreign Ministry then refused to approve a residence permit for Gregory. In Gregory's first few weeks of life, articles began to appear in *The Wall Street Journal*, *The Washington Post*, *The Economist* and other publications about him as "China's youngest hostage." We didn't ask fellow journalists to write about Gregory, but we didn't discourage it either, and the Foreign Ministry grew embarrassed. Sheryl finally carried baby Gregory to the Foreign Ministry and asked our handlers: "Why are you afraid of this cute little baby?"

Soon afterward, the Foreign Ministry capitulated. "We have decided to grant a residence permit to your baby," an official told us. "It's a special effort to accommodate you."

After the failed attempt to pressure us through Gregory, the authorities took on Sheryl. They refused to renew her journalistic credentials, meaning that she could still live in Beijing but could not work. We assumed that if she wrote articles without credentials, they would expel both of us and maybe close the *Times* bureau, and presumably they hoped that our solution—having her report only from outside China—would eventually wear us both down and lead us to leave the country.

Sheryl spent months reporting in Myanmar, Australia and elsewhere while we worked on getting her credentials back. Initially, a *Times* editor came to Beijing and threatened our Foreign Ministry interlocutors with harsh coverage in the paper, but that backfired and made them more obstinate than ever. What finally succeeded was a two-step process. William Safire, a *Times* columnist who had good ties with Chinese officials, came to Beijing and gently asked the deputy prime minister for help resolving the situation. Second, the American ambassador, Jim Lilley, delayed giving a journalist visa to the new *People's Daily* correspondent in the United States. This infuriated the Chinese authorities and could have escalated into a situation in which neither side gave anyone a journalist visa. But at that point Lilley issued the visa to the *People's Daily* reporter, and his concession gave face to the Chinese authorities. They grumpily gave Sheryl her credentials back.

Prime Minister Li Peng still wanted us out of China, though. We soon heard through our networks that the authorities were seeking new excuses to expel us from the country. The next effort involved auditing our taxes. Almost nobody in China paid income taxes then, and when we arrived in Beijing the authorities had simply asked us to submit a letter disclosing our salaries; we would then pay income taxes each year on that amount. Journalistic colleagues suggested submitting a letter listing an extremely low salary, partly to save us money and partly to avoid getting them in trouble by comparison. Most other reporters "disclosed" absurdly low sums, and a predecessor as *Times* bureau chief had claimed his salary was $27,000 a year. The Chinese Foreign Ministry knew that correspondents were cheating on their taxes, so it ordered an audit of us so it could expel us as tax cheats. However, in a burst of honesty, we had actually disclosed our full earnings; the authorities were aghast to discover that we had committed no tax fraud.

I protested the constant surveillance in a letter to Jia Chunwang, the minister of state security, with copies to other senior officials:

> I would like to respectfully request that State Security agents stop tailing me when I go around Beijing. I'm sure the tailing is the result of a low-level decision, but it leaves a sour taste in my mouth . . .
>
> When I took my wife out for dinner on her birthday, for example, we had a little tail following us the whole way. This kind of silliness unfortunately reinforces the image among some people abroad

that China is not sincere in its reforms and is a hard-line, repressive country. Naturally, the tailing is newsworthy and I will be forced to write about it if it goes on. But I'm sure it's the result of some minor official being overzealous, so I am taking the opportunity to ask for your assistance in ending the tailing.

A response came in the *People's Daily:*

There is indeed a small number of foreign journalists who, regardless of China's laws and regulations, conduct activities incompatible with their status. They distort facts, spread rumors, maliciously attack the Chinese government and deliberately jeopardize the security of the country.

Ultimately, it was a reformist official inside State Security—the very agency that was tailing me—who found a way to keep me in Beijing. A vice minister of State Security whom I knew pulled me aside at a reception and told me that some officials wanted to expel me, while he and others feared that an expulsion would damage Chinese-American relations. "It's extremely delicate," he said. "It could go either way. But it would help the people who are arguing in your favor if they had something to hold up, something they could point to, to say your attitude had improved."

He urged me to write a letter to the Foreign Ministry. "Don't apologize," he said. "Don't write a self-criticism. Just say that you have noted the Foreign Ministry's concerns and that you believe that journalists should engage in fair and accurate reporting. At least your supporters could point to that, and it would help them in the internal arguments that are now going on."

I didn't like the idea of writing such a letter. It felt like playing games. But I also felt I owed it to the *Times* to do everything possible to avoid getting expelled, and I was already playing games. I had enlisted the help of three visiting American delegations, each of which had warned their Chinese interlocutors that expelling me would be a blow to Sino-American relations. So, grumpily, I wrote the letter as he suggested, and it worked. I was still tailed, and Li Peng still smarted at my coverage, but the authorities stopped looking for an excuse to kick us out.

ONE OF THE THINGS I disliked about Li Peng and the hardliners was the way they cultivated nationalism as a new national glue to hold China together as Communist ideology faded. They revved up "humiliation education" in school textbooks, portraying foreign powers as having constantly sought to dismember and humiliate China when it was weak. The hardliners wanted every international disagreement seen through that prism, as one more effort by arrogant foreigners to hold China back. The result was a surging, unruly nationalism targeting the United States and Japan. The most painful result for me came many years later, after the 9/11 terror attacks on the Twin Towers. I read the Chinese Internet message boards that day in disbelief. On a chatroom at Sina.com, a leading portal, the first of six thousand commenters about the terror attacks said in Chinese: "Just one word: cool! Now the day has come for the American dogs."

"Excellent!!!!!!!!" added another gleefully. "But the hijacked planes didn't carry a nuclear bomb."

"Just great. Really fantastic. Serves 'em right."

"So cool to see America bombed."

"I'm waiting for the third plane, the fourth plane, the fifth plane, the sixth plane. Ha, ha!"

Not until the forty-fourth message was there a reproach: "Do you people here have no shame?" someone wrote. "Do you have no morality?"

I worry that as China assumes a greater role in the world and builds up its military forces, that nationalism creates growing risks of clashes over Taiwan or the South China Sea. One of the great risks for the world in the coming decades is that of a war between the United States and China over Taiwan, for China's increasing military capacity is accompanied by a dangerous political immaturity: an aggrieved, chip-on-the-shoulder nationalism. Leaders like Xi Jinping have stoked this ideology, but it will also make it more difficult for them to compromise and settle any crisis that does arise. As the Chinese saying goes: *Qi hu nan xia*. It's easier to mount a tiger than to dismount.

19

An Escaped Felon

I slipped quietly out of our Beijing apartment one day and took the stairs down to the lobby so that the State Security cameras wouldn't see me. By prearrangement I jumped into the back seat of a Chinese friend's car and lay on the floor under a blanket as he drove out past the guards. When my friend had driven around for miles and we were satisfied that we were not being followed, I had him drop me off. This evasion strategy was effective, but I couldn't do it often because it put my Chinese friend with the car at some risk.

After walking around and making absolutely sure I wasn't tailed, I entered a quiet coffee shop with a front and back entrance to facilitate a hurried departure if necessary. I took a table in the corner, away from anyone else, and ten minutes later the man I was waiting for walked in and sat opposite me. He was a slight figure with outsize charm, a warm sense of humor and a provincial accent. He teased me about my accent in Chinese, and I teased him about his. In his thirties, he was working at a military-controlled company and was involved in China's secret export of M-11 missiles to Pakistan. He showed me that he had documents and photos to verify the missile transactions—but he wouldn't give them to me.

"Here are the contracts for the sales to Pakistan," he told me. "Here's the shipping information. And here are some photos of the missiles in shipment." He gave me a glimpse of each, and I found them tantalizing. China swore up and down that it was not providing Pakistan with the

M-11s, weapons that could be destabilizing because they are capable of carrying nuclear warheads.

"You can publish all this," my source said. "You just have to pay for it."

"*The New York Times* can't pay for information," I told him. "That's a sacred rule. We don't want to create incentives for people to make stuff up."

This is indeed a sacred rule in American journalism, but it's also a self-serving one: It saves news organizations money. Journalists in other countries don't have this rule. Japanese news organizations, for example, routinely pay for interviews. And American journalists do offer nice meals to coax information out of people.

Sure enough, my source was unimpressed.

"Make stuff up?" he repeated. "I'm not just telling you things. I'm willing to give you photos and documents. But why should I give it for free? I'm taking a risk. You need to pay me."

"I'd like to pay you, but I just can't. It's an ironclad rule."

"Oh, come on! *The New York Times* is a rich company. Of course it pays for news. It's paying to keep you in China. It's paying for my coffee."

I laughed. "Yes, I can pay for your coffee," I acknowledged. "I can pay for lunch. But I can't give you cash in exchange for information or documents. That's one thing that separates us from spies."

He paused and looked at me in exasperation.

"So how do I meet some American spies?" he asked plaintively.

"Look, you've already shown me the documents," I said. "How about if you just let me photocopy them? I can give them back to you in twenty minutes. This will all come out eventually, anyway."

"No way. Pay me first. I know these are worth a lot of money to you, so just pay up. Then they're yours."

So I tried to build a rapport with my source, in the hope I could use that relationship to extract information. I inquired about his family, his interests, his hopes. He showed me photos of his wife, a beautiful woman who smiled warmly in all the photos. "She doesn't know anything about what I'm doing," he said hastily. He told me about their young child and his dreams for the child. His frustration was that his friends and neighbors were in private business and getting rich, while he felt left behind.

"If my neighbor's kid gets a toy, then my kid wants it, too," he told me. "Life's a competition now. Everybody's trying to make money. Everyone! Hey, I'm just trying to cash in on what I have."

I met the man several times in my effort to wheedle information out of him. He also asked to meet American diplomats or spies, and I wouldn't make the introduction; I didn't want to be seen as a pawn of the intelligence community.

Yet the more I spoke to the man about his family in my effort to woo him, the more I was troubled by the thought of what might happen if I got the photos and documents. Sure, I would make every effort to protect my source—but Chinese officials would mount a huge effort to find the leaker, and there was obviously some chance they would identify him. And then they would imprison or execute him.

"You know what?" I told him in our last meeting. "Just go back to your family. Forget about selling these documents or even giving them away."

"What?" He looked at me and tilted his head in surprise. "What are you saying?"

"Hug your wife and child. Burn any paper with my name or contact. Forget about making money. I don't want something terrible to happen to you."

Interviewing dissident workers by candlelight in Beijing.
Photo by Du Bin.

"You're really not going to pay me?" He had been wooing me as assiduously as I was wooing him, but we both had failed.

It felt very unprofessional to drive a source away. But as far as I know, he did what I advised and never got into trouble. What I did wasn't good journalism, for I may have missed a great story. But in places like China we journalists have to operate by an ethical code that is more about being human beings than reporters. That made for wrenchingly difficult choices.

LIU XIANG, the student from Tsinghua University who had helped us cover Tiananmen and its aftermath, had gone underground, and I had heard from him just once. He had telephoned from a detention center in Hong Kong without using his name: "Nikko, Sherry," he said, and I immediately recognized his voice. He explained that because of fear of arrest at Tsinghua University, he had fled south to the city of Shenzhen, and then sneaked across the border into Hong Kong. Police there had detained him as an illegal immigrant, and he was calling from a detention center. Now he needed a document to show the British authorities in Hong Kong that he deserved refugee status. I immediately faxed over a document confirming that he was a dissident and at risk. I didn't hear back, so I assumed that he was lying low in Hong Kong and didn't want to contact me because of State Security bugs on my phone.

Now after almost a year of silence, I heard the same voice on the phone. Liu was in Beijing. I promptly agreed to meet him. I evaded surveillance by hiding under the blanket in my friend's car. My testimonials to the Hong Kong authorities had done no good, Liu told me, and he had been forcibly returned to China. On the bus carrying him back, Liu frantically tore up my faxes and shoved the pieces through the grate in the window.

On the Chinese side of the border, Liu gave a false name. Chinese authorities locked him in a detention center where he shared a room with forty other people and was forced to work all day. In the meantime, he became a gangster. Chinese prisons often have cell bosses, inmates who bully others and control the cell. Liu was lucky that in his cell, the boss was a fellow northerner and Mandarin-speaker, and Liu became his henchman. When a new prisoner arrived in the cell, Liu would rough him up and search for any money or valuables that he had hidden. The money could be used for food, cigarettes or bribes for special treatment.

Soon the cell boss was transferred to another prison, and Liu took his place: The former Tsinghua engineer was now master of the cell. He ordered other prisoners to wash his underwear and give up their money or food. If they disobeyed, he had his henchmen beat them.

"If you don't beat them up, then others will beat you up," he told me. "And then you'll end up washing their underwear."

While in the detention center, Liu was obsessed with trying to escape. "I decided the best time to escape was during a rain, because then it's harder for them to drive their motorcycles around looking for you, and they won't try as hard to find you," he said. One rainy day when the prisoners were scattered on a large field with only three guards minding them, Liu made his move. He slipped behind a hedge, preparing to say if caught that he was simply relieving himself. From there he crawled along to a road, then caught a ride to Guangzhou and hid with friends. He realized that he needed more help if he was going to escape to Hong Kong and get refugee status, so he came to Beijing and reached out to me.

"Can you help?" he asked.

Alarm bells sounded in my mind. There are gray areas in journalism, but helping an escaped prisoner flee the country is clearly illegal. If I were caught helping Liu, I would probably be kicked out of the country. I might also be prosecuted for breaking the law, and the *Times* might be evicted from China. Helping him felt like a betrayal of my employer, as well as crossing a red line.

On the other hand, here was a young man who had gotten into trouble only because he had helped the *Times* and its readers, and if we didn't help him he would likely be caught eventually and face terrible consequences. I wanted to consult with Lelyveld and other editors, but our phone lines were tapped and we didn't have any way of communicating securely. And in any case, I realized, no editor could possibly say that it was fine to help an escaped felon.

I hate to admit it, but I also didn't entirely trust Liu's story, especially his supposed escape from prison. I had never heard of such an escape. I wondered if this was an elaborate Chinese government ruse to set me up. The tax audit had failed to generate a pretext to expel me, so maybe this was the new plan. Perhaps Liu had been coerced under torture to entrap me into committing a crime.

Sheryl was away—this was the period when her credentials were suspended, so she was reporting in Australia—and I waited impatiently for her to return to Beijing. I needed to talk this through with someone I trusted, and that was Sheryl. When she returned, we took a long stroll through Ritan Park, and I filled her in. I was genuinely at a loss, but Sheryl argued for helping Liu.

"What if we get caught?" I asked. "What if we're arrested, or the *Times* bureau is closed? And anyway, should we really be helping escaped prisoners?"

"He helped us," Sheryl answered. "And now he needs us. Nobody else can help him, and he's in trouble only because he went out on a limb and helped us and the *Times*. That has to count for something."

"But, Sheryl, what if it's a setup?"

"I can't imagine he'd be setting us up, but we can talk to him and test him," Sheryl said. "And anyway, we can't just abandon him after all the help he gave us. Then he'll be caught for sure, and he'll spend a lifetime in jail. The guards will pulverize him. How can that be the right thing to do?"

We went back and forth for several days. Finally, we wrote Liu a letter to show the Hong Kong police in case he was caught again at the Hong Kong border. The letter attested to his status as a dissident and hinted that we would create a public stink if Hong Kong returned Liu to China. The letter was signed by Sheryl, for we figured that since her credentials were suspended she was not presently a journalist in China and had a little more leeway. That was our rationale, but it may also simply be that Sheryl was braver than me. We also gave Liu $300, enough to get to the border and cross over into Hong Kong.

I was fearful that we would be immediately apprehended when we handed Liu the letter and money, but that didn't happen. We walked back to our apartment without incident and breathed easier.

Liu was able to join a Chinese tour group to get to the China–Hong Kong border, and he then slipped into Hong Kong. He had chosen to cross on Christmas Day 1990, on the theory that it would be a holiday in Hong Kong with fewer police on duty. That evening, the phone rang in our apartment in Jianguomenwai.

"Hello?" It was a familiar voice. "Is that Nikko, Sherry? I am Liu. I'm in Hong Kong." It was the best Christmas present we could have wished for.

I flew to Hong Kong the next morning to make sure that Liu was not sent back to China and to try to get him safe passage to the United States. Washington quickly agreed to give him refugee status, but the British authorities in Hong Kong declined to help in any way. They reserved the right to expel him back to China, and they would not allow him to leave Hong Kong for the United States. Senior officials up to Lord Wilson, the governor, refused to be helpful—because they were fearful of offending Beijing. It was sad to see the British government kowtow to China.

While we tried to work out Liu's exit to America, I wrote a *Times Magazine* story about his journey, but of course it could only run when he was safe in the United States. We edited it and shot the photos, but the British intransigence forced us to wait. When I was back in Beijing, with Liu's case still in limbo, I got a note saying that the next week's magazine cover story had fallen through and mine would run in its place.

"Whoa!" I telexed back. "We can't run it until he's in the United States. You know that." I had to be elliptical since my telexes presumably were read by Chinese State Security.

"I'm sorry but we didn't have anything else. It's decided."

"We absolutely cannot run this until I give word. The person in it would be in jeopardy. Find a different cover."

"I'm sorry, but it's too late. The decision is already made. We can't make changes now."

I felt a deep sadness. I didn't see how I could stay at the *Times* if it betrayed Liu by running the article now and putting him in danger. Protecting sources was sacred. I knew that as soon as the Chinese authorities saw the article, they would apply enormous pressure on Lord Wilson to return Liu to China. And Lord Wilson would cave. After all our efforts, Liu was again at risk to spend decades in prison. Perhaps melodramatically, I recalled the case of a prisoner in Yingshan Prison in the Guangxi region who was kept for two years in solitary confinement in a cell that was never cleaned. The prisoner died, and authorities were unsure whether he had frozen to death in his unheated cell or been overcome by fumes from a fourteen-inch pile of his own excrement. Was this Liu's future?

I loved the *Times*, but I couldn't stay at a paper that endangered my source. And I couldn't explain my case clearly to editors because of the surveillance and bugging.

I reached out to the magazine editor, Warren Hoge, an editor with whom I had warm ties because he had been my first foreign editor. I called Warren and pleaded with him to hold the piece, telling him it was a matter of safety for the person featured in it and that I had given my absolute commitment that the piece would not run until the person was safe.

"I'm sympathetic," he said, "but we do need a magazine cover, and we're right on deadline. I don't know that there's time to find something else." I didn't tell Warren I was likely to resign if he went ahead—I should have, for it would have been unfair to quit without warning him—but I made clear how much I cared about this matter. Sometimes great editors, even if they don't fully understand why, defer to reporters, and that's what Warren did.

"You're normally easy to work with, so this is obviously something you really care about," he said finally. "I'll see what I can do." He telexed me soon afterward that he would hold my piece until I gave approval to run it, and I never told him or any other editor that I'd been ready to resign if they'd gone ahead.

After weeks of tense negotiations, with the invaluable help of the late Robin Munro of Human Rights Watch, a compromise was reached. British officials wouldn't give permission for Liu to leave Hong Kong, but they would avert their eyes. A United States diplomat escorted Liu through the airport, bypassing an immigration officer who looked the other way, and led him onto the plane. Liu had no passport, but the authorities at John F. Kennedy Airport in New York were waiting for him and welcomed him to America.

When Liu was safe, I came clean with editors about how Sheryl and I had helped him flee China. To my surprise, they were unconcerned, even congratulatory and grateful. Abe Rosenthal, now a columnist, told me that there was a precedent: In 1959, a Polish staff member of the *Times* bureau in Warsaw was in political trouble, and Abe and the paper had helped him escape to the West. Other editors noted the newspaper's shame that it hadn't found a way to help its Cambodian assistant, Dith Pran, escape when the Khmer Rouge seized the country. Dith Pran starved during the Khmer Rouge genocide and was almost killed, an experience chronicled in the hit film *The Killing Fields*. Eventually, he was able to escape to Thailand in 1979 and was hired by the *Times* as a photographer. We all loved and admired Dith Pran as a colleague, and perhaps one element of our admiration was our regret that the paper had left him behind.

The Liu Xiang episode reminded me how lucky I was. Somehow, everything had worked out, and I emerged with credit within the *Times* for having done the right thing—even though it was really Sheryl whose moral compass was true.

I've often struggled to understand what the right thing to do is in journalism, or in life itself. Sometimes I've made errors, been duped, missed stories or overplayed others. Helping Liu was particularly egregious, for it's clear that we should avoid helping escaped prisoners or making consequential decisions without consulting editors. Yet while this was one of the most unprofessional episodes in my career, it's also one of those that I'm proudest of.

WE SPENT FIVE YEARS in Beijing, and for all our distress when friends were imprisoned and tortured, it was also obvious that there was another side to the country. Education standards were soaring, and the government was showing an impressive commitment to building high schools and universities and to improving the caliber of teaching. I'm a strong believer that the best predictor of where a country will be in twenty-five years is its education system, and it was difficult not to be dazzled by China's progress there.

More broadly, China also managed its economy well. Its day-to-day leaders were engineers and problem-solvers who were pragmatic and forward-thinking in handling routine challenges. We could see the results. China lifted hundreds of millions of people out of poverty and raised more people from illiteracy than any country ever. Health standards were rising quickly, so that today a newborn in Beijing has a longer life expectancy than a newborn in Washington, D.C.

Sheryl and I covered the economic boom, but I wondered sometimes if we focused enough on it. The repression was real, particularly the cruelty and cultural genocide toward Muslims in Xinjiang, but so was the explosion of wealth and economic and educational opportunity. Families in Gansu and Ningxia that had been living in caves got houses or apartments, villages got electricity, and leprosy was eliminated as a public health threat.

Lu Lin, the dissident who spent six years in prison after our journalist friend was found with papers that incriminated him, had become a clothing trader because no other job was open to an ex-convict. But traders thrived in the free market and booming economy, and Lu Lin was very good at what he did. He kept his retail stalls in the markets but moved into the wholesale clothing business, opened a branch office in Moscow and began exploring opportunities to do business in the United States. I contrasted his economic success with the struggles of some of my old friends in rural Oregon, and I began to wonder what made the difference. Attitudes? Drive? Opportunities?

We debated how long to stay in China. *Times* correspondents typically remain in one location for three to five years, and we were approaching five years. There would be openings soon in both Moscow and Tokyo, and it seemed we could claim either. But there was also a good argument for staying in China indefinitely. We were well sourced and spoke Chinese, and we both felt that the most important story in the world was the rise of China. What convinced us to move was exhaustion at being constantly tailed and fear of getting Chinese friends in trouble. We had managed to avoid getting any of our sources sent to prison, but we didn't know how long we could keep that up. After much discussion, we told Lelyveld we wanted to transfer to the Tokyo bureau.

We weren't sure it was the right call, but soon afterward the Chinese authorities raided the offices of *The Washington Post*, searching the safe, notebooks and papers of its correspondent, Lena Sun. While Lena was not herself arrested, China did arrest two of her best Chinese friends, Bai Weiji and his wife, Zhao Lei. The authorities sentenced Bai to prison for ten years for supplying documents to Lena, and Zhao was sentenced to six years. With no one to care for their baby daughter, Melanie, the girl was almost put in an orphanage; at one point, Zhao asked Lena to adopt Melanie. In the end, a family member cared for the girl.

That news devastated us. That could have happened to our friends. Yes, it was time to leave China.

Those five years in China were transformative for me. Seeing an army fire on its own people changed me, and the experience of being constantly tailed left an indelible imprint on my psyche. Living in China was a chance to witness an economic revolution that hugely empowered hundreds of millions of people, but it was also a reminder that principles rarely defeat machine guns. Time and again after Tiananmen, from the Arab Spring to Myanmar, I heard variations of "the people united will never be defeated." Take it from me, it's not true.

That said, in the words of the Chinese writer Lu Xun, "Lies written in ink can never disguise facts written in blood." In my mind's eye, daydreaming about some day in the future, I envision a new statue at Tiananmen Square: It is of a rickshaw driver carrying a wounded student.

China helped shape my belief in purpose-driven journalism that exposes injustice. In recent years in the United States, as democracy has struggled, as some elected leaders and television pundits seemed more committed to undermining democratic government than to preserving it, I've thought often about those Chinese who risked everything in their failed bid for greater democracy.

It's sometimes difficult to know how to navigate our responsibilities as people are massacred or as democracy is attacked. But journalism does not operate in a vacuum. It can be harnessed to some larger vision that gives it meaning, and—particularly since Tiananmen—that's what I've aspired to do. That kind of journalism is messy to pull off in practice, though, and I haven't always gotten it right.

20

Frequenting a Brothel

For our son Gregory's fifth-birthday party in 1997, in Tokyo, we invited twenty of his classmates from his Japanese kindergarten. After China, we had undergone a year of intensive Japanese language training, and I was now the Tokyo bureau chief of the *Times* while Sheryl covered business and economics in the region. We also had another child: two-year-old Geoffrey, born during our language training.

What's a great birthday party game for young children? Musical chairs! So we set out folding chairs, and I tried to explain the rules; it's not a game played in Japan. The kids seemed to understand, so we started the music, and they trundled around, with Gregory followed by his five-year-old girlfriend, Chitose-chan. I stopped the music, and Chitose-chan happened to be standing in front of a chair. But she politely stood and waited for Gregory to be seated first. Gregory scrambled into her seat, and Chitose-chan beamed at her good manners. Then I walked over and told Chitose-chan that she had lost and was out of the game. She stared at me, her eyes widening in shock.

Japanese kids proved awful at musical chairs. The Japanese moms on the sidelines looked distressed, too. They were too courteous to say so, but I could imagine the thought bubbles forming: *You mean the purpose of this game is to reward rudeness?* Yabanjin! (*Barbarians!*) I grew embarrassed at how good Gregory was at musical chairs, and at the end of the game we gave all the children prizes and announced that they had all won. I was becoming more sensitive about cultural differences, because in his nursery school all the Japanese kids used Lego bricks to make schools or fire trucks, and Gregory had made a gun.

Living in Japan was a window into how a society can be ordered to promote harmony, or *wa*. More than any society I had encountered, there was a strong cultural emphasis on subordinating the individual to the collective good, and in some ways it worked. Japan has more than one-third the population of the entire United States crammed into an area smaller than California. In the United States, we'd have long since shot and clubbed each other. Yet Japan typically has a single-digit total of gun murders in the whole country in a year; the United States has that many in a single school shooting.

Around the world, societies tend to have either high suicide rates or high murder rates, and in Japan it is suicide that is common because of all the internal pressure to conform. When Japanese get fed up and explode, they don't kill their neighbors or ex-girlfriends. They kill themselves. The United States is an exception in having both high murder rates and high suicide rates; that's largely because we have 400 million guns, and firearms are effective at killing other people as well as oneself.

There's much we can learn from Japan. It has an excellent system of public nursery schools that function as day care, as well as strong health care and elementary schools focused not just on education but more broadly on nurturing good citizens. Japanese schools also don't have custodians, for the kids themselves have time set aside each day to clean classrooms, hallways and even toilets (they alternate toilet duty among themselves). The result is not pristine, but children prove less likely to scrawl graffiti on desks or toilet stalls that they themselves clean.

Sheryl and I grew so impressed by Japanese child-rearing techniques that we decided to adopt a local tradition. One day Gregory was playing at the swings in Arisugawa Park in Tokyo when he dived to the ground and came up with a 100-yen coin in his palm. It was worth a bit less than a dollar. The next day I took Gregory and Geoffrey to the local police station and pushed Gregory forward.

"I found a coin," Gregory squeaked in Japanese, holding it up.

The police officer, a stocky man with piercing eyes, treated six-year-old Gregory with great respect. He examined the coin and nodded gravely.

"Thank you for reporting it," he said to Gregory. "You're a very honest young man."

The policeman pulled out a "found property" form and began to fill it out.

"When did you find the coin?" he asked Gregory.

"Yesterday."

"What time?"

That stumped Gregory, who could not really tell time, but I jumped in to say that it was 5:50 p.m.

"What's your address?" the policeman asked. "And your occupation?"

"Hiroo Towers," Gregory answered nervously. "I'm a kindergarten student."

The policeman noted exactly where in Arisugawa Park Gregory had found the coin and then telephoned a central office to explain that a very honest citizen had turned in a 100-yen coin. The policeman jotted down an administrative record number for the file and took some time to complete the paperwork before looking up.

"Here's a receipt," the police officer said, handing it to Gregory. "If no one claims the coin in six months, then you can get it back. Thank you for reporting this found property."

We walked out, with Gregory beaming and Geoffrey enormously impressed by his older brother. The police officer had spent thirty minutes handling the business, so some might consider it a colossal waste of time. But Japanese see it as an investment in values education, and I agreed.

Nothing is as simple as it seems. Three days later, I was walking Gregory home from kindergarten when he leaped into the bushes by the sidewalk and emerged with a 10-yen coin, worth less than a dime.

"Look what I found!" he said, thrilled. "Let's get Geoffrey and go back to the police station."

I put Gregory off, explaining that I was heading off on a trip, but it got worse. Every time we went outside, Gregory and Geoffrey kept their eyes downward, looking for coins. Tragically, they often found them. Gregory and Geoffrey were prepared to go by the police station every couple of days to turn in coins; I dissuaded them. As it happened, Gregory's kindergarten class was then collecting money for needy families, while stipulating that the money had to come from the kids rather than their parents—another effort to inculcate values—so

I told Gregory that it would be fine to donate the coins. He was a bit confused about why it was now okay to give away money that I had previously taught was not his, but I said something about Robin Hood and muddied the waters. I was coming to appreciate that nurturing Japanese-style values is more complicated than it had seemed at first.

Six months after we found the first coin, I took Gregory and Geoffrey back to the police station, and Gregory nervously handed over the receipt. Had the owner claimed the coin? The policeman consulted his records and announced that it was unclaimed. He dug into the files, located the coin, and then had Gregory sign for it. The police officer again praised Gregory for his honesty.

A week later, we were walking home from kindergarten when he dived to the ground. "Daddy," he shouted gleefully. "A coin!"

I HAD NOW BEEN at the *Times* for more than a decade, and I was full of thoughts about how we in journalism needed to cover the world differently. My posting in Japan was a time to test these ideas.

Journalism is famously described as "the first rough draft of history," but what is history? Traditionally, history was what kings and presidents and prime ministers did. It was the chronicles of "great men" and diplomatic and political events; neither Plutarch nor Shakespeare paid much attention to ordinary places and people. Yet perhaps because I was from so inconsequential a place as Yamhill, it seemed to me that the "great men" mattered largely because of their impact on ordinary lives. I thought we should do more to illuminate the texture of societies, even quotidian matters such as birthday party games and institutional mechanisms to teach children right from wrong.

On university campuses and in the literary world, notions of history had changed. The field of "social history" emerged and focused on how people actually live—but I felt that we in journalism hadn't adjusted enough in framing our first rough draft of history. Newspaper headlines and television news shows still focused on pronouncements from Washington and other capitals. Those are important, of course, but we didn't adequately follow through on those pronouncements to see how they affected the lives of ordinary people in the Yamhills of the world. We didn't sufficiently cover family, sex, faith, health, domestic violence, education, mental health, addiction, alcoholism, immigration, gender gaps, race, gender, same-sex relationships—or kids.

Because the *Times*'s audience was mostly well-heeled, we covered charity banquets and the challenges of installing a swimming pool inside one's house. But it seemed to me that we didn't convey the challenges of the other 99.999 percent of the world. We needed to get out of the office and quote fewer university-educated men in their sixties and more high school kids. Maybe even more six-year-olds.

My notion of this different kind of journalism was tested shortly after I moved to Tokyo when the Foreign Ministry arranged for me to interview the prime minister, Tomiichi Murayama. We spoke for forty minutes in the prime minister's residence, but Murayama was so guarded that he said nothing noteworthy. I could have written an article beginning something like "Japanese prime minister Tomiichi Murayama said yesterday that he values Japanese-American relations and hopes they will steadily improve." But this would have been the stenography that I was complaining about internally at the *Times*. So I sent a note to editors saying that I'd interviewed the prime minister but wouldn't file an article because he had said nothing. That raised eyebrows but felt liberating—though I did have to deal with fallout from an irritated prime minister.

I tested my ideas about journalism by "adopting" a small town called Omiya, two hundred miles southwest of Tokyo. Every few months I visited Omiya and tried to write about the texture of Japanese life. What kind of kids are cool in high school in Omiya? How do husbands and wives interact? How does religion shape daily life? In South Korea, I did something similar, visiting a village and asking people in every house what they thought of wife-beating. To my surprise, every household except the pastor's acknowledged that the husband sometimes beat the wife (other villagers confirmed that the minister was the exception). I figured that was a pattern of violence that shaped lives more than many other topics that I wrote about for the front page.

I was becoming increasingly focused on the role of women as one of those topics that we in journalism didn't adequately cover. My awakening came partly in 1990 after reading an academic study that estimated that 39,000 infant girls died in China *each year* because they didn't get the same access to food or health care as boys. That number astounded me. It meant that the number of girls who died of gender discrimination every month was far greater than the number of people killed in the Tiananmen crackdown. Yet while I had written innumerable articles about the massacre, I hadn't written a single column inch about these girls.

That same year the great Indian economist Amartya Sen, one of my intellectual heroes, wrote an essay explaining that it was worse than that. We tend to assume that there are more females than males in the world, because women live longer. In the United States and Europe, there are indeed more females. But because of lethal discrimination in access to food and health care, coupled with sex-selective abortion, there are about 100 million women and girls missing from the world. That means that globally there are actually more males than females. That's staggering, yet we in journalism had missed the story.

Japan was a prestigious base for a correspondent, but it wasn't necessarily home to the most important stories—particularly those like this that carried a moral urgency. Our bureau system in journalism also resulted in a fragmentation of global coverage, and I didn't want to write just about the Japan angle to this or that. So I began to push to do more global articles, covering an issue not just in one country but from a worldwide perspective. My editors, sensing that I was also getting professionally impatient with the harmony in Japan, gave me the green light to travel to other countries with less *wa*. Those trips would be among the most consequential of my career.

The first of these trips took me across Asia to report on girls and boys forced into the sex trade. This struck me as the kind of tragedy that we in journalism should be covering more, even if prime ministers didn't talk about it. By some official estimates, 1 million children were forced into the sex trade each year in Asia alone.

I knew about trafficking intellectually, but nothing could prepare me for what I found in a village called Svay Pak in Cambodia. I came across brothels imprisoning young teenage girls and auctioning them off for their virginity. In one brothel, the owner—a dour woman in her thirties who beat the girls regularly—perceived me as a potential customer and tried to interest me in purchasing Miss Nguyen, a Vietnamese girl whom she had acquired three days earlier. The owner was holding Miss Nguyen off the market until she could find a buyer for the girl's virginity.

"It's $500," the owner told me through my interpreter. "It's not so expensive. After all, she only loses her virginity once. This is a once-in-a-lifetime opportunity."

Miss Nguyen was shy and looking down at her hands. She seemed mortified by the business discussion of her virginity. She was wearing a long purple dress, heavy makeup and gold costume jewelry. All this seemed out of place, for while she said she was fourteen years old, she was slight of build and looked like a prepubescent American eleven- or twelve-year-old. The effect was of a young girl playing at dress-up, and she looked terrified.

The owner told me that a foreigner, perhaps an Overseas Chinese, would probably buy Miss Nguyen's virginity. There was a belief among some men that sex with a virgin would make one more youthful and virile, even that such an encounter could cure AIDS.

Several girls were seated near Miss Nguyen, and one was a fifteen-year-old Vietnamese girl who was also new to the brothel and seemed to have taken on the task of looking after Miss Nguyen.

"A man from Singapore paid $500 for my virginity a few days ago," the girl piped up. "It hurt a lot and I cried. It still hurts me. But it's not quite so bad now."

Miss Nguyen shuddered and leaned against the fifteen-year-old. She finally looked up and into the girl's eyes.

"I'm scared," she said softly. "I'm scared."

It felt as if I were visiting a nineteenth-century slave auction. One big difference was that these girls would be dead of AIDS by their twenties. I talked to customers who, as I saw it, paid to rape these children. The customers denied that it was rape, saying that the kids consented and that the age of consent was customarily much lower in Asia. If local people agreed that this was fine, why should sanctimonious foreigners like me get involved and moralize? They noted that poor children suffer through many difficult, dangerous and stigmatizing jobs, and the money a girl earned in the sex trade could be transformative for her family.

"I'm doing these girls a favor," one customer memorably told me. "I'm giving them more money than they'll make any other way." To me this was a toxic mix of nonsense, self-delusion and myopia, and of course in most cases the money went not to the girl but to her trafficker. I imagined a Mississippi plantation owner venting with similar indignation: *I give these slaves food and housing! They like it! And I let them take Sunday off. I'm doing them a favor.*

In one brothel in the Tuol Kork red light district in Phnom Penh, I spent a humid late afternoon talking to two girls through my interpreter. One was a thirteen-year-old whom I'll call Sophea, and the other was her fifteen-year-old best friend; we'll call her Bopha. The brothel was deserted at this hour, which made it easier to talk. We sat in rickety folding metal chairs at a card table as the hot sun slowly descended.

Sophea was unusually outgoing with a lovely, mischievous personality, and she teased me for not understanding the Khmer language. She wore a white knee-length dress and too much makeup—including a smear of lipstick that had smudged—and fingernails and toenails painted bright red. As long as I kept buying overpriced drinks for the group, the brothel owner let me speak to them.

The girls were full of life and seemed surprisingly cheerful, for they joked, teased and flitted from topic to topic. A pornographic video was playing on a mounted television in the bar area, presumably to arouse customers, and sometimes the girls pointed at the action and whispered to each other and shook with laughter. In another context, they would have come across as teenyboppers.

Sophea said she had been sold by her stepfather. Bopha recounted that she had been kidnapped by a neighbor and sold. I asked them about escaping, and they said that girls sometimes did try to flee but were usually caught and returned, often by the police. Girls who were returned faced beatings and were starved, locked up inside small rooms inside the brothel and never let out. Customers were brought to them. Sophea pointed to the shell of a brothel next door. It had burned down recently, and the incinerated bodies of two girls were found. They had been locked inside as punishment for trying to escape.

The brothel owner, a woman in her late twenties, came over, trying to press a sale. I was a good target, for while local customers often paid just $1 or $2, a foreigner might pay much more.

"Ten dollars, okay?" the brothel owner suggested. "All night? Okay?"

"No, no," I said. "More Cokes. Four Cokes."

"You like?" the brothel owner asked me, gesturing to the girls. "You like?" Then she reached over and pulled down the neckline of Sophea's

dress to expose her breasts—or rather the nipples of what would eventually become breasts if she survived to maturity.

"You like?" the brothel owner asked me, as Sophea looked to the
side in embarrassment. "You take girl, okay? Okay?"

"Just a Coke," I replied. "No, four Cokes."

The brothel owner switched to Khmer and spoke to my interpreter,
telling him how young and fresh the two girls were. Then the brothel
owner pulled down the top of Bopha's dress, to expose her flat chest
as well.

"Just four Cokes," I said. The brothel owner wandered off to get
the drinks, and the girls readjusted their dresses and tried to recover
their dignity. They resumed their joking with me and my interpreter,
but beneath the surface there was also a deep melancholy. I sensed that
another reason they believed escape to be impossible was that they felt
stained as prostitutes who would be forever scorned by society and
unable to marry or have families.

When Bopha went missing, her mother had searched all over Cambodia for her—and if your teenage daughter disappears there, you look
in the brothels. So after venturing into many red light districts, the
mother happened to visit this very brothel the previous week, and she
and her daughter had a joyful reunion.

"So why are you still here?" I asked. "Why didn't your mom take
you home?"

Bopha shrugged and smiled sadly at my naïveté. "The brothel owner
explained that she had paid good money for me, and my mom would
have to buy me back. And my mom didn't have the money."

Sophea was listening quietly. She seemed to think that at least Bopha
had a family who loved her and wanted her back. I asked Sophea how
she came to the brothel.

"Dad died in the war, and everything changed," she said. "Mom
married another man, and he didn't like me. I wasn't his girl, so he
didn't want me in the house. He tried to get rid of me. He used to
beat me."

She paused and shook her head ferociously. The sun in her personality disappeared behind a cloud, and a storm brewed.

"I hate my stepfather," she snarled. "I hate him. I hate him. I hate
him. He was the one who wanted to sell me. He forced my mom to

sell me. He made her go along with it. Mom was sick, and she needed money. We didn't have the money for a doctor, and she would have died."

I asked what the sickness was. The answer was convoluted and involved a folk description of what was probably tuberculosis.

"We wanted to take her to a doctor, but we didn't have money," Sophea continued. "So my stepfather said he had to sell me. Mom didn't want to sell me, but my stepfather made her. She was too weak to do anything."

So Sophea had been sold, at the age of about eleven, to one brothel that auctioned off her virginity, then she was resold to another brothel, and finally she was resold to this one. She had heard that her stepfather had indeed used some of the money for medical care but that her mom had still died.

"What do you think of your mom?" I asked.

"Mom's dead now. I can't say anything bad about her."

"But what do you think of your mom allowing you to be sold?"

There was a long silence. Sophea's eyes grew distant.

"Mom was sick and needed money," she said finally. "I don't hate her."

"No anger at all?"

Sophea did not answer, did not lose her serenity, and she seemed lost in thought. But she used her fingers to play absentmindedly with a piece of brittle plastic on the table, breaking it with slender fingers, violently tearing it into smaller and smaller pieces.

That girl haunted me. She's probably long since dead of AIDS, but when I returned to Tokyo and was interviewing cabinet ministers, it was difficult to forget her. I had thought that my reporting on children sold to the sex trade would be a single article about a topic I found important if unpleasant, but I have continued to report on sexual exploitation ever since. For so many of us lucky people, sex is wrapped up with pleasure, love and intimacy, but for millions of unfortunate children it is all pain, degradation and death.

I walked out of that brothel wondering about my own moral responsibility. Sophea was a thirteen-year-old prisoner, effectively a slave, and every day strange men walked into the brothel and exploited her and then walked away. In my own journalistic way, I had done something similar. I spent time in the brothel, gathered up the girls' stories and satisfied my needs, and then left the girls behind. I remember walking out of the brothel knowing that I had a good front-page story, and that they would die of AIDS.

I wondered, too, about the ethics of my interviews. When I cover conflicts, I'm wary of interviewing prisoners of war trotted out before me, because they can never say no. Is a child slave different? Is it appropriate to interview a child in such circumstances, even without using a full name? What is meaningful consent for a child in a brothel, not to sex but to an interview?

These are complicated questions and I wasn't sure how to answer them. But I did feel that I had witnessed something profoundly wrong, and that I should use my journalistic toolbox to address it. This would probably not help Sophea but might encourage a crackdown on child trafficking that would help other girls and boys. And I thought that Sophea and Miss Nguyen and others I spoke with would be willing to have their stories told if this might help other children avoid a modern form of slavery.

It was also clear that girls were preyed on in part because they were girls—because they didn't matter as much as boys did—and so I became more alert to broader issues of gender inequity from education to law enforcement, from hiring to health care. These would play a much larger role in my reporting in years to come.

I also wondered if maybe the real force for change in the world didn't have more to do with women and kids than with aging male prime ministers. It wasn't obvious to me that Prime Minister Murayama was having much impact on Japan. But as I looked around the region, it was hard to avoid the revelation that what had been transformative in recent decades was the education of girls and the mobilization of those educated women into the labor force.

East Asia hadn't soared because of any particular economic policy—South Korea, Hong Kong, Taiwan and China all adopted very different development strategies—but a common thread was investments in education and the migration of young women from low-productivity jobs in agriculture to high-productivity jobs in industry. Women, it seemed, shouldn't be seen so much as a tragedy as an opportunity. But first we reporters had to cover them.

At this time, my interest in gender issues was inchoate and I worried that "women's issues" might seem small-bore. I wanted to write serious articles that provoked discussion, and I knew the graying doyens of the Council on Foreign Relations wouldn't inquire about each other's views on female genital mutilation. "Women's issues" traditionally weren't part of the serious agenda. But I couldn't shake the idea that in these topics was something profoundly important that the world wasn't paying adequate attention to.

21

Journey into a War

The *Times* had another correspondent in Tokyo aside from Sheryl, plus stringers who contributed articles in Tokyo and Seoul. The paper was doing just fine with me as an absentee bureau chief, so I continued to lobby my editors for the chance to cover global stories. That's when they asked if I wanted to go to Congo during the civil war there. A correspondent was needed to help chronicle the disintegration of the old regime and the emergence of whatever came next.

I leaped at the chance, promised Sheryl (who was now pregnant with Caroline) that I would be careful—"No, honestly, I really will be"—and set out for Nairobi, where I met up with the photographer Steve Crowley. Then we boarded the plane chartered by the United Nations Refugee Agency. And that's how I ended up with Steve on a damaged plane, the body of the man we'd hit still wrapped around the right landing gear, as it descended toward a crash landing.

Steve and I were in the brace position, looking at our shoes, and had no idea what was going on. I had worked out a plan to unbuckle my seat belt and rush a few steps to the emergency exit and force it open before fire engulfed all of us, but I was skeptical of my own plan. I had seen what plane crashes do to occupants, and they're not usually able to jump up and open doors. Steve felt the same way but had his own plan: He had his camera on his lap to document our roasting in the conflagration when we crashed.

As we looked at our shoes, muscles tensed, wondering if this was the end, we suddenly felt the plane touch ground violently and bounce. Dale, the pilot, had managed to bring the plane down on a grassy field near Entebbe Airport in Uganda, landing on the intact left landing gear. This was a tribute to his brilliant piloting skills, but as the plane slowed it couldn't stay upright without a right wheel. So it collapsed on the right side, the right wing touched the ground, and the plane spun wildly, with the luggage inside flying all over the place. The seat belt tugged at my belly and took my breath away, but I kept my hands clasped over my head and eventually the plane came to rest. I was able to jump up and open the emergency door, with others, and we stumbled out. The plane never caught fire.

We stood on the field looking at the mangled plane, and at the corpse on the right landing gear. I set up my satellite phone to call Sheryl in Tokyo.

"How are you?" I asked, somewhat breathlessly.

"I'm fine," she said. "Thanks for calling. Kids are fine. All good with you?"

"Yup, all good. Just wanted to check in. The baby good?"

"Doing fine."

"Me too." I had decided that I would wait until I got home before telling Sheryl about the plane crash. Plane crashes, I thought, fell into the category of things you tell your spouse when you're together and she's sitting down.

Sheryl spoke for a couple of minutes and then said she had to get off to take a call. I hung up and messaged the *Times* foreign editor, Bill Keller, to explain that because of a plane crash, I wasn't in Kisangani in central Congo, and had no idea how I would get there. "Glad you're okay," he told me. "We won't look too closely at your next bar tab."

But Sir Walter Scott was right: "Oh, what a tangled web we weave, when first we practice to deceive." A couple of hours later, an editor on the foreign desk was speaking to Sheryl on the phone.

"That was terrible about Nick's plane crash," the editor said.

"What plane crash?"

I was busted. One lesson learned: Immediate honesty is the best policy with a spouse, and there isn't an exception for plane crashes.

IT TURNS OUT that if you crash-land in a country, officials give you a visa because there's not much else they can do. The United Nations Refugee Agency sent another plane a few days later to Uganda that ferried us to Kisangani. Steve and I found a cheap hotel—every other hotel had been taken over by rebels who had seized central and eastern Congo and were winning the civil war—and spent several days covering the Rwanda refugee crisis. There I absorbed another lesson in journalism, this time from the legendary Brazilian photographer Sebastião Salgado.

Most of us journalists were staying in Kisangani and making day trips to a makeshift refugee camp an hour away where 85,000 Rwandan Hutu were starving. These were a different kind of refugee, a morally complicated strain, for many had participated in Rwanda's genocide. When the genocidal forces were defeated, these Hutu had fled and were now enduring terrible privation themselves. It was difficult to imagine people suffering more wrenching hardship than these refugees dying of hunger and cholera, yet also difficult to imagine people who, collectively, had more blood on their hands.

The refugees were morally troubling in another way as well. The young men most involved in the genocide dominated the refugee camp and monopolized what little food there was. They often seemed to still be hale and hearty even as women and children starved. One husky thirty-five-year-old, Bizumana Faustin, introduced me to his three starving sons, aged two to seven years, the youngest of whom was near death.

"Why are they so hungry when you're so well fed?" I asked.

"When we get food, I eat first," Faustin explained.

"Why do you eat ahead of your starving children?"

Faustin didn't take offense. He laughed good-naturedly. "I've become thinner, too," he boomed, as his children looked on with vacant stares.

Salgado was documenting this nightmare but didn't stay in town with the rest of us. He camped with the refugees and spent all his time with them, beautifully capturing the pulse of their daily lives: the haircuts, the deaths, the love, the grief. I felt as if I had done everything I could possibly do to tell this story of the refugees, traveling halfway around the world, enduring a plane crash, staying in a crappy hotel, journeying down unsafe roads, surviving on bananas and canned tuna because that's all that was available, interviewing from morning to night—and then Salgado showed me how a real pro got even closer to the story.

No other journalist or aid worker stayed with the refugees, and we all understood the risk Salgado was taking: Among the refugees were many who had already committed murder and might not flinch at one more killing. In Salgado's case, a local person tipped him off that a group of men were planning to murder him the next day for his cameras and clothes. So that night at 3 a.m. he fled the camp with the help of two boys with bicycles to carry him and his gear to safety in Kisangani.

The lesson from Salgado reinforced my instincts: To get the story, we can't just drop in for a few hours, grab some quotes and depart. We need to embed ourselves among those we're covering—but also make sure we survive to file.

After the plane crash entering Congo, I liked the idea of driving out rather than trying to fly out. The rebels had recently repaired a road through eastern Congo so that they could invade from the east and overthrow the government. Rumors in Kisangani were that the road should be passable all the way to Uganda, if we didn't get killed by army soldiers, rebel soldiers or independent Mai Mai warriors.

This was one of the most remote areas in the world, and if I believed in getting out of the capitals and seeing how people actually lived in the villages, this seemed a way to do that. We would be passing through an area that few foreigners had visited for decades.

Steve and I found a good Land Rover with an experienced driver who promised he could go anywhere. He insisted on bringing along an assistant, which made me suspicious: I worried that two of them would be better able to rob us and leave us in the jungle. But it turned out to be normal in Congo for drivers to have assistants, and when we first set off, I learned why. The dirt roads would frequently traverse long puddles. The driver would stop in front of each puddle, and the assistant would jump out and wade through it. If he made it through the puddle and it was no deeper than his knees or his thighs, then the Land Rover would follow him and plow through the water. But if the assistant suddenly disappeared under water, we would stop and carve a new path around the puddle.

We also found an interpreter, Dr. Ndomba Benda, a professor of English at the University of Kisangani. The university wasn't func-

Steve Crowley and I encountered a traffic jam on our journey through Congo, because of a truck that had turned over. We carved a path around it.

tioning, so Professor Benda moonlighted by interpreting for foreigners, and we couldn't have found a more astute interpreter and guide. He was an albino, so when he was with us, local people sometimes assumed he was a white foreigner. He was quick to correct them in the local language, Lingala.

As Professor Benda kept reminding us, Congo was blessed with gold, diamonds and tremendous natural wealth. King Leopold of Belgium had ruled it brutally in the nineteenth century, then Belgium as a country had governed it, and it had been independent since 1960. The Belgians had been discriminatory and had ruled Congo for their own benefit in ways that were demeaning and damaging to Congolese. But it was also true that Congo had gone downhill in much of that period since independence, so some elderly Congolese expressed nostalgia for Belgian rule—which was achingly sad.

Benda took me to the Kisangani zoo as a window into the country's decline. Founded by the Belgians in 1954, the zoo had been a center of local life and schooling. Benda remembered it as a vibrant place where local city dwellers could learn about elephants, hippos and animals living in the forest. The star attraction was Alfonse, the chimpanzee, who delighted crowds by smoking a cigarette or chugging a beer. But when we showed up, the zoo had twenty-two unpaid keepers, and nothing else.

"The zoo isn't closed," the senior worker there explained to me. "The zoo is open. There just aren't any animals."

He said that the animals had starved to death, one by one, except for the elephant, which had been eaten by soldiers. The last inmate to survive was the crocodile. "We tried to feed him snakes, but he wouldn't eat them," said another zookeeper. "We knew he would starve, but he lasted a long time. He was a tough guy."

The zookeepers showed me Alfonse's skull and spoke lovingly of his talents and fondness for beer. Professor Benda was whispering to me that this was all rubbish about the animals starving to death.

"The zookeepers were hungry," he explained. "They ate the animals." The keepers grew indignant when I asked about that, but one of them did acknowledge that he had heard that Romeo, another chimpanzee, had "tasted good."

"It's a sign of the collapse of everything," Benda told me sadly as we drove away. "How can people feed the animals when they are hungry themselves?"

The Belgians built roads in part to exploit the country and remove its resources, but these roads also provided channels for the provision of health care and education. In Belgian days, Congo had 88,000 miles of usable roads; by the time of my visit, there were almost no roads that could be negotiated year-round in an ordinary car. The mayor of Kisangani jabbed at an ancient map from 1958, the only one of the city available, and pointed to outer areas where roads were so overgrown that they had returned to jungle. "This area is full of forgotten villages," he told me. "Nobody even knows about them anymore."

I asked at the Kisangani bus station about making an overnight visit to Buta, a provincial center that used to be a six-hour drive by ordinary car from Kisangani. The head of the bus station looked at me with amusement.

"There are no vehicles going to Buta anymore," he said. "If you want to go, first you'd have to buy gas for the ferry halfway there and pay it to take you across the river, because the ferry has stopped, too. Then on the other side of the river, the road is so bad that to get to Buta it would take a month, maybe two or three."

So much for my trip to Buta. But Steve and I did make a day trip to a diamond mine. Except that it wasn't a day trip. We became stuck in the mud repeatedly and finally had to hike three and a half hours to the mining camp, where 120 men were digging for gems. The government had barred foreigners from visiting diamond mines, but Professor Benda gave a stirring speech telling the miners about the revolution now taking place across the country and telling them that a new Congo was emerging. "This is your country now," he told them. "It is up to you to decide." The miners took a vote and chose to let Steve and me visit and spend the night—and promptly began lobbying us to obtain American bulldozers for them so that they wouldn't have to dig by hand. It was backbreaking work on the mountain to remove the top-soil, dig deep holes and sift through the sand for diamonds, and these holes sometimes collapsed and killed miners. The stories reduced the glamour of diamonds for me.

Steve and I shared a grass hut that hadn't been used in months, and I wondered if the previous occupants had been killed in a mining accident. There was a rough-hewn woven cot, with just enough room for both of us.

"Normally I have a policy of not sleeping with colleagues," I told Steve. "Except one."

"I won't tell Sheryl," he promised.

We spread little sheet sacks we had brought and got in them for the night. I had a lantern, and as I was about to put it out, Steve pointed in horror at the thatch roof.

"Look at the size of that," he said, pointing to a tarantula in the thatch directly above him.

As it happens, there are a few scary things about Congo aside from warlords and plane crashes, like puff adder snakes, mambas and the venomous and possibly mythical Congolese Giant Spider, or *j'ba fofi*, which is supposedly the size of a monkey. What if that tarantula was actually a baby *j'ba fofi* whose mother had stepped away briefly?

"I can't sleep under that thing," Steve protested.

I pointed the light at it, and it didn't move.

"Oh, come on, Steve," I said, a bit scornfully. "It's been dead for months. It's just a dead skeleton."

"How do you know?"

"Just look at it. It's dead." Here I adopted the standard journalistic tactic of compensating for lack of knowledge with a tone of absolute authority.

Steve looked at the spider suspiciously in the feeble light.

"Maybe leave the light on in case it jumps me?" he suggested.

"Come on, Steve. It's dead. Dead!"

"Okay, okay," he grumbled. I turned the light out, and thirty seconds later there was a light "pat" sound of something falling, followed by a scream from Steve.

"Ahhhhhh!" he roared. "A tarantula on my face! My flashlight! Where's my flashlight?"

We turned on our flashlights. Sure enough, the "dead" tarantula was gone from the thatch roof. Steve didn't trust me so much after that.

One of the reasons for lack of development in places like rural Congo is corruption and insecurity. As we drove toward Uganda, we'd periodically come across soldiers of one kind or another who would request "donations." And when a soldier has a rifle pointed at your chest, it seems churlish to refuse.

There are other security concerns when driving through a war zone, such as land mines. "This road is mined for the next sixty kilometers," our driver explained early on. "But I think the mines have probably been discovered. Anyway, I'll just follow in the tracks of cars that have gone ahead of us." A mile later, large mud puddles became frequent, so the driver began swerving wildly to avoid them. Steve and I held our breath.

On the first day after leaving Kisangani, we came across a large rebel encampment with child soldiers who operated a checkpoint. I introduced myself—following my risk-management principle that I should always shake hands and exchange names with people who might kill me—and asked them what they were doing.

"We're capturing Rwandan refugees," said one, a scrawny boy of about thirteen carrying an AK-47. "We're catching them and killing them."

"You're executing refugees?"

"Yes," he said proudly. He pointed to a truck loaded with Hutu men, their hands tied behind their backs, squatting and looking miserable. The men on the truck stared at me, faces blank; they knew they were going to die.

"You're going to kill those men on the truck?"

The boys all nodded.

"Every day we kill them," the kid with the gun said. "They fled, so they must be bad people. So we catch them and take them back to our commander, and then we kill them.

"There are so many of them," he added wearily.

I was appalled but also eager to get the full story. It's often difficult to piece together culpability for mass atrocities, but here rebel soldiers were admitting on the record to massacring civilian refugees and were happy to talk about how many they had killed. The fact that they were child soldiers, thirteen to fifteen years of age, added a notable element.

I interviewed them for a while and then thought how nice it would be to have the warlord confirm all this. Icing on the cake. "Could we talk to your commander?" I asked.

"Yes," the boy said, shrugging. "I'll take you to him."

Unfortunately, the warlord was more savvy about the implications of two reporters showing up in the middle of his massacre.

"What are you doing here?" he asked angrily. "Who authorized you to be here?"

The warlord was a Rwandan Tutsi who didn't speak the local language, but Professor Benda was able to communicate with him in Swahili and plead with him to let us go. It was not a happy conversation. The warlord was furious and detained us. I suddenly felt that not only were Steve and I in peril, but that I had also endangered Professor Benda and the driver and his assistant.

One of the basic principles of journalism is that we never lie. We're in the truth business. So we don't lie to sources, we don't pretend to be people we're not, we don't lie about what authorizations we've obtained. But there's an exception when you're detained in the Congolese jungle by a menacing warlord who is massacring refugees.

"Laurent Kabila sends his regards," I said, referring to the uber-warlord in command of the entire region, whom I had never met.

"You know General Kabila?" he asked, taken aback.

"Of course," I lied. "He told us this road was passable and that we should take it. He said to give you his regards."

"I will get him on the radio and ask him what to do with you."

That worried me. I had taken a gamble by claiming approval by Kabila, guessing that the commander had no easy way of checking my statement. Now I hoped that his radio was out of batteries or that

Kabila's was. I also thought that even if they did make radio contact, Kabila was unlikely to use an open radio transmission to order the execution of American prisoners. The greater the number of people who learned that we were detained, I thought, the less likely we would be executed on the spot.

The warlord couldn't get ahold of Kabila, so after an hour he released us on condition that we not take any photos on the trip. We were willing to agree to anything to save our skins, even if we had no intention of honoring that pledge.

So we drove on toward Uganda. A few hours later, the warlord was able to reach Kabila, who of course had never heard of us. The warlord dispatched a truckload of soldiers to arrest us, and they pursued us for the next five days on the narrow red clay track through the jungle to Uganda. We got stuck in the mud for hours sometimes, but so did the rebel truck, and it never caught up with us. We were unaware that we were being pursued until after we reached safety at the Uganda border. Then our vehicle turned around to drive back to Kisangani and almost immediately ran into the pursuers. They were looking for Steve and me and did not harm those in the Land Rover, but Benda passed the message on to me about the pursuit.

When we reached the Uganda border, we took this photo of our vehicle and crew. *From left:* Steve, the driver's assistant, me, the driver and Professor Benda.

Somewhere on the journey through eastern Congo, I was bitten by a malarial mosquito. I learned that a week later when I was back in Tokyo. My temperature soared, I found myself shaking uncontrollably, and I had to be hospitalized with the most lethal form of malaria. Sheryl was pretty much ready to finish me off.

"You've got to think of us," she said. "You can't just take these risks now that you have a family."

"I'll be careful," I promised between shivers. "I really will be." And I meant it. I always did.

Driving through Congo made me skeptical of the widespread notion that impoverished countries today lag simply because of the legacy of colonialism. That seemed too glib. Those countries that were not much colonized by outside powers, like Ethiopia, Thailand and Liberia, did not do noticeably better than their many neighbors that were colonized by European powers, and I'd seen how fast countries could develop when they had the right policies in place. South Korea had once been as poor as India or most of Africa, and it was now an industrial power. Within Africa, Botswana had been one of the world's fastest-growing nations in part because of excellent leaders.

So I came to think that the two crucial factors for development are mass education and good governance and leadership. They explain why East Asia generally thrived, with its ancient reverence for education, but why North Korea did not (awful governance) and why much of Africa did not (weaknesses in both education and governance, which in fairness did relate to the colonial inheritance).

Governance is complicated, of course, and includes corruption as well as sensible policies. There's an old joke about differences in corruption, and I thought of it often as I drove through Congo. Two friends from graduate school, one from Indonesia and one from Congo, both rise to become finance ministers of their countries. The Congolese minister travels to visit his old friend in Indonesia and stays at his mansion. The Congolese says: "You've done so well, my friend. This house is gorgeous. But tell me how. You didn't build this on a government salary!"

"You see that road there?" the Indonesian says, pointing below. "Ten percent!"

A few years later, the Indonesian visits the Congolese finance minister. The Congolese minister's home is even grander, like a palace. The

Indonesian is stunned, and congratulates his friend. "You've done so well, old buddy," the Indonesian says. "But tell me how. This wasn't built on a government salary."

The Congolese minister nodded sagely. "You see that road?" he said, pointing out the window.

The Indonesian looked out the window and frowned. "No, what road?"

"That's just it. One hundred percent."

22

"We Have to Kill Them"

S ecurity. It's like oxygen: You don't notice it until you don't have it. To grow up in middle-class America is to feel, most of the time, reasonably safe. There may be murders, recessions and natural disasters, but we don't typically think much about home invasions or drive-by shootings. We worry even less that a warlord will sweep through our neighborhood, that our children will be kidnapped, that ATMs or gas stations will run empty, that everything we have will be seized, that we will be forced to flee as refugees.

In college, I read the political philosopher Thomas Hobbes, who theorized that life in the state of nature is "solitary, poor, nasty, brutish and short." Hobbes believed humans were prone to aggression and war, and that even small numbers of ruthless figures could create chaos in society unless they were restrained by strong government. All that seemed unnecessarily gloomy. I thought of Hobbes as a pessimist and a patriarch of conservatives, so as an optimistic liberal I dismissed him.

Then I became a reporter. And I came to see civilization as a thinner veneer than we might like to admit.

The Asian Economic Crisis of 1997–98 offered a chance to test my theory that correspondents should spend less time in capitals and more time in the field. I covered the crisis in part by talking to finance ministers, but I also traveled to villages to gauge how this economic collapse was affecting ordinary people. I spent time in Indonesia, where incomes had collapsed by more than 90 percent in dollar terms, reporting on the decline in nutrition and health care. That I expected. What I hadn't anticipated was the unraveling of the social fabric, with whispers that sorcerers were to blame for the economic pain. And next came the discussion of how to find and kill sorcerers.

One day the area exploded in violence, centered on a town called Turen. If Japan exemplified harmony, Turen seemed to offer a lesson in how society can unravel.

I drove with my interpreter on a rainy morning in a cheerful blue taxi, but traffic thinned and then disappeared as we approached Turen. Nervous, we stopped at a regional police station to see if an officer might accompany us.

"No, I'm afraid not," said the local police chief, a tall, pompous man in a crisp uniform. "All the police officers are staying inside the compound."

"Why?"

He paused, sighed and deflated. "They think it's too dangerous to go out in the streets."

The police were terrified. Equally scared, we drove on to Turen and stopped at a central intersection where a group of young men were standing. I told our driver to leave the engine running in case we needed to leave quickly, and to leave the windows down so that anyone could see this was just a taxi and not, say, a sorcerer-mobile. I left my black camera bag in the car in case someone mistook it for a sorcerer's kit.

I have a routine for approaching people who may kill me. I wear loose clothes and running shoes, in case it doesn't go well and I need to flee. I wear only a cheap watch, because of a story I'd heard in the Philippines of a Japanese man there who wore a Rolex—and encountered a thief with a machete who whacked off his forearm and ran off with it. As I mentioned earlier, I also carry a decoy wallet so that if I'm robbed at gunpoint I have some modest sum to hand over without losing all my money and credit cards. I don't carry anything else that might look worth stealing. I don't show anything that looks like a weapon. I approach in a friendly way and try to shake hands with each person and give my name and get theirs. My theory is that it's harder to murder someone you've just shaken hands with. I explain that I'm a reporter and want to hear their stories and share them with the world. Usually the kind of people who kill others are egotists who consider themselves interesting to others, and I want them to understand that I can tell the world how great they are only if I survive. I try to establish a symbiosis.

This particular group was flattered by my interest, and a rickshaw driver named Sukiando recounted what had happened the previous day. "There was a big crowd, hundreds of people, and we all had our own weapons," he said. "Sickles. Knives. Machetes."

"How did you know who to attack?" I asked.

"We attack the ninja," he said, using another term for the sorcerers.

"How do you tell who the ninja are?"

"It begins when people see someone suspicious and try to chase him. Sometimes the ninja turns into a cat, and sometimes he stays human. If he stays human, then they cut off his head." Several ninja had been beheaded the previous day, he said, offering a vigorous pantomime of beheading someone in front of him with an imaginary machete.

Sukiando paused and concentrated. "You hear that?" he asked me. "They're coming." I could hear a faraway clamor, like the roar of a crowd at a soccer match. I needed my camera from the car but didn't run for it because that might be what a ninja would do. Instead, I beamed and trotted backward to the car, looking Sukiando in the eye the whole time, then grabbed my camera just as a crowd of men on motorcycles arrived. They waved bloody sickles and machetes, and one young man in the center carried a head on a pike. The head had belonged to a young man with bushy eyebrows and thick black hair. The motorcyclists were soon followed by a car that was dragging a naked, headless body, presumably one that matched the head on the pike. I snapped photos, but my mind had trouble processing all this.

I had stepped into *Lord of the Flies*. Until that moment, I had simply worried about being killed. But as I faced the mob, I felt an acute fear of this degradation of the body: I didn't want my head to be paraded on a pike or my naked corpse dragged behind a car. If the day ended badly, I caught myself thinking, let it end with a simple execution rather than this humiliation of the corpse. And I couldn't believe I was thinking this.

I continued to chat with the men, trying to understand this descent into violence. I loved Java. This wasn't far from Mount Bromo, where I had proposed to Sheryl. Comfortable one- and two-story homes lined the road, and a billboard down the street promoted "Sun Silk Shampoo" with a photo of a beautiful young woman with shining, luxuriant black hair. Someone in the mob was thoughtful enough to try to buy me fried-rice takeaway from a cart. I couldn't eat after just seeing a head on a pike, so I explained that my sensitive foreign stomach was giving me trouble.

One man, who carried a club, told me that the sorcerers were reproducing wildly, and that each one who was killed spawned a thousand more.

"But then isn't it counterproductive to kill them?" I asked. Several men looked at me suspiciously. "You kill ten, and now you have ten thousand to deal with."

"We have to kill them," the club carrier replied hotly. "Last night, I saw it with my own eyes. There were three ninja, and when we shone a flashlight on them, they vanished."

"So if they disappear or turn into cats, that means they really are ninja," I agreed. "But if you kill them and cut off their heads and they don't vanish, doesn't that mean that they were just ordinary people and you made a mistake?"

My interpreter didn't want to ask that question and probably toned it down, but it still turned the crowd sullen. Winning debate points with a machete-wielding mob didn't seem productive. I bought a round of snacks for everyone because another of my theories is that people are less likely to kill you if their stomachs are full and they've accepted a gift from you. And then, shaking hands with everyone again, I got in the car and we took off.

That evening I showered away my fear in a room in the Surabaya Hilton. I called Sheryl to hear her voice and sent my story and photos to New York. My story about the beheadings ran on the next day's front page, and by coincidence my friend Marcus Brauchli had a story from Indonesia on page one of *The Wall Street Journal* that day as well. Marcus is a terrific journalist who later was the top editor of both the *Journal* and *The Washington Post*, and he had a smart, deeply reported story about rice shortages affecting tens of millions of Indonesians— but it's hard to compete with a mob chasing sorcerers.

"You really screwed Marcus," another journalist told me. "He worked on his piece for months, he gets it on page one, and he has to compete with your Indonesia story involving naked, headless bodies?"

I've thought many times about the sudden collapse of norms and security that I witnessed in Java, in Darfur, in Myanmar, in Congo and in other places. It's impossible to fight poverty when there's chaos and violence. In Central African Republic, I saw a clinic that had an engraved sign in front: "Gift of the German people." But that was all that was left of the clinic. It had been looted by bandits and burned to the ground.

In urban neighborhoods in the United States, I've seen something similar. People live in fear of crime, and sometimes of law enforcement as well. A friend who owns a gun shop, Mike Weisser, has customers who come into his store all the time to buy firearms, explaining that they need a gun for protection. Then Mike did a series of interviews with sixty-one juvenile offenders who had committed serious crimes. "I asked them why they carried a gun, which they all did," he recalled, "and everyone said they needed a gun to protect themselves." Where there's violence and insecurity, whether in Chicago or in Central African Republic, businesses don't invest, kids fear walking to school, and there's a risk of a downward spiral.

American liberals are, rightly, skeptical of military interventions. What happened in Vietnam and Iraq should leave us deeply skeptical. But it's also fair to point out that some interventions to establish security have been positive and transformational. President George W. Bush dispatched 150 troops to Liberia and they helped end a brutal civil war there. Britain did the same in Sierra Leone, saving thousands of lives. We should have intervened militarily in Rwanda in 1994, and it's good that we intervened in Kosovo in 1999. So it seems to me that the best course is not to be dogmatic about the use of force but to understand that sometimes it is helpful and sometimes it is catastrophic.

Another lesson I've drawn from coverage of chaos and insecurity is that when stressed enough, human society is capable of unimaginable convulsions—and we shouldn't assume that any society is immune.

I thought of all this during the attack on the United States Capitol on January 6, 2021. I have friends in Oregon who feel so alienated from the government and so distrustful of institutions—and consequently so willing to believe a demagogue like Donald Trump—that they supported the January 6 insurrection. Two of them have talked about taking up arms to fight in a new American revolution. Probably this is just angry bluster and bravado, but I've witnessed enough societies disintegrate that I can't entirely discount it.

What I've seen over and over in my reporting career is that our norms and values may be more contingent than we would like to admit, and that civilization can unravel with frightening speed. That's why robust institutions are so necessary, why laws are (as a plaque declares at Harvard Law School) "those wise restraints that make men free" and why journalism is essential to provide accountability—but also why we in journalism have to do a better job. I came to think more about that in the following years, for my reporting at home and abroad has left me with a deeper appreciation of Hobbes.

EVEN WHEN I WASN'T reporting on mobs carrying heads on pikes, much of my reporting was shattering. Child malnutrition particularly pained me, partly because it's so widespread. About 2.2 million children worldwide die each year from malnutrition—one every fourteen seconds—and one-fifth of all children under the age of five are physically stunted from malnutrition. It's preventable with simple interventions like school lunches, micronutrient supplementation and support for exclusive breastfeeding. Up to 600,000 children's lives would be saved each year just by helping moms with optimal breastfeeding.

Children dying of starvation are eerily quiet. They are in enormous pain but they don't cry. Their hair has fallen out, they have sticks for limbs, they suffer painful skin rashes, yet they are almost completely passive. They don't frown and barely move, simply following me with their eyes, showing no expression. The medical explanation is that the body is using every available calorie to keep the major organs functioning. It doesn't waste energy on tears.

We forget how recently we in America and Europe lived a similarly fragile existence. In 1924, President Calvin Coolidge's sixteen-year-old son, Cal Jr., got a blister on the third toe of his right foot while playing tennis with his brother on the White House court. That was before antibiotics, and a week later the president's son was dead of sepsis.

Jimmy Carter and I talked once about how many schoolchildren around the world are listless, anemic and malnourished because they have worms in their gut. Every now and then after international travels, I take an albendazole pill to deworm myself, but Carter noted that it wasn't so long ago that such parasites were ubiquitous in America as well.

"When I was growing up in rural Georgia," he told me, "we had similar problems. We had worms. We had blinding trachoma. We had unsafe water. We had poor sanitation. We forget how recently some of these problems have disappeared in the United States. It has been in my lifetime."

Carter led a heroic effort to eliminate some of these ailments around the world. It was largely because of him that cases of river blindness, a painful disease caused by a parasite, have fallen by more than 90 percent. Carter also made a major push to eradicate Guinea Worm disease, an excruciating ailment in countries like Chad and South Sudan, in which a three-foot worm grows under the skin and finally pops out— and then must be pulled out, about an inch a day. If you pull too hard, it breaks and the remainder is left inside the body. Carter told me he was determined to eradicate Guinea Worm before he died, and it became a race with enormous impact. When I first traveled in Africa in the 1980s, there were 3.5 million human cases of Guinea Worm disease each year, and in 2022 there were just thirteen.

I witnessed Carter's efforts firsthand in countries like Liberia, Ethiopia and South Sudan, and in 2007 I was invited to travel with Carter to Ethiopia. His staff had told me that this would be his last major foreign trip, and that felt historic. So I sat down with Carter in rural Ethiopia by a creek linked to river blindness.

"I understand that this is your last major foreign trip," I began, and Carter interrupted. He was normally friendly, but now he glared at me.

"Whatever would give you that idea?" he asked icily, as his aides looked in every other direction. Carter clearly planned to continue traveling to places like Ethiopia until he was 150 years old—and I loved him for it. He gave me hope, not only because of what he had achieved in attacking some of these diseases but also because of the progress that he had witnessed in his hometown. If Georgia can deworm children successfully and make progress on public health, so can the rest of the world.

Health doesn't get enough attention in journalism—we tend to see everything through the prism of politics—but my travels deeply impressed on me the urgency of addressing such issues. On another trip, this time in rural Cambodia, I came across a grandma named Nhem Yen who was looking after her young grandchildren because her daughter had just died of malaria. Nhem Yen showed me her one bed net to protect the children from malarial mosquitoes. The problem was that the bed net could accommodate only two children, and she was caring for two grandchildren as well as five children of her own. Every evening, she had to decide which of the children could sleep under the bed net, and which would risk malaria by sleeping outside of it.

"It's very hard to choose," Nhem Yen said softly as her children clustered around her. "But we have no money to buy another mosquito net. We have no choice."

The idea of Nhem Yen having to make such a choice each evening has haunted me ever since. I solved her problem by leaving money with her at the end of the interview: We can't pay for interviews, but I sometimes left money afterward with people in desperate need. I never wanted to create an expectation that people would get money if they told me a heartbreaking story, but I also didn't want a child to die if I could help it. My help for Nhem Yen wasn't enough, though. With Bernard Krisher, a friend who was a Holocaust survivor and had a deep humanitarian impulse, I started a fundraising effort to provide bed nets to Cambodians. For $5, we could buy a bed net that would accommodate three kids. Bernie's line was "Save three lives for $5." We surely managed to save some lives and help some Cambodians avoid the equivalent of Sophie's choice.

When journalism projects an issue onto the agenda and forces people to pay attention, it can have an impact. In 1997 I traveled through Asia and Africa and wrote about how routine ailments unnecessarily kill vast numbers of children. I noted that 3 million children a year died from diarrhea, typically from contaminated water. That piece didn't make much of a ripple at first. But for two readers in Seattle, a young couple in the tech world, the article resonated, because they had been dabbling in philanthropy but hadn't found the right cause yet.

"Three million kids a year!" Bill Gates ruminated later, reflecting on my article. "How could that many children be dying from something that was, as far as we knew, little more than an uncomfortable inconvenience? We learned that the simple lifesaving treatment for diarrhea—an inexpensive liquid that replaces the nutrients lost during an episode—wasn't reaching millions of children. That seemed like a problem we could help with."

Bill and Melinda Gates sent my article to Bill's father with a note: "Dad, maybe we can do something about this." One consequence of that article was that Bill and Melinda studied global health and poverty and eventually made these the focus of their foundation. Today, Bill and Melinda are saving millions of lives from malaria, AIDS, diarrhea and pandemics, while helping to empower women around the world. My article about diarrhea is displayed in the lobby of the Gates Foundation offices in Seattle. Because of its galvanizing effect on two particular readers, it's by far the most consequential piece I ever wrote.

23

"Do They Play Baseball in America?"

Joe Lelyveld, now the executive editor, was nudging us to come home. Joe argued that Sheryl and I had covered the world but could use more time in the United States to learn about our own country. We listened to Joe, for he had been right to send us to China, and his instincts had been unerring on almost every issue on which we had worked with him. But we also wanted our kids to have as much international experience as possible, soaking up languages while they were young, and we weren't sure we were ready to give up the overseas life just yet.

We had spent most of fourteen years with the *Times* in Asia—Hong Kong, Taiwan, Beijing and Tokyo—and we now had three children, for Caroline had been born in Tokyo. The kids were multilingual, jabbering away in Chinese, Japanese and English, although this had meant that they were slow to start speaking as toddlers. Many of our friends had kids at the same time we did, so we were inadvertently caught up in cycles of competitive parenting. We were initially at a disadvantage, because of our kids' slowness in talking. When we were on a visit back to New York and Gregory was about two, a friend visited with her daughter in tow, and I knew Sheryl was going to have a tough time because the friend's daughter was much more verbal than Gregory. So I coached Gregory, who at that point could pronounce the number "two" but could not say "one" or "three" or "four." I trained him at my signal to shout out "Two!"

After the friend had told us all the wonderful things her daughter was doing, as Gregory sat silently in the corner, I said that Gregory didn't talk too much but he was quite interested in math.

"Hey, Gregory," I said, attracting his attention. "What's the, oh, say, cube root of eight?"

"Two," he said instantly.

Our friend was still thinking it through: *What is the cube root of eight?* Later, she pulled Sheryl aside.

"Does he really know all his square roots and cube roots?" she asked.

When our kids eventually did speak, of course, it was in multiple languages, but they still didn't have a national identity. In the elevator in our Tokyo apartment building, a neighbor asked Gregory in Japanese where he was from, and poor Gregory looked like a deer in the headlights. Where was he from? He didn't know. He had been born in Hong Kong, had lived in China and Japan, spent summers on a farm in Oregon, but wasn't really *from* anywhere.

One day I was walking Gregory home from elementary school and we passed a park where Japanese men were playing baseball. "Dad," Gregory asked me, "do they play baseball in America?"

That answered the question of where we would go next. It was time to return home and turn these kids into Americans. So we talked to Joe Lelyveld about what post to take up.

"What would you like to do at the *Times* in the long run?" Joe asked me.

"My dream is to be an op-ed columnist," I told him. "Or else to be a top editor."

"Both are reasonable ambitions for you," he replied. He said he would mention my interest in a column to Arthur Sulzberger Jr., Punch's son, who had taken over as publisher, and he urged me to write to Arthur as well. As for becoming an editor, Joe would keep an eye out for a good role.

I did write Arthur about a column, and he responded promptly: "Your interest in becoming an op-ed page columnist is intriguing. You have the writing skills and the insights to be a very good columnist, so be assured that I take your interest seriously." The *Times* was close to appointing a new foreign affairs columnist, Tom Friedman, so Arthur urged me to get more domestic experience as a reporter or editor.

We moved back to the United States in 1999, and our move coincided with roughly the end of the golden age of foreign correspon-dence. Newspapers and news magazines for decades had spent lavishly to treat their foreign correspondents as ambassadors—*Time* magazine particularly pampered its overseas bureau chiefs—and at *The Wall Street Journal*, Roger Cohen was once scolded for flying business class. *Journal* foreign correspondents, he was told, should never think of fly-ing less than first class.

Yet that epoch was ending. By the time Sheryl and I concluded our careers as foreign correspondents, the *Times* and other news organi-zations were cutting back. Foreign correspondents were asked to fly economy, and we knew we had to take that edict seriously when the foreign editor, Bill Keller, flew coach from New York to Delhi to visit the staff in India.

News organizations were also changing the nature of overseas coverage. Instead of sending veteran reporters overseas at the height of their careers with enormous expense accounts, head offices hired younger people and sometimes refused to pay for housing, education and moves. The new system of more junior correspondents nurtured some first-rate journalists, often experts in a region who had superb language skills and stayed in a bureau for long periods. But the glamour days in which foreign correspondents enjoyed vast freedom to shape coverage was coming to an end.

This was partly because news organizations increasingly were being run by executives trying to squeeze out more money for shareholders by running the companies in more efficient ways. When I started at the *Times*, editors mocked the idea of budgets for newsrooms. How could you plan your spending when you didn't know what the news would be? What if a war broke out that required costly coverage? Jour-nalists themselves largely decided how to spend money, which is why foreign correspondents flew everywhere business class and turned in expense statements substantially greater than their salaries. When I was Hong Kong bureau chief, I earned less than $100,000 a year but my expenses exceeded $200,000. (Of course, $100,000 then is worth more than $260,000 in today's dollars.)

Reining in expenses became more important after the mid-2000s, when the Internet brought fundamental challenges to the news busi-ness model. Classified advertising, a major revenue source for news-papers, collapsed first, and then other advertising began to drift to

Google and Facebook. Print circulation started to decline as well, while online news sites like Buzzfeed were often more adept at reeling in young people. News organizations abruptly realized that they might not have a future, and they frantically cut costs. The *Times* closed its in-house medical clinic, farmed out its cafeteria to contractors and ultimately ended the system of copy editing that was a last line of defense against misspellings and errors. Scrutiny grew on foreign correspondents: Did the Tokyo bureau chief really need to live in a $12,000-a-month apartment? The answer was no, and this cost-cutting made economic sense and to some degree brought news management in line with other kinds of companies. It also meant that the glory days of the foreign correspondent—traveling and spending money with no adult supervision—were soon history.

UPON RETURNING to the United States, Sheryl and I found our initial entertainment walking through large supermarkets. "Look at this, Sheryl," I'd say excitedly. "Eight kinds of peanut butter." But she'd be impossible to pull away from, say, the bakery section. "There are more varieties of bread in this single store than in all of Asia," she'd say breathlessly. "And look at the muffins." The consumer choices some Americans enjoy can be intoxicating when you've been away for many years.

We moved to Yamhill to write a book about Asia. We had earlier added a wing to the farmhouse for ourselves and the children, and it was refreshing to spend time with my parents and my old friends after being away so long. I saw more and more of both my parents in myself: their social justice concerns, their passion for the farm and their love for dogs. I wasn't a hunter like my dad—he would disappear into the mountains to hunt elk even in his late eighties—but I channeled that enthusiasm for the outdoors into backpacking. Sheryl still wasn't getting her vacations in Tuscan vineyards: Instead, she and I took our first family backpacking trip up Eagle Creek Trail, a beautiful path that passed a series of waterfalls, when Caroline was not yet two years old. I carried Caroline, but five-year-old Geoffrey hiked all thirteen miles up the first day and all thirteen down the next day. He and Caroline shared a sleeping bag and we all slept in the open and counted shooting stars until we fell asleep.

Backpacking with the kids on Oregon's Eagle Creek Trail.

With Sheryl and my parents in front of the farmhouse. *Photo by Gerry Lewin.*

Sheryl and I began taking the kids on longer trips into the wilderness. It was also convenient parenting: During their elementary school years, Gregory and Geoffrey were often at each other's throats while on car rides, but backpacking left them too exhausted to feud. We hiked most of the Pacific Crest Trail in Oregon with them and began taking Caroline along as well. The trail seemed a way for the kids to test themselves and find maturity.

My dad's passion for scholarship was also familiar. He was always reading and writing, in one language or another. On his desk he had a quote from Petrarch in 1361: "By night and by day I read and write, finding relief in alternating my work so that one labor serves as repose and solace for another. . . . My labor is certain; the results uncertain." Hmm, I thought, that sounds kind of like me.

JOE LELYVELD THREW ME into the presidential campaign of 2000 to get political experience in the United States. Al Gore was the presumptive Democratic nominee, and on the Republican side George W. Bush was duking it out with John McCain. I covered all three, and after years of enjoying the freedom of a foreign correspondent, a political campaign resembled incarceration. I'd stay at the same hotel as the candidate, then board a press bus and follow along listening to the candidate make the same speech several times a day. We reporters would wait in the back, perking up during the questions and answers, waiting to pounce if the candidate misspoke.

This descended into stenography and reflected a gotcha culture that I found unhealthy and not particularly illuminating, yet it was difficult to do deeper reporting. Every time I thought about escaping for a morning, I reminded myself of the legend of the reporter assigned to cover President John Kennedy in Dallas on November 22, 1963, who did other reporting instead and missed the assassination. That tale is probably apocryphal, but it frightened me and other reporters into dutifully staying on the campaign bus.

I had been away from the newsroom for fifteen years, and in the meantime new technologies had rippled through journalism, and the *Times* had become more editor-driven. Campaign reporters like me all had mobile phones and pagers, and after each major speech by a candidate we would hurriedly write our stories on our laptops and then transmit them to New York. I felt chained to whichever candidate I was covering that week.

The *Times* had an insatiable appetite for coverage of each major candidate, so editors wanted articles even if nothing happened. The candidates knew that, so they would try to manipulate us by creating "news" for each cycle: an endorsement, a policy proposal, a speech, a new line of attack, a denunciation of someone. These usually didn't offer anything substantial for voters, but we reporters resigned ourselves to covering them rather than being left out. I did not feel I was playing an essential role in a robust American democracy.

I particularly felt like the generic *New York Times* reporter one day when I finished a week with George W. Bush and ended up in a town in South Carolina; I forget which one, for campaign stops blur. It was past 10 p.m. on a Friday night when the campaign press bus unloaded us at a Hampton Inn where we were all staying, and in the lobby we lined up to pick up our room keys from a campaign worker.

"New York Times," I told the woman, and she handed me the key to my room. I rolled my carry-on bag to the hotel room, looking forward to flying back to New York the next day to be with family. I opened the hotel room door and walked in and fumbled for the light and—

"Ahhhhh!" a woman screamed. "Who's that? Get out!"

"I'm sorry," I said, stepping back. "They gave me this room and said it was mine."

"Nick?"

It was Alison Mitchell, a colleague, who was taking over from me in the morning. She had flown in earlier that day, so of course the campaign had given her the *Times* room. We were widgets.

The most interesting candidate to cover in 2000 was John McCain, for he was (along with Bill Clinton) among the most complicated, admirable and occasionally maddening politicians in my lifetime, and he was at his best in the 2000 campaign. McCain traveled in a bus called the Straight Talk Express, in which he was constantly talking to reporters on the record. He wouldn't shut up, in fact. McCain liked reporters, and we mostly liked him. He was funny, charming and outrageous, and he teased reporters and everyone else nonstop.

"I enjoy it," he said of his time with reporters. "I apologize for enjoying being around a group of Communists and Trotskyites."

It was also obvious that McCain had a strong moral compass, even if he sometimes felt forced by politics to ignore it. In January 2000, he had called the Confederate flag a "symbol of racism and slavery," but he backed away from that as he approached the must-win primary in South Carolina, where the flag flew over the statehouse. After the South Carolina primary, McCain gave a speech acknowledging that he had dissembled for political reasons.

"I feared that if I answered honestly, I could not win the South Carolina primary," McCain said. "So I chose to compromise my principles. I broke my promise to always tell the truth."

That staggered me—a candidate speaking honestly and apologizing for demagoguery. McCain showed similar qualities eight years later when he was running as the Republican nominee against Barack Obama. One of the finest moments in American politics in my lifetime came in August 2008 when McCain held a campaign rally at a high school in Lakeville, Minnesota.

McCain's appearance in Lakeville came at a tense time in the 2008 presidential campaign when it seemed the election could go either way. Republican suspicions of Obama were widespread, with many believing he had been born abroad and was not eligible to become president. Some subscribed to fantastical conspiracy theories such as that Obama was a Muslim planning to impose Islamic sharia law on the United States. A few conservative commentators like Glenn Beck wondered aloud whether Obama was the Antichrist. McCain's running mate, Sarah Palin, raised ugly doubts about Obama at rallies where people shouted that Obama was a "terrorist" and cried "Off with his head!" That grotesque fear of Obama probably helped McCain politically, and it was evident in the questions voters in Lakeville asked of him. A middle-aged man who said his wife was pregnant took the microphone and expressed his anxiety about bringing up a child in an America led by Obama.

"Frankly, we're scared," the man told McCain. "We're scared of an Obama presidency."

McCain took the microphone and responded as seriously as I've ever seen him.

"First of all, I want to be president of the United States," he said. "And obviously I do not want Obama to be. But I have to tell you, I have to tell you, he is a decent person, and a person that you don't have to be scared of as president of the United States."

The McCain crowd booed McCain. An elderly woman named Gayle Quinnell took the microphone.

"I can't trust Obama," she said. "I have read about him and he's . . . he's an Arab."

McCain stopped her, took the microphone and shook his head.

"No, ma'am," McCain said. "He's a decent family man, citizen, that I just happen to have disagreements with on fundamental issues. And that's what this campaign is all about."

"I will fight, but we will be respectful," McCain told his supporters, adding: "I admire Senator Obama." At this, the crowd booed more loudly.

McCain's rebuke of his followers was a high-water mark in American politics.

I took time off to investigate McCain's past. His heroism was well known: In 1967, McCain had been shot down over North Vietnam and endured more than five years of torture and brutal mistreatment. When North Vietnamese officials realized that McCain was the son of a top navy admiral, they offered to release him early—but he refused to go home unless his fellow POWs were released as well. What wasn't as well-known was how McCain could fall infuriatingly short of his own standards, and I wrote about that, too. His wife, Carol, had been a tall, slender model, and she had raised their three children while he was a prisoner in Vietnam. But she nearly died in a terrible car crash in that period, surgery left her four inches shorter and medications led her to put on a good deal of weight. After his return to America, McCain, now a handsome war hero, spotted a twenty-five-year-old blonde at a reception.

"John and I were talking, and then somebody tapped me on the shoulder and I turned around and exchanged a few words," Albert Lakeland, then a Senate staff member, told me. "When I turned around, John was gone. I looked around, and he was making a beeline for this very attractive blond woman. He spent the whole party talking to her, and he kept avoiding me when I approached." After the reception, McCain took the young woman, Cindy Hensley, to dinner, and courted her aggressively. Soon he told Carol that he wanted a divorce. She was in shock but acquiesced; their kids were less forgiving, and none of them attended the wedding with Cindy.

"I was certainly disappointed and mad at Dad," his son Andy told me, adding that it took almost four years for his anger to dissipate. But it was impossible to stay angry at John McCain, because he was so funny, charming and penitent. McCain was also lucky that Carol continued to adore her ex-husband and donated to his campaigns. "I'm crazy about John McCain and I love him to pieces," she told me, and she refused to say a word against him.

John McCain then used his new wife's base—Arizona—and her family money to mount a political campaign that leveraged his celebrity as a POW. Once in Congress, he was tireless, traveling constantly around the world and developing expertise and influence on security issues. He was early to recognize the threat from Vladimir Putin of Russia, and he was a powerful force for improving treatment of veterans in America. I disagreed with McCain on many issues and voted for Obama over him in 2008, but I never doubted that McCain was one of the greatest political figures of my lifetime.

I also spent time in that 2000 campaign on *Air Force Two* with Al Gore, who was less effervescent than McCain but still a substantial and impressive figure. Gore cared deeply about the environment and once advised my son Gregory to consider civil disobedience protests as a tool to fight climate change. Gore was also surprisingly talented at balancing a stick on his nose.

But he was still a big letdown after a president with the political and intellectual skills of Bill Clinton. When Clinton spoke to you at an event, he always pretended you had his full attention. Clinton was also exceptionally smart and analytical, though he camouflaged it with his Arkansas twang and folksy aphorisms like "If you see a turtle on a fencepost, it had help getting there."

As for Bush, he was not the dummy of liberal caricatures, and he was far more than the entitled rich heir that many Democrats perceived. In the primaries, I'd watch him talk with real feeling to affluent white audiences about the need to improve educational opportunities for Black and brown kids (as Texas governor, he had focused on raising education standards and done a good job at that). Bush would also refer in campaign speeches to young single moms as having the "hardest job in the world"; his audiences would applaud but look a bit mystified.

Bush and I formed a brief rapport by talking about China. Bush told me about visiting China in 1975, when his father was the top American diplomat there, and he mentioned one of his frustrations then as a single young man. "You just couldn't meet Chinese girls," he told me, adding that he'd tried unsuccessfully to find the bar scene in Beijing and Shanghai.*

Beyond China, though, Bush was singularly uninterested in chatting about ideas with a *Times* writer, and he turned out to have a chip on his shoulder about "elites," a class that turned out to include me but not to include him. I sat down with Bush for a series of biographical pieces about him that I was writing, and I quickly realized that we were at cross-purposes. I saw myself as an Oregon farm kid interviewing a wealthy Yale- and Harvard-educated governor and scion of one of America's leading families. And he saw himself as a hardworking guy from Midland, Texas, who was being picked on by a snotty Harvard-educated elitist from the *Times*.

One of his answers still troubles me. In probing his views of religion, I once asked him whether he believed in evolution. He looked at me with some amusement, as if to say *I see your trap*. He was a product of Andover, Yale and Harvard—and he said, "I think the jury's still out." My take was not so much that Bush himself didn't believe in evolution, but rather that he wasn't much interested in evolution one way or the other. And he wanted to get votes from fellow evangelical Christians.

I spent months interviewing Bush's old friends and girlfriends and colleagues for my series about Bush, and in retrospect that campaign of 2000 was the last one in which mainstream journalists still functioned as gatekeepers to determine what rose to the national agenda. There were all kinds of rumors that I heard in my reporting about Bush, but because I couldn't confirm them I didn't report them and neither did other journalists. For example, there was a persistent rumor that Bush had fathered an illegitimate child, but the mother wouldn't discuss paternity and all we knew was that the child looked like Bush. I have

---

* I was amused that an American could think of trying to pick up Chinese girls in the middle of the Cultural Revolution, and I mentioned this to our friend Zhang Hanzhi, who at the time of Bush's visit in 1975 had been a top Chinese Foreign Ministry official and the wife of the foreign minister. Zhang told me that the Chinese security authorities had noticed Bush's interest as well. She recounted that officials had tried to set a "honey trap" to film George W. Bush in bed with a local woman and then blackmail him into spying for China. While George W. Bush was simply a business school student then, the Chinese thought he might be able to access some of his father's documents. The honey trap did not succeed, Bush soon returned to the United States, and his father moved on to become CIA director, vice president and president. There was a long pause in my conversation with Zhang as we tried to imagine what might have happened if the honey trap had succeeded. I don't believe that President Bush is aware that the Chinese tried to trap him.

no idea if it was true, and I generally think that politicians should be allowed a measure of privacy about family life. I'm not sure that evidence that Bush had fathered an illegitimate child would have revealed anything significant about Bush's character (unless he had refused to pay child support, or had urged the mother to get an abortion even as he opposed abortion rights for others). In any case, none of us in the mainstream journalism world were able to confirm it or report it, Al Gore didn't raise it, and Twitter and Facebook weren't around to circulate rumors. So almost no voters heard about the allegation—and that was the proper outcome.

Just four years later, some people on the far right succeeded in getting a great deal of attention for false allegations aiming to discredit the Vietnam War record of John Kerry, the Democratic nominee for president. The critics claimed that Kerry had not earned his medals for his command of a Swift Boat during the war, and they vilified almost every aspect of his service. That led to a new verb, "swift-boating," to describe a host of lies used to try to discredit a politician. Veterans who served on the Swift Boat that Kerry commanded told me that the allegations were unequivocally false, and news organizations would not have published them without substantiating evidence. But by 2004, it was possible to do an end run around us, and then newspapers covered the resulting controversy in ways that spread the lies further.

Four years after that, in 2008, when Barack Obama ran for president, voters heard widespread lies that he had been born in Kenya. Partly that was because of the increasing irresponsibility of Fox News, but more broadly it was because mainstream news organizations were losing their gatekeeper function and could no longer keep preposterous allegations off the national agenda.

I was proud of my series about Bush in 2000, and Lelyveld nominated it for a Pulitzer. The conceit of the series was that biography helps us understand what kind of president a candidate would become. If so, I missed the mark. My reporting led me to believe that Bush would become the kind of president he was from his inauguration until the 9/11 attacks—a center-right president with disdain for the establishment, some instincts about education (raise standards) and taxes (cut them in hopes of boosting growth), but without a focus on foreign affairs. Then along came 9/11 and he became determined to invade not just Afghanistan but also Iraq, in ways that defined his presidency and the country. The Iraq war was a catastrophe that my series would not have predicted, and neither would it have foreseen Bush's pathbreaking program to fight AIDS, which has saved 25 million lives so far and is one of the best single policies of any recent president.

I got President Bush wrong, and I think in part that's because the 9/11 attacks changed him. He kept hearing intelligence briefings with worst-case scenarios—a month after 9/11, for example, I'm told that he was briefed in the Oval Office that terrorists had nuclear weapons in New York City and were ready to set them off. That turned out to be untrue, but officials were very scared.

Fear of follow-up attacks and a determination to prevent them became an obsession. Bush didn't know security policy and Dick Cheney did, so Bush let Vice President Cheney mold his foreign policy for several years to come. Cheney historically had been a creature of the establishment, but he too had become unhinged, as I saw it, by all the intelligence warnings. My friend Brent Scowcroft, who had been national security advisor to the first President Bush, bluntly said of Cheney: "I've known him for thirty years. But Dick Cheney, I don't know any more."

It was a tragedy that Bush didn't rely more on his father, who had a deep and nuanced understanding of foreign policy and was a genuinely good man, but in his first term Bush instead turned to his vice president, with disastrous results.

As I covered Bush and his drive for war in Iraq, I lost confidence not only in my own journalistic powers and in the usefulness of biography as a tool to judge the future. Covering politics also made me more suspicious of political coverage more generally.

The upside of being a political reporter is that everybody pays attention to what you do. The downside is that it is sometimes stenography, and that's something good reporters always try to escape by offering their own more creative takes. The problem is that those creative takes are regularly wrong. Sometimes they suffer from perennial faults like bothsidesism or false evenhandedness. Other times, they further a narrative that is intriguing but not quite right.

One of the great land mines of all kinds of reporting is the narrative. Our brains need patterns to process data about the world and make sense of it, so that's how reporters cover the world—but when those narratives are flawed, we mislead the public.

When Gerald Ford was president, a narrative started that he was a klutz. This was absurd, for Ford had been a star football player on consecutive national championship teams at the University of Michigan. Indeed, Michigan retired his No. 48 jersey. Later, Ford was a football and boxing coach at Yale and an athletic director in the navy. In the White House, he swam daily and played a good game of tennis. But he once slipped and fell in the rain while climbing the metal stairs to board *Air Force One*, and *Saturday Night Live* poked fun at this. That nurtured a perception that Ford was clumsy, and from then on, any stumble by Ford or tumble when he went skiing made the television news—and when the cameras follow you every moment, it's inevitable that you will occasionally stumble. Somehow the media turned an unusually athletic president into a klutz.

The narrative about Jimmy Carter as a hapless wimp was likewise unfair and wrong. One day when Carter was fishing from a boat in a pond, a rabbit swam frantically for his boat. Carter fended off the rabbit with an oar and apparently didn't think more about it. A few months later, Carter's press secretary happened to mention the incident, and the result was a deluge of articles about a "killer rabbit" or "wet bunny" intimidating an American president. It was comical, and it unfairly became a metaphor for Carter's presidency, using a frightened rabbit to cement the notion of a lightweight president overwhelmed by whatever came along. Carter was much better than his reputation, for he resolved tough issues like ownership of the Panama Canal, established diplomatic relations with China, negotiated the Camp David peace accord between Israel and Egypt, made human rights a thread in American foreign policy and endorsed renewable energy (installing thirty-two solar panels on the White House roof; Ronald Reagan removed them). Carter was also one of very few American presidents who managed an administration without waging war somewhere in the world.

George H. W. Bush faced his own "wimp factor" headlines, ridiculous for a war hero who had been shot down over the Pacific and then led a coalition in the Gulf War. Then during the 2000 campaign, there was the false narrative that George W. Bush was a dummy, and likewise the false narrative that Al Gore routinely dissembled and exaggerated.

Gore did not exaggerate more than any other politician, but all politicians periodically make claims that stretch the truth. He was mocked for claiming to have invented the Internet, although he had supported its development. And once the narrative of a serial exaggerator was started it was easy for reporters to polish off a day's story about Al Gore's latest "whopper." It was a little like high school all over again, and it's easy for good people in the media world to fall in love with their own narrative and snark. In the exceedingly tight election of 2000, I thought we journalists collectively were sucked into a juvenile role of skewed narrative framing that may have changed the outcome of the presidential election and damaged the country.

24

I Become an Editor

I'd like you to become weekend editor," Joe Lelyveld told me. "You'd be in charge of the Sunday *Times* and help plan the Monday paper. And I'd like you to help us think more broadly about our weekend editions and how we can make them better. You'd also be part of the masthead and help guide the paper as a whole."

I think Joe was worried that I might say no to any editing position, since I had recently declined an invitation to be deputy foreign editor. I loved writing, and I had balked at leaving reporting to sit at a desk and implement someone else's vision of international coverage. This time, Joe was making an offer too good to turn down.

"And I know you have three small kids," he added. "So if you get articles in shape for the Monday paper, you won't have to work Sundays, just Saturdays."

"I'm in," I told him immediately. "I'll miss reporting, but I'd love to take that on."

Joe was nearing the end of a brilliant tenure as executive editor, and he wanted to position some of his mentees in senior positions. He hoped Bill Keller, his managing editor, would succeed him, and he also wanted to line up a potential next generation after Bill while he still had time. Joe and I were close and had followed a similar trajectory—growing up in the middle of nowhere, making Phi Beta Kappa at Harvard, joining the *Times* as young reporters and then serving as foreign correspondents in Hong Kong and elsewhere. Joe had been weekend editor before taking over as managing editor, and he saw it as a key role in the paper. He and I were both reporters at heart, and he was forever suspicious of all editing except his own; he saw in me a kindred spirit. Once when he was weekend editor, he had posted on the wall a printout of a story as I had filed it and beside it the edited version, with a scrawled notation that the editing had made it worse. We reporters loved him for that.

Joe had considered naming me metro editor but decided, correctly, that I didn't know New York City well enough to make that work. "We thought of you because Abe Rosenthal came back from abroad and was a brilliant metro editor," Joe told me. "But Abe knew New York like the palm of his hand. It wouldn't have been fair to put you in that position." By making me weekend editor, Joe found an alternative path to pry me from reporting and usher me into the ranks of senior editors. There was a pay bump with the masthead job and a significant boost in other benefits: bonus, executive health care, free membership in a health club, and 15,500 stock options a year. Alas, the options were issued at the top of the market, so I never made a penny on them.

I missed writing, but I came to love editing and managed to spend much of my time working with reporters and editors on weekend stories. After years spent manipulating editors, I now had to learn to manipulate reporters.

Editor management is a key skill set for any reporter, and it generally mirrors the way cats control their owners: You want them to feed you and care for you and clean up your messes, but they should never presume to give you instructions. Reporters have long been skeptical of editors, reflecting H. L. Mencken's sour dismissal of editors as "literary castrati who never leave the office."

The suspicion of editing among *Times* reporters was captured in a satirical guide to editors that a *Times* reporter, Ralph Blumenthal, wrote in the 1990s after he was lamenting with a colleague, Peter Kaufman, about what editors sometimes do to reporters. "I went back to my desk and knocked this out in ten minutes, and sent it to Peter," Blumenthal told me. "And then he shared it, and it went around the world." It became an instant classic at the paper, forwarded to me in Asia and to every corner of the *Times* empire. It advised staff on how to edit:

1. Your lead here. Write what you think you know about the subject, what you feel happened, what your gut tells you.
2. Move reporter's second graf down to bottom where it can be bitten off in the composing room.
3. Fashion new second graf from material deep down in story, preferably with a mysterious second reference to someone not introduced yet.
4. For a quote, get the reporter to put into someone's mouth what you believe or suspect happened.
5. Write and complete the sentence: At stake is . . . Something must be at stake here. Or unfolding against a backdrop of something. Be sweeping—use the word "sweeping" if necessary. Take a step back. What's really happening here? Even if it isn't. *Especially* if it isn't.
6. Move a lot of stuff around.
7. Order up a mountain of new reporting. *Could* something unlikely possibly happen? Why? Why not? Who hasn't commented on this?
8. Now cut this all for space.
9. Cut the kicker [the last paragraph]. If the reporter left it for the end it couldn't be important.
10. Sked the story.
11. Hold the story.

Over my sixteen years at the *Times*, editor management had become increasingly important. When I first joined the paper, reporters were largely on their own, simply filing when they finished a story and then answering a few questions. But editors did the hiring and often felt that the highest priority addition was another editor rather than a reporter. So while copy editors were pushed out, the ratio of first-line editors to reporters (or to columnists) multiplied, and editors now increasingly do fact-checking and get involved in story planning and execution. This means that it is less crucial that a reporter be a good writer, since editors can always do some rewriting. Hence an influx of strong reporters who aren't necessarily great writers, requiring even more editors. The editors start asking for story memos, so they can track their reporters, and then it becomes necessary to hire more editors to read all those memos. And all these editors now require meetings to coordinate their work, and invariably in these meetings they discuss story ideas. Slowly, subtly, story generation has shifted in part from the correspondent or beat reporter to the editing ranks.

Editors assume that whatever is of interest to them will be of similar interest to all their readers. If a top editor develops gum disease, then expect a front-page story about periodontal ailments. If an editor's dog is diagnosed with cancer, then prepare for a series about the scandalous cost of veterinary care. Sure enough, when I was weekend editor, I commissioned a page one story about backpacking.

These may be perfectly fine story proposals, but the risk is that if a top editor offers a dumb idea based on some personal encounter, then a sycophant will pop up with "Oh, that happened to my neighbor, too!" And in journalism, beware: The plural of anecdote is trend.

This "trend story" will then be transmitted a couple of levels down to a correspondent or beat reporter, gaining enthusiasm and misinformation as it travels, and it'll be left to the reporter to excavate the mess and find a path out. I saw this when I was an editor and asked innocent questions about a metro story I wanted to run for the front page. I was excited about the story, and my questions simply reflected things I was wondering about. But they morphed into "Kristof wants these points addressed high up," even though, as it happened, they didn't make sense to address. I had discovered what my colleague Jon Landman called the "megaphone effect"—it's very difficult for a senior editor to ask a question without it being transmitted as a bellow to change the story.

So the savvy reporter at the receiving end engages in jujitsu, leveraging the high-level enthusiasm for the general topic by reinterpreting the story suggestion into something that is actually real and relevant. The hope is that by the time the story is written, the editors will have forgotten the specific suggestion and will recognize a good story when they see it. In fairness, good editors have themselves mostly been reporters and believe in such jujitsu.

The most aggravating experience for a correspondent is to write a pathbreaking story on some subject, then be followed by *The Washington Post* playing catch-up a couple of weeks later, and then get a note saying "WashPost is reporting xxxx. Looks like a good story. Can you match?"

Some correspondents responded to such inquiries with rage: *Don't you read our paper as well as theirs? I had that story three weeks ago, and the* Post *is just catching up to us. You really want me to match them matching us?* Unfortunately, reporters don't have much credibility in assessing the value of a story by a competitor. Even if a rival publishes a scoop that is Pulitzer-worthy, the tendency is to scoff: *Nothing really new there, but meanwhile you've been sitting on my feature for two weeks. How about running that?*

Reporters also lose credibility because of their tendency to write too long and then howl when their copy is cut to fit space. Invariably, reporters file x words, where x is a whole number approximately four hundred words greater than the number allotted. They then insist that the top can't be cut because that's what the story is about, the middle can't be cut because it's essential background, and the end can't be cut because anyone with half a brain can see that the kicker is what makes the story sing.

My shift to manipulating reporters involved flattery and cajoling them to undertake big projects that would be ready for the Sunday paper—and then, when unexpected big news came along on Saturday to occupy the front page, calling them up apologetically and explaining that I'd have to hold the story for a week, and could they please update it next week. Oh, and please cut it by six hundred words. My friend Len Apcar, a fellow Armenian American who worked on the international desk, told me that his wife had given him a self-help book to read: *How to Talk So Kids Will Listen and Listen So Kids Will Talk*. The book is essentially about manipulating grumpy kids into having real conversations, and the idea was that it would help Len communicate with their two teenage kids.

"It didn't help much with my kids," Len told me. "But it was very helpful in talking to reporters."

I had strong opinions about the Sunday paper, which I thought had become complacent and tired, and it was exhilarating to try to modernize the *Times*. The bane of page one story selection then was lack of data. "Everyone's going to read this," a department head would say, but there was no way of knowing then what people actually did read in the print paper. Then as the Internet unfolded over the last couple of decades, the bane of story selection has become too much data: Now we know just how much better a story about Meghan Markle will do than one about famine in Somalia, so it becomes more difficult to argue for worthy, important stories that readers are less interested in. It becomes less likely that we take risks with story selection.

I argued that we could get data and resist being corrupted by it—indeed, we could use the information to figure out how to pitch important stories more effectively to readers—but that takes great willpower, and I may have been naïve. As time has unfolded and newspapers have gone digital and obtained better data, it has become apparent that news organizations have indeed been corrupted: Just as food companies get more excited about candy bars than spinach, media companies find compelling reasons to give readers more articles and videos about Kim Kardashian.

I began laying out the Sunday page one in a more horizontal format, with three- and four-column headlines, while seeking trend stories, investigative pieces or analyses that I thought people would read and that would have impact. I forged an alliance with Glenn Kramon, the superb business editor, who understood what I was looking for and came up with important stories about young consumers, about car safety, about women exceeding men in law schools. And I used visuals more than ever before, sometimes employing photos rather than an article to tell a story. I relied less on Washington stories, on the stenography about what the president had said the previous day, and on pieces about horse-race politics. I argued that we were not adequately covering myriad other forces shaping the country, such as religion, family structure, race and ethnicity, education and economics. James Fallows, the journalist and press critic, describes the challenge as "the mainstream press obsession with *politics* over anything else. ('Martians land on Earth. Here's what it means for the midterms.')"

The Washington bureau became mutinous—as it periodically did, for there was a long history of tension in the *Times*'s between New York and Washington. I flew to Washington to have a brown-bag lunch with reporters there and try to explain my vision, but Washington correspondents were experienced at dealing with sweet-talking visitors, and tensions were soothed only modestly.

The culture of the *Times* was cautious, partly because everyone was understandably proud of producing an extraordinary newspaper. Editors didn't want to tamper with success, but the caution discouraged and drove away some great stylists: David Halberstam, Bill Geist, Molly Ivins and many more. Molly epitomized a writer with voice, and she started off awkwardly at the paper back in the Abe Rosenthal era when she walked the newsroom barefoot along with her dog, whose name was Shit. She was instructed to leave Shit at home.

Molly once wrote about a man with "a beer gut that belongs in the Smithsonian," and it was edited into "a man with a protuberant abdomen." She wrote about someone who squawked "like a $2 fiddle," and it was changed to "like an inexpensive musical instrument." Her career at the *Times* ended when she wrote a feature about a chicken-plucking party in New Mexico and described it in her original draft as, depending on which version you hear, either a "gang pluck" or a "cluster pluck."

"They hired me because I could write, and then they wouldn't let me do it," she protested to the *Chicago Tribune*.

By the time I became an editor in 2000, there was increasing recognition that voice wasn't so bad, and reporters were given more license to write with humor and tell stories. I favored more of that. The enforcer of standards at the *Times* was Al Siegal, a legendary editor of editors, and Joe Lelyveld put my desk right next to his. Perhaps the idea was that the guardian of the paper's values could tutor and restrain a young revolutionary like me. Al distributed postmortems that scolded people for grammatical mistakes and infelicitous wording.

"As if written by pedants from Mars," he scrawled indignantly about one headline. About another, he wrote: "If this was intentional, it's beneath contempt. If it was unintentional, it rises to contempt."

Yet Al, too, knew that the paper needed to modernize, and he and I shared a view that this could be done in a way that didn't yield to sensationalism but preserved the focus on the most important stories. He also was both amused by and respectful of my efforts to actually draw up the Sunday front page, working out each headline size and font, a task that previously had been left to news editors. Despite his reputation as a curmudgeon, Al was an unsung pioneer in some ways: He mentored journalists of color and helped the *Times* bring in announcements of same-sex unions on the weddings page (this was long before same-sex marriages were permitted). I regarded Al as a crucial ally to cultivate, both because of the credibility he enjoyed within the paper as an institutionalist and because he knew the system well enough to understand how to change it.

Every Friday evening I would meet with Lelyveld and his second in command, Bill Keller, to outline what I planned for the Sunday front page. Sometimes they agreed with my choices, and sometimes they didn't, but Lelyveld mostly let me run the Sunday paper as I saw fit. He wanted change and was willing to let me experiment, even if he sometimes wondered about my choices.

Then Joe retired and Arthur Sulzberger Jr. chose as the new executive editor not Bill Keller but Howell Raines, the editorial page editor. Keller was probably the better journalist, but he had never gone out of his way to charm the Sulzbergers and had occasionally dissed them. In contrast, Howell courted the Sulzberger clan and argued, rightly, that the paper was complacent and needed to be shaken up.

A stocky fly fisherman and natural storyteller, Howell proved both a brilliant editor and a catastrophic one. A student of politics and former Washington hand, Howell hailed from Alabama and retained a southern accent that strengthened whenever he spoke of his home state. I identified with that, and we both thought that the *Times* needed to do a better job covering mainstream America outside New York: college football, auto racing, rural America, life in the South and West, religious faith. Howell took over the job as top editor in September 2001.

On the morning of September 11, 2001, I was preparing to fly to Louisville, Kentucky, to give a speech. A car service picked me up to take me to LaGuardia Airport, and the driver mentioned a bit of news. "A small plane just hit the World Trade Center," he said. "Don't know if anyone was hurt."

"Keep the radio news on as we drive," I suggested. "I'm curious what happened."

Soon the news coverage suggested that the plane wasn't a small one after all. And by the time we reached the Whitestone Bridge and could see lower Manhattan, a large plane had hit the second tower. A huge cloud of smoke was rising from the towers, and it was obvious that this was not a random accident. We turned around and I returned home— and for me and so many others, life was changed. Along with the entire *Times* staff, I threw myself into covering the catastrophe.

Howell's news instincts initially seemed well placed for 9/11. He wanted a quicker pulse of activity, faster responses to news and more photos—all of which I agreed with—and the *Times*'s coverage over the next month was masterful. In fairness, much of the credit belonged to others, including Jon Landman, the metro editor, and Joe Lelyveld, who had hired the staff that made Howell look good.

For all his achievements, Howell erred in pushing the staff too hard and pushing too hard for his own narratives, sometimes at the expense of the truth. Reporters and editors were working fourteen-hour days, and instead of sending herograms he scolded them for missing stories—or topics that he believed, rightly or wrongly, were stories. He perceived himself as a strong leader, but this periodically crossed into bullying autocracy.

"I don't understand what you're doing," he told an editor one evening, ordering her to crack down on reporters and get them out in the field filing stories. Then he went home—and the editor, at 10 p.m. that night, was still calling reporters and trying to follow Howell's guidance without triggering an open rebellion.

"I've just about had it," she told me between calls. She was near tears and seemed to be approaching a nervous breakdown.

Several national correspondents quit or were pushed out and were quickly snapped up by the *Los Angeles Times.* Howell didn't recognize that our most important assets walked out the door each evening and needed to be nurtured and cultivated; instead, he systematically antagonized them. Howell also exacerbated the morale crisis by playing favorites even more than usual. Editors always had reporters who got better assignments and were more likely to vault onto the front page; I had benefited from this favoritism. But Howell took this further than ever, installing one of his acolytes, Pat Tyler, as an unofficial lord of the Washington bureau, while undermining the Washington bureau chief, Jill Abramson.

Howell turned another of his stars, Rick Bragg, a beautiful writer and storyteller also from the South, into a fixture on page one. Eager for stories that people talked about, Howell pushed too hard for pieces that were provocative but short on sourcing. One result was flawed reporting by Judy Miller, a star reporter, about Iraq and weapons of mass destruction, supporting those who wanted to go to war with Iraq. Judy was smart, well sourced and experienced, but she needed an editor holding her back, not pushing her to connect dots. It didn't help that Howell didn't know much about foreign affairs and didn't appreciate his limitations. I had repeatedly seen how Joe Lelyveld had used the editing process to ask hard questions of reporters and rein them in (as he had done with me after my Canton migrants story). Now I saw how Howell did the opposite, using the editing process so stories leaned even farther beyond their skis.

In some ways, Howell was an echo of Abe Rosenthal, yet without people around to restrain him. To be managing editor, Howell chose Gerald Boyd, a pathbreaking journalist who grew up poor in St. Louis and enjoyed a rapid rise, and their enforcer was often Andy Rosenthal, Abe's son, prodigiously talented but lacking a warm bedside manner. While Abe had had people around him like Seymour Topping and Arthur Gelb to soothe the newsroom and undo the damage, Howell surrounded himself with people who empowered him more than they questioned him.

Others on the masthead did their best. Soma Golden Behr, an assistant managing editor, bravely pushed back at Howell, but he dismissed her, sometimes caustically. He made clear in masthead meetings that he didn't fully respect her. Howell had admired my work as a foreign correspondent and he knew that Arthur Sulzberger Jr. liked me, so he did listen to me and sometimes I was able to influence him on foreign coverage. But there were limits.

Still in the thrall of Rick Bragg, Howell sent Bragg to Pakistan to cover the arrival of war. Bragg had no understanding of Pakistan and wrote a series of pieces that I considered embarrassing. I would refuse to put them on the Sunday front page, Howell would order them on, I would argue, and I would be overruled. Matters came to a head when Bragg wrote a feature about Pakistanis with small heads. A group of us sat in Howell's office as I outlined the five stories I planned to put on the Sunday front page.

"What about the Bragg story?" Howell asked. "The shrunken heads."

"Yeah, it's well written," I replied cautiously. "But we have a war in Afghanistan, anthrax attacks at home, arrests and detentions of Muslims, a reorganization of airline security, and so much more. Pakistan is seething. Not sure page one needs a small-bore piece on Pakistanis with small heads."

"Everybody will read it," Howell responded icily. "It's a break from the war news."

"But there's so much going on that is far more important, don't you think? And the tone of Bragg's piece strikes me as mocking more than inquisitive."

"No, Nick, it's a great yarn," Howell continued stonily. "That is going on the front page of the Sunday paper." Later, he told someone, not unreasonably, that as long as he was executive editor of *The New York Times* he was damn well going to determine the front page of the single largest edition, Sunday's.

It was increasingly obvious to the newsroom that while Howell and I had a grudging respect for each other, we were in opposing camps. I was a leftover from Team Lelyveld and an obstacle to Howell's blitz-krieg through the newsroom.

I had known that my job might be in danger with Howell's ascension, for he had grumbled to colleagues about Lelyveld acting near the end of his tenure to choose me as weekend editor. "This is one of the most important newsroom jobs, and I should be able to choose my own person to fill it," he told another editor. So before Howell took over, I had written again to Arthur Sulzberger Jr. reminding him of my interest in an op-ed column.

25

I Begin My Column

Opinion columnists were pretty much at the pinnacle of the *Times*. Punch Sulzberger used to say that he had a half-dozen reporters who wanted to be executive editor of the paper, and a hundred who wanted to be columnists. When James Reston was forced to choose between his column and the job of executive editor, he chose the column. The *Times* traditionally had just seven columnists, each writing twice a week. The publisher selected columnists, and they reported to him.

If the columnist wrote something outrageous and refused to change it, the copy editor would call in the editorial page editor, who would remonstrate with the columnist: *That's libel! That's inappropriate! You can't write that!* But the columnist could still veto the editorial page editor, who would then call the publisher—and only the publisher could force a change. Of course, the publisher could also kill the column or fire the columnist. That had happened occasionally, as when Punch ended Sydney Schanberg's column in 1985 or, closer to home, when Arthur canceled Abe Rosenthal's column in 1999.

Abe had been suffering from dementia and memory loss, and his columns grew weaker, more emotional and sometimes embarrassing. Within the paper the name of his column, "On My Mind," was sometimes referred to as "Out of My Mind." I never said that; I admired Abe too much and owed him too much, but I wished he would retire.

Arthur's move to cancel the column was the right decision, but a wrenching one. The *Times* tried to portray it as Abe retiring, but Abe resisted and sent an anguished note to many colleagues, including Sheryl and me, saying that he had been fired from the paper he had served all his life. He later began a column for the *New York Daily News* that was shrill and forgettable, and it underscored that Arthur had been right to nudge Abe out the door.

My respect for the Sulzbergers had grown as I'd had more interaction with them. In the late 1990s, the *Times* had clashed with the authoritarian government of Singapore, where the international edition (then the *International Herald Tribune*) was printed, and the paper offered a craven apology. I thought that was a mistake that signaled weakness and would invite other autocrats to target the *Times*. So I wrote Punch a letter saying so—and then waited nervously to see if I would be reprimanded. I soon received a letter back from Punch saying that in retrospect he agreed with me. "You won't see any more of those" apologies, he wrote, and he urged me to write again if I saw something that bothered me.

Then when I was weekend editor, we planned a long article that amounted to a takedown of Linda Wachner, the CEO of Warnaco Group—and one of Punch's closest friends, whom he socialized and traveled with. The reporter, Leslie Kaufman, wrote a devastating piece:

> Mrs. Wachner also developed a reputation for demoralizing employees by publicly dressing them down for missing sales and profit goals or for simply displeasing her. Often, many employees said, the attacks were personal rather than professional, and not infrequently laced with crude references to sex, race or ethnicity. . . . The Warnaco Group, as the company is now known, has almost completely collapsed. . . . Mrs. Wachner's management style has hurt and perhaps even killed the company. . . . One former executive, raising a common theme, said, "The only people who survive at Warnaco were people who were abused children."

We edited the piece and prepared it for the Sunday paper, but I asked Joe Lelyveld, who was still in charge then, how to handle the fact that we were going to run an article that would infuriate one of Punch's best friends.

"Just show the piece to Punch," Joe advised. "Give him a heads-up. He deserves that. But he won't abuse it."

So I printed out Leslie's article and on the Friday morning before publication took it up to Punch's office. After a few pleasantries, I told him we had a tough story about Linda Wachner that we were planning to publish Sunday. With that, I handed him the printout, and I sat back as he read it slowly and carefully. I watched his face as he read it, and I thought he was both deeply pained and trying very hard not to show it. After he had finished, he handed it back to me.

"Thanks for showing me," he said graciously. He was trying mightily to remain cheerful and warm for my benefit, but he wasn't entirely succeeding. I waited half a beat for him to say something more, but that was it.

"No problem," I said with immense relief. "Have a great weekend."

In fact, I knew that Punch would have a terrible weekend, because the newspaper he owned was going after a volatile person who was his friend—or would be his friend until that article appeared. Yet he gave no sign of wanting me to change so much as a comma. In fact, Punch could have made a reasonable request to take out anonymous quotes savaging Wachner—we had a policy of not lightly allowing anonymous sources to make personal attacks—but he made no request at all. His paramount loyalty was to the institution of *The New York Times*, even when it caused him great pain. (Leslie Kaufman's piece was right on, and Wachner was fired later that year.)

That loyalty to the institution sometimes meant disloyalty to individuals and to rifts in the family. Punch had fired his cousin John Oakes as editorial page editor, and had allowed mandatory retirement to end the tenure of another cousin, Cy Sulzberger, as foreign affairs columnist. A generation later, Arthur Sulzberger Jr. had gone on a long walk with his cousin Dan Cohen, a senior *Times* executive who was also one of his closest pals, and told him that things weren't working out; Cohen stepped down. The *Times* also targeted another of Arthur's closest friends, Steve Rattner, in an investigation about kickbacks in pension fund management. Rattner denied any wrongdoing, and the reporting strained their friendship, but Arthur never interfered with the coverage. Those were all probably the right decisions, but they were excruciating for all involved.

There were other times when editors pushed people out in ways that seemed profoundly unfair. One of my friends learned that the *Times* had laid her off by reading about it in the *New York Post* on her commute to work.

Yet the paper could be utterly loyal to its people. When correspondent John Tagliabue was shot by a sniper in Timisoara, Romania, in December 1989, as the Communist regime there collapsed, the *Times* moved mountains to get him evacuated by ambulance to Belgrade. When four colleagues were kidnapped in Libya in 2011, the *Times* again made every effort to get them freed. Because members of the ruling Qaddafi family were believed to be movie buffs, I was asked to reach out to George Clooney and other film stars I knew to see if they might help. Clooney offered to help in any way, but Libya freed my colleagues a day or two later, before he could assist.

An indelible example of loyalty came when a *Times* contract photographer, João Silva, was on assignment in Afghanistan in 2010. A compact, quiet man from Portugal, João was a legend for his work across Africa as well as in Iraq and Afghanistan. I was in Kabul at the time and had dinner with João in the Kabul bureau. "We're leaving for an embed with U.S. troops in Kandahar," João told me, and he was clearly relishing a trip to the field. I wished him luck.

While with the troops in Kandahar, the military commander tried to keep João in the rear for his own protection—but João was having none of that. He explained that he needed to be at the front to get good photos. There he stepped on a land mine. There was a thunderous roar and João went flying to the ground. He retained consciousness and saw that both his legs had been shredded. He suffered massive internal injuries yet continued to shoot photos from the ground until he lost the strength to hold the camera. While awaiting a helicopter evacuation, João spoke to his wife by satellite phone, a possible goodbye.

João was rushed to a military hospital in Germany. "I'm good," he told the *Times* photography director, Michele McNally, not at all truthfully. "I'm good." He was then airlifted to Walter Reed Army Medical Center in the United States, where Michele met him as he arrived—and he asked her what had happened to the memory card in his camera (it had been rescued). The *Times* ensured that João had the best possible care as he underwent amputations of both legs and more than eighty surgeries. Afterward, when João had learned how to use prostheses, the *Times* hired him as a full-time staff photographer and assigned him to cover the White House. That made me proud. I understood the brutal side of the *Times* that fired people or laid them off, but it was good to know I was part of an institution that also showed heart.

Arthur Sulzberger Jr. was sometimes mocked as a lightweight (just as his father, Punch Sulzberger, had been a generation earlier), but that was unfair and off base. He impressed me with his efforts to modernize the paper and support a web presence. Arthur also had made the company much friendlier to women and to gay reporters, and he had pushed editors to hire more people of color. That created a demographic revolution in the reporting ranks.

Sheryl had been the first Chinese American reporter at the paper, but soon there were many Asian Americans as well as a growing number of Black and brown reporters on staff. Arthur was a relaxed and collegial presence who tried to put reporters at ease, and he also managed to read the entire newspaper more carefully than anybody I knew.

In one period when I was banned from North Korea, I devised a strategy to get a visa by using Arthur as bait. The North Koreans were very status conscious, and I said that the publisher of *The New York Times* was interested in going to North Korea before he visited South Korea—but I was part of the package deal. The North Koreans unbanned me, and Arthur and I traveled to North Korea for a week. We had no Internet access while in North Korea and hadn't been able to read the *Times*, so on the way home as we transited the Beijing airport, Arthur had the week's editions of *The New York Times* delivered to us. I watched as he went through the entire paper, page by page, day by day.

The public sometimes thought newspapers bowed to pressure from advertisers or government officials, but I repeatedly went after institutions that happened to be major advertisers, and the *Times* never winced. I went after friends of the publishers, and they never flinched. And all three publishers in my career at the *Times* stood up to presidents and cabinet officials—after listening respectfully—when necessary to preserve journalistic independence.

Arthur Sulzberger Jr. had just started a Chinese-language website for the *Times* and had high hopes for it as potentially a long-term moneymaker when in 2012 a few reporters wrote a devastating exposé of official Chinese corruption that infuriated leaders in Beijing (the article revealed that the family of China's prime minister had amassed $2.7 billion). The Chinese government retaliated by blocking access to this new website. Bloomberg News responded to similar pressure by refusing to publish articles that would antagonize Chinese leaders, but that was never a question at the *Times*. Arthur never asked whether reporters or columnists could dial back tough coverage of Chinese leaders; he was willing to sacrifice commercial interests for the sake of journalism, even when the newspaper's business model was in desperate shape.

We went out of the way to avoid even appearances of conflict. I was once set to write a *Times Magazine* cover story extolling Taiwan's emergence as a model of democracy for Asia, and then Taiwan's government bought a special advertising section in the *Times* promoting itself. I was horrified when I saw that, for I knew that now I couldn't write my article any time soon; it might be seen as a quid pro quo. I waited a year before writing my magazine piece about Taiwan.

On the staff, the tendency among journalists is to roll our eyes at our bosses, whoever they are, and there were periodically unkind things said about the Sulzberger family. But to me the real test of the family ownership came in 2009 when the *Times* suspended its dividend, which many in the family had come to rely on for income. It would have been easy for the family to simply lay off a few dozen reporters instead—as many other newspaper companies did—but the Sulzbergers bit the bullet and felt the pain themselves. That was heroic.

The Sulzbergers did make some grievous mistakes. The *Times* bought *The Boston Globe* at the top of the market, and it didn't invest in the right Internet companies that represented the future (if only we had made an early investment in Google). The *Times* purchased its own stock as it was falling, an awful investment. Publishers sometimes chose the wrong people for top positions in the newsroom, opinion section or business side. But these were honest mistakes, and they were utterly scrupulous about putting the paper and its journalism above their friends and their bank accounts.

———

MY JOURNALISTIC HERO, Anthony Lewis, had become a *Times* columnist by accident, even though he was widely regarded as one of the most brilliant people in journalism. When Tony covered the Supreme Court earlier in his career, Justice Felix Frankfurter observed: "There are not two justices of this court who have such a grasp of these cases." (Presumably Frankfurter believed that he himself was the one justice whose wisdom exceeded Tony's.) Tony was also a fast, lucid writer on deadline.

One evening, Tony hadn't filed his column by deadline so the copy editor, Linda Cohn, called his home. Tony's wife answered and said he was out at a dinner at someone else's house and provided the number. Linda reached Tony, and it turned out that there had been a mix-up in scheduling.

"I'm so sorry," Tony told Linda. "I hadn't realized I was due for a column tonight."

"That's okay," Linda said. "We'll find an op-ed and run it in the space."

"No, hang on," Tony said. "I'll come up with something. Hmm. Yes, I can file. Can you take dictation? I'm ready to go." Linda typed away as Tony dictated an eight-hundred-word column off the top of his head.

Given his brilliance, you might think that Tony got the job of columnist as the result of a search by Punch Sulzberger to choose the best person for the job. It was messier than that. In 1969, as James Reston stepped down as the top editor and handed the keys to Abe Rosenthal, Reston offered Tony the No. 2 editing job under Abe. But the job wasn't Reston's to award. An imbroglio erupted, and to soothe feelings and get Tony an off-ramp from the newsroom, Punch gave Tony a column. And now something similar happened to me.

While Howell was never rude or dismissive toward me, he was fed up with me. He didn't want a weekly battle over which stories should be on the Sunday front page. Understandably, he wanted a compliant weekend editor who would do his bidding, run Rick Bragg articles and not push back. But Howell also didn't want to oust me and see me defect to *The Washington Post* (the thought had crossed my mind). So Howell now proposed that I be made an op-ed columnist for a year to write about terrorism and the aftermath of the 9/11 attacks. I was delighted, and Howell noted to Arthur and Gail Collins that there was now appetite for more global coverage than Tom Friedman could provide and that I would be the rare columnist comfortable covering a war in a place like Afghanistan.

Everybody liked the idea, and Gail was eager to have more international expertise on the opinion pages. However, Gail said that there wasn't money in the opinion budget for another op-ed columnist—so Howell volunteered that the newsroom would continue to pay my salary, plus my expenses, while I wrote for the opinion section. He was that desperate to get rid of me.

It was agreed that I would write about terrorism and international security for a year and then return to the newsroom. Presumably Howell's thought was to move me then to some distant bureau where I would be out of his way. As for Gail, she was determined that my op-ed stint not become permanent: There was growing recognition within the paper of the need for more diverse columnists, and Gail didn't want yet another white man as a permanent columnist on her roster. There was then just one female columnist, Maureen Dowd, and one Black male columnist, Bob Herbert, along with four white men.

For my part, I was eager to escape the demoralized newsroom and cocky enough to think that I had a shot at working my way into a permanent column. It was especially poetic that the spot I would be taking had belonged to . . . Tony Lewis, who stepped down as a columnist in December 2001 as I began. I couldn't fill his shoes, but I relished the idea of wearing them.

So after seventeen years as a *Times* reporter, I escaped the third-floor newsroom, moved up to the tenth floor, where the editorial page team worked, and became an (acting) opinion columnist. Meanwhile, the newsroom—with ever fewer people willing to stand up to Howell—spiraled out of control. Eventually, Howell was ousted after a young reporter named Jayson Blair was found to have plagiarized articles. The Blair scandal was the tipping point, but the fundamental reason Howell was forced to resign was a staff revolt. Although Howell had changed the *Times* for the better—stronger visuals, a better website, a faster pulse—he had run the paper as a dictatorship and had lost the goodwill and loyalty of the staff.

A different kind of leader, one who forged a mutual respect with editors and writers, would have easily survived the Blair scandal. Instead, people turned on Howell when he was vulnerable. It was a great management lesson, one that I don't think the *Times* or other news organizations ever fully absorbed, about the need for newspapers to operate as a partnership resting on the goodwill of the staff.

As for my column, I wanted it to be based on shoe-leather reporting rather than pontificating. I didn't want to sit in New York or Washington talking to "experts" and rehashing and debating the conventional wisdom. Nor did I want to preach to the choir and repeat liberal bromides, however much I believed in them. I wanted to challenge readers and play with ideas.

One of my favorite quotations is from John Maynard Keynes: "The ideas of economists and political philosophers, both when they are right and when they are wrong, are more powerful than is commonly understood. Indeed, the world is ruled by little else. Practical men, who believe themselves to be quite exempt from any intellectual influences, are usually slaves of some defunct economist."

I was determined to hit the road internationally and talk to a broad range of people, including young people and women and others whose concerns were not sufficiently represented in our pages. It seemed to me that nearly everyone quoted in newspaper columns was a powerful man over the age of fifty who had a university education, spoke English and lived in a major city—yet such people represented a tiny fraction of humanity. After having spent much of my journalism career pushing against stenography, I wanted to offer opinion journalism that escaped the bubble and engaged with people who weren't foreign ministers or taxi drivers. So I decided to begin my column in Afghanistan, where the American-backed rebels had just captured Kabul from the Taliban.

ON A CHILLY, CLEAR DAY in November 2001, I looked down on Afghanistan through the window of my small United Nations plane. The countryside was endlessly brown with only occasional smudges of green where fields had been cultivated. As we dropped in altitude, the destruction was overwhelming: Vast neighborhoods of Kabul had been blown to smithereens in years of civil warfare. The Kabul airport was itself demolished and the runway pitted, so we dropped toward Bagram airfield an hour away. The pilot chose a corkscrew descent, spiraling steeply to avoid anti-aircraft fire from any Taliban still in the area. After my Congo crash, sudden descents made me very nervous, but now I was exhilarated as well as scared: This was the kind of on-the-ground opinion journalism I believed in.

I felt the money belts under my shirt and in my pants to make sure the stacks of hundred-dollar bills were still there. In addition to looking for column topics, I was there to resupply the *Times*'s troops. Reporters and photographers who had been following the rebels were converging on Kabul and were desperate for equipment and dollars. So I carried almost $60,000 plus three cameras and three satellite phones. It was terrifying to be lugging so much cash.

On arriving at Bagram, the United Nations and aid officials on the plane disappeared into the cars sent for them. "Sorry, old buddy, I'd like to give you a ride," one told me. "But we're a stickler for rules and can't take passengers. Too dangerous."

I made my way to the airport gate. A handful of private cars were offering rides to Kabul. Who was Taliban and who was an entrepreneur? And were any of the entrepreneurs inclined to murder a passenger for his bags? I had no idea. Should I engage in ethnic discrimination? Pashtuns were more likely to support the Taliban, so should I choose a Tajik? Was a bearded driver more likely to be Taliban? Was it offensive that I was wondering these things?

"How much to Kabul?" I asked the group of drivers assembled.

It took a while to convey that, and a while to understand that they wanted $30 for a ride.

"Thirty dollars!" I said, trying to look too impoverished to be worth robbing. "I can't afford that!" I spent the next forty-five minutes haggling with the drivers, emphasizing my poverty, until they regarded me as a charity case. Finally one driver agreed to give me a ride to Kabul for $15, and when we got to the house that the *Times* was renting he was pleased when I gave him $30. I was deeply relieved to hand over that $60,000 to Barry Bearak, the brilliant correspondent who was setting up the Kabul bureau.

"Now you can keep all this cash safe," I told Barry, and I kept pulling hundred-dollar bills out of hiding places.

"Sure," he replied, "but we haven't been able to buy a safe yet, so here's where I keep valuables." He led me to his bedroom and we stowed the wads of hundred-dollar bills in the corner of the room under his pile of dirty laundry.

I made many trips to Afghanistan during the war, and my reporting left me endlessly frustrated. The Taliban had been a disaster for the country; in one district, a woman had a 50 percent lifetime risk of dying in pregnancy or childbirth. But while the American military and aid presence allowed girls to study and sharply lowered mortality rates, the American forces often seemed to have little idea what they were doing. On one of my early trips, some entrepreneurial Afghans told me of the latest get-rich-quick scheme. They would set up a fake campsite on a hillside, with a few empty tents around a fire, and then collect a cash reward from Americans for offering intelligence about a Taliban camp there. The Americans would drop $10 million worth of bombs on the fake camp, and the Afghans would go the next day on horseback and collect the scrap metal from the bombs and sell it for a few hundred dollars.

The more I reported in Afghanistan, the more determined I became to leave the American bubble and spend time with ordinary Afghans. Many were ambivalent: They often liked the Taliban's stance against corruption and the sense that it was an authentic nationalist force, but they were offended by its brutality.

I once spent an afternoon with a group of men from Helmand Province who were thinking about joining the Taliban. One man had almost done so after an American air strike accidentally killed his wife, three sons and two daughters. On the other hand, he was also mad at the Taliban for drawing fire by attacking Americans from the village and thus endangering his family. He and others were also sickened when the Taliban beheaded seven men in his village. In the end, he decided against joining because he thought there would be more economic opportunity if he supported the government. He thought wrong: The government wasn't providing expected economic benefits, while the Taliban was recruiting men not just by telling them that they would be good Muslims fighting against invaders, but also by offering several hundred dollars a month plus free food, tea and sugar. That's why he was again inclined to fight for the Taliban.

So where did the Taliban get the money to pay its fighters? From the Americans, I learned.

A young Afghan woman named Soora Stoda told me how she despised and feared the Taliban. When she was in the seventh grade, the Taliban had raided her secret girls' school, beaten the girls and killed the teacher, who was also her aunt. With the Americans in power, Soora was able to form a company and earn a good income as a military contractor—yet she acknowledged that in practice the United States was financing the Taliban.

For example, Soora had won a $200,000 contract to transport equipment to the American forces in Kandahar. But the roads were insecure, and the Taliban seized the shipment—so Soora had to pay $150,000 to the Taliban to recover it. Routinely, she said, she must make large payoffs to the Taliban to be able to do her work for the Americans. On average, she estimated that for every $1,000 she received from the United States forces, $600 went to the Taliban. One security expert told me that of the $1 million the United States spent annually on each soldier deployed in Afghanistan, enough leaked to the Taliban to support ten Taliban fighters. So the United States provided one soldier and indirectly paid for ten Taliban soldiers trying to kill that American. I once asked Soora about the impact of the American presence, and she put it in fatalistic terms: "In one way, it hurts the Taliban," she said. "In another way, it helps the Taliban."

No wonder we lost. We helped defeat ourselves.

26

The Iraq War

The Baghdad airport was full of posters glorifying President Saddam Hussein, and on that warm September night I was the only
Westerner in sight. It was the fall of 2002, the United States was moving toward an invasion of Iraq early the next year, and I wanted to
understand how an invasion might play out. For weeks I had lobbied
Iraq for a visa, sweet-talking the Iraqi diplomats at the United Nations.
I also tried to charm a group of doves in the United States, such as
former senator Mike Gravel, whom the Iraqi government listened to.

The key to getting a visa from a dictatorship lies not in convincing officials that your visit will be good for their country, but rather
in assuring them that they will not personally get into trouble for
approving your visa. The nightmare for an Iraqi bureaucrat was that
I would visit Baghdad and insult Saddam Hussein, leading Saddam's
office to inquire whose signature was on the visa approval. So it's
most effective to seek a visa in a way that leaves no one responsible
for granting it. To accomplish this, I managed to be named to a delegation of nonprofit dignitaries visiting Iraq—meaning that no official was personally approving my visit. That got me my visa, even
though the rest of the delegation had already left Iraq by the time
I received it.

I flew in from Jordan on a plane full of Jordanian laborers. I had been
told that communications were difficult without a satellite phone, but
that satellite phones were banned. So I had brought two: one Thuraya

sat phone to be confiscated at the airport (and returned to me when I left the country) and another to keep with me and use. I figured that the authorities wouldn't expect the second one and wouldn't look hard for it.

Sure enough, a customs official named Ahmed promptly found my first Thuraya, confiscated it, gave me a receipt, and told me I could pick it up on departure. Unfortunately, Ahmed—a big man with a paunch and, like most Iraqi men, a Saddam moustache—also found my second Thuraya.

"Oh, come on," I explained. "I need it to communicate with my head office."

"I'd like to help," Ahmed said, "but it would be dangerous for me. You'd have to help me a little bit."

"I'm very grateful," I told him, and I put a $50 bill on the table.

"That's 'grateful,'" Ahmed said cheerfully. "Not 'very grateful.'"

"I am indeed *very grateful* for your help," I told him, taking back the $50 and putting a $100 bill on the table. He nodded and smiled and pushed the Thuraya back over to me.

I hesitate to describe this incident of bribery. Here I am, a columnist who regularly denounces corruption, and now I'm admitting to offering a bribe? The blunt truth is that in corrupt dictatorships, I sometimes had to offer "tips"—to get through a checkpoint, to keep my passport or phone, to keep soldiers from shooting my interpreter. I have reluctantly engaged in such actions for security reasons—but never for personal benefit. And, as I said earlier, I have never paid for information.

Communications tools like the Thuraya are critical in insecure countries, not just to be able to exchange emails or file stories, but also to reach editors or summon help in an emergency. In some places, you might be detained a month before anyone even gets around to interrogating you.

That's why I was determined to keep a satellite phone with me. Unfortunately, Ahmed was still rooting around in my bag, and before I could put it away the chief of customs came into the room for a moment. Seeing the second Thuraya, he took it and put it in the cages where confiscated sat phones were kept and then handed me a receipt. He then swept out of the room, and I motioned to Ahmed to give it back to me.

"I can't do that now," he whispered. "The boss has seen it. It's too late."

"So give me my $100 back," I replied.

"No, too late."

"Ahmed, give me my money back," I said firmly. "Or I'll report you for taking a bribe."

Ahmed grinned at me, unafraid, and explained things as if I were a slow learner: "You can report me for taking a bribe, yes. And then I will be executed. And you? You will be arrested, too, as a spy sneaking in a satellite phone."

"You'll be dead!" I retorted.

Ahmed had a penchant for drama. With a gleam in his eye, he solemnly drew a finger across his throat before adding, "So we are both dead."

He looked at me triumphantly, and I realized that I couldn't out-bluff him. I pocketed my receipts, changed dollars into dinars with Saddam's portrait on them, and walked out to the taxi stand to find a ride into Baghdad and the Al Rasheed Hotel. In those days before the war, Iraq was safe from kidnappings and bombings, whereas just a few years later it cost $10,000 for a single one-way trip from the airport to the city because of the security necessary.

Upon arriving at the Al Rasheed Hotel, I faced a challenge. Saddam's minions had installed a mosaic of President George H. W. Bush in the floor at the hotel entrance, to force visitors to step on the first President Bush (who had defeated Saddam in the Gulf War). I didn't want to step on the elder Bush, whom I liked, and I certainly didn't want to be photographed doing so. But neither did I want to give the Iraqis the satisfaction of seeing me tiptoe around the edge in an elaborate effort to avoid tromping on the president's noggin. So I looked down at the mosaic, shook my head in exasperation in a way that I hoped would ruin any Iraqi propaganda photo, and marched on ahead.

I spent the next ten days traveling around Iraq, trying to gauge what would happen if the United States invaded. This was challenging, partly because my Arabic had deteriorated sharply, with strange intrusions of Japanese. For some reason my brain stored Japanese and Arabic in the same compartment reserved for languages with complex grammar. I'd ask a question in Arabic, and it might involuntarily include a few words of Japanese.

My government minder escorted me everywhere and interpreted for me, and ordinary Iraqis were terrified of speaking openly in front of him. Fortunately, my interpreter was lazy and liked long meals and coffee breaks, so I periodically could interview people on my own.

Najaf is one of the most holy cities for Shiite Muslims, home to the vast Imam Ali Mosque. I prowled the old city and market, taking advantage of every moment I could sneak away from my minder, and my sense was that most Iraqis—especially Shia and Kurds—hated Saddam, but also hated the idea of an American invasion. Iraqis were nationalists who believed that America was trying to steal Iraqi oil and occupy their country. Moreover, Saddam provided order, and it looked to me as if our invasion would leave the country in chaos. In one of a series of columns warning against an invasion of Iraq, I wrote:

NAJAF, Iraq—As soon as American troops are rolling through Saddam Hussein's palaces, the odds are that this holy Shiite city 100 miles south of Baghdad will erupt in a fury of killing, torture, rape and chaos.

The Shiite Muslims who make up 60 percent of Iraq—but who have never held power—will rampage through the narrow streets here. Remembering the whispers from the bazaar about how Saddam's minions burned the beard off the face of a great Shiite leader named Muhammad Bakr al-Sadr, then raped and killed his sister in front of him, and finally executed him by driving nails through his head, the rebels will tear apart anyone associated with the ruling Baath Party.

In one Shiite city after another, expect battles between rebels and army units, periodic calls for an Iranian-style theocracy, and perhaps a drift toward civil war. For the last few days, I've been traveling in these Shiite cities—Karbala, Najaf and Basra—and the tension in the bazaars is thicker than the dust behind the donkey carts.

So before we rush into Iraq, we need to think through what we will do the morning after Saddam is toppled. Do we send in troops to try to seize the mortars and machine guns from the warring factions? Or do we run from civil war, and risk letting Iran cultivate its own puppet regime? In the north, do we suppress the Kurds if they take advantage of the chaos to seek independence? Do we fight off the Turkish Army if it intervenes in Kurdistan?

Unless we're prepared for the consequences of our invasion, we have no business invading at all. . . . The most ticklish challenge ahead is not overthrowing Saddam but managing the resulting upheaval for a decade afterward.

I was not persuasive. Most of my fellow pundits on the center-left backed the war, with caveats, joining what Bill Keller termed the "I can't believe I'm a hawk club." The *Times* itself wrote editorial after editorial about the war without ever taking a decisive position against it. Among major national columnists, I was one of those writing most frequently against the war, and I became steadily more opposed as the war approached.

My initial appointment as a columnist had been for one year, and I worried that my opposition to the war was coming across as strident. My future as a columnist was up in the air, and some senior editors thought I was falling into the role of knee-jerk leftist Cassandra.

"I didn't find that at all convincing," one top editor snapped one morning after my umpteenth column against the war. The tone worried me. With war looming, Arthur Sulzberger Jr. had extended my appointment as op-ed columnist, but I didn't know how much longer I would have before being tossed back into the Howell Raines newsroom—although it probably helped that Howell never wanted to see me again.

Gail Collins, as editorial page editor, won Arthur's backing to offer a column to Richard Rodriguez, a Latino writer from California, and that seemed likely to mean the end of my presence on the op-ed page. I deeply believed in more Latino voices on the editorial page, but I wanted my own voice to be present as well. Fortunately, Rodriguez eventually turned down the job, and Gail steadily warmed to my kind of heavily reported column. I also argued to Arthur that it would be inappropriate to return me to the newsroom after I had been expressing opinions for more than a year. That was so disingenuous that Arthur smothered a laugh.

While I expected the criticisms I got from Fox News about my opposition to the Iraq War, it was harder to take critiques from journalistic colleagues I admired. I knew the writer Andrew Sullivan from our time together at Magdalen College, Oxford, and I regarded him as smart and thoughtful. His pioneering argument for same-sex marriage had changed my mind. So it was painful to read his take on my Iraq reporting:

USEFUL IDIOT WATCH: Nick Kristof goes to Baghdad and finds people ready to attack the U.S. *Quelle surprise!* In a police state where the tiniest dissent on the tiniest matter can have you disappeared and tortured, Kristof deduces no support for a U.S. invasion. Let's check in and see what happens if we do invade, shall we? We have long memories in the blogosphere, Nick. And little pity.

What if Andrew were right? It was possible that I was wrong and that the invasion would succeed. But I felt the hawks were intoxicated with hubris, reflected in the cockiness of a writer like Andrew who as far as I knew had never been to Iraq and spoke no Arabic but scoffed at the reporting of a columnist on the ground in Baghdad. (To his credit, Andrew later acknowledged that he'd been completely wrong and apologized to me.)

The Iraq hawks weren't the only people who didn't like my reporting. While I was still in Baghdad, a senior Iraqi security official summoned me to his office.

"I understand that you have written lies about our country," he raged. "We give you a visa as a friendly gesture of respect, and then you betray that trust and write lies and act like a spy!"

I didn't know how to judge the risks, but my minder seemed terrified. I adopted my most soothing bedside manner, and I asked the Iraqi official to explain his concerns. "I'll be sure to discuss them with my editors, and I'd like to get back to you," I suggested.

The official did not speak English, and as we discussed my sins it seemed to me that he had simply heard a somewhat garbled version of my Najaf column. So I took a gamble.

"I'm not sure you've seen my full column," I told him. "I have a copy here in my laptop. Do you want to know exactly what I wrote?"

Suspiciously, he agreed. I handed my laptop to my minder, who proceeded to interpret the column aloud for the official. I noted with satisfaction that my minder was greatly softening my column, leaving out whole paragraphs. I had guessed correctly that the minder had a twofold interest in me not getting into serious trouble. First, if I were arrested for spying or slandering the state, he might be arrested as well. Second, I had told him I would pay him $100 a day, at the end of my visit; nominally this was a tip for his help as an interpreter and fixer (he was on the government payroll), but it was mostly a way to win a bit of his loyalty and get him to take long lunch breaks so I could report. If I were arrested, he would be out $1,400. So he had a major financial incentive in having this blow over, and in that meeting with the security official, he earned his pay. We walked out of his office simply with a warning.

On occasions like that, I saw that the curse of dictatorships is their lack of access to reliable information. Autocracies breed sycophants, and even top officials end up misled and basing decisions on misinformation. Saddam Hussein's regime ended because he was surrounded by yes men and didn't realize that the United States was poised to invade his country and topple him from power. He could have easily taken his wealth and relocated with his family in another country, but his brutality cowed subordinates so that he received flawed intelligence that cost him and his sons their lives.

On the eve of the invasion of Iraq, I visited the site of ancient Troy in Turkey. The *Iliad* and the *Odyssey* have always moved me, and I wanted to reflect on the coming war—and the failure of journalists to prevent it—on the site where Hector and Achilles had battled and bled. Troy fills a vast space in literary history and in our minds, but the area within the ancient city walls was much smaller than Yamhill. It is surreal to walk around and think about the history that unfolded here. Indeed, there is still a spring, which Homer describes as the place where Trojan women washed their clothes.

One of the preeminent lessons of the Trojan War, I reflected, is that even when there are legitimate grievances, war isn't always worth it. Achilles knew that, asking, "Why must we battle Trojans?" Agamemnon and Odysseus also expressed doubts, but they were overruled by the hawks of the day. The hawks won by offering an early version of the arguments that drove us into Vietnam and Iraq alike: *If we let the Trojans get away with kidnapping Helen, they'll steal our women again.* And so the Greeks set sail on "this insane voyage," as Achilles put it, "fighting other soldiers to win their wives as prizes."

Both sides were overly optimistic and resisted a negotiated compromise. The Greeks won, of course, but at enormous cost; meanwhile, the

Trojans lost everything, and Hector's baby son, Astyanax, was hurled to his death so that Troy would never rise again. The Trojans' loss was a consequence of their failure to listen to skeptical voices. Cassandra and Laocoön warned against Greeks bearing gifts, and if the Trojans had waited and observed the wooden horse for a week, the Greeks inside would have died of thirst. But the Trojans dismissed the warnings as "windy nonsense"—and this overconfidence destroyed them. Higher walls would not have saved Troy, or more spears; intellectual humility might have. That's a lesson that would have saved many American lives in Vietnam, Afghanistan and Iraq.

THE KUWAIT-IRAQ BORDER IS a flat, desert moonscape. After the Iraq War began in March 2003, it became a cacophonous, terrifying land filled with choking black smoke.

I drove from Kuwait into Iraq in a rental car, against the terms of the rental contract, passing through Kuwaiti checkpoints and then through unmanned, destroyed Iraqi checkpoints. Iraqi army helmets were on the ground where soldiers had thrown them and fled, trying to blend into the civilian population. Smoldering Iraqi tanks and artillery pieces littered the roads. The Iraqi army had melted away and offered no resistance to American military convoys passing through, but Iraqi troops in civilian clothes periodically fired at press vehicles or other foreign civilians. Several journalists had been shot or disappeared. So I drove at ninety miles per hour on the highway through southern Iraq, on the theory that Iraqi troops hiding on the side wouldn't have time to figure out if I was a target or not.

I had spent a couple of days embedded with American troops but had given up on that approach. Embedding oneself was a great way to cover the experience of the American forces, but many reporters were doing that. I wanted to cover the Iraqis who were on the receiving end of the war. I wanted to know how many were being killed, what the survivors thought of the invasion, and what they believed would happen next. That wasn't possible when traveling with the Americans, so a number of us journalists decided to go "unilateral," renting a car and driving through Iraq. Some of these reporters covered their vehicles with signs saying "PRESS," but I thought that amounted to a sign saying "Please rob this vehicle full of unarmed people carrying large amounts of cash and expensive cameras; we won't shoot back." I favored old and unmarked cars that didn't look worth robbing.

In the center of Basra, I found a large mob in front of a bank building, squaring off against British troops backed by tanks and mounted machine guns. I asked a group of Iraqis what was going on.

"We're here to rob the banks," one paunchy middle-aged man said.

"What do you mean?" I asked.

"We used grenade launchers to break into the bank buildings, but we needed more time to break into the safes with the money. Those British soldiers came and won't let us do that. We're very upset."

My most perilous moment in Iraq didn't come at the hands of bank robbers or Saddam's forces. It was an American soldier who almost killed me. Several of us reporters had hired an Iraqi to drive us around, since he knew the area (and in theory knew where it was safe). American troops were jittery because of the looting, bank robberies and attacks on foreigners. Our car approached a checkpoint guarded by a young American soldier who looked very nervous. He shouted at our car to stop, but our driver for some reason only slowed while continuing to move forward. I'm not sure if the driver didn't understand the command "stop"—he didn't speak English—or if he thought that by

Interviewing an Iraqi early in the war, with smoke filling the skies.

going slowly he was complying. The young soldier saw a car driving toward him that refused to stop; understandably, he perceived a threat.

"*Halt!*" the soldier shouted, raising his M4 carbine and pointing it at us. I was in the back seat, likewise shouting "Stop!" and telling the driver in my awful Arabic (or perhaps Japanese) to stop at once. The driver continued to inch forward. He seemed overwhelmed by all the people shouting at him. I reached over the seat and tried to force the car into Park, but I couldn't quite manage it. At any moment, the soldier seemed ready to spray our windshield with automatic gunfire.

We had our windows down, so maybe the soldier heard our screams in English for the driver to stop. Perhaps that made him pause for just long enough. Finally the driver stopped, looking bewildered, and I poked my head through the left window and shouted to the soldier that we were American journalists. He approached, still suspicious and pointing his weapon at us, but relaxed when he saw our passports and press credentials.

"Never, ever do that again," he told us. He seemed almost as relieved as we were that he hadn't shot us.

MANY IRAQIS SAY THAT the original site of the Garden of Eden was the village of Qurna, a onetime oasis in southern Iraq. When it flourished, Qurna must have been an idyllic place with fruit trees and ponds. But Iraq's marshes were drained decades ago, turning the village into a sad desert town. Gusts of wind carried dust and sand through the streets, and when I visited everything was a shade of brown. Houses were dilapidated, and I didn't see a single fruit tree.

Qurna boasts "Adam's tree," which legend says was the tree that produced the fruit that tempted Adam and Eve. I looked it over skeptically.

"So this is the tree that got us all expelled from paradise?" I asked my local guide.

"Yes, this is the one. Adam's tree."

"It doesn't look thousands of years old," I objected.

"But it must be. Otherwise it wouldn't be Adam's tree."

"And how can it have been the tree that bore the fruit that tempted Adam and Eve?" I asked. "It's not even a fruit tree. It looks like a cedar."

"Of course it doesn't bear fruit *now*," the guide explained. "After all, it's thousands of years old."

In any case, Qurna was no longer an Eden, and living there seemed punishment more than paradise. It also seemed, like so much of Iraq, full of loathing for Saddam—but also for Americans.

"Life is worse than before the invasion," complained Jabbar Sabeeh, a villager. Another man, Ahmed, added sourly: "The Americans are useless."

Soon afterward I visited some American troops, and we watched a hookup they had arranged to view Fox News. We slumped in our seats exhausted and nervous as gunfire cut through the night, bewildered as we watched commentators in the safety of their Fox News studio in New York City celebrating the "success" of the invasion and declaring how Iraqis were welcoming us all with flowers. We stared, incredulous, at the screen.

Such hawks seemed to live in their own bubble, impervious to contrary information. It was true, of course, that many Iraqis were happy to see the end of Saddam, but there wasn't much correlation between the grim reality on the ground and the peaceful Iraq that the hawks conjured in their minds. The *Wall Street Journal* opinion page mockingly quoted something I had written from the chaos of Iraq, seeing it as self-evidently wrong because it contradicted the rosy view of *Journal* editorial writers in New York City.

The hawk echo chamber was striking for both its arrogance and its ignorance. The hawk ranks included few people who spoke Arabic and knew the Middle East well, and there was often an inverse relationship between familiarity with the region and confidence that the war would go swimmingly. One journalist from a news organization clamoring for the Iraq War told me that he had filed an article and then gotten a question back from a copy editor unfamiliar with foreign reporting:

"What is our preferred spelling for this place anyway? I've seen it both ways. Iraq and Iran. Which is it?"

Sigh. We Americans seem fated to learn geography through our foreign wars.

Yet we doves also could live in a bubble. I spoke that spring at a Senate retreat, and over dinner chatted with another guest speaker, Ambassador Joe Wilson, who was there with his wife, Valerie Plame. Joe told Sheryl and me that he had firsthand knowledge that President Bush had lied about Iraqi weapons of mass destruction in his State of the Union address. My ears perked up because in my column I had been asking plaintively where those WMD were.

Ambassador Wilson told me that Vice President Dick Cheney had sent him to Niger on a mission to investigate reports that Iraq was seeking uranium from there. Wilson told me that he had investigated and reported back that this was untrue, and that Iraq had neither sought nor received uranium from Niger. But Bush had ignored his report, Wilson said, for the president had declared in his State of the Union address that the British had learned that "Saddam Hussein recently sought significant quantities of uranium from Africa."

"It was a lie," Wilson told me. "A lie to get us into a war."

Joe Wilson initially didn't want to go on the record but after some weeks of negotiation he let me tell the story attributed to "a person involved in the Niger caper." I did some fact-checking and corroboration and wrote a column relaying Wilson's version of events: The White House had sent an ambassador to Niger, the ambassador had refuted the allegations of an Iraq connection, and Bush had made the claim anyway.

In fact, it's now clear to me that Wilson's central story was right but that he laid it on thick. As best I can figure it out, Cheney expressed interest in reports (later shown to be based on false documents) that Iraq was seeking uranium from Niger, and as a result the CIA dispatched Wilson to investigate. Cheney himself was apparently unaware of Wilson's trip. Afterward Wilson delivered a report that overall cast doubt on the Iraq-Niger connection but didn't unequivocally discredit it. In other words, Wilson somewhat exaggerated both his role and how firmly he disproved the intelligence about Iraq seeking uranium.

When Cheney and other top Bush administration officials saw my column, they were initially puzzled. They were unaware of the Wilson trip and weren't quite sure what I was referring to. Meanwhile, Wilson was growing bolder, and I arranged for him to write an op-ed in the *Times* in which he went public and told his story. Cheney and his staff asked around, and what they heard was that Wilson's trip was a boondoggle arranged only because Valerie worked at CIA. Then Richard Armitage at the State Department unwittingly leaked Valerie's CIA connection to a reporter, and a special counsel was called in to investigate.

My own take is that the truth was more complicated than either side acknowledged. Bush was wrong when he accused Iraq of seeking uranium in Africa, but he was not "lying": He believed his statement to be true, and at the time both the American and the British intelligence communities judged it true. As for Cheney and his aides, they were wrong to think that Wilson was chosen for the Niger trip as a boondoggle, but the White House did not conspire to punish Wilson by leaking Plame's CIA connection.

I wondered why Cheney or his aides didn't just call me when they saw my not-quite-right column and tell me, at least off the record, that I was overstating things. The reason, I think, is that they simply didn't trust me. They saw me as a die-hard opponent of the Iraq War who was working to bring them down. That distrust hurt them, but it also hurt me and my readers, for it meant that I was slow to correct my reporting. Even today, the standard liberal version of events in the Joe Wilson affair, which I'm heavily responsible for, is that Bush lied about Iraqi WMD and that the White House leaked Plame's CIA job as revenge against her husband. The truth is messier; truth usually is.

One of the lessons to me of the Iraq War was the paramount importance of humility. In 1991 many doves had warned against the Gulf War, while hawks predicted correctly that it would be an easy and popular victory. So in 2003, the hawks confidently predicted that the Iraq invasion would again go smoothly, while past doves like Joe Biden or the *Times* were reluctant to oppose the war. Then a few years later, those of us who had opposed the Iraq invasion felt vindicated and mostly also opposed President Bush's "surge" of forces into Iraq, warning that it would never work; in fact, it did succeed.

The world is complicated. Nothing goes as planned. If anybody tells you with certainty what's going to happen, run.

Humility also seemed in order because my career benefited from the Iraq War, just as it had earlier benefited from the brutal Tiananmen Square crackdown in China. Once the Iraq War was imminent, it became clear that the op-ed page could benefit from a columnist who traveled in war zones and spoke Arabic (albeit sometimes sprinkled with Japanese). As the war in Iraq was beginning, Arthur Sulzberger Jr. and Gail Collins told me I would be made a permanent columnist. An office shuffle meant I soon gained a palatial office suite that had belonged to Abe Rosenthal when he worked as a columnist; it had a private bathroom and shower. I had never imagined that a journalism career would lead to such a nice office, but more than the luxury it meant a great deal to me that I had inherited Abe's former lair.

Another lesson I learned from my time in Iraq, which I should have learned already in Ghana and Congo and Indonesia and elsewhere, is that journalists must work harder at staying safe. Journalistic colleagues, including Michael Kelly, died in the Iraq War, and it was no consolation for me to then win the Michael Kelly Award.

"You don't want a journalism award named after you," my friend and colleague Tom Friedman mused as we strolled through Kuwait as the war was about to begin. "You want to get the story, but you also want to get back."

I've known Tom since the 1980s, and he offered helpful guidance when I gained my column six years after he got his. Once, when we were talking about bulletproof vests, he told me: *Any time I needed a flak jacket, I was too close.* That isn't always literally true, and I have two sets of helmets and body armor—one for domestic riots and lesser weaponry, and a heavy-duty set for wars and automatic weapons. But Tom is right that we journalists too often are inclined to rush toward gunfire. Early in the Iraq War, I calculated that journalists there were dying at ten times the per capita rate of American soldiers, and partly that was because the American military worked very hard to reduce risks even in a dangerous mission. In Iraq and elsewhere, I tried to counsel fellow journalists to be more careful, to always ask questions before going down uncertain roads, and to always remember that we put not only ourselves at risk but also our drivers and interpreters. I know it doesn't sound like much of an ambition in life—not to have a journalism award named after me—but it's the least I can do for Sheryl and the kids.

27

Covering Genocide

On the fringe of the Sahara Desert in western Sudan, the Darfur region is an endless expanse of sand and brown hills interspersed with mud-brick villages. Arriving on a trip there in early 2004 to investigate reports of atrocities, I found thousands of villagers who had fled their homes and were sheltering under trees with no food and little water. I did what journalists do: I went from tree to tree, interviewing survivors.

Under the first tree I met Magboula, a twenty-four-year-old woman with a beautiful round face, jet-black skin and a soulful smile that ached as it neared her eyes. She had belonged to one of the most prosperous families of a Darfur village called Ab-Layha: Magboula and her husband had owned three hundred cattle and fifty camels. In the predawn darkness one morning, as she was preparing for prayers, she heard a plane overhead. That was very rare in rural Darfur, so the villagers came rushing out—to see an Antonov plane dropping bombs on them. Shortly after, a force of about a thousand militiamen swept in on horses and camels, backed by two helicopters.

"We will not allow Blacks here," the men shouted repeatedly. "This land is only for Arabs." The attackers belonged to the Janjaweed, a government-backed militia that Sudan's leaders harnessed to kill or drive out members of three non-Arab ethnic groups. This was not a religious conflict, for perpetrators and victims alike were Muslim, but that made it no less brutal.

Magboula grabbed her children and ran for a nearby forest as gunshots flew around her. Her father and mother stayed to protect their animals—they were yelling, "Don't take our livestock"—and were both shot dead. The father's body was thrown into a well to poison the water, so survivors could not drink from it.

About a hundred people were killed that day in Ab-Layha, and the survivors hid in the forest. Magboula was now caring not only for her two small children, but also for her young sister. Her husband, Ali, helped forage for wild plants, but soon the survivors were so malnourished that they were eating grass. Magboula's mother-in-law died of starvation. Cobras killed some of the survivors, and scorpions stung many of them. Then a Sudanese military plane spotted the survivors, and the Janjaweed mounted an attack.

"Ali had told me, 'If the Janjaweed attack, don't try to save me. You can't help. Don't get angry. Just keep the children and run away,'" Magboula told me. She says she hid with the children in a hollow and saw the Janjaweed round up dozens of villagers, including Ali and his three younger brothers. "They tied their hands like this"—she showed me her hands in front of her—and then forced them to lie on the ground. Then, she said, the men and boys were all shot dead, and the women were taken away to be raped.

When the Janjaweed left, Magboula said, she and the other survivors crept out. Forty-five corpses of men and boys were on the ground. Magboula, now a widow, decided that the only hope for the children was to walk to Chad, traveling at night to avoid detection. Eight days later, half dead with hunger and thirst, Magboula arrived with her two daughters and her young sister. They collapsed under a tree at the Chad-Sudan border, and that is where I found them.*

Magboula's tree was the first one where I did interviews. I moved on to the next tree, and I found two young orphans, both barefoot. Nijah Ahmed was just four years old, but her parents and older brother had been murdered, so she carried her thirteen-month-old baby brother on her back and trudged through the Sahara with the other survivors

---

* Women like Magboula who survived Janjaweed attacks often insisted that they had hidden and observed atrocities but had never been captured themselves. Sometimes this was true, but it's worth noting that it would have been deeply stigmatizing for Magboula or any woman to admit capture by the Janjaweed, for people would then have guessed that she had been raped. And in the Darfur culture, especially in the early years of the genocide, to have been raped was perceived as perpetual defilement, shame and ruin.

from Ab-Layha. Other families had helped her with food and water, but this heroic little girl had carried her baby brother for eight days to Chad and saved his life. I thought of my children, prone to quarrel with each other. I thought of how I was whining to myself about camping on the ground nearby, and how I fretted about scorpions—and I was around for just a few days while conducting these interviews. I tried to tell Nijah how brave she had been and how proud her parents would be. She listened politely, but all she wanted to know was where she could get food for her baby brother.

Under the third tree, I found a thirty-year-old woman, Zahra, tall, thin and emotionally shattered. She told me that the Janjaweed had shot dead her husband, Adam, and their seven-year-old son as well as three of her brothers. Then they grabbed her four-year-old son, Rasheed, from her arms and cut his throat in front of her.

Zahra said that the Janjaweed had then kidnapped her and her two sisters, Kuttuma and Fatima, and gang-raped them for days. Afterward, they shot Kuttuma dead and cut the throat of Fatima, but they decided to release Zahra after mutilating her—so that others would know what would happen to women in her Zaghawa ethnic group.

"You are a slave to the Arabs, and this is the sign of a slave," one Janjaweed fighter told her, slashing her leg with a sword before letting her hobble away, stark naked. Other villagers confirmed that they had found her naked and bleeding, and she showed me the scar.

These were simply the first three trees under which I did my interviews. In every direction as far as I could see there were more trees and more survivors with tales like these. Many thousands of people were sheltering, an endless panorama of suffering. That's when I understood not only the horror of what was unfolding but also the scale.

I had covered other atrocities, but Darfur evoked particular horror because it appeared to be a genocide. That's a word that is thrown around a great deal, but this was a deliberate effort by the Sudanese government to wipe out villages that were home to three Black African ethnic groups in Darfur: the Zaghawa, the Fur and the Masalit. Some people in these tribes supported a rebellion against the largely Arab government, so this genocide was a scorched-earth counterinsurgency campaign that consisted of murder, pillage and rape.

"They took the cattle and horses, killed the men, raped the women, and then they burned the village," a sixty-year-old man told me. A

Interviewing Darfuris who had fled their villages for Chad.

woman whose husband had been murdered said: "They want to exterminate us Blacks."

The slaughter horrified me, and the passivity of international officials infuriated me. In Chad, I was struck by how ordinary peasants who lived in huts and seemed to have nothing shared their nothing with the Darfur refugees. One impoverished Chadian farmer was sharing his well with the refugees and told me: "If we have food or water, we'll share it with them. We can't leave them like this."

I visited Magboula repeatedly to make sure she was okay, and each time I approached she offered me the only things she had: a sad smile and a cup of brackish water. It tore me apart that a homeless widow refugee perceived moral obligations to a stranger better than leaders around the world.

It was wrenching to hear these stories from survivors, while I had a car with bottles of water and bags of nuts to eat, and I could sleep in my sleeping bag. And I knew that if it was hard to hear these stories, it was a hundred times harder to tell them, and a million times more difficult to live them. I shared my nuts and water with Darfuris I met, but my supply couldn't make a meaningful difference.

Given that my family had lost loved ones to both the Nazis and the Soviet Communists, I thought I knew about atrocities. But witnessing this genocide shook me. I had reported on the war in Congo, which cost far more lives, yet there was something particularly sinister about mass torture and slaughter of people because of their ethnicity and skin color. I came back from Darfur and hugged Gregory, Geoffrey and Caroline. I wrote about other issues in the headlines but couldn't get Darfur out of my mind.

I kept thinking of families out there in the desert. I had interviewed parents who were desperate for water, but wells were rare and the Janjaweed sometimes surrounded them and used them as killing fields. If a man from one of the targeted tribes went to a well, he was shot. If a woman went to a well, she was raped. That meant that in some areas families had no safe way to get drinking water. Some sent their young children—just eight or ten years old—miles across the desert with donkeys to fetch water from the well, because the gunmen often did not bother to kill young children. I watched as families dispatched their children and waited, terrified, to see if the youngsters would come back. I wondered what I would do. My children were then seven, ten and twelve years old, and I tried to imagine sending them with donkeys across the desert to try to get water from wells where gunmen were standing guard, ready to kill, rape and mutilate. Just thinking of this horrified me. I was anxious sending Caroline off for the first day of school; these families knew that they might never see their children again.

I had never imagined that I would make another trip to such a remote and obscure part of the world as Darfur, but the genocide occurring there nagged at my conscience. I made three trips in 2004 alone, and each time what I saw was so harrowing that it drove me to want to do more to bear witness. I began sneaking across the border from Chad into Darfur, terrified of the risks but determined to document every atrocity and capture every outrage.

With each trip, I saw more horror. A farmer who had been held down as his eyes were gouged out with a bayonet. An old woman who had been set alight. A young girl shot in the chest. Villages torched. I brought back a charred oil lamp that I recovered from a still-smoldering village and put it on my desk as a reminder of the human capacity for evil (it is a few feet away from me as I write this), and I began to needle officials to do more and shame them when they didn't. I urged President Bush to speak of the crisis, and I prodded an Illinois senator named Barack Obama, who took up the cause. Another senator,

Joe Biden, was all in and was irrepressible; as I tried to tell him what American policy should be, he told me what columns I should write about Darfur. I pushed United Nations secretary-general Kofi Annan, whom I admired, writing in one column: "I hate to say it, but the way things are going, when he dies his obituary will begin: 'Kofi Annan, the former U.N. secretary general who at various points in his career presided ineffectually over the failure to stop genocide, first in Rwanda and then in Sudan, died today.'"

That was unfair—and Kofi's obituary did not begin that way when he died in 2018—but I was trying to use every bit of leverage I could to get him and everyone else to confront this genocide. In retrospect, I regret that line about Kofi. It's easy as a columnist to snipe from the sidelines, harder to get things done when you are secretary-general of the United Nations. In any case, shortly after the column appeared, my phone rang.

"Nick," a familiar voice said. "This is Kofi Annan. We have to talk." To his credit, he did work harder to get peacekeepers into Darfur and to pressure Sudan to stop the slaughter.

President Bush wanted to do more, but there were drawbacks to all potential steps and there was concern that too much pressure on Sudan would lead it to renege on the recent landmark peace deal that ended the war in South Sudan. No one, including me, thought we should attack Sudan and start a war in yet a third Muslim country, and officials were reluctant to use the bully pulpit without evidence that it would make a difference. Sanctions had some impact, but not enough. The killing, pillage and rape persisted, albeit at a somewhat slower pace. The United States and Europe helped fund an enormous relief operation, and there was an African Union peace operation that morphed into a United Nations peacekeeping force, and these helped displaced Darfuris living in camps. But the Janjaweed continued to attack villages periodically.

I was fortunate to be at a news organization like the *Times* that had the resources to send me to Sudan and supported me as I covered an obscure humanitarian crisis. The paper's higher-ups never questioned the time and sums I spent reporting on Darfur. Well, almost never. One time I came back from a grueling trip in Darfur and arrived at night, parched, at the Acropole Hotel in Khartoum. The only potable substance was a couple of bottles of water in the room, and I drained them. When I checked out, the hotel listed them rather grandly as "mini bar" on my bill.

A few weeks later, I had an email from the accountant who processed expenses submitted by the columnists. I had thought he might be in touch, for I had hired an illiterate itinerant driver who had no fixed address, email or cell phone number, and certainly no receipt book. So I had simply written in English on a sheet of my reporter's notebook: "Received from Nicholas Kristof US$1,000 for pick-up truck and driver for one week in Darfur." The driver had signed it in childlike Arabic: "Muhammad." But that actually wasn't what the accountant was emailing about; he never mentioned the driver. Instead, he cited the bottled water.

"Your hotel bill included $3 for a hotel minibar," he noted. "And we don't cover minibar expenses."

I made more than a dozen trips to the Darfur area, mostly with Naka Nathaniel, a video journalist who was an essential partner in my coverage. I was acutely conscious of the need to reach younger audiences if I was to have greater impact, so I had pushed to experiment with new platforms. A *Times* colleague and social media whiz, Soraya Darabi, had helped me get on Twitter early, and I'd also been the first *Times* blogger and the first person to make a *Times* video; later, I would

Sneaking into Darfur from Chad on a local pickup truck.

be the first to file a story on the *Times* Snapchat channel. In the case of Darfur, I thought that videos could convey the brutality in a way that prose never could, and Naka was central to that effort.

Naka is an ethnic Hawaiian who managed to be perceived as a local almost everywhere we went. On one trip to Iran, we were detained as spies, and the security authorities were particularly suspicious of Naka because to them he looked Iranian.

News photographers and video journalists like Naka tend to be dangerous to travel with, because when they hear gunfire, they rush toward it. One of my basic rules of covering conflicts, therefore, is to never get a ride from one.* Once, in the Amazon, I interviewed a native who was brilliant at firing darts with a blowpipe, and my video journalist got a gleam in his eye. "I have a great idea," he said, and soon he was filming the man firing a blow dart at a papaya balanced on my head.

"I'm imagining my call with New York," the video journalist explained as he set up his camera. "I'll tell the editors, 'There's good news and bad news. Bad news is Kristof got killed by a blow dart to the head. Good news is that I got it on video.'" On another occasion, Naka and I were rafting down a river in the Arctic National Wildlife Refuge for a reporting project. Suddenly a huge Alaskan brown bear appeared in the river directly in front of us. "Row to the right!" I yelled to Naka, as I tried frantically to steer around the bear rather than hit it dead on. But Naka had put down his oar to shoot video.

One challenge for Naka and me as we reported together in Sudan was our names. As I've mentioned, "Nick" in Arabic means "fuck." Unfortunately, "Naka" is the third-person past perfect of the same verb. When we introduced ourselves in Darfur, we were "Fuck" and "Fucked."

Naka overcame that, and his videos from Darfur offered indelible glimpses of what a genocide looks like. We traveled together repeatedly. It was enormously difficult to get visas and travel permits from Sudan to enter Darfur legally, but we sometimes sneaked in from neighbor-

---

* Conflict photographers and video journalists are heroes for our age. One of those I most admire is Lynsey Addario, whom I've known for two decades since we met in Afghanistan. She's fearless. She's an artist. And did I say she's fearless? She has been kidnapped in Iraq and in Libya and has done extraordinary work in South Sudan, Afghanistan, Ukraine and many other places. I love to work with her, even if I'm always scared she'll drag me into a shootout. Then one day we were staying in adjoining rooms in a "hotel" in a remote part of the Central African Republic, and Lynsey knocked on my door. "There's a spider in my bathroom," she said. "Can you get rid of it?"

ing Chad and sometimes figured out ways of getting in directly. Kofi Annan made a trip to Darfur on a United Nations plane in 2005 and agreed to take Naka and me; Sudan gave us visas as part of the traveling press corps. Kofi was going to stay on the ground in Darfur for only a few hours, and as we were about to land I approached him and his press aide.

"I just want you to know," I said gingerly. "I think we're going to miss the plane out. I don't want you to think we've been kidnapped or detained if we don't board the plane this afternoon."

Kofi looked at me for a long moment, but he understood how difficult it was for a reporter to get access to Darfur and what an opportunity this was. He sighed. "Okay, I understand," he said. "Be careful."

A few hours later, Naka and I watched from the back of the crowd as Kofi's plane took off again. We felt free, for the Sudanese authorities had no idea we were still in Darfur, but we still needed a way to get through military checkpoints. In watching United Nations aid workers pass these checkpoints, I noticed that they had English-language UN passes dangling from lanyards on their necks and displayed them to soldiers. I doubted that the troops spoke English, so I took my sunglasses lanyard and dangled my library card and United Airlines Mileage Plus card from it. As we approached the first checkpoint, I told the driver to slow down but not stop, and I rolled down the window and waved it at the soldier. No problem. It's amazing the respect soldiers have for United Airlines.

The interviews we recorded with Darfur villagers were chilling.

"You are Black people," one rapist told a woman I interviewed, Nemat, after she had been gang-raped by men in uniforms. "We want to wipe you out."

This was a policy of rape meant to advance a genocidal agenda. A Sudanese doctor I knew who protested rapes of young Darfuri girls was herself gang-raped and warned by her rapists that they were acting on orders of the country's intelligence chief. Sudan barred Western aid groups from bringing in rape kits to support survivors, and the government periodically arrested women and girls who reported rapes. Unless they could provide three adult male witnesses to confirm the rape, the government regarded survivors as having admitted to illicit sex, so they were subject to punishment for fornication or adultery.

A seventeen-year-old girl reported to a French-run clinic to seek treatment for a rape that had left her bleeding and traumatized. The Sudanese government had an informer in the clinic who alerted the authorities, so the police barged into the clinic and carried the girl off to a police hospital—over the heroic resistance of two Frenchwomen working in the clinic. At the police hospital, the girl was chained to a cot by one leg and one arm, and a police doctor declared that she had faked the rape. The police proposed that she be charged with filing false information.

On another visit to Darfur (this one theoretically to cover a trip there by Robert Zoellick, the deputy secretary of state, who helped me get the visa), Naka and I found a nineteen-year-old university student to translate for us. He was eager for the income and the chance to help spotlight atrocities, and he did a fine job. We traveled to a village that had been attacked, and on the way back we saw Janjaweed marauders passing freely through government checkpoints. We weren't so lucky. At one checkpoint, a commander noted that while we had permits, our interpreter wasn't mentioned on the permits—so they would detain him.

"You go on," the commander told us. "We're just going to hold him for investigation. Nothing to do with you." The student was a member of the Fur ethnic group that the government was slaughtering, and it seemed likely that the investigation would end as soon as our car was out of sight, with a bullet in his head.

"We need him!" I told the commander. "We can't leave without him. We'll stay here while you investigate."

"No, you go on," the commander said. "We don't need to stop you." (The student was interpreting for us, and he was terrified that he was perhaps chronicling his last moments.)

Naka and I tried joking with the soldiers and ingratiating ourselves with them. We gave the troops food and water from our car. We tried offering the commander a bribe to let the student go. We tried warning them that we would write about the incident. Nothing worked. Finally, we said we just would not leave without our interpreter.

"So we keep all of you," the commander said, still speaking through our interpreter, who was at least relieved to have company. The commander used his radio to summon a general—it was a higher-pay-grade decision to kill foreigners—and confined us to a detention cell while we all waited. The cell was not reassuring: A crude mural on the wall showed a man held down, writhing as a stake was pounded through his stomach.

Was this mural depicting how they tortured detainees? Was this meant to get people to confess? Or was it just meant to play with our minds? Was this some obscure Koranic or historical allegory? We had no idea.

Eventually the general showed up and agreed to let us all go, while keeping the interpreter's cell phone. In the meantime, our vehicle had become stuck in the sand, so the general made some soldiers push the car out. That was satisfying. I was even more surprised when one of the soldiers approached me.

"Hi," he said, speaking through the interpreter whom he previously was prepared to execute. "Can you help me get a visa to the United States?"

28

Where's the Line?

Naka and I traversed terrain in Darfur where there were typically no police and no aid workers, and we often struggled to understand our moral obligations. One day Naka and I came across a village in Chad that had just been attacked by the Janjaweed. As it happened, the villagers had had a few guns to protect themselves, and they fought off the attackers and even managed to wound and capture two of them. One was a man who had been slashed with a machete, and the other was a teenage boy who had been shot.

Normally, I would have taken the two injured attackers to a hospital, but that would have taken all day and I desperately wanted to reach another village, Koloy, that I had heard was about to be attacked. I also didn't brim with sympathy for two people who had been hurt while attempting to massacre this village. So I made the villagers promise not to kill their two prisoners and to turn them over to the Chadian authorities, and then we drove on to Koloy. (The villagers handed them over to the authorities; a few weeks later, the Janjaweed raided the prison and freed them.)

As Naka and I arrived in Koloy, the police force was fleeing, along with almost everybody who could walk. Those remaining in the town were the infirm, and they were waiting to be killed. "Any moment, they will attack us here," one elderly sheik explained. I told my driver to point our Toyota Land Cruiser toward the road out and leave the engine on.

One of those unable to leave was Adam Zakaria, the sheik of a nearby village, for he had been shot twice when the Janjaweed attacked the previous day.

"I know the man who shot me," Adam told me. "He used to be my friend." That man was an Arab neighbor who had joined the Janjaweed the previous year and now regularly attacked non-Arabs.

"I told him, 'Don't shoot me!'" Adam recalled. "Three or four times, I pleaded, 'Don't shoot me.' And then he shot me."

Adam's two wives and four children were still missing. "In my heart, I think they are dead," he said.

It was nerve-racking to report in Koloy, knowing that the Janjaweed might raid at any moment. But I also knew that I might be the last person here before the attack, so I wanted to document every last person waiting to be massacred. My driver and interpreter were getting increasingly anxious and telling me that we had to go.

"Just a few more minutes," I kept telling them.

"No, we've got to go," my interpreter said, now with urgency. "Now. If the Janjaweed come, they may kidnap you. They know you have value. Somebody will pay ransom for you. But me? They'll just shoot me. So I want to go. Now."

He was right. We jumped in the vehicle and drove off. But I've rarely felt so helpless as when I drove away from a village full of people waiting to be slaughtered. I thought of what it would be like to huddle with my family, paralyzed by fear, waiting for the shouts, the gunshots, the smoke, the end.

I never had writer's block on the subject of Darfur. The things I'd seen poured out of me. The great sports columnist Red Smith had said: "Writing is easy; you just open a vein and bleed." That was me on Darfur.

I WANTED AS MUCH attention as possible on Darfur, for I noticed that whenever interest subsided the pace of killings increased. So one of my frustrations was that the media weren't much interested in covering the slaughter. My colleagues on the foreign desk did a fine job, as did *The Washington Post* and some European publications. But most ignored it, and *Christianity Today* ended up covering Darfur more assiduously than either *Newsweek* or *Time*.

Most frustrating, American television networks paid little heed to the genocide. In all of 2004, according to monitoring by the Tyndall Report, ABC News offered only 18 minutes of coverage of the Darfur genocide in its nightly newscasts—and that was a tribute to Peter Jennings, the anchor. NBC News provided only 5 minutes of coverage, and CBS News only 3 minutes. In contrast, the three networks had provided 130 minutes of coverage of Martha Stewart.

I had been railing at President Bush for not speaking up more forcefully about Darfur, but in fact he and his administration addressed the slaughter more than American television networks did. That in turn had to do with the broader question of what television covered and what was good for ratings. Television executives knew that covering global crises like Darfur was expensive and dangerous and would result in fewer viewers. I could wag my finger at them, but I couldn't change the business model they operated within.

Anderson Cooper of CNN traveled to eastern Congo in 2006 and anchored from there for three nights. It was hugely expensive and logistically complicated, and it presented some risk, but Anderson did excellent work and illuminated what was often described as the most lethal conflict since World War II. Yet his ratings fell during those evenings. As a result, CNN hasn't let Anderson anywhere near Congo since.

Maybe the most depressing glimpse into television news judgments came after the Bill and Melinda Gates Foundation awarded a grant to ABC News to cover global health issues for a year. This was controversial, for why should the Gates Foundation allocate scarce dollars to reward ABC executives for doing their job, as opposed to using the money to vaccinate children or distribute anti-malaria bed nets? But ABC News did outstanding reporting with the grant, covering everything from maternal mortality to micronutrient deficiencies. So a year later, the Gates Foundation went back to ABC News to offer to extend the grant. ABC declined. It explained that when it ran these important stories, viewers switched channels.

I did find a partner in the networks who shared my passion for covering neglected humanitarian stories: Ann Curry of NBC. Ann had grown up in a working-class family in Ashland, Oregon, and then climbed her way up the television world to the *Today* show. I was initially wary of joining forces with a hotshot television anchor. Would

she require a hair-and-makeup trailer? Would she be sticking microphones in the faces of dying children? But I wanted to do anything
possible to encourage more Darfur coverage, so Naka and I traveled
with Ann and her crew, and I needn't have worried that she was a
pampered television star.

We stayed at a $1-per-person "guest house" on the Chad-Sudan bor-
der that had no electricity or running water. The "toilet" was a gopher
hole in the ground with a grass mat around it for privacy, but nobody
had stayed at the "guest house" for months, so bats had moved into the
gopher hole. When disturbed by one of us doing our business, the bats
flew out indignantly. This was disconcerting to both bats and humans.
But Ann was uncomplaining. She did powerful reporting from Darfur,
and was willing to stand up not only for stories that needed covering
but also for women who had been harassed by her co-anchor, Matt
Lauer. In the end, Matt and NBC pushed her out—and, characteristi-
cally, Ann was less concerned about herself and more worried about
whether former *Today* colleagues might lose their jobs as her ouster
caused ratings to tumble. If all television anchors had her integrity and
commitment, journalism would be held in higher regard. Meanwhile,
NBC was eventually forced to fire Lauer in 2017 because of his pattern
of sexual harassment.

One conundrum we all faced in Darfur and elsewhere was whether
to use graphic photos. There's a misperception that newspapers like to
use sensationalist photos because these sell papers. Almost the opposite
is true. People don't like to see images of bloodshed, and companies
don't want to buy advertising that might end up next to a disturbing photo. There are also legitimate questions about whether graphic
images rob victims of dignity. But as the genocide in Darfur continued,
I became impatient with those strictures and increasingly felt that we
should show readers and viewers what a genocide looks like—or, in
other contexts, what a famine looks like, or what AIDS looks like. I
feared we were sanitizing horrors.

In 2005 an American named Brian Steidle contacted me. Working
for the State Department, he had shot thousands of photos in Darfur
after being posted there with an African Union peacekeeping group.
The photos had been kept secret by the State Department, but Brian
thought that if Americans could see the slaughter, they might try

harder to end it. So he gave me this classified genocide archive and permission to publish anything I wanted.

My next fight was with editors. They understood the importance of the images and were willing to publish four large photos, taking up most of the space on the op-ed page. But they were reluctant to publish the most haunting images and preferred more sedate photos of bodies at a distance with faces not visible. One of the most disturbing images, for example, was of a five-year-old boy who had been beaten to death, his face a bloody mess. I agreed that we couldn't run that one, or the one of a ten-year-old girl staring up lifeless from the ground. But I was open to running a photo of the manacled hands of a teenage girl who had been burned alive along with others at the school for girls in the town of Suleia.

One of the arguments against running graphic photos was that we wouldn't do so after a gun massacre in the United States, so it would be a double standard if we were willing to do so only when Black children were killed in a distant land. I thought that was a pretty good argument—for running tougher images of gun violence in America. I

Photos like this one from the Brian Steidle genocide archive raised difficult questions. I argued that we should be bolder about showing what genocide looks like, in hopes of ending it. *Photo by Brian Steidle.*

wanted every tool available to galvanize the public so as to save lives, whether in America or abroad.

In the end my editors and I compromised on the Darfur photos. We ran four photos: one of a dead child facedown, one of a corpse of a man whose head was in a bush, one of a skeleton of a man or woman whose wrists were still bound and whose clothes had been pulled down, and a village scene after a massacre that claimed 107 lives. Those photos did indeed have a power that my words lacked, and they were displayed and discussed by John McCain and Barack Obama on the floor of the Senate. Brian Steidle later acknowledged that he had been my source, and that's why I'm naming him here even though my original article did not.

The genocide continued. On one trip, I met a man who had just fled a Janjaweed massacre. But his wife was eight months pregnant and could only hobble, so she was still in the village along with their four children, ages three to twelve.

"There's no way for people to escape," the man told me. "The Janjaweed will kill all the men, women and children, take all our blankets and other property, and then burn our homes. They will kill every last person. The Janjaweed will rape and kill my family. And there's nothing I can do."

I drove off, and I never found out what happened to that man or his family. There were no mobile phones in rural Darfur or Chad then, no Internet, no way of following up. Elie Wiesel once said, referring to victims of genocide, "Let us remember: what hurts the victim most is not the cruelty of the oppressor but the silence of the bystander." I had no illusions about Sudan's brutality but I did have expectations of the West—and I found its silence maddening.

It was never a question of intervening in Darfur with military force, but the West didn't even have the fortitude to speak up forcefully and regularly at the highest levels, to use our intelligence community to gather evidence, to name and shame the killers, to pressure China to stop arming Sudan, to rally African countries against the genocide. For modest sums and with limited political capital, we could have saved significantly more lives.

My passion for covering Darfur won praise and awards. But in my heart, I wondered whether my drive to get to dangerous places in Darfur was entirely high-minded or whether it was in part shaped by a reckless pursuit of glory.

Prizes are the holy grail of journalism and also the curse of journalism. They properly reward extraordinary work that might not otherwise get noticed, and they are a way for journalists at smaller papers like *The Indianapolis Star* or *The Oregonian* to get noticed. But because prizes can make the career of a reporter or editor, the drive for them shapes the way news organizations cover the world. Newspapers reallocate resources from local beat coverage to six-month-long investigative projects. Reporters and photographers take risks in hopes of winning prizes and occasionally they die. Look at any major newspaper in the last two weeks of December, and you'll see one amazing front-page piece published after another. That's because each paper is trying to wrap up its Pulitzer entries. Submissions are for the calendar year, so you want to make sure the whole series appears by the end of December. For the same reason, January always represents a drought of prize-winning journalism.

I had been a finalist for a Pulitzer in 2004 and 2005 before winning one in 2006 for Darfur columns, and I valued that prize above all others. But I realized that I was not only putting myself in danger but others as well: Naka, my interpreter and my driver. In this light, was my reporting a bit selfish?

Another question I asked myself was whether I was going rogue: Was I breaching journalistic ethics and protocol by investing too much of myself in this story? I was exerting power to advance my own goal of ending a genocide. Is it appropriate for a journalist to engage in public policy in this way, however admirable the goal? Aren't we supposed to be observing from the bleachers rather than rushing into the arena to assist the underdog?

"A reporter spent his life sitting in the best seat in the house to watch the rest of the world playing its fascinating games, but the price of that wonderful seat was tremendous: The reporter could only sit there; he could never play," the great *Times* columnist Russell Baker wrote in his memoir.

Yet stepping occasionally into the arena has been an uneasy thread throughout much of my journalistic career, even when I was a reporter rather than a columnist. Getting an all-male dining club to admit women is not an obvious job for a Los Angeles correspondent. Helping an escaped felon flee China is not part of the foreign correspondent's job description. And in Darfur I felt I was stretching my role on a regular basis as I poured my soul into the effort to fight a genocide.

The truth is that our moral obligations as journalists are complicated. Russell Baker's caution is generally a good one, but journalists do leap out of the bleachers to intervene in extreme situations. Foreign correspondents, photographers and columnists don't simply stand by with notebook and camera to chronicle the death of a child. We do everything we can to save that life, because we're human beings first and journalists second.

In 1993 a photographer named Kevin Carter took a famous photograph of a starving boy in Sudan with a nearby vulture that was seemingly waiting for the boy to die. Carter was criticized for not doing more to assure that the child got help. He said he had chased the vulture away, and he won the Pulitzer Prize for that photo. Three months later, he killed himself. "I am haunted by the vivid memories of killings & corpses & anger & pain . . . of starving or wounded children," he wrote in his suicide note.

I admire Carter. I respect his determination to travel to remote places to take such shattering photos. I don't think any of us know enough about the circumstances of the vulture photo to criticize his actions. But I do believe that one thing that emerged from that controversy was some consensus that in such circumstances, journalists are not only allowed to intervene to save a life but are expected to do so.

That's my practice. In Mali, I was once reporting on malnutrition when we dropped in on a village at random and found a shriveled three-week-old infant who was barely alive. The young mom had been unable to take the baby to a clinic, so we rushed them to a hospital in the nearest town, Mopti. I worried that if the child died while in my vehicle, I might be accused of killing the child, putting me and my team at risk. Yet it would be repugnant to chronicle a death that we might prevent.

On the way to the hospital, the mother told us that she didn't have enough breast milk and had bought cow milk to try to save her child's life, but the baby wouldn't drink. When we arrived at the hospital, the doctor saw the baby right away, because I was a foreigner and was paying.

I wasn't sure the baby was still alive, but the doctor opened the baby's mouth and put it firmly on his mother's breast—and hallelujah, the baby got a few drops of milk and almost magically revived in front of us. "The mother doesn't know how to breast-feed properly," the doctor explained. The mother was thrilled to see her baby come to life, and the doctor showed her how to reposition her arm and make sure the baby latched on properly. I had written about how more than 600,000 babies die each year around the developing world because of lack of optimal breast-feeding, but it was incredible to witness how quickly the baby was restored.

Domestically, as well, we're human beings first and journalists second. Most reporters who witness an assault will call 911 and perhaps even intervene. When I was an intern at *The Oregonian*, I interviewed a prison inmate who intimated to me that he was likely to murder another inmate; after much discussion and debate, I told the warden so that the two inmates could be kept apart.

At the same time, our primary job is reporting, not law enforcement. While working on stories, I have come across drug use and other illegal behavior, and I haven't run to the police. It's when a life is at stake that our human imperatives transcend our journalistic roles, but that's often a difficult demarcation to honor in practice.

With a genocide unfolding, and more lives at stake than anybody could count, I sometimes pushed my role even further. I wasn't just trying to help a child here or there, and wasn't just expressing opinions about issues, but I was veering uncomfortably close to a crusade. I felt near the edge of what a journalist should do. The *Times* didn't seem to worry about this, but I did.

Because I had visited Darfur so often, policymakers reached out to me for advice. I declined to testify before congressional committees, because that felt too political, and I declined to be a speaker at a huge demonstration on the Washington Mall against the Darfur genocide because it felt too much like being a leader of a movement that I wanted to be in a position to criticize. But when senators and White House aides called, I told them what I thought they should do about Darfur, and I found myself in meetings at the United Nations with Kofi Annan and groups of nonprofit leaders and agency heads discussing what could be done. I wanted to keep my independence and distance, but at times I also offered advice.

Television networks often invited me to talk about the issues in the headlines, and I tried to bargain with them. I'll talk about Iraq or Congress, but how about just one question about Darfur?

I knew that there were precedents for campaigning about a genocide. The *Times* had aggressively covered the Armenian genocide in 1915, and Tony Lewis had thundered regularly against the Bosnian genocide in the 1990s. Tony's columns about Bosnia were predictable—normally a great sin among columnists—but they were magnificent because of their moral force, and they helped push President Clinton to act. In contrast, the paper was embarrassed that it hadn't covered the Holocaust with greater force, nor the 1994 genocide in Rwanda.

I worried that my columns were becoming shrill, not sufficiently acknowledging how difficult it was for policymakers to stop a slaughter half a world away in a country in which they have little influence. This lack of subtlety was found among politicians as well. When Bush was president, Democrats like Barack Obama and Joe Biden excoriated him for inaction on Darfur and sometimes implied that solutions were simpler than they were; then when Obama and Biden moved to the White House, Republicans returned the favor. Whether in politics or journalism, critics rarely acknowledged adequately that policymaking is a Sisyphean task, with never enough information, and invariably it entails risks that have to be weighed as well.

For my part, I wanted to be a journalist, not a crusader. When journalists become zealots, they risk identifying with a particular side and failing to adjust when new information comes in. They become less judicious, less independent, less reliable, less useful. Yet while I didn't want to become an activist or crusader, I also worried that if I erred on the side of caution and didn't leap into the arena, people would die unnecessarily. My family and I existed only because a French diplomat and French journalists had skirted the lines of what was appropriate and helped my father when he was a refugee. I was glad that they hadn't simply been wringing their hands from the sidelines and refusing to help.

So, often doubting that I was weighing the trade-offs correctly, I called attention early to the Save Darfur movement, which became a major force on university campuses and in the Jewish community. Synagogues that had previously been hostile to me because of my tough criticism of the Israeli occupation now invited me to speak about Darfur, and I couldn't handle all the university invitations. When Harvard's

Kennedy School of Government invited me to give the commencement address, I did agree, and I took nine-year-old Caroline with me. As we walked over to the Kennedy School, we saw swarms of people crossing the street, going in the other direction.

"Where's everybody going?" I asked a young woman.

"Oh, didn't you know? Bill Clinton is speaking in Harvard Yard in a few minutes. He's the Class Day speaker for undergraduates."

Oh, no! I stopped and stooped down to look Caroline in the eye. I wanted to explain that her dad was going to be humiliated by an empty array of seats, because no one would be there to listen to him.

"You see, at the same time that I'm speaking in this building, Bill Clinton is going to be speaking just over there," I told her. "And everybody would rather hear Bill Clinton than me."

Caroline looked thoughtfully into my eyes.

"Daddy," she said, "can I go hear Bill Clinton?"

It has been almost two decades since I began writing about Darfur, and killings and rapes continue in the 2020s. Hundreds of thousands have been killed, and millions have been displaced. Yet it is also true that the pace of killing has subsided—the large-scale slaughter has mostly stopped—and the architect of the genocide, President Bashir of Sudan, has been imprisoned.

On my trips back to Darfur, I saw rows of planes from the United Nations, the International Committee of the Red Cross and other aid groups, not to mention African Union and United Nations peacekeepers. Billions of dollars were allocated for aid, and an industry emerged to keep displaced Darfuris alive. It all felt inadequate because atrocities continued, albeit at a slower pace, but it was a tribute to the power of journalism and citizen movements to shake people up and reallocate resources. Articles, videos, television coverage, protests, reports by Amnesty International and Human Rights Watch—these did have an effect. They raised the cost to Bashir of genocide, they raised the cost to China of supporting Bashir, and they raised the cost to the West of doing nothing.

The world didn't save enough lives and many died unnecessarily, but relief efforts and peacekeepers and political pressure did make a difference. I was proud of the Pulitzer and other prizes I received for calling attention to Darfur, but moved above all by an account by Robert DeVecchi, the past president of the International Rescue Committee, that my writing had singlehandedly mobilized world attention to the Darfur genocide and saved the lives of hundreds of thousands of people. Compared to that, any prize shrivels to nothingness.

IT WAS ALWAYS STRANGE to return home from Darfur. I spent much of my time there scared for my physical safety—Samantha Power, the writer who later served in the Obama and Biden administrations, had once said that I was the person the Janjaweed most wanted to kill, a compliment of sorts. I'd spend the morning in Darfur talking my way through checkpoints, a knot constantly in my stomach, seeing smoke rising from burning villages and then interviewing survivors. Then I'd take a late-afternoon domestic flight from Darfur to Khartoum, followed by the night flight on Lufthansa to Frankfurt. When the plane took off for Germany, I'd feel relief sweep over me and the knot would untangle.

I befriended an American aid worker in Darfur. She was a tough young woman, and I never saw her flinch or show any sign of weakness in the field. She had once visited an area controlled by the Janjaweed where, in public, everyone insisted that things were fine. Then she spoke privately to two sisters, both of the Fur ethnic group, who explained that the Janjaweed were enslaving the Fur villagers, forcing them to work in the fields and even to pay protection money to be allowed to live. The two sisters were forced to cook for the Janjaweed fighters and to accept being raped by them. The girls' father, while terrified, had finally summoned the courage to approach the Janjaweed commander and beg him to free his daughters. That's when the commander had called the sisters over—and beheaded their father in front of them.

My friend had asked the sisters what she could do for them. "There's nothing you can do for us," one told her. "We just want to die."

That gnaws on you, that impotence, that frustration at the world turning its back on people in need, but it also offers perspective on our own lives. Over Christmas vacation, my friend was back in the United States, sitting in her grandmother's backyard, thinking about all she had seen in Darfur. And suddenly this strong aid worker, for all her fortitude, collapsed on the ground in tears.

What had happened? She explained that her eyes had fallen on a birdhouse that her grandmother had set up, and she had found herself thinking how lucky she was to be in a country where we mostly take security for granted, where we typically have enough food and clothing—and where we even have enough extra that we can help wild birds get through the winter. That's when my friend suddenly felt an epiphany about how lucky she was, and she burst into tears as she contemplated this good fortune and her responsibility to pay it forward.

I identify with my friend's story. Every time I see a birdhouse on our farm in Yamhill, I think how lucky we are—and also how we bear moral obligations when we win the lottery of birth.

29

What I Learned from Genocide

I was frustrated that so many of my columns from Darfur landed with barely a ripple. Meanwhile, New York in 2004 was engrossed by the story of two red-tailed hawks who had lived in a luxury apartment building on Fifth Avenue just across from Central Park. The building management, annoyed by the bird droppings, dismantled the hawks' nest—and suddenly all of New York was up in arms about the suffering of two homeless hawks. The hawks, dubbed Pale Male and Lola, became the objects of pity and activism, celebrated in articles, a documentary and multiple books. Mary Tyler Moore helped lead a campaign that won widespread sympathy for the homeless raptors, and the Audubon Society described Pale Male as the most famous red-tailed hawk in the world. The pressure worked, for the building management capitulated and allowed the hawks to return.

"What's wrong with my writing?" I asked Sheryl as I watched that story unfold. "Why can't I generate the same outrage over hundreds of thousands of people killed in Darfur?"

To answer that question and sharpen my writing, I turned to social psychologists for research on what makes us care. Some of the best work on this had been done by Dr. Paul Slovic, and he found that what moves us isn't rationality but emotion, and in particular individual stories.

We know that as Stalin supposedly said (there's no proof he did), "One death is a tragedy, a million deaths is a statistic." We care about a single child who falls into a well, not about a million children at risk of starvation. But Slovic found that the point when we begin to be numbed is not when n equals 1 million or even 1,000. It's when n equals 2. In other words, even if there are just two people suffering, our empathy ebbs. We're hardwired to care, but to care for a person in front of us, not for groups of people we read about in a newspaper column.

Slovic also found that we're turned off by situations that seem hopeless. We're more likely to get engaged with a situation that, however bad, seems as if it might improve if we helped.

The implication is that journalists and aid workers get storytelling about crises exactly wrong. We focus on scale—"millions are at risk!"—and emphasize the problems so much that we don't fully acknowledge the opportunities for improvement. All this is a turnoff. So increasingly I began to tell individual stories, and then broadened the scene to describe the larger problem. I also tried to show that these crises are fixable and to outline steps that readers could take to make a difference.

I realized I needed to find new ways to reach the public that were less formal than my *Times* column, and that led me to plunge full bore into social media, video, audio, blogging, 360-degree photography and any other pathway I could find. I also proposed a "win-a-trip" contest to take a student with me on a reporting trip to Darfur.

"Why don't you run that by legal," advised Gail Collins, the editorial page editor. So I dropped by the office of my friend David McCraw, an in-house lawyer.

"I've got a great idea!" I told McCraw. "I'll hold a competition to choose a student to travel with me to Darfur! Then the student will write on my blog about the trip."

McCraw looked at me, and there was a long pause. "So you want to take a student into a war zone?" he asked.

Hmm. This effort needed rebranding. So I reconceived of "win-a-trip" as an annual contest to take a student on a reporting trip to the developing world, and that was approved. For my first trip, in 2006, the winner was Casey Parks, a student from Millsaps College in Mississippi who had grown up poor and never traveled outside the United States. With Naka, Casey and I traveled through Equatorial Guinea, Cameroon and Central African Republic, which was then next to Darfur and also dissolving into chaos. We were held up twice at gunpoint.

Naka (with the camera),
Casey and me on my first
win-a-trip journey, on a bad road
in rural Cameroon in 2006.

Even more shattering, we watched a mother of three, Prudence, die
in childbirth after we donated blood and money to try to save her—
a reminder of the toll of maternal mortality. Casey wrote powerful
blog posts and helped attract new interest to these issues among young
people, and I've continued to hold the win-a-trip journey almost every
year since.

The winners are carrying on the kind of journalism that highlights
important but neglected issues. Casey is now a reporter at *The Washington Post* along with another winner, Tyler Pager. A third winner, Dr.
Leana Wen, is a medical commentator and columnist at the *Post*, and a
fourth, Mitch Smith, is a reporter at the *Times*. Another, Dr. Saumya
Dave, is a novel-writing psychiatrist, and still another, Austin Meyer,
is an outstanding filmmaker. Nicole Sganga and Cassidy McDonald
are both reporters for CBS News.

Watching Mary Tyler Moore's efforts on behalf of the red-tailed
hawks also underscored the power of celebrities to channel public
attention, so I began to recruit some to the cause. Celebrity is not my
natural ecosystem, and I'm not a movie buff. My assistants used to
laugh at my ignorance of popular culture. When I was slated to mod-

erate a panel on refugee issues that included Angelina Jolie, I was led over to a couch on which three women were sitting.

"This is Nick Kristof," my guide said, but he didn't tell me which of the women was Angelina Jolie. I looked blankly from one to another and had no idea who to stick out my hand to. Fortunately, Angelina recognized my plight and with amusement jumped up to say hello. I've worked with her many times since on issues ranging from refugees to sexual violence.

Another co-conspirator was Mia Farrow, whom I met in Darfur on an airstrip when we were both traveling there. I admired her fearlessness. Once she was driving in a United Nations car near the Chad-Sudan border and saw a big local man beating a woman.

"Stop!" Mia shouted, and her driver pulled over. Mia jumped out of the car, ran over and leaped on the man's back. He stopped beating the woman, who ran off, and the United Nations driver managed to distract the man and recover Mia before she was ripped in half.

Bono has particularly impressed me with his mastery of global poverty issues, from AIDS policy to anti-corruption initiatives. While Bono is eloquent in front of the television cameras about the need to address poverty, I've also seen that he is equally effective in boardrooms with corporate executives or in meetings with senior politicians. A pragmatist, Bono went out of his way to build bridges to Republican lawmakers so that humanitarian work could be bipartisan, and he helped make the ONE Campaign a particularly potent advocacy organization for addressing AIDS and extreme poverty. Bono also understands better than most the importance not only of haranguing politicians to do more, but also of thanking them for doing the right thing. His music made him famous, but I would argue that his greatest legacy is his humanitarian efforts that have saved lives all around the world.

Another celebrity came to me by voicemail. I was in a remote village in Pakistan one evening when I used my satellite phone to check voicemails on my *Times* office line. It was the usual collection of story pitches, publishers asking me to write about a new book, families asking me to write about a prisoner who they said was innocent, television producers asking me to come on a show to speak about this or that, and then there was someone whose name I didn't catch but who was interested in Darfur. I forwarded the message to my assistant, Winter

Miller, explaining that I couldn't hear it well and asked her to follow up if necessary.

"I know you don't know pop culture, Nick," Winter emailed me. "But I thought you'd know the name of the guy who left that message you forwarded. It was George Clooney. He's an actor."

I actually had heard of Clooney. I would even have been able to pick him out of a three-person lineup on a couch.

George's father, Nick, had been a television and print journalist, and George cared deeply about bringing attention to neglected causes. We traveled together to the Chad-Darfur border area at a time when it was insecure and the Janjaweed was attacking villages with impunity. We drove through a lonely area that had sometimes been subject to attacks, and he didn't flinch.

"I'm always followed by cameras, so if they're going to follow me anyway let's see if we can shift some of the attention to Darfur," he said to me.

George and I slept on mattresses on the floor in front of what looked like a large bloodstain on the wall. George became an eloquent advocate for Darfur, and he shared my view that Darfuris weren't just passive victims but inspirational figures who had plenty to teach us. One woman we met, Suad Ahmed, particularly moved us. A blunt, plain-spoken woman in her mid-twenties, she had been gathering firewood with her younger sister, Halima, who was then about ten years old (we heard different accounts of Halima's age), when Janjaweed gunmen approached on horseback, firing in the air and shouting "Stop!"

"Run!" Suad told Halima. "Run back to camp!" Then Suad made a decoy of herself, running in the other direction to draw the attention of the Janjaweed. She was herself already married with two children and another on the way so she thought she could survive rape, while if Halima were raped she might be unable ever to marry.

Suad's strategy worked. The Janjaweed saw her and ran her down, and eight of them gang-raped and beat her. But Halima escaped, her reputation intact. After the Janjaweed left, people from the village came out and carried Suad back to camp. She refused medical attention because she didn't want people to know that she had been raped; everyone might suspect it, but no one would ask. Suad didn't even tell her husband about it, yet she told me.

George and I talked about how reporting rape stories can be an ethical minefield. It could humiliate a survivor and even lead her to be prosecuted for being raped, under the crimes of fornication or adultery. Yet if we didn't use names and told stories only generically, the accounts would be shorn of emotional impact. If we wanted to raise the cost to Sudan of a policy of rape, it helped to publish individual accounts—only with the woman's full consent, of course.

If a woman was sure she wanted to share her story, I worked out ways to shield her identity so that the authorities could never trace her. I might give a first name if it was a common one, but never a second name or a home village. Suad said she was willing to be identified and to tell her story on video; indeed, she was determined to do so. Still, I worried about the impact on her: I doubted that she understood what the *Times* and the Internet were, and I wanted to make sure that her consent was meaningful. I asked her repeatedly if she understood the risk of stigma and punishment, and she said she did. Still, I had reservations; I didn't want to put her in danger.

"So why do you want to tell your story?" I asked.

"This is the only way I have to fight genocide," she replied. "This is my only way." I understood that, and I let her tell the story—while doing everything I could to keep anyone from figuring out who she was. Thankfully, I was successful in that.

In a world that had responded so cravenly to genocide, Suad's courage inspired me. Her actions reminded me that when we humans are tested, we are capable of extraordinary courage, generosity and magnanimity. She's also a reminder that we journalists can tell stories and galvanize the public only with the help of people who are willing to share their stories, even painful and humiliating ones. Suad undertook greater risks for *Times* readers than I did.

George became increasingly active on Darfur issues, and television networks were eager to have him on their shows—and then he'd divert the conversation to Darfur. He was arrested at a protest outside the Sudanese Embassy in Washington, and that drew more attention. George knew storytelling and used his communications skills to engage people who weren't otherwise interested in a distant genocide, and all that attention added to the pressure on Western governments.

Journalists traditionally were wary of advising readers about how to help. The thinking was that we should illuminate problems, but that it was sappy and might seem like finger-wagging to tell people where to donate. But people were always asking me how they could help, and readers were frustrated when they read an account of a problem and didn't get any useful information about how they could make a difference. It seems to me a service to readers to advise them how they can chip away at a problem we write about. I also think that news organizations should try to cultivate readers as a community, and that involves supporting them and building relationships with them.

So I began experimenting with offering readers a pathway to help. This wasn't always smooth. When I offered to forward donations to a Pakistani rape victim, Mukhtar Mai, who had started a school in her village to fight the attitudes that led to her rape, readers contributed more than $1 million. But much of the money was in the form of checks made out to her, to me, to the *Times* or to entities that didn't exist like the "Nick Kristof Fund for Mukhtar Mai." I had a box full of checks but no idea what to do with them. The *Times* chief financial officer was able to bail me out of that mess, and henceforth I made sure that I was never handling money. Instead, I always found an aid group to take on that task.

After some experimentation, my journalistic efforts to nurture reader philanthropy evolved into an annual "holiday giving guide" suggesting a few aid groups to which people might donate. My editors were initially wary. The *Times* had a holiday drive, the Neediest Cases Fund, but should individual journalists be in the business of soliciting funds? The *Times* didn't allow columnists to speak at nonprofit fundraisers, on the theory that this lessened our independence, so why allow a columnist to recommend who to donate to?

My view was that we were overthinking it. News organizations should provide services to readers, including offering advice on effective organizations to give to, and this was part of the *Times*'s role as a public good. My editors were skeptical but let it go. I began partnering for my holiday giving guide with a nonprofit called Focusing Philanthropy, and soon we were raising more than $6 million a year and recruiting large numbers of volunteers as well. I felt I was paying forward my parents' good fortune.

My thinking had also shifted about where journalists can have the most impact. When I began the column, I had anticipated weighing in on the issues of the day and had naïvely assumed that I'd be changing people's minds twice a week. But I soon realized—my Iraq War columns cemented this realization—that when I wrote about issues that readers had already thought about, I rarely changed minds. I could write about the Arab-Israeli conflict, or abortion, or the political disputes in the headlines, and people who started out agreeing with me would nod in approval, and those who started out disagreeing would scoff: *Kristof completely missed the boat today.*

The public may exaggerate the ability of any individual pundit to influence the issues of the day. When Robert Samuelson, a *Washington Post* columnist, retired after fifty years of superb writing, he declared in his farewell column: "So far as I can tell, nothing that I have written has ever had the slightest effect on what actually happened." Samuelson protested too much, for he was a wise observer who influenced many of us, but it is true that while writing about the issues of the day generates page views, it doesn't often change the course of events.

Where I found I could have an impact was projecting onto the agenda issues that were neglected. These generated fewer page views, but they nagged at readers. Once people were forced to think about a genocide, or about obstetric fistula, or about human trafficking, it was hard to remain indifferent. In some ways, these humanitarian issues were poorly suited for a column, for what was interesting wasn't the

With my *Times* colleague Adam Ellick, making a video about the oppression of Rohingya villagers in Myanmar.

opinion ("genocide is bad") but the underlying reporting about atrocities. I also risked coming across as a sanctimonious moralizer on global issues readers weren't deeply interested in. However, reporters in the newsroom often couldn't get much attention for such global human rights stories, while I could use my column to force policymakers to take notice.

So after the slaughter in Darfur subsided, I continued to highlight other conflicts. I sneaked into the Nuba Mountains of Sudan to cover a brutal war there, and I hiked through marshes to cover massacres in South Sudan. I evaded checkpoints in Myanmar to report on the oppression of the Rohingya—which in time became a genocide against the Rohingya.

The Arab Spring drew me in for similar reasons. After World War II my dad had been stuck in Eastern Europe, a collection of countries that systematically denied people both political freedom and economic opportunity. Today, much of the Arab world seems the same. It's a region that holds its people back instead of empowering them. Then, in 2011, political and economic frustrations parallel to those that had led my dad to flee Romania ignited a mass movement in Tunisia that then spread to Egypt, Libya, Yemen, Syria and beyond. I caught a flight to Cairo.

30

The Arab Spring

One morning in Cairo in February 2011, I arrived by taxi at Tahrir Square, the center of the Arab Spring democracy movement. I had spent a week reporting on the Arab Spring protesters, and Tahrir had been full of joyful families daring to hope that they could have a better future. The police had kidnapped individuals here and there but had not cracked down on the protest as a whole. But now I saw government thugs attacking pro-democracy protesters. The thugs carried knives, swords, straight razors and clubs with nails sticking out. Bodies of people they had attacked were being carried away on stretchers.

"Go thirty meters, and let me out," I told the driver. I stepped out and watched, and the goons evidently thought I was harmless enough—looking more like a lost tourist than a pro-democracy protester—that they didn't attack me.

Then I saw two local women trying to make their way to the square to join the protests. The two women turned out to be middle-aged sisters, Minna and Amal, and they wore headscarves in the conservative Muslim style. They looked timid, frail and out of place, and my heart sank as the thugs surrounded them. I approached and watched as the goons tried to intimidate them with weapons and shouts.

"You bitches," one man shouted in Arabic.

"Go home!" another yelled in Minna's face.

"You want trouble?" another shouted, waving his club at Amal.

But the women answered mildly and listened calmly.

"We just want democracy," Amal said soothingly. "That would be good for all of us."

"What you need isn't democracy, it's a beating," one of the men shouted back. But when jostled and screamed at by these men, Amal and Minna refused to be cowed. When blocked, they simply listened patiently to the men without saying much, and the thugs seemed unwilling to club conservatively dressed women on a city street; perhaps it helped that I was there. Eventually the men rushed over to attack a different target, and I moved in to interview Amal and Minna. I introduced myself and jotted down their names, and then asked them why they were taking this risk.

"We need democracy in Egypt," Amal said simply. "We just want what you have."

Seeing me interview the two women drew the thugs back over to us. One of them was stroking a straight razor, and it was no longer plausible that I was just a tourist.

"I'm a reporter from *The New York Times*," I explained in Arabic. "I'd like to interview you. Can I ask you what you think of this?"

I'd learned over the years that one way to defuse a threat is to pull out a notebook or camera and begin an interview. Almost everyone is flattered at being asked their opinions, so instead of cutting your throat, the assailant will pontificate. Sure enough, the goons competed to tell me how they were protecting Egypt from terrorists, and Amal and Minna saw their chance and slipped into Tahrir Square to join the embattled protesters there.

The next day, Tahrir turned into an even worse battleground. I sneaked into the square and found thousands of protesters inside—surrounded by a similar number of government thugs who hurled rocks and clubbed anyone they could get their hands on. It looked like a war from the Middle Ages. A field hospital in Tahrir Square was staffed by a corps of 120 volunteer doctors, including an elderly physician who walked with a cane and said he had written his will before driving all night to the hospital.

I interviewed a carpenter named Mahmoud who was in the field hospital getting a bloody head wound patched up.

"This is my seventh time for medical care," he explained. He looked it. Mahmoud's left arm was in a sling, his leg was in a cast, and his head was currently being bandaged.

"How are you going to get out of the square to get home?" I asked.

"Home?" he asked indignantly. "I'm not going home!" He tried to gesture with his left arm, forgetting it was tied up, and then did so with his right arm. "I can still fight. And as long as I can fight for democracy, I will. I just want these doctors to hurry up with the dressing on my head, and I hope they don't let the wound bleed into my eyes so I can't see. Then I'm back to the front line."

"Can I take your photo?" I asked Mahmoud.

"Sure, as long as you don't delay me."

As I framed the photo, I inadvertently backed into a wheelchair. Another fighter being bandaged, Amr, was in it, so as Mahmoud rushed back to the battle I asked Amr about his backstory. Amr said he had lost his legs years ago in a train accident, but he was determined to fight for democracy along with others in the square. So Amr rolled his wheelchair to the front lines to throw rocks at the government forces. He was now being stitched up for a wound from a chunk of concrete hurled by a government agent, but he was impatient to return to the fray.

I asked Amr, as politely as I knew how, why a double amputee in a wheelchair was battling government thugs armed with Molotov cocktails, clubs, machetes, bricks and razors.

"I still have my hands," he said firmly. "God willing, I will keep fighting."

People like that—Minna and Amal, Mahmoud and Amr—left a deep impression on me. They were willing to risk everything for democracy, even as so many Americans don't even bother to vote, even as some Americans seem intent on undermining the democracy that they have. The people who most value democracy, I reflected, are those who lack it.

I flew to Bahrain, traditionally one of the most relaxed and fun countries in the Gulf, a beautiful, prosperous and traditionally tolerant society whose ambassador to Washington was a Jewish woman. Bahrain was a close ally of the United States and home to the U.S. Navy's Fifth Fleet. Alcohol was abundant and rules were relaxed, making it a playground for Saudis, but there was an inherent tension because the royal family was Sunni Muslim while the population was mostly Shiite. Not surprisingly, the Shiite population wanted more representation, and protesters set up peaceful pro-democracy encampments. Saudi Arabia, which wields enormous influence over the Bahrain royal

Covering a pro-democracy protest in Bahrain during the Arab
Spring. I thought the government might be less inclined to attack
protesters if foreign reporters were visible; it didn't much matter.

family, demanded a crackdown, so Bahraini troops broke up the pro-
democracy camp, clubbing first protesters and then doctors trying to
treat the injured.

On a beautiful sunny afternoon, on a pleasant road in Bahrain, a
throng of pro-democracy protesters walked down the street chanting
"Peaceful, peaceful." Many had their arms in the air. Without warning,
Bahraini troops opened fire and shot them in cold blood.

Here was a United States–backed government crushing peaceful
protesters, creating a considerable awkwardness for American officials
(who I thought were too measured in their reactions). I spent the day
reporting and tweeting about the shootings and beatings. In the hospital that evening, my phone finally ran out of juice, but I continued
to interview people who had been injured and the loved ones of those
who had been killed. The hospital morgue steadily filled with corpses
of men with bullet holes and shattered skulls. As I was about to return
to my hotel, I heard whispers that an American man was among those
shot. I combed the hospital and morgue and couldn't find him, but the

rumors grew. He was an American journalist and had been shot in the back, and he was fighting for his life.

"Do you know anything about this American journalist who supposedly was shot?" I asked doctors, nurses, guards, anyone I could find. Most had heard the rumor and some added details—he was conscious; no, in a coma; Americans were trying to evacuate him—but I could not verify it or find where he was. Finally, I gave up and returned to my hotel. After entering my room, I plugged in my phone and was reminded again that social media is not reliable as a news source. On Twitter, I found out who that American was: me. When I had abruptly stopped tweeting, a rumor had somehow started that I had been shot, and then it took on details and gained authority as it was repeated. I reassured friends that, as best I could tell, I was alive.

The Arab Spring started full of hope, but ultimately it backfired and mostly brought less freedom to Arabs rather than more. It was a reminder of the principle I had absorbed at Tiananmen: When one side has principles and the other has guns, weaponry usually prevails. Syria had been one of my favorite countries, because of the desert oasis at Palmyra and the citadel in Aleppo. Syrian protesters started out handing flowers to police, as a symbol of their goodwill. But the government cracked down brutally, and after 2012 Syria dissolved into a civil war marked by torture, rape, starvation and murder, with hundreds of thousands of lives lost. I argued that President Obama should do more to support rebels in Syria (and many of his advisors, including Hillary Clinton, David Petraeus and John Kerry agreed), but in fairness I also called for and welcomed the intervention in Libya, which turned out to be messier than I had foreseen. Foreign policy always has more problems than solutions, and Obama grew frustrated by critics like me, who shared his general worldview but whom he regarded as too inclined to take risks on slippery slopes like Syria.

"Even if we get criticized, I'm not interested in the crowd in Tahrir Square and Nick Kristof," Obama told aides, according to a memoir by Ben Rhodes, his deputy national security advisor.

Obama was, along with Bill Clinton, the brightest of recent presidents, but far more disciplined than Clinton and less swayed by politics. I got to know Obama when he was a senator involved in the Save Darfur effort, and I was impressed. He did his homework, and my sense was that both Barack and Michelle Obama were genuine idealists who engaged in the political world for the right reasons. Yet over time, I sensed that Obama became more cautious, perhaps because he was the subject of so many unfair attacks. I saw the unfairness firsthand after I interviewed him and wrote a column in 2007 that included these paragraphs about his upbringing partly in Indonesia:

> Mr. Obama recalled the opening lines of the Arabic call to prayer, reciting them with a first-rate accent. In a remark that seemed delightfully uncalculated (it'll give Alabama voters heart attacks), Mr. Obama described the call to prayer as "one of the prettiest sounds on Earth at sunset."
>
> Moreover, Mr. Obama's own grandfather in Kenya was a Muslim. Mr. Obama never met his grandfather and says he isn't sure if his grandfather's two wives were simultaneous or consecutive, or even if he was Sunni or Shiite.

For years afterward, commentators on the far right claimed that my interview proved that Obama was a Muslim whose native language was Arabic. Conservatives kept demanding the tape of the interview, as if it would prove something important. But most people who have lived in a Muslim country can recite the opening of the call to prayer; you hear it five times a day from mosques. Obama had a good accent because he was a boy when he heard the call to prayer and children excel at accents, but of course he didn't understand Arabic (he did speak reasonable Indonesian). For me, that was one glimpse of the way Barack and Michelle were battered by unfair attacks constantly, and I think that not only grayed his hair but also made him more careful.

He would occasionally invite columnists to the White House for off-the-record briefings, but these tended not to be very effective at winning people over. Obama is impressive in his mastery of topics, and he can be funny, but he's not an innately warm person like Bill Clinton or even Joe Biden. He's a bit aloof, and his natural voice is dispassionate analysis. He would come across in the White House meetings as a cool law school lecturer, brilliantly examining issues but sometimes with a whiff of arrogance. He appealed to minds more than hearts, and while I admired his intellect I sometimes wished his public-facing messaging were a bit less cerebral.

The arrogance was real in the sense that Obama could be cocky, but at the same time he was very self-aware and knew that his career had benefited from good luck. He always acknowledged that some racists voted against him because of his race, but also said that there were probably some other Americans who cast ballots for him because of his race. Obama thrived with complexity, and I admired that about him. Politicians are usually trying to simplify everything to squeeze it into a ten-second sound bite, while Obama never lost his appreciation for nuance. In that sense, he was a breath of fresh air in politics, and that sophistication made him popular among the university educated. But it perhaps wasn't an accident that the Obama presidency also marked a transition in the United States to a society in which education increasingly became the political fault line: Particularly with white voters but not exclusively so, educated people vote Democratic and the less educated vote Republican, the opposite of the traditional divide.

Obama had an acute appreciation for how predictions can go wrong and everything can go south, and that had been helpful in leading him to oppose the Iraq War. But this caution also made him wary of leading internationally as much as he might have, and many of his aides were deeply frustrated by his caution in Syria. They wanted to arm the moderate Syrian resistance, which might have toppled the Syrian regime and at least would have given John Kerry some leverage in his negotiations with the Syrian authorities. Because the moderate Syrian resistance got no support, it collapsed, and its fighters grew beards and joined extremist groups supported by the Gulf states, because those groups did take on the Syrian army.

The truth is that distant humanitarian crises in countries where we have little leverage are a policy nightmare. That was true of the Armenian genocide, the Holocaust, the Cambodian and Rwandan genocides, and of Darfur and Syria. If we're not going to dispatch American troops, and we mostly won't and shouldn't, then we don't have many ways to stop a government from killing its people. Sanctions can help, as can naming and shaming, and here and there we can support rebel groups that seem credible, but these options require boldness and a certain amount of good luck to succeed.

We journalists may have helped produce that caution in Obama and other presidents by seizing upon gotchas and elevating partisan accusations from the other side. Even as I protested what I saw as

Obama's paralysis on Syria, I worried that columnists like me were unremittingly negative and failed to offer positive reinforcement when presidents did the right thing. I excoriated President Bush for not doing more in Darfur, yet didn't heap praise on him for ending the north-south civil war in Sudan or for successfully intervening in Liberia to help end a civil war in 2003. Those were humanitarian triumphs.

Likewise, I repeatedly reproached President Obama for not doing more in Syria and South Sudan, but I didn't adequately praise him for one of the best foreign policy moves he made: a military intervention in 2014 at Mount Sinjar, on the border of Syria and Iraq, to block a genocide by the Islamic State against the Yazidi people. That intervention saved thousands of lives, yet few people have even heard of it. Bleeding hearts like me should have done more to give presidents credit when they took political risks to save lives.

31

Covering Genocide and Poverty
Left Me an Optimist

When I reported from Darfur, Congo, Yemen or other places inhabited by people of color, woke critics sometimes scoffed that my reporting was that of a "white savior." The same charge was made against other white writers and photographers reporting in the developing world, and against white doctors and aid workers there. It reflected the notion that white American busybodies preen as they engage in moral crusades abroad, without acknowledging their own severe problems at home. There was a kernel of truth to this. It became "cool" for Americans to volunteer in Rwanda or Tanzania rather than at a prison or school in their hometown, and journalists and aid workers alike can be condescending or disrespectful to people abroad.

Then again, the fundamental conceit of the white savior critique—that white people are eager to help people of color—doesn't ring true to me. The blunt truth is that the big problem isn't white saviors but white indifference. Americans intervened in 1999 to protect white Kosovars and in 2022 to protect white Ukrainians, but did much less to help Black Rwandans, Black Darfuris or Black Ethiopians, or to rescue Arabs in Syria or Yemen, or to support other dark-skinned people like Guatemalans or the Rohingya. Given all that, is it really true that the fundamental problem is a surplus of white saviors? White activism, particularly from the Jewish community, saved many lives of Black people in Darfur, and anything that discourages white people from activism against atrocities against people of color is likely to mean more people dying unnecessarily in places like Tigray or Myanmar.

Another thread of the white savior critique emphasizes that coverage or activism often portrays those suffering as two-dimensional "victims," and that the right to tell these stories belongs to people from these countries rather than to Western journalists or aid workers. Again, there's some validity to this critique. Simplistic narratives abound in journalism and the humanitarian community, and too often we drop into countries and report without knowing enough about local conditions.

That said, the critique is also simplistic. How would it work to have stories told primarily by local people? Were Germans really the best people to cover the Holocaust? Should Rwandans have been the voice of the genocide there? Should European newspapers have hired only Southerners to report on the American civil rights movement, and if so, which Southerners? If a news organization wanted to hire a local person to cover the genocide in Myanmar, where repression of the Rohingya was popular, the majority of those local people would have said that there was no genocide at all and that the Rohingya didn't exist as a people.

I'm also shaped by my interactions with extraordinary people who are sometimes perceived as "white saviors" but in my view are heroes. A white Australian doctor named Catherine Hamlin moved to Ethiopia in 1959 and started a hospital to repair obstetric fistulas and treat some of the most forgotten women in the world. Dr. Hamlin became the world's leading advocate for women and girls with fistulas and raised enormous sums for corrective surgery (credit Oprah Winfrey, who put Dr. Hamlin on her show and also contributed personally). Even during the most perilous periods of the Ethiopian dictatorship, Dr. Hamlin continued her work as so many others fled. For six decades she gave her all, enduring danger and difficulty, to alleviate suffering in Ethiopia. Dr. Hamlin, who died in 2020, was regarded by many Ethiopians as a saint.

Likewise, when I reported on the civil war in the Nuba Mountains of Sudan, I heard legends of "Dr. Tom," an American named Tom Catena who ran a hospital in a rebel-held area and provided the only medical care in one of the most dangerous and disease-ridden parts of the world. I was scared reporting in the area for just a few days at a

Children hiding in caves in the Nuba Mountains to protect themselves from bombs.

time. Sudanese government planes dropped bombs in the rebel areas, so we camouflaged our vehicle so it couldn't be easily seen from the air. When we saw a plane overhead we would rush for caves in the rocks. The caves had spitting cobras, so even hiding from a bomb could be lethal. The only road into rebel territory in Nuba was a dirt path, and the day before I took it on one occasion government soldiers ambushed civilian vehicles and opened fire on them. Dr. Tom endured all this year after year after year.

Dr. Tom treats bombing victims and leprosy patients, he delivers babies and sets broken arms, he pries shrapnel from women's bellies and amputates their children's limbs. Somehow he manages a 435-bed hospital with no reliable electrical power or running water, not even an X-ray machine. He is always on call, except when he periodically falls unconscious from malaria—and then the entire Nuban community holds its breath to pray that he will survive. Dr. Tom is motivated by his conservative Catholic faith to save lives half a world away, and I am in awe of him. It's easy for Americans sitting on a university campus to scoff at missionaries like Dr. Tom, but impossible when you see him working by himself in a hospital that has been bombed eleven times.

"He's Jesus Christ," a Muslim paramount chief told me. The chief explained that Jesus healed the sick, made the blind see and helped the lame walk—and that is what Dr. Tom does every day. It's because of witnessing people like Dr. Tom that I'm more friendly to evangelicals and conservative Catholics than most liberals are. Yes, there is religious intolerance and bigotry, but there's also irreligious intolerance when people on the left mock people of faith.

American university students sometimes complain to me that American news coverage of humanitarian crises is exploitative. They see news organizations profiting off the suffering of people in the developing world. But in truth, coverage of overseas crises invariably loses money. For me, one striking moment came when I filed a Yemen column back-to-back with one about the nomination to the Supreme Court of Brett Kavanaugh. The Kavanaugh column, which I whipped off in an afternoon with no dangerous travel, had *seven times* as many page views as the Yemen column.

That's why most news organizations don't cover Yemen, which at the time the United Nations called the world's worst humanitarian crisis. George Bernard Shaw wrote many years ago: "The worst sin towards our fellow creatures is not to hate them, but to be indifferent to them."

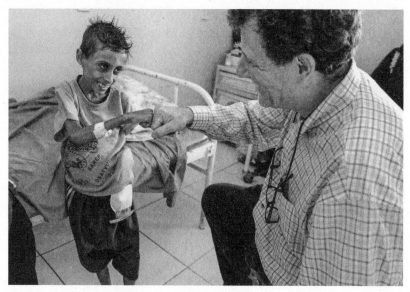

A fist bump with a malnourished child whom I interviewed, with his family's permission, in Yemen. *Photo by Giles Clarke.*

And that indifference, toward people of any complexion, strikes me as a far more urgent concern than the willingness of some doctors or aid workers to help people of a different race. If Western news organizations weren't willing to lose money to cover these crises, the suffering would be even greater.

IF IN GENERAL I was skeptical of progressive critiques of foreign news coverage, there was a strand that I found important and valid. I came to think that we in the media had a bias toward negative news that often harmed poor parts of the world. If I think of the places in Africa that I have principally covered over the last quarter century, they are the crisis spots: southern Africa during the AIDS crisis, Darfur, Congo, South Sudan and so on. Somebody reading my columns might get the misimpression that all of Africa is starving or fighting, when in fact some parts of Africa have done well. I undercovered countries like Ghana that were democratic and making progress in education and health care.

That's a way in which journalism can be misleading: We cover planes that crash, not the far greater number of planes that land. There's a media bias toward bad news, layered on top of a cognitive bias toward threats. In the context of global development, our audiences learn primarily about failure and setbacks, not the progress that is often the backdrop. As former Treasury secretary Larry Summers once told me, "Events are 75 percent bad, and trends are 75 percent good." And we cover events more than the trends.

I fear that journalists and aid workers, by focusing on crises, genocide and famine, further a narrative of Africa as a dangerous, failed continent and that this makes it more difficult to attract tourism and investments. So I've tried to also write about the successes there, and in my win-a-trip journeys we normally include a stop that highlights progress as well as challenges.

This penchant for bad news misinforms the public. In polls, a majority of Americans say that world poverty is getting worse. That is false. One of the most stunning trends of my lifetime has been an extraordinary decline in global poverty, disease and illiteracy. When I graduated from college, more than 40 percent of the world's people were still living in "extreme poverty"—equivalent to a bit more than $2 per person per day in today's money. Adjusted for inflation, fewer than 10 percent now live at that level.

People meeting me for the first time often expect me to be dour and pessimistic, the Eeyore of journalists, because I spend so much time covering war, genocide, poverty and disease. But the truth is that my travels have left me with a deep appreciation for this positive change—and for the capacity for further improvements. Much of the change in my lifetime has been positive for most of the world's inhabitants.

Just about the worst thing that can happen to any person is to lose a child. Until the early nineteenth century, almost half of all humans died in childhood. Now that's down to about 4 percent.

For most of the last twenty years or so, we could have run a front-page headline reading "Another 170,000 People Moved Out of Extreme Poverty Yesterday." Or: "Another 200,000 People Get Piped Water for the First Time Today." Or: "Another 325,000 People Today Get Electricity for the First Time." Those are the real figures for the number of people lifted out of extreme poverty or gaining running water or electricity on an average day around the world.

The 2020 COVID-19 pandemic marked a setback in this global march forward, and the number of people living in extreme poverty increased. Children also dropped out of school, hunger increased and girls were forced to marry early. But this was a setback of a few years, not longer, and preliminary evidence suggests that global child mortality actually continued to decline during the pandemic, though more slowly than before. Meanwhile, other trends, such as the declining cost of solar panels and improved access to the Internet, continued apace.

We in journalism focus mostly on villains, which is fair enough. But side-by-side with the worst of humanity, you see the very best. You encounter evil, but also heroism. For every genocidal warlord burning a village or throwing a child on a bonfire, there is a Dr. Tom Catena or a Dr. Catherine Hamlin, or some nameless hero showing undaunted courage.

When the Lord's Resistance Army attacked St. Mary's College, a girls' boarding school in northern Uganda, and kidnapped 139 teenage girls, tying their hands and leading them off into the bush, the police and army refused to help. They were terrified of the LRA and its reputation for killing and raping without hesitation. But an Italian nun at the school, Sister Rachele Fassera, refused to be intimidated. She set out, armed only with a rosary, and followed the trail of the kidnappers, in part by the litter they left behind. On the second day, Sister Rachele caught up with the kidnappers and begged them to release the girls. She pleaded, she browbeat them, she refused to give in—and the kidnappers released 109 of the girls to Sister Rachele. Sister Rachele didn't accomplish all she had hoped, but with raw courage and a rosary she accomplished what the Ugandan army could not.

Sister Rachele, and so many other selfless souls struggling to do justice around the world, inspire me. They remind me of one of my favorite quotations from Robert F. Kennedy: "Each time a man stands up for an ideal, or acts to improve the lot of others, or strikes out against injustice, he sends forth a tiny ripple of hope, and . . . those ripples build a current which can sweep down the mightiest walls of oppression and resistance."

Despite the setback from the pandemic, if you had to pick one time to be born in the roughly 300,000 years since the emergence of modern humans, it would probably be this decade. Yes, climate change presents enormous challenges, and there are risks of nuclear war and eroding democracy. But you still would probably be less likely to die, less likely to be malnourished, and more likely to be educated than at any point in human history.

Those aren't just numbers. I've seen the progress in my reporting. When I first traveled through West Africa with Dan Esty in 1982, when I wasn't being held at gunpoint by soldiers in Ghana what pained me the most was the beggars in every town. Some were blind from cataracts, trachoma or river blindness. Others were disfigured by leprosy. Still others were crippled by clubfoot. Now these terrible ailments are all disappearing.

Cataracts are repaired in a quick $50 surgery by groups like Cure Blindness and Seva Foundation. Blinding trachoma is prevented with inexpensive azithromycin, by groups like Helen Keller International. River blindness is prevented with ivermectin, used to deworm dogs and horses in America, thanks to the work of the Carter Center and others. For less than $1 a person, we can prevent devastating and excruciating causes of blindness.

Leprosy has also declined more than 90 percent, and leprosy hospitals are so empty they are taking on patients with new kinds of ailments—fistula, Buruli ulcer and more. Bravo to Leprosy Mission International for its work! As for clubfoot, it is easily treated in infants by organizations like Miracle Feet, leaving children able to run and play like everyone else; they can grow up to become doctors or teachers instead of beggars.

A journalist following in my footsteps today may never see the leprosy, blindness and genocide that I've spent decades covering—and it's that sense of progress that fills me with hope, and with determination to keep pushing for further gains.

32

A Day in the Life of a Columnist

Dawn. Cocks start crowing. A call to prayer sounds from a distant mosque, then a second mosque joins in. Somewhere outside, two women start arguing loudly. I roll over. My eyes flutter open. Any hope of getting another thirty minutes of sleep?

A truck revs its engine outside my window. Nope, sleep is out. Since this is a "typical" day in the life of a columnist, and there is no such day, this is a composite that we'll place somewhere challenging like Mali or Guinea. So I'm in a rural "guest house" for $10 a night. There is a generator or solar panel that provides electricity for a few hours each evening.

I disentangle myself from my mosquito net and pull myself out of the sheet sack. It's still almost dark, but my headlamp spent the night on my forehead so I wouldn't lose it. I turn it on, quickly dress and brush my teeth with bottled water. I dig out my toilet paper and use the pit toilet. Then I ask someone in French if there's anywhere to get a cup of coffee.

There isn't. So I dig in my pack for dark-chocolate-covered coffee beans—the next best thing.

I check to see if the photographer with me is awake. She is, even though she was up late downloading photos from a camera card onto her laptop. I have often traveled with a female photographer or female win-a-trip journalist, and sometimes I wonder if there's a risk of a

#MeToo problem. It can be awkward: Sometimes we plan the next day's journey in my hotel room or hers, because there's nowhere else. There are usually no toilets available during the day, other than a bush. The "shower" may be a bucket of water behind a reed mat with a few holes in it. I'm periodically called upon to stand guard on one side of a bush or mat while a colleague attends to her business on the other. Alternatively, there may not be enough rooms in the guest house, so several of us pile into a room together, sleeping on the floor.

My female assistant, Winter Miller, once persuaded me to take her along on a trip to Darfur, but Winter was traveling on her own dime and couldn't afford the hotel where Naka and I were staying in the Chadian capital. I had two beds in my room, but sharing a hotel room with my female assistant was not the kind of thing I wanted to read about on Twitter. Fortunately, Naka offered the extra bed in his room to Winter. We've always managed to work problems out like that: There can be some awkwardness about men and women working together, but it works out if everyone is professional. And it's important to do so, for a male-female pairing often is particularly effective at getting stories, as it may be easier for a female journalist to talk to local women and girls.

While waiting for the team, I set up the satellite phone outside and

Interviewing rebel soldiers in Sudan.

download emails, while emailing my assistant that we're setting out for the day and advising her roughly where we're headed. If we go missing, I want people to know where to look for us.

For most of my career as a columnist, nobody but my assistant would know where I was in the world, but these days the *Times* has more oversight and, in the case of dangerous places, protocols and security consultants. Initially, I took a dim view of security consultants after watching them work with television networks, especially at NBC with Ann Curry. One of her security advisors put us at unnecessary risk at a checkpoint at night in Darfur by getting out of the car and approaching some very jittery soldiers after curfew. Another made Ann buy a month's supply of water for a five-day trip, so that there was no room in her vehicle for anything else. A third was so hopeless that Ann left him behind in a South Sudan refugee camp as we sneaked across the border into the Nuba Mountains of Sudan.

The *Times* brought in security consultants after my brilliant colleague Anthony Shadid died of a medical condition on a reporting trip to Syria in 2012, and my attitude warmed to security advisors after I made my own trip to Syria in 2014. Two security consultants accompanied me and, frustratingly, didn't allow me to go very far into Syria. They had intelligence warning of the risk of kidnappings. A few weeks after that Syria trip, reporters started getting kidnapped in Syria by extremist groups and were held hostage, sometimes tortured and killed—and I'm very grateful for having been restrained.

After a breakfast of protein bars and almonds, I'm ready to go, and we drive off to an area we hear has acute malnutrition. If I'm traveling with the help of a local aid group, as I sometimes am, we may take two vehicles. That's for safety if one breaks down and also to deter bandits (including soldiers). As we approach a checkpoint, one car hangs back to watch and witness that everything goes smoothly. I use my kids' old walkie-talkies to communicate between the vehicles.

I plan to be out for the day and return to this guest house for the evening, but I still load my pack in the vehicle. Maybe we'll get a lead and go in some other direction, or maybe the car will break down; it's always good to have your belongings.

On trips like this, I carry a large shoulder bag packed with my laptop, BGan satellite phone for email, Iridium satellite phone for voice, American iPhone, a second iPhone with a local SIM card, files, books, a Kindle, charger cables, power inverter for charging devices in the vehicle, adapter plugs, extra passport photos if necessary for permits, copies of my passport, and various press passes.

My main pack is usually a long carry-on duffel, for I try never to check a bag. Once I checked a bag to Bamako, Mali, and had to leave for Timbuktu before it could catch up with me—and I've been too traumatized to check a bag since. I carry a ski lock so I can run it through the padlock on my duffel and tie it to something immovable in my hotel room. You never want your bags to walk off without you.

The duffel can be packed in the back of the vehicle. It includes a small mosquito net to keep malarial mosquitoes at bay at night and a tightly woven silk sheet sack to sleep in, reducing the risk of assaults by bed bugs. An encounter with bed bugs in Central African Republic left me never wanting to repeat that experience, and I don't know that Sheryl would forgive me if I brought bed bugs home.

I aim for clothes that don't show dirt and minimize the risk of being pickpocketed. That means zipper pockets or hidden pockets for a passport and real wallet (though I also carry my decoy wallet with $20 and a couple of expired cards in case I get robbed at gunpoint). A company called Clothing Arts makes pants that are a challenge for pickpockets.

Some of my travel clothing comes from the backpacking world, because it's light and can be washed in a creek or hotel sink and will dry overnight. That includes quick-dry synthetic underwear and thin socks that don't take up space. I wear dark khakis and dark running shoes, and sometimes pack a very light blazer in case I meet the president of a country. I also bring a wide-brim backpacking hat that looks a bit silly but is light and folds up to almost nothing. And of course I bring sunscreen and insect repellent.

Somewhere in the pack is a small first aid kit, with water purification tablets, duct tape, medicines and a tourniquet. I began carrying tourniquets after journalists Tim Hetherington and Chris Hondros were killed in 2011 while covering the Libya war. Tim bled copiously from a leg injury, and the advice I got was that tourniquets significantly improve the odds of surviving if you're bleeding badly from an extremity.

———

AFTER A COUPLE OF HOURS of driving, we spot a school and a health clinic next to each other. "Let's stop!" I suggest, and we pull over and walk into the school. The principal turns out to be absent along with much of the staff, but we find a congenial teacher to chat with.

Then, with the teacher's permission, I chat with some students. I ask them about school fees. I ask why the pump over the school well isn't working. I ask a few students if they have any schoolbooks, and I may quiz them: What is four plus eight? Can they read simple words? Do they have a pen or pencil?

I deeply believe in this kind of questioning because so often I've found a huge gap between the official reality that exists in national statistics and the practical reality on the ground. Interviewing officials and academics in the capital is important, but they sometimes aren't fully attuned to the complexities of village life—just as I don't think officials in Washington have a proper understanding of the struggles of my friends in Yamhill. That's why well-meant policies often don't work, whether in America or in Algeria. I've learned to pore over academic studies and statistical reports that offer the view at 30,000 feet, but also to spend a good deal of time interrogating villagers at a distance of just three feet. In rural Pakistan, I discovered "ghost schools" that exist on paper but were never actually built; the money was diverted into someone's pocket along the way.

Then we drop in on the clinic, with similar questions. Can we see what medicines are in stock? Do kids get dewormed? Do they get vaccinated? Is birth control available? Where do women give birth, and who delivers babies? If it's a traditional birth attendant, does that person have any training? Does she use a new razor blade with each birth, or does she use the same one each time? If female genital mutilation is practiced here, is she the one who does the cutting?

The teacher has mentioned a village that he says is so poor that almost no one goes to school from there. The clinic director agrees that it's very poor and names another village five miles beyond that is even poorer.

"Is the road there safe?" I ask. "Are there bandits? Rebels?"

"It's safe," they agree.

I ask the driver to speak with them and get directions, and then we set out. Nothing seems alarming in the first village, so we continue to the next one. A bridge has collapsed, so we leave the vehicle, wade through the creek, and walk on. We pass a street market, so I pause and take a look at what's available, closely examining the medications for sale: Do they look real, or are they counterfeit?

Too often I've seen desperate parents sell a goat to raise money to buy anti-malarial medicine to save a sick child. But then the medicine turns out to be fake and the child dies anyway. One study found that in some African markets, up to 70 percent of basic medicines like antibiotics and anti-malarials are counterfeit, and in South America contraceptive pills are often faked so that women face unwanted pregnancies. Often the counterfeits are produced by Chinese or Indian companies and sold to poor countries that can't detect the fakery.

I'm also interested in what's in the market generally. There will usually be cigarettes and, especially if it's not a Muslim country, alcohol ranging from the national beer to homemade sorghum liquor. Candy will be available as well. But what about things that can save a life, like bed nets? Or what about deworming medicine? I always want to understand—not in an accusatory way, but to better grasp how to solve problems—why impoverished people have the resources to buy candy but not schoolbooks. Or I'll talk to men who can afford to buy sex from prostitutes but say they can't afford condoms. Money is usually controlled by men, and in many cultures there's a tradition of men pampering themselves while not spending much on women or children; these traditions seem to be changing as women become more educated and gain more earning power.

When we arrive in the village, people are happy and surprised to see us. The chief prepares to slaughter a goat to honor me with a feast. I frantically get the interpreter to explain that I don't eat meat: Please, please, please, don't slaughter the goat. The last thing I want to do is impoverish the village further.

Fortunately, the village chief agrees, but he does offer me some banana beer and cassava. I feel that it would be impolite to refuse him, so I take a bit. I cheerily dissemble and tell him how tasty his village's cassava is. I steer the conversation to why children don't go to school, to whether crops are failing because of a changing climate, and I ask if any children are going to be married soon. He tells me that a twelve-year-old girl is about to be married, because her father's crops have failed and he can't feed her. She will be the second wife of a man in his forties.

"Can I meet this girl and her family?" I ask.

He leads me to a hut where the family is preparing for the wedding. It turns out that the groom will pay a bride price of sixteen goats, and the family desperately needs the money from the sale of the goats for medicine to save the mom, who has an ailment that doesn't translate but sounds as if it might be schistosomiasis, caused by parasitic worms.

I am planning on doing a column about child marriage and how it is linked to poverty and climate change. I know there are lots of global statistics that I can get from the United Nations, but I want to see what's happening on the ground and find examples of the problem.

"What do you think of being married?" I ask the girl.

"It is God's will," she says, but she looks fearful. I ask her a few more times, but I can't get her to express an opinion. I ask for her documents to verify that she is twelve, and the parents show me an ID that would make her sixteen years old.

The ID was issued two years ago, and the dad explains that he gave the birth date to the government office and may have gotten it wrong. "She's fourteen," he says. I ask the girl herself, and she says she thinks she's fifteen. I try to work out the age of her older and younger siblings, but their ages are equally uncertain.

Child marriage is illegal, and the village chief now senses that I might get him in trouble. National law, which no one pays attention to, says the marriage age is eighteen.

"Actually, she is eighteen," the village chief says. "I remember now, she is eighteen."

I wander over and talk to the people in the next house. After asking some unrelated questions, I ask them about the girl getting married. How old is she?

The village chief interjects something at that point.

"The chief is saying to the neighbor, 'Tell him she's eighteen,'" my translator advises me. The neighbor then pipes up, "She's eighteen."

This isn't going to work. I huddle with the photographer and work out a plan. "We'd like to get a photo of you with the other village leaders who make the important decisions," I tell the chief, trying to flatter him. "Can we gather them in front of your house?"

The photographer obligingly distracts the chief with a photo shoot, and I return with the interpreter to grill other neighbors. Finally, we find a new neighbor who says he knows how old the girl is because he has a son the same age, born just a week later. That boy has a government ID that lists a year of birth, without month or day, making him thirteen or fourteen. It was issued just a year later and seems credible. We're getting somewhere.

"Does the girl seem happy with the marriage, or is she unhappy?" I ask. "Does she cry often, or does she laugh a lot?"

I try to frame questions broadly like that, rather than give people a chance to answer "Yes," because sometimes people want to agree with whatever I ask. If I ask if she's happy, they'll say yes; if I ask if she's unhappy, they'll likewise nod and say yes. I learned early on in my travels that if I asked "Is this the way to the train station," it always was.

"Oh, she's laughing and smiling these days," the neighbor says. "She's very happy to be getting married."

I'm deflated.

I ask, "How do you know?"

"Oh, she was begging her father to let her be married," the neighbor says. "She was happy when he agreed."

Flummoxed, I ask the neighbor's wife, who has been silent, what she thinks. She agrees and explains further: "The girl's father beats her, and he is poor and doesn't give her much food. Her new husband has a reputation of being a kind man, and he is rich and has more food. So she is eager to be married and live a better life."

A girl under the age of fifteen is married approximately every seven seconds, Save the Children says, and here I've found a child marriage— yet this girl's story doesn't reflect the challenges of child marriage. Maybe I can use this girl as a paragraph or two to explain that it's complicated, but that's it.

One of the hardest parts of reporting in developing countries is getting facts right. If you let little things like ages slide, you can't be counted on for accuracy on the big things. Yet verification is awkward. You feel like a heel trying to verify the account of a rape survivor. In many cases, uncertainty lingers. "Journalism is always the art of the incomplete," Anthony Shadid once said. "You get bits and pieces."

In this case, there's no doubt that child marriage is a problem, and I'm still intrigued by the idea of doing a column on it if I can find the right story.

"Are there any other young girls who have just married around here?" I ask. "Or girls who will get married in the next week or two?"

"Oh, there's a very young girl getting married tomorrow, two villages over," the neighbor says. "The imam was talking about it. He thought she was too young. But what could the girl do after the teacher made her pregnant?"

"The teacher made her pregnant?" I ask. "Is she marrying the teacher?"

"Yes, he is a bad teacher. If the girls couldn't pay school fees, he would use them and let them stay in school. But this is the first time he got one pregnant."

"Will he get in trouble?"

"Not since he agreed to marry her. He didn't want to, but the village chief made him marry her. Otherwise, no one else would ever marry her. She was ruined."

"What about the girl? Did she want to marry him?"

The interpreter and the neighbor go back and forth; the neighbor seems to have trouble understanding the question. Finally, the interpreter explains: "He says he doesn't know."

I ask the interpreter to get as much information as possible, including the name of the village and whether it's possible to drive there.

Back at the guest house that night I get on the satellite phone and give New York my whereabouts, and my plans to visit the village the next day. For my next column, I email my assistant and ask her to dig up any statistics and journal articles on child marriage, and I send notes to a couple of experts asking their views on child marriage. Are the numbers going up or down? What age do they think constitutes child marriage? Is it cultural imperialism for us to object to fifteen-year-old girls getting married when Shakespeare has Juliet marrying Romeo at the age of thirteen? I tell them that I'm planning on writing a column describing child marriage as a huge global problem and asking them to push back if they think I'm wrong.

My assistant has also emailed with updates about visas. She has made another fruitless trip to the Venezuelan consulate, where my visa application has been languishing for two years, but there's some hope for a visa to Turkmenistan.

I spend a huge amount of time trying to extricate visas from countries that don't want to give them. Then after my visit, I'm usually banned for writing about human rights abuses, and it takes years to get me un-banned. North Korea once issued a statement that not only was I banned but all *New York Times* reporters would also be banned "for life." That took many years to unwind.

China in recent years has been recalcitrant about journalist visas, but even India once denied me a visa, because I wanted to write about health problems in the country. "We know we've got sick people," a top government official snapped. "We don't need Kristof to tell us that." But at the Indian Embassy in Phnom Penh I managed to get a transit visa good for seventy-two hours in India, and that got me inside the country. In Delhi, U.S. ambassador Frank Wisner invited me to a dinner party, seating me next to the Indian minister of health. I arrived straight from the airport, and the minister looked at me in surprise. "How are you here?" he asked.

"We are like ants in the kitchen," I explained. "You can't keep us out."

I'm not thinking about visas now, though, but about child marriage. Over dinner, we chat with three people at the next table about the appropriate age for marriage; they say that the average age for girls is rising as more girls go to school, but many still are married in their early or mid-teens. Dinner is meant to be goat stew, but since I don't eat meat, the restaurant owner offers me chopped cassava leaves. Much like chopped spinach, but better. So I relish the dinner as much as the conversation and am relieved not to have to raid my dwindling supply of protein bars. Another triumph: I arrange for a pot of coffee in the morning. Sated, I contemplate the prospect of finding people to interview tomorrow; I want to follow up on that idea of child marriage and of a teacher abusing his power with students—I believe that goes on often. What I've heard may be true, or it may not be, but I'll sort that out tomorrow.

Under my mosquito net, in my sheet sack, mosquitoes and bed bugs at bay, dreaming of good stories, I am secure and content. But tomorrow will bring new checkpoints to be negotiated, new risks of banditry or drunken soldiers, new encounters that will shake me to the core and gnaw at my gut, new stories that will demand to be told.

33

Exorcising Our Ghosts

In 1989, Jim Markham, a Rhodes Scholar a generation ahead of me who was Paris bureau chief of the *Times*, died by suicide. He shot himself with a hunting rifle in the stately home that was the official residence of the bureau chief in Paris (beautiful homes given to bureau chiefs disappeared with later cost-cutting). Markham was a brilliant journalist who had reported bravely from Iran, Vietnam and many other places and spoke several languages, including Hindi and German. The *Times* had just named him deputy foreign editor, and at age forty-six he was climbing the ladder and headed for a leadership position. But along the way, something went wrong.

Journalists (me included) traditionally feign toughness and are reluctant to acknowledge complications in our physical or mental health. We pretend we are invulnerable. After Markham's death, the paper became more sensitive to mental health burdens and offered more support.

In 1995, I reported on an enormous earthquake in Kobe, Japan, that had flattened neighborhoods and killed six thousand people. I worked almost around the clock for several days and was exhausted, but I had just filed an article well after midnight and was drifting off to my first good sleep in five days. Then the phone rang.

It was the deputy foreign editor, Steve Weisman. He beat around the bush for a bit, and I could tell he was getting to something awkward. Finally, it came. "We know you've seen some really difficult things,

Nick," Steve said. "And we've started a program to give correspondents confidential access to counselors. So if you want to take advantage of it, I can tell you how to do it."

I thanked him. But I wanted to shout: *I was doing just fine until you called and robbed me of my sleep. Now I'm jumping out the window.*

I'm glad I didn't say that, because Steve was right to make the call. Many years later, I wrote about Iraq and Afghan veterans struggling with PTSD, and some of their stories and symptoms felt familiar. I might have scoffed at the idea that I had suffered trauma from my reporting, but I had noticed that I had become quicker to tear up. Likewise, I grind my teeth at night and sometimes clench my jaw when I'm thinking or writing. I also developed a gastrointestinal problem that one doctor said was probably driven by stress.

I'm not sure what to make of all this, but I wonder if in the course of reporting I picked up the mildest case of PTSD. Like some of the veterans I wrote about, I was shot at and seared by terror more times than I can count. Steve Weisman knew what he was talking about after all.

The truth is that the things you see do haunt you. The sense of powerlessness when you're held at gunpoint, or when bullets are flying about, or when your plane is coming down for a crash landing—you feel you've lost all control, and that sense of vulnerability is hard to shake off afterward. The fear that clenches your gut may subside, but after many such clenchings your gut may never fully recover. "The body keeps the score," in the words of the psychiatrist and writer Bessel van der Kolk. I found that over the years I developed a protective emotional armor when speaking to survivors of terrible violence, perhaps in the way an emergency physician does. I can listen to a Rohingya mom talk about being gang-raped or losing her child, and most of the time I'm totally professional, getting the details and making sure I have names spelled correctly. And then something may set me off. Perhaps she mentions that the way she lost her child was that soldiers threw her baby on a bonfire and she begins weeping—and I find myself weeping, too. Children are the chink in my protective armor.

This is embarrassing! I'm supposed to be the grizzled columnist, veteran of a thousand traumas, and then with a photographer and an interpreter I'm interviewing an innocent kid who is sharing a story of pain and loss, and I find myself surreptitiously dabbing at tears.

I also find it very difficult to move on when I have put someone else at risk. That may be an interpreter, like the one detained with me in Darfur, or it may be a woman like Suad who wants to tell of her rape. Writing about the Vietnam War in *The Things They Carried*, Tim O'Brien observed: "The bad stuff never stops happening: it lives in its own dimension, replaying itself over and over." That's true of soldiers and also of journalists.

In my reporting, I was struck by the penchant of some traumatized people to repeatedly drift back to danger. Freud talked about this "compulsion to repeat," and it baffled me when it was veterans seeking out new wars, trafficked women returned to pimps or my old Yamhill friends returning to crime. Van der Kolk says that this addiction to danger may arise because the brain recalibrates what it needs to get a thrill, and I suspect that is sometimes true of war correspondents finding new conflicts to cover. My old friend and colleague in covering wars, Chris Hedges, once wrote a book about our trade with the resonant title *War Is a Force That Gives Us Meaning*.

I couldn't take my family into war zones, but I did try to ease the loneliness of relentless travel by pulling the kids out of school to accompany me on certain reporting trips abroad, to expose them to different worlds. The travel together left a deep impression on them and offered bonding opportunities. When post-election riots flared in Kenya in 2008, I took sixteen-year-old Gregory with me to interview survivors in the western part of the country. One survivor was a boy, also sixteen, from the Luo ethnic group (the same as President Obama) who had been chased by a mob from the Kikuyu ethnic group. The Kikuyu circumcise boys, and the Luo traditionally don't, so the mob seized the Luo boy, pulled down his pants, and circumcised him with a machete. (I don't know if this meant that they removed just his foreskin or if they hacked off his penis; the Luo boy was too traumatized to query about the details.) For Gregory, meeting a boy who had endured such mob violence was a lesson in the good fortune of attending a secure American school.

On that same trip, on the Sudan–South Sudan border, a group of gunmen tried to detain Gregory and me, but fortunately we had gunmen escorting us and escaped. On a different trip, Geoffrey and I were arrested in China while trying to interview the wife of an imprisoned labor leader. After that, Caroline complained that I had failed in my parental duties by never getting her arrested with me. When she was

Iranian women in the conservative city of Mashhad warmly welcomed Caroline.

fourteen, I did manage to lose her in Iran, in the holy city of Mashhad. She was unflustered and enjoyed touring the Mashhad shrine until I finally tracked her down. A group of Iranian women, on learning that she was American, bought her sweets and embraced her; I think she learned something about how there are good people even in countries we often consider our enemies.

On one trip with Caroline to Honduras, we were driving with a local priest through a particularly dangerous gang-controlled neighborhood in the capital, Tegucigalpa. The priest knew the gangs, but every time we got to a gang checkpoint and saw armed kids who were high on drugs or glue, we got nervous. After several such checkpoints, Caroline turned to me.

"You know, Dad," she said, "when my friends go on vacation abroad, they mostly go to the Caribbean." So for our next family vacation, over Thanksgiving, we all went to the Caribbean—to Haiti to help me cover the cholera outbreak there. For several days I led the kids through cholera hospitals, and they never asked to go back to the Caribbean.

I OFTEN TRIED to return from overseas reporting trips to heal my soul on the farm. But increasingly I'd come from a humanitarian crisis abroad and find another at home. When farms consolidated, sawmills closed, factories moved abroad and good union jobs were eliminated, many of my Yamhill friends found their lives shattered. Bob Bansen, my dairyman friend, would catch me up on grim news about old acquaintances.

"We used to talk about how this person or that person had been arrested for drugs," Bob observed. "Now we're talking about how this friend or that has died."

He was right: Of the kids on my old No. 6 school bus, three of the Green kids are gone, along with four of the Briggs kids. Farlan Knapp died from substance abuse, and then one of his daughters drank herself to death. My neighbor Bobby Stepp was sentenced to life in prison for raping his girlfriend's daughter. Bobby wrote and asked me to put money in his prison account. "My family has abandoned me," he said. "I don't have anyone else." I was horrified by what Bobby had done but deposited money into his prison account so he could buy tennis shoes and food, in honor of a shared childhood when we were all buddies walking to and from the school bus.

I had trouble coming to grips with the fact that Bobby was one of two boys on my old No. 6 school bus who were imprisoned for raping very young girls. How could a single school bus end up with two child rapists? Meanwhile, two other boys had cooked meth. Others had gone to prison for armed robbery and a brutal assault. After the Stepps moved out of their old house, another family had moved in, and the daughter went to prison for attempted murder in a meth deal gone wrong.

I sometimes mythologized Yamhill because I needed it as a retreat from the Yemens and Darfurs of the world, but it was difficult to sustain that when I thought of Bobby raping a young girl. Growing up, we had thought of places like Yamhill as the heartland, the repository of traditional values, the land of barn raisings and mutual support. Now a dysfunction was ripping through working-class households.

My friends suffered greatly but also inflicted great suffering. Billy Beard, who had taught me to look out for Bigfoot, was high on meth in the beach town of Lincoln City one day when he walked into a store and attacked the shopkeeper. "I don't remember it a bit," Billy told me. "I just remember waking up after the police arrested me." Billy was sentenced to twenty years in prison for that, got out and started a successful wine country chauffeur business, and then was cheated by his partner and retired. He soon was fighting cancer, and we stayed in touch by phone, text and visits. He was a good man, and I struggled to understand how someone as smart, talented and decent as Billy could have committed such an assault. He died in October 2023, at the age of sixty-four.

I have words to describe the chaos and upheaval that I encounter in poor countries, but we lack the vocabulary to describe the distress in working-class America. It's a broad, interlinked pathology that includes mental health problems, homelessness, addiction, loneliness, chronic unemployment, suicide, crime, educational failure, unraveling of the family, conspiracy theories, political extremism and early death. We in journalism sometimes address elements of this, but I don't think we fully acknowledge how much these are pulling the country down.

How could it be that a newborn boy in Mississippi has a shorter life expectancy than a newborn boy in Bangladesh? Why are one in seven prime-age men out of work, a higher share than during the Great Depression? What is the link between deaths of despair and a drift toward QAnon? Is the embrace of right-wing extremism among working-class men in particular today parallel to the rise of fascism among desperate Italians, Germans and Spaniards between the world wars? I don't think we fully know what's going on, and I don't think we've tried hard enough to understand this pathology or address it.

Liberals too often dismiss all this as simply a crisis of the white working class, but it's more complicated than that. While the rise of extremism is most pronounced among white working-class men, it has also been growing among people of color, especially men. I wish we had a name for this pathology, because it might help us recognize it and respond to it. The Great Misery? The Great Unraveling? I'm not sure what term to use, but I believe that educated Republicans and Democrats alike have not come to terms with the despair among many of the least educated in America.

One of the things I've learned from the distress in old friends is the cost of America's failure to invest in early childhood, in social services, in job training, in addiction treatment, in mental health services. That was primarily a conservative failure. But liberals also betrayed timber towns, mining counties and factory towns, cutting out traditional sources of income without investing in alternative business models or in job training. Liberals then compound the myopia with stereotypes about hillbillies, rednecks and people of faith.

In much of America, local churches play a crucial role in helping the needy. Churches run food pantries, offer hot breakfasts, hand out clothing and shelter the homeless. In Yamhill, it was difficult not to observe that the only local institution that seemed to provide full protection was the Mormon church: Kids raised Mormon didn't struggle with drugs in the same way, partly because they had so many eyes on them enforcing strict standards. I've talked with my friend Tara Westover, author of the wrenching memoir *Educated*, about the challenges of our rural hometowns, and we wonder if hers came through better partly because it was full of Mormons.

At a larger level, the only institution that did not abandon Americans left behind was the United States military. Kids who enlist in the army, marines or another branch can learn a skill, gain discipline and find a path to a better life. The military has been a particular lifeline for Native Americans, who have been betrayed by virtually every other government agency. But when Sheryl and I encouraged at-risk young people to sign up for the military, we found that many didn't qualify. They hadn't graduated from high school, or they had a criminal record, or they couldn't pass a drug test, or they couldn't pass the physical fitness test, or they had some other disqualification. Only a minority of young adults today qualify for the United States military.

YAMHILL WAS ASSOCIATED with another kind of pain, a personal one. My father had aged well, and in his late eighties he was still climbing Douglas fir trees on the edge of our property to photograph our cherry orchard in bloom.

"Be careful!" I'd shout up, and Sheryl and I would watch nervously and hope he didn't fall. He still disappeared into the mountains to hunt deer and elk, and at the age of eighty-nine he rolled the tractor and broke his leg. He was in great pain but managed to dislodge himself and walk away.

"I think I'd better go to the hospital," he said—and that was a pretty good indication that he was half-dead. I hoped I would be rolling tractors at the age of eighty-nine.

By the time he reached ninety-one, though, he was suffering the beginnings of dementia. He spoke frequently of his childhood home in Romania, and one day he suggested we all drive over to his native village.

"We can't drive there," my mother said. "It's in Europe. We're in Oregon."

"Oh, yes, of course," my dad replied, embarrassed. "Of course."

One day he was feeling unwell and underwent several procedures at the hospital. The doctors debated whether to keep him overnight or discharge him. In the end, they released him with a supply of medications. The next morning when he woke up, he pulled out his .308 hunting rifle and shot and killed himself.

It's painful to write these words. How could a man with such a strong survival instinct, who so loved his family, who had endured war and concentration camps with an indomitable spirit of survival, kill himself? My dad was a warm and happy man with a deeply ingrained optimism and no history of depression. We worried that my father's suicide would traumatize our kids—Gregory was just graduating from high school, and Caroline from middle school—and for some time we didn't tell them it was a suicide (when someone dies at ninety-one, the cause of death doesn't much arise).

So why had my father killed himself? The best answer the doctors could offer was that his medications had had an unexpected interaction with his age and psyche, spurring sudden depression or psychosis. That, and the fact that he had a hunting rifle at hand.

I had written for years about the toll of guns in America, feeling that I had a special obligation to advocate for gun-safety measures since I grew up with firearms and for a year as a teenager was even a member of the National Rifle Association (membership came free as a perk of the gun-safety course I took at age thirteen). More than half of gun deaths each year in the United States are suicides, and they are one reason for the high suicide rates in America: Most suicide attempts fail, but suicide attempts with guns invariably succeed.

Losing a family member to gun violence is a reminder of America's failed gun policy. America has lost more people to gun violence, including suicide, since I graduated from high school in 1977 (some 1.5 million) than in all the wars in American history dating back to the Revolutionary War (1.4 million).

Many of my friends in rural Oregon are strong gun-rights advocates who see the issue differently than I do. But I've found it is possible to have constructive discussions even with such people—and if we can talk in a civil way about guns, surely we can discuss just about anything. I start out my gun conversations by noting that we all recognize that there has to be some minimum age to buy handguns—we don't want eleven-year-olds buying firearms—and that in Oregon this minimum age is eighteen for private sales. Meanwhile, in Wyoming—one of the most gun-friendly states in the country—it's twenty-one. I suggest: Shouldn't we follow Wyoming and raise the minimum age to twenty-one? And if people with felonies are barred from possessing guns, what about those with violent misdemeanor convictions? What about those who have engaged in stalking, have a history of drug and alcohol abuse, or have a domestic violence protection order against them? People are at least willing to have these knotty, respectful conversations—and we're all better off when we can have them and listen to each other.

REPORTING ON GENOCIDES and losing my dad and many old friends took a toll on my mental health. Perhaps because of my rural roots, I sought help not from therapists but from what might be called wilderness therapy. Backpacking became my refuge. It's where I heal.

Gregory and Geoffrey drifted toward other activities as they moved into their teenage years, so Caroline became my main hiking companion. The trips got longer as she grew older. When she was fourteen, she and I disappeared into the woods for a two-hundred-mile backpack on the Pacific Crest Trail. Unfortunately, there were late snows that year that left us unable to find the trail in the Three Sisters Wilderness. We spent a couple of days lost in the woods, hiking north by map and compass on three feet of snow and having little idea whether we were near the trail or far from it. Once I was elated to find some footprints: We must have found the trail! We followed the tracks until Caroline noticed that the footprints had claws.

"Dad," she said, "I think that's a bear you're following."

We eventually found the trail again, and soon we decided to finish the Oregon segment of the Pacific Crest Trail, then the Washington segment as well. When we had done those, we figured we might as well do California as well. So over a half-dozen years, Caroline and I hiked

Hiking with Caroline on the Pacific Crest Trail.
Photo by Barney Scout Mann.

the entire 2,650-mile Pacific Crest Trail. It was the best parenting I ever did. Neither of us could get lost on our screens or in calls with our friends; we were stuck with each other. We chatted about all kinds of things, and it was on the trail that Caroline persuaded me to follow my principles and give up meat-eating.

Caroline became an adult over the course of our six-year hiking adventure; she became her own person. In a piece we published jointly for *Backpacker Magazine*, she lovingly skewered me:

> Dad's idea of "a good campsite" doesn't always align with mine. Dad will point to a vaguely level site dotted with rocks and elk feces and exclaim, "Caroline, this is perfect. All those weeds and roots will serve as nature's mattress." I relent, and then Dad whips out the air mattress he needs for his "sensitive back," even though I couldn't bring extra underwear because we're "ultralight." I have a fun night being jabbed by sticks and Dad wakes up perfectly rested from "nature's mattress."*

* The article is "Growing Up on the PCT," August 2019, and it's also online. Caroline teases me in it quite unmercifully.

Together on the trail we were rained on, we went thirsty, we slipped on snow and we experienced the spiritual exhilaration of the wilderness. We rose each morning with the sun, carried everything on our backs, drank from creeks, bathed in lakes and rivers, rested in alpine meadows dazzling with wildflowers, forded creeks swollen with snowmelt, cursed mosquitoes, lamented forests ravaged by forest fires, and in the evening laid out a ground sheet and our sleeping bags to sleep under the stars. We didn't carry a tent; if it looked as if it might rain, we put up a tarp to shield us. We marveled at springs burbling water from the ground, at the sheer beauty of the mountains, at the ability of water to seep into our shoes and through our tarp, at the relentlessness of mosquitoes seeking Caroline's tender skin.

"Dad, I just counted," she told me once. "I have forty-nine mosquito bites on my forehead alone!"

I fear that if the United States were being formed today, the most beautiful spots of wilderness would be privatized and sold off to tycoons. But our forebears were more public-spirited. People like Theodore Roosevelt and Gifford Pinchot were wealthy and could afford their own wilderness refuges, but they wanted to ensure public access to wild places—and the result is that much of the American West is publicly owned. So that's my natural therapy: When I'm troubled by what a mess the world is, I disappear into the mountains, for they offer perspective. They were here a thousand years ago, and they will be here a thousand years from now. In our daily lives, we're in control, and we can move the temperature up or down a single degree; in the mountains, we're always too hot or too cold, and all trails seem to be mostly uphill. We're not lords of the universe but atoms in the firmament. That vast green firmament is salve for my soul; the wilderness is my cathedral.

34

Women Hold Up Half the Sky

M y reporting on crises abroad and at home underscored to me again and again how central women's stories are to—to, well, everything.

In Darfur, as I said, women didn't initially speak much about rapes because of the shame they would suffer. But gradually so many women became pregnant after their husbands had been killed that it became obvious what was happening. Darfur women were typically raped when they left their camps or villages to gather firewood, so I asked why it was always the women who collected firewood.

"It's simple," one woman told me. "When the men go out, they're killed. The women are *only* raped."

What a statement! Too often, sexual violence is simply accepted as part of the landscape. A United Nations survey found that almost a quarter of men in six Asian countries acknowledged that they had raped someone, and 37 percent of men in a South African province said that they had raped.

On a trip to Pakistan I encountered a woman who had been walking to school at the age of fourteen when she was hit on the head—and woke up in a brothel at the other end of the country. She spent six years in the brothel being raped before she finally managed to escape. The brothel owner said he would capture her, torture her and kill her—and then he bribed the police, who arrested the woman and were about to return her to him. I quickly wrote a column that won the woman her freedom. That was satisfying, but there were millions of women and girls still locked up in brothels around the world.

Readers sometimes had a hard time understanding that "modern slavery" isn't hyperbole. So on a trip to Cambodia, I asked David McCraw, a *Times* lawyer, about the legality of buying human beings: If I purchased a girl from her brothel and freed her, was I breaking any American law? He didn't think so. So to make a point, I ended up buying two girls from their brothels in a town called Poipet—$150 for one, and a bit more than $200 for the other—and helped them return to their families. I was staggered when I got written receipts for them: It was like buying a farm animal.

Some readers sent me messages along the lines of "Buy one for me, too." In fact, I didn't believe in buying girls their freedom as a general practice, because that would simply incentivize traffickers to kidnap more girls. I wanted to bankrupt traffickers, not enrich them. In this kind of reporting I knew I was navigating along the very edge of what was appropriate. I wanted to shake people up and call attention to a humanitarian crisis, but I came close to tabloid sensationalism. I wasn't entirely sure what I myself thought of what I was doing.

Times editors generally trusted my judgment on these issues, with perhaps one exception. In postwar Sierra Leone, which had undergone an epidemic of sexual violence, I happened to come across a fifteen-year-old girl who was trying to report her pastor for repeatedly raping her and other girls. The girl was brave for speaking up and seeking to prosecute the pastor, but the police couldn't find him to arrest him. Then the girl had a suggestion: If I as a foreigner called up the pastor and asked to meet him, he would be flattered and would agree to meet—and then the police could swoop in and arrest him. I wondered about the ethics of that. Should a journalist help the police arrest a suspect? Shouldn't a journalist remain on the sidelines, observing?

This is a question that bears revisiting. It reflects a constant tension in the work of journalists, and reporters must debate these questions to help navigate an ethical path. In this case, I feared that if I didn't help, the pastor would hear the police were seeking him and would disappear and prey on other girls. My view of journalistic ethics has always been that a simple test is What would it look like on a billboard? I figured that "Kristof helps nab child rapist" was a billboard I could live with.

So I called the pastor. The *Times* has guidelines that its journalists should never lie but need not volunteer information, so I was careful to avoid saying anything untrue. It all worked smoothly: The pastor agreed to meet me, and the police arrested him. That evening, the neighborhood had a spontaneous celebration, and more girls acknowledged that the pastor had raped them as well. The actress Eva Mendes sponsored the girl who had first reported the pastor at the best boarding school in Sierra Leone so she could continue her education, and on returning to New York I wrote about the incident, disclosing my own role.

Andy Rosenthal, the editorial page editor, was startled to read that I had helped arrest someone, and that morning he called me into a meeting with Arthur Sulzberger Jr. to talk about it. I think it was meant as an intervention to yank me back from cowboy journalism. I argued that I had followed *Times* policy, but they were both clearly uncomfortable with what I had done. Fair enough: I agreed that if something like that came up again, I would give Andy a call before careening off into some course of action that he would read about in the paper. It helped that the public seemed entirely supportive of what I had done, and that bolstered my general view that our paramount ethical obligations are as humans rather than as reporters.

THE MORE SHERYL AND I TALKED about the challenges facing women worldwide, the more we wanted to write a book about the topic. We came to feel that women and girls were systematically held back in ways that hurt them, their children and entire societies. As Simone de Beauvoir said, "Her wings are cut and then she is blamed for not knowing how to fly." We also believed that the best way to remedy many international problems was to invest in educating girls and then usher those educated women into the labor force. Women represented not just tragedy but also opportunity, and we made that point in our 2009 book *Half the Sky*.

Perhaps one reason I saw acutely the benefits of empowering women was simply that I was surrounded by strong women—Sheryl, my mother, my forebears. One of my British female ancestors was arrested in the suffragette movement for breaking a window at 10 Downing Street to demand women's rights. Our family tells that part of the story with pride and then mumbles the rest: Her husband was so irritated at her action, and at the fact that she used his umbrella to break the glass, that he didn't bail her out until the next day.

My mother was one of the early female PhDs at Columbia University, and she deeply believed in taking action to solve problems. When she tutored Black children in reading and found that in the 1960s there weren't many children's books with Black protagonists, she wrote an excellent children's novel, *Steal Away Home*, about two Black boys who escape north on the Underground Railroad in 1858. She always hounded visitors to our home to sign petitions on behalf of political prisoners around the world, and for half a century she was active in the Yamhill County Democratic Central Committee. I had a model at home as I was growing up of how an educated woman can contribute to society and household, yet too often what I saw around the world was squandered potential.

We were proud of *Half the Sky*, but in retrospect I wonder if we should have written more about gender in the United States. There's no doubt that women in some foreign countries experience worse problems, but we don't have the moral authority to protest other countries' shortcomings unless we make greater efforts to address our own.

Five years after *Half the Sky*, Dylan Farrow reached out to me. I was a friend of her mother, Mia Farrow, and of her brother, Ronan Farrow, and of course I knew about the allegations that Woody Allen had sexually assaulted Dylan when she was a young child. Dylan herself had never addressed the allegations but now, as an adult, she wanted to. Woody Allen had just won a Golden Globe lifetime achievement award, and she had written an essay in which she expressed her frustration. Could I help her publish it?

Dylan sent me the essay, and I offered it to the *Times* op-ed editors, who declined to run it. She likewise offered it to the *Los Angeles Times*, who also rejected it. I thought that was a mistake: The allegations involving her had been a topic of national debate, but we had never heard from the alleged victim. Was it right to deny her a platform, after we had heard from so many other people? And the lifetime achievement award had revived the debate, so it wasn't about a dispute two decades earlier but about a present question of whether we should honor people who have such a cloud hanging over them.

I ran Dylan's essay in full on my *Times* blog and wrote a column excerpting it. Her essay began:

What's your favorite Woody Allen movie? Before you answer, you should know: when I was seven years old, Woody Allen took me by the hand and led me into a dim, closet-like attic on the second floor of our house. He told me to lay on my stomach and play with my brother's electric train set. Then he sexually assaulted me. He talked to me while he did it, whispering that I was a good girl, that this was our secret, promising that we'd go to Paris and I'd be a star in his movies. I remember staring at that toy train, focusing on it as it traveled in its circle around the attic. To this day, I find it difficult to look at toy trains.

This was a backdoor way of getting her essay out to the public after editors had rejected it, and it was fraught because of my relationship with members of her family (I disclosed that, of course). Plenty of readers thought this inappropriate, and there was a stark gender gap in the response. A statistician, Emma Pierson, analyzed the online comments below the article and found that female commenters overwhelmingly believed Dylan; male commenters were evenly split.

A problem with the piece—and the larger debate—is that none of us can be sure what happened between Woody and Dylan. I believe Dylan, and most #MeToo allegations have proven credible, but one study suggested that between 2 percent and 10 percent of sexual assault allegations are false. So we're in this messy situation where either Woody or Dylan is not telling the truth, and a shadow is hanging over Woody that can never be confirmed or dispelled. I understand how his backers feel I was unfair to him, but I think that credible allegations should be aired. And a starting point in presenting an honor like a lifetime achievement award should be that the winner is indisputably honorable.

In the case of Dylan Farrow, the public dispute continued because the facts were murky, but that was not true of the next maelstrom involving sexual assault. In 2017, I had a call from my *Times* colleague Jodi Kantor. She swore me to secrecy and said she was working on an investigation of sexual assaults by Harvey Weinstein. Jodi believed that Weinstein had made unwelcome advances toward my friend Ashley Judd, so would I ask Ashley if she would talk about it? I made the introduction, and Ashley showed enormous courage in speaking on the record. The two-part series about Weinstein began with Ashley's story:

Two decades ago, the Hollywood producer Harvey Weinstein invited Ashley Judd to the Peninsula Beverly Hills hotel for what the young actress expected to be a business breakfast meeting. Instead, he had her sent up to his room, where he appeared in a bathrobe and asked if he could give her a massage or she could watch him shower, she recalled in an interview.

"How do I get out of the room as fast as possible without alienating Harvey Weinstein?" Ms. Judd said she remembers thinking.

The exposé about Weinstein was a brave one for the *Times*, for Weinstein's lawyers and friends were pressuring the paper to kill it or tone it down. Weinstein was one of the two or three biggest advertisers in the *Times*. Arthur Sulzberger Jr. was besieged with messages and warnings not to run the Weinstein investigation—yet the *Times* went ahead. That article, along with another one in *The New Yorker* by Ronan Farrow, resulted in Weinstein being sent to prison for many years and sent shock waves through the business and cultural world. A number of people I had respected in the media world, including Charlie Rose, were credibly accused and lost their jobs. The reverberations of this #MeToo movement opened my eyes to how widespread sexual harassment was, and it began to end the impunity that had followed powerful men. I've long been a believer that the way to bring about change isn't sensitivity training, but to create consequences. Fire or prosecute some bad actors, and others will learn morals.

IN *HALF THE SKY*, we had written about human trafficking abroad. As I began to report on the issue at home, I found so many young Americans traumatized because they were pimped out or forced into survival sex when they ran away from home. As Rachel Lloyd, who was herself a trafficking survivor, told me, it's not as sensationalist as people imagine. Girls aren't kidnapped off the street and chained to radiators to provide sex. Often the people pimping them are men they think of as their boyfriends. But girls who don't meet their "quota" are still beaten.

Backpage, a major classified advertising website, ran prostitution ads that in most cases involved consenting adults. But it also routinely ran ads for the sale of underage girls, and I interviewed many girls who were sold there. When parents of a fifteen-year-old told me that she was missing, I found her offered for sale on Backpage; the police rescued her that night at a hotel, where she was controlled by an armed pimp. And Backpage did everything it could to frustrate investigators trying to locate trafficked girls, because it made money on them.

While Backpage was privately owned, I was able to obtain internal documents showing that a number of mainstream financial firms had invested in it. Among them was Goldman Sachs, which also had a managing director on the board of directors controlling Backpage. I called up Goldman for a comment, and it dumped its holding in one day; I'm told that when it couldn't find a buyer, it gave the shares away. But soon after, it promoted the managing director who had been on the Backpage board to partner.

I don't think that Goldman partner was an evil person, any more than pharma executives who marketed opioid painkillers were necessarily evil. But I do think that people watching PowerPoint presentations in corporate conference rooms don't ponder—or care enough about—the human devastation they cause. Accountability, delivered by journalists or by civil society, can change their calculations.

Technology was changing the trafficking business, and increasingly the companies engaged in exploiting children were international websites with vast audiences. After my campaign against it, Backpage was the target of a bipartisan congressional investigation and federal and state criminal inquiries. The FBI soon closed down Backpage. But other websites emerged to exploit children in their own ways.

Pornhub and XVideos are two of the most visited websites in the world, each with more traffic than Amazon, Netflix or Yahoo. I didn't have anything against porn. But after hearing about trafficked children whose rapes had been posted on Pornhub for the world to see, I spent a few hours investigating the site.

I couldn't believe what I found: The site was infested with rape videos. A search for "14yo" returned more than 100,000 videos. I watched a drugged woman being raped, with the rapist lifting his victim's eyelids and touching her eyeballs to show that she was truly unconscious. There were videos of women and girls being tortured, and of obviously underage children being abused. I began calling around.

One girl I spoke to, Serena Fleites, told me she had been thirteen and an A student in Bakersfield, California, when she developed a crush on a boy a year older. He asked for a naked video of her, and although at the time she was completely innocent—she had never made out with a boy—she sent it to him, and then another, and another. "That's when I started getting strange looks at school," Serena told me. The boy had shared the videos with other students, and someone had posted them on Pornhub, which of course profited by running ads beside them. One of the videos had 400,000 views, and despite Serena's pleas to remove the videos the company dithered or allowed them to be reposted.

Serena's world imploded. She quit school, attempted suicide three times, self-medicated with drugs, began cutting herself, and became homeless. When I spoke to her, she was living in her car with three dogs.

Here were companies like Pornhub trying to monetize the humiliation of Serena and other children. Search engines like Google were complicit. I asked Google why on earth it should answer a search for "rape unconscious girl" with videos on sites like Pornhub of unconscious girls being raped. After all, if you searched for "how do I poison my husband," Google didn't provide how-to instructions. If you searched for "how do I kill myself," Google led you to a suicide hotline. So why should Google lead pedophiles to illegal videos of unconscious girls being raped?

I wrote several columns about this, and the outcry after the first piece forced Pornhub to remove 80 percent of its videos—some 10 million of them—because it hadn't obtained consent of people in them. Visa and Mastercard curbed ties to Pornhub because of apparent criminal behavior, and Google stopped pointing people to Pornhub videos on searches for "rape unconscious girl." One commentator tweeted: "New York Times columnist @NickKristof, a pro-pornography liberal Democrat, has done more to reduce the actual flow of pornography online than every Republican in the entire country combined in the last twenty-five years."

The removal of the nonconsensual videos infuriated many porn fans, and I was accused of being a prudish moralizer. As I saw it, the problem wasn't porn but rape. Just as the issue with Harvey Weinstein wasn't sex but coercion, my concern with Pornhub and XVideos wasn't nudity but the monetization by a corporation of rape videos of children. We can be sex positive and exploitation negative.

I ended up getting more death threats after the Pornhub piece than I had ever gotten from a single article, but most didn't seem very credible. My favorite was from a Japanese man who wrote, ever so politely: "Please die for the time being."

On the other hand, victims were extraordinarily grateful. One woman wrote me that for years she had been trying to get Pornhub to take down a naked video of her, and now it had finally done so. She added exultantly: "I can breathe again."

Times are changing, often in a good way—#MeToo and the closure of Backpage are examples of that. But sometimes the campaigning has gone too far, for we don't always see shades of gray and distinguish between misdemeanors and felonies. I don't believe Al Franken should have been forced out of the Senate after unproven allegations of touching women inappropriately, and the concept that we should "believe women" sometimes morphed into the unrealistic variant "believe all women." But on balance, there were huge improvements at home and abroad.

A next step, I believed, was to take on child marriage. After writing about underage marriage in other countries, I gradually came to realize this was also a problem in the United States. In 2017, I began to write about the fact that in every state in America, children under the age of eighteen were allowed to marry in at least some situations. I told the story of an eleven-year-old girl in Florida who was raped and impregnated by a twenty-year-old man in her church—and then forced by her family to marry him. One clerk refused to issue a marriage license to a girl so young, but the next one did grant the license. Too often, judges and clerks just won't help these young girls.

"Don't cry," one clerk told a sixteen-year-old bride before issuing a marriage license. "This is supposed to be the happiest day of your life." When girls under the age of eighteen are married, they also find themselves helpless if the relationship falls apart or becomes violent. In some states, they cannot get a domestic violence protection order without a parent's support, and women's shelters often don't take girls who haven't reached adulthood at eighteen.

Because of that publicity and the work of nonprofits like Unchained at Last, which focuses on the issue, ten states have since banned all child marriages, and similar efforts are underway in many more states. We're making progress. Highlighting a problem isn't sufficient to engineer change, but it's a necessary first step.

Sheryl and I speak regularly on college campuses about *Half the Sky*, and we saw the progress. Just two decades ago, no one had heard of an obstetric fistula, and there was little interest in maternal mortality or domestic violence. Women's rights were perceived as a soft, touchy-feely second-tier issue. Now many people know what a fistula is, and international efforts plus groups like Fistula Foundation have helped enormous numbers of women recover their lives—even as maternal deaths around the world have fallen by 40 percent. There are about as many girls in elementary schools worldwide as boys, and presidents discuss human trafficking in their speeches.

Gender gaps are complicated, however, and a simple diorama of men repressing and exploiting women doesn't capture the nuances of the landscape. In the United States, some outcomes are better for women than for men. Incomes are greater for men, but American boys and men are more likely than girls and women to drop out of school. Boys and men are more likely to be arrested, imprisoned, commit suicide, overdose or die young. Sixty percent of students in American colleges are now female, and there are also more female than male students getting law degrees, medical degrees and PhDs.

Many of us on the left are attuned to inequities faced by women, but a bit oblivious to those faced by men. Partly that's a legacy of the past, including the architecture we built in times of greater gender discrimination. For example, we have the American Association of University Women, which does excellent work calling attention to pay discrimination and reproductive rights, but there's no equivalent for men at a time when males are hugely underrepresented in college and professional schools. And just as women's rights were never just a "woman's issue," the despair and struggles of so many men are not just a "man's issue." The fundamental truth is that there is no war of the sexes—there's too much sleeping with the other side—and both men and women will benefit when we join forces to provide opportunity to girls and boys alike.

Gender differences are complicated, of course. When I give a lecture at universities with mostly female student bodies, indeed even at women's colleges, the first question or two will inevitably come from a man. In the question-and-answer period, I'll point to a woman and she'll look around uncertainly, trying to figure out if I mean her, and meanwhile some man in the vicinity will jump up and confidently ask his question. I don't know what to make of this gap in assertiveness, but it shows how difficult it is to overcome gender gaps.

When college women do ask questions at our talks, the queries are sometimes quite personal: *How do you make it work? How do you as a couple juggle your causes, your careers and your kids?*

The blunt truth is that my frequent travel imposed a burden on the family, but Sheryl and I tried to look out for each other. When I called from some far-flung country and needed a fact checked, Sheryl would look it up for me. And when Sheryl took on high-powered jobs as an executive on the business side of the *Times*, I took over household responsibilities for paying bills so she could focus on her work. I kept that up when she worked long hours in the investment division at Goldman Sachs. Later, when she started her own consulting company— advising companies on how to incorporate social values and display a mission larger than simply quarterly profits—she had more flexibility and took those responsibilities back.

Sheryl has had a pathbreaking career first in journalism and then in business: *Newsweek* named her one of 150 "women who shake the world," PBS said she was one of "the leading women who make America," and Harvard Business School named her one of its most eminent graduates. She has been on the boards of three Ivy League universities, which may be a first, and she's now also on the boards of a banking company and Oregon Public Broadcasting. I'm very proud of what she has achieved and of what she does to make corporate America work better. On the wall of my home office here on the Yamhill farm as I write this, I have a poster of Sheryl from *Fast Company* naming her to "the league of extraordinary women."

Like any long-married couple, Sheryl and I have been through so much together. Joys and sorrows. Triumphs and losses. So many thrills, including the birth of the three kids. And so many scares, including my bouts with skin cancer and with a kidney tumor in 2010 (it turned out to be benign). There were also so many adventures.

Once, when we were staying together at a hotel in Hue, Vietnam, we were in bed, reading with the lights on, when a rat tumbled down from the false ceiling onto the floor and began running around. Then another rat tumbled from the ceiling as well. Sheryl's view was that rat wrangling was a husband's responsibility, despite my mumbling about women holding up half the sky, so she offered directions from the bed as I ran around the room trying to chase the rats into the bathroom. I finally managed to do so and shut the door to lock them in. I felt quite proud, for my trapping them seemed the epitome of manliness.

I went down to the front desk and explained to the man dozing there what had happened. He didn't speak English, but he understood my pantomime immediately. Evidently rat rain was a regular complaint. He was a slight, frail man, much smaller than me, but he took a machete from behind the counter and followed me up to the room. He removed his sandals and slipped barefoot into the bathroom and hurriedly closed the door behind him. Then there was a furious sound of blows for several minutes, as Sheryl and I waited to see who would win the battle. Finally there was silence, the bathroom door opened and the man came out carrying the dead rats in one hand and the machete in the other. I realized that I had been seriously outperformed.

In 2016, we had another hotel adventure. We were in Philadelphia at the Franklin Hotel for the fall meeting of the American Philosophical Society, whose members, other than us, seem to be mostly septuagenarian or octogenarian, many of them Nobel laureates. I woke up at dawn and went down to get coffee in the lobby, but to avoid waking Sheryl by closing and opening the hotel room door, I left it slightly ajar. At the elevator down the corridor, another man was waiting, but when it came he told me to go ahead: He was waiting for his wife.

I returned from the lobby a minute or two later, walked down the corridor to our room and pushed open the door—and there was the man, inside our room. The layout of the room was such that all I could see was the entry, and I was confused. If the man had shouted at me *What are you doing in my room?* I would have apologized profusely and backed off and tried to figure out which was my room. But instead he said, "Hotel maintenance" and tried to step past me. That seemed ridiculous at this early hour.

"Sheryl," I shouted, "are you okay?"

The man tried to push past me, but I blocked him and was shouting at him. Sheryl woke up to our fight in the doorway. At that point, the man got past me and ran for the stairs. He had a backpack, and I feared he had stolen things from our room.

"Call hotel security," I shouted to her. "I'll chase him down."

We were on the ninth floor, and he ran down the stairs with me a few steps behind him. I didn't want to get into a fight in the stairwell—especially when he shouted at me that he had a knife and would stab me. He ran out on the second floor, where the restaurant was, and charged through the breakfasting Nobel laureates with me behind him. Then he knocked down a decorative screen and rushed down the grand stairway into the lobby, with me shouting, "Thief! Stop, thief!" I tackled him just as he reached the lobby, and a bellman helped restrain him until the police came.

He turned out to have a long criminal history, and a judge later sentenced him to four years in prison for trying to burglarize our room. Sheryl and I laugh about that memory now whenever we stay at a hotel, and she teases me to make sure I never leave a room door ajar when she's asleep.

Yet in some ways, Sheryl and I divide our parenting and labors in quite traditional ways. She's a tiger mom, while I believe in more laissez-faire parenting (Sheryl might suggest that's a euphemism for "neglectful"). Sheryl does most of the cooking and managed the children's book clubs and play dates; I take out the garbage, kill cockroaches, set mousetraps and fix broken towel racks. I also do 95 percent of the driving when we're together. The traditionalism of our roles bothers me more than it does Sheryl; I consider myself a feminist, while Sheryl doesn't identify that way (she sees it as an outdated term that carries lots of baggage). Sheryl thinks men should hold doors open for women, which strikes me as very nineteenth century—but I still hold doors open for Sheryl because I like to make her happy.

35

Covering Donald Trump

As a presidential candidate in January 2016, Trump came by the *Times* to speak to the opinion writers and editors. He brought Ivanka, and we sat around a polished wood conference table. In a nod to Trump's celebrity, the room was full of editors who rarely turned up for these meetings.

I had interacted with Trump only once before. "I *love* your work," he had told me after we were both guests on a television show, speaking in an obsequious tone. "We should get together for lunch."

Trump greeted everyone in the conference room warmly and sang our praises. It was meant to be charming but was so at odds with his public comments that it was obviously disingenuous. There was a fundamental tension in the room: We thought he was a charlatan, and on the campaign trail he thundered against the *Times*.

At this point I had been a *Times* journalist for more than three decades and had interviewed countless demagogues and shallow, self-absorbed politicians. That conference room had been the scene of innumerable officials lying to us. But when we began to ask Trump about policy, he was in a league of his own: He was an all-time champion of prevarication. I respect people with whom I disagree, but I don't respect people who are dishonest.

Trump dodged questions, then careened off on wild tangents and finally promised outcomes without ever explaining how he was going to achieve them. I jousted with him. Ivanka looked pained; she wanted my respect and that of the *Times*. At one point, Trump said—on the record—that he was going to impose a 45 percent tariff on all Chinese goods. That was a ridiculous assertion, and we reported it. Trump then denied ever making the statement.

"That's wrong," Trump said. "They were wrong. It's *The New York Times*. They are always wrong." So we released the audio of Trump calling for the 45 percent tariff on Chinese goods.

Pakistani president Pervez Musharraf was the only other politician I had known who would look you in the eye and flatly tell you something that you both knew was a lie. Musharraf was at least a knowledgeable, competent manager who understood how to manage risks. Trump had the same utter indifference to truth, but he knew nothing about governing. Worse, he was running against democracy as he ran to lead a democracy. So while there had been many venal politicians around the world whom I deplored, Trump was unique. He was a con artist. I had never known an American politician so uneducated about policy, so self-absorbed and so deceitful.

I waded through hundreds of pages of documentation and wrote a long essay in July 2016 concluding that he was a racist. This was out of character for me, for I prefer to critique policy rather than sling insults. Yet after sifting through decades of evidence, I concluded:

> My view is that "racist" can be a loaded word, a conversation stopper more than a clarifier, and that we should be careful not to use it simply as an epithet . . . And yet. Here we have a man who for more than four decades has been repeatedly associated with racial discrimination or bigoted comments about minorities, some of them made on television for all to see. While any one episode may be ambiguous, what emerges over more than four decades is a narrative arc, a consistent pattern—and I don't see what else to call it but racism.

The initial media response to Trump in 2016 was, in my judgment, pathetic. As Margaret Sullivan, then of *The Washington Post*, put it, media coverage that election year was "an epic fail." Cable television in particular put Trump on screen interminably: By March 2016, Trump had received $1.9 billion worth of free media coverage—190 times as much as he had paid for. Channels were desperate for an audience, and Trump provided it; like a wreck on the highway, he was impossible to turn away from. So television executives handed him the microphone. Cable television and Donald Trump exploited each other, with the broadcasters making money off Trump's ratings and Trump riding the wave of uncritical publicity. As Leslie Moonves, the CBS president, said about Trump's run: "It may not be good for America, but it's damn good for CBS." Cable television executives wouldn't have let a charismatic entertainer urge viewers to stay young by drinking rat poison, but they gave free airtime to Trump.

Coverage of Trump's speeches would have been fine if television channels had also provided fact-checking and issues coverage. But they didn't do this in a serious way. Andrew Tyndall, whose Tyndall Report monitors the evening broadcast network news shows, told me that in all of 2016, the three broadcast networks—CBS, ABC and NBC—provided a collective total of just thirty-six minutes of independent issues coverage, defined as that not arising from a candidate's statement.

I think we in the media simply failed the American people—the *Times* included. One study found that in just six days before the 2016 election, the *Times* provided more page-one coverage of Hillary Rodham Clinton's emails than it had of all policy positions combined in the sixty-nine days before the election. Even the most prudent news organizations didn't wake up to the possibility that Trump would be the Republican nominee and might become president until relatively late, and we covered the candidates traditionally.

Traditional coverage did not work. Discussing each candidate's allegations against the other was a sideshow when one candidate was running against democracy itself, and we were too slow to use the word "lie" to capture Trump's deliberate, repeated falsehoods. Polls suggested that the public believed that Trump and Clinton dissembled at about the same rate, but every reporter knew that Clinton exaggerated like any presidential candidate, while Trump was off the charts. He lied, was caught, and then repeated his lies. He was pathological.

Journalists like to think that they are advancing both truth and fairness, and normally those qualities go hand in hand. But that is not always the case: Sometimes there is tension between truth and fairness. On three occasions in the postwar period before Trump, the journalistic impulse for fairness and quoting both sides in a neutral way constituted a disservice to democracy, and we ended up fair but not truthful.

The first instance was in the Joe McCarthy era. When television covered McCarthy's Communist witch hunt and then quoted denials from people he slimed, the public misunderstood and thought there must be something to McCarthy's attacks. White House officials and members of Congress refused to stand up adequately to McCarthy, so there was a vacuum in opposition to him. Journalists knew the truth—that McCarthy was a lying bully—but did not convey that truth until the great Edward R. Murrow famously spoke up in 1954:

> The line between investigating and persecuting is a very fine one, and the junior senator from Wisconsin has stepped over it repeatedly. . . . We must remember always that accusation is not proof and that conviction depends upon evidence and due process of law. We will not walk in fear, one of another. We will not be driven by fear into an age of unreason. . . . We cannot defend freedom abroad by deserting it at home.

The second instance was the civil rights movement. It didn't work to quote George Wallace in one paragraph and Martin Luther King Jr. in the next. Reporters knew that Wallace lied and King spoke the truth about the Jim Crow South—but they didn't always convey the revealing details that would make this clear to the public. It took reporters both Black and white, including Claude Sitton of the *Times*, to wake the public.

The third instance was Vietnam. The United States government tried to control the narrative with upbeat propaganda and phony body counts, and the public began to understand the truth of the war only when American reporters captured the grim, faltering reality in the field—and photographers like Nick Ut, David Hume Kennerly and Larry Burrows were an enormous part of conveying that horror.

Trump put us in a fourth crisis, and I argued in public and private that once again we journalists had to recognize that our paramount obligation was to the truth—which meant eschewing bothsidesism, in which journalists quote first one side and then the other to create a false equivalency. When democracy is at stake, you can't simply walk down the middle and pat yourself on the back for being criticized by both sides.

Ever since Galileo was hauled before the Inquisition for contending that the earth revolves around the sun, it has sometimes been the case that truth does not lie in the middle. That was the case with Trump.

AFTER TRUMP WAS ELECTED, I kept in touch with some Trump insiders, including Jared Kushner and John Bolton, because I wanted to understand what was going on in the White House.* But the Trump administration grew more extreme and less constrained by sensible aides, and my reporting indicates we came much closer to a war with North Korea than most Americans realize.

President Trump poisoned the Republican Party and instilled deep divisions between principled conservatives and those willing to follow him down his dangerous path for short-term gain. But he also poisoned liberal organizations. Many organizations disproportionately staffed by urban liberals underwent bitter internal conflict, with young people sometimes accusing an old guard of not standing up firmly enough for progressive values and against the racism and authoritarianism that Trump represented. That was true of the Sierra Club, Time's Up and the Guttmacher Institute, and in Oregon a Latino rights group dissolved because of internal conflict. News organizations, including the *Times* and *Washington Post*, endured similar tumult.

At the *Times*, a furor erupted in 2020 after the opinion page published an essay by Senator Tom Cotton, "Send in the Troops," urging a crackdown on protests against racial violence. I was untroubled by the *idea* of a Cotton op-ed. In general, I think newspapers like ours should run *more* pieces by conservatives, including essays that outrage liberals. I've periodically helped conservatives place pieces on the opinion page, including pieces I completely disagreed with, and internally I've long argued that we should run tougher and more critical letters to the editor. We rightly lose credibility when we dish out excoriations but don't allow letter writers to criticize us in equally harsh terms.

One reason I'd like to see mainstream news organizations publish

---

* John Bolton was far to my right and, from my point of view, wrong on every possible issue. But I kind of liked him. I got to know him during the Bush administration, when he would come into the *Times* and make hawkish arguments about Iraq and North Korea. I would listen and then write articles slamming his approach—and yet he would return and try again. He was knowledgeable, smart and sincere, and I benefited by dueling with him intellectually. I thought the same of Paul Wolfowitz and Condi Rice. I was glad when Bolton went to the White House as Trump's national security advisor because I thought he would push back when necessary—and that's what he did, which got him fired.

more conservative op-eds and letters, including more denunciations of liberal columnists like me, is that it just might build trust and give our work more influence. When *60 Minutes* did an exposé on corruption in the administration of Governor Ron DeSantis of Florida, he was not only unembarrassed by it but called attention to it; he knew that criticisms from mainstream news organizations would be so scorned among Republican voters that they would actually benefit him.

Republicans disproportionately died during the coronavirus pandemic, and that's partly because of Fox News's egregious coverage. But another factor was conservative distrust of news organizations like my own, driving them to read, watch and listen to blowhards with lethal advice. Only 7 percent of Republicans said they trusted the news media to provide reliable information on COVID-19, and it's not good for any of us when that figure is so low. Mainstream news organizations might be taken more seriously by conservatives and would have more credibility if we let conservatives criticize us harshly even on the issues we are most passionate about.

Still, it's complicated. I was unimpressed by the *actual* Tom Cotton op-ed and thought it a mistake to run it in its present form—it was knee-jerk right-wing outrage that didn't illuminate conservative thinking or hold us liberals accountable—and we should have pushed to make it more thoughtful. But I also thought the staff outrage was greatly overblown: We run dumb op-eds all the time, often by liberals, and we had already run several in favor of the protests. It was perfectly appropriate to run an op-ed denouncing the racial justice protests or calling for a tougher law-and-order response, even if I was not a fan of the Cotton one.

Many *Times* people didn't agree with my take. The newsroom was up in arms, with the fury greatest among young people and the digital and audio people who were less steeped in journalistic traditions. More than eight hundred staff members signed a letter protesting the Cotton op-ed, and there was enormous pressure on A. G. Sulzberger, who had taken over as publisher from his father, Arthur Sulzberger Jr. I like and respect A.G. a great deal and think he has wise instincts about journalism leavened with humility. Perhaps I am biased because he had trained as a reporter at *The Oregonian* and still carries a cell phone with a 503 area code from Oregon.

Later A.G. had been a metro reporter for the *Times* and an outstanding correspondent for the paper in the Midwest, based in Kansas City. I thought his vegetarianism suggested good liberal values while the Midwest seemed to nurture his innate civility and a respect for rural, conservative America that I thought the *Times* could model more often. A.G. then became an editor and presided over a team that produced a pathbreaking report on how to adapt the newspaper to the digital age. The ninety-seven-page *Innovation Report* was initially confidential, and I despaired when the paper issued a bland press release about its completion.

For years, I had been an in-house revolutionary arguing that the *Times* needed to embrace social media, search engine optimization, video, headline beta testing and other digital strategies. I also thought our writing was sometimes formal and stodgy in a way that turned off younger readers accustomed to more informal writing.

I feared that we were so risk-averse about change that we were actually risking our future. When Ben Smith joined the *Times* after editing *BuzzFeed News*, he said he was greeted with the warning "Do not, under any circumstances, try to change anything." There was at the time too much of that mindset. I was discouraged from using photos with columns and discouraged from promoting stories on social media. I would periodically come up with new ideas—"How about running a Chinese-language headline?" "How about running this video clip in the column?" "How about running a QR code with the column online so readers can go to the right website?"—and editors would run for cover and hope someone talked sense into me.

Fortunately, the full *Innovation Report* was leaked to *BuzzFeed News* and turned out to be nothing like the press release. Instead, it was a clarion call for change. Since everyone knew that A.G. had written it and that he represented the future, the paper quickly pivoted and embraced digital. The timing coincided with the replacement of one executive editor, Jill Abramson, with another, Dean Baquet, so the past traditionalism was somewhat unfairly blamed on Jill's regime and innovation was embraced with Dean. The push for change in the *Innovation Report* left me feeling optimistic that A.G. was also a revolutionary who favored change in platforms while upholding traditional journalistic values.

After the Tom Cotton op-ed, some of the newsroom rage was directed at A.G. and some at James Bennet, the editorial page editor.

Many reporters protested on Twitter that the Tom Cotton op-ed column put them in danger. Really? *Times* reporters are genuinely put in great danger all the time, covering the Ukraine War, covering Ebola outbreaks, drug dens, riots and natural disasters. *Times* reporters in Syria or Iran or North Korea were in danger, yet didn't demand that the paper not run op-eds critical of those countries. Likewise, publication of liberal op-eds may create risk for reporters who then go out and interview white supremacists, but we don't let that dissuade us from running those op-eds. When others engage in fits of hysteria, journalists keep their heads down and do their work—and, yes, sometimes that entails risk.

Despite the newsroom's anger, most of us thought it would run its course and subside. Then a couple of days later, I had a phone call from James Bennet. He was a talented journalist who had risked his life for the *Times* in the Middle East (he was once almost kidnapped in Gaza) and had later been a much-admired editor of *The Atlantic*. He was the brother of Michael Bennet, the senator from Colorado. A good man and a terrific journalist, James sounded brokenhearted as he explained he was being pushed out because of the upheaval.

"There must be something that can be done," I said. "You want me to call A.G.? Should I try to round up several columnists?"

"It's too late," James said. "It's decided. My departure is going to be announced in the next few minutes."

That was a blow. To me, the ouster of James seemed a surrender of op-ed principles, a sign of weakness and an implicit warning that editors should be wary of publishing conservative views that might outrage liberal staff members. Many of us in the columnist ranks were horrified, and we discussed among ourselves what to do and whether to protest in some way. We chose not to, because we thought it wouldn't do any good and would drag out an already ugly situation at the *Times* that needed healing. Among the columnists, only Roger Cohen spoke up publicly for James in a forceful way; when I saw Roger's column, I thought he was right and wished I'd been less deferential to the paper.

Less than a year later, a distinguished health reporter, Donald McNeil, was pushed out of the *Times* after a forty-five-year career at the paper. Donald had used the N-word in a discussion about racist language with students, but he hadn't used the word as an epithet. Rather, a student had asked Donald if her classmate should have been suspended for using the N-word, and Donald repeated it to try to clarify what exactly the classmate had said. That nuance was lost, and it didn't help that Donald was as prickly as he was talented and had offended many editors over the years. An agitator in the reporters' union, he had often been ferociously critical of management, sometimes unfairly so.

Donald's defenestration, too, seemed to me an overreaction, particularly as the *Times* itself periodically used the N-word in print in ways parallel to Donald's usage, such as when quoting a racist or the title of a work of art. Donald shouldn't have used the word, but the paper shouldn't have ousted him. It was unfair, and as a practical matter, readers were not well served by ejecting one of the nation's leading health reporters in the middle of a pandemic.

There seemed to be a generational divide. Many reporters of my generation felt as I did, for we were shaped by an era when it was conservatives who wanted to censor speech and liberals who argued for a free market in ideas. Younger journalists often disagreed. They argued that words, like sticks and stones, can indeed do damage—and of course they have a point.

I couldn't help but observe a paradox here. For decades, I had been arguing internally in the *Times* that we should be more willing to exercise moral authority. I thought that some of our greatest moments—such as coverage of the Armenian genocide in 1915, of the civil rights movement in the 1960s, or of the Balkan slaughter in the 1990s—reflected a willingness to recognize the moral weight of certain stories, and that our greatest failings involved a reluctance to elevate moral questions about the Holocaust, Japanese-American internment, Jim Crow segregation or mistreatment of livestock and poultry. There is something to what Marguerite Duras wrote: "Journalism without a moral position is impossible. Every journalist is a moralist. It's absolutely unavoidable." Yet now a wave of this moralism was washing through the *Times* and other newsrooms and leading to results that I thought were neither fair nor good journalism. It was a reminder for me of how carefully we must harness that moral view to traditional journalistic tools of fairness, independence and skepticism—and of how we must constantly remind ourselves of our proclivity to make mistakes.

All this is an echo of the same question I wondered about in conversation with Sir Isaiah Berlin: How can we act boldly to advance our values, yet still be humble enough to accept that our ideas may be wrong?

How do we reconcile responsibility and humility? Too often, I think, older journalists of my generation throw up our hands and engage in false equivalence and bothsidesism, simply quoting each side on an issue in the hope that the reader can figure it out. That often works, but not always: I don't think we should accept being loudspeakers for crooks or bigots, yet I also recognize that my assessment of who is a crook or bigot may prove incorrect. Judge Learned Hand put it well eight decades ago: "The spirit of liberty is the spirit which is not too sure that it is right."

One reason I aim—not always successfully—for intellectual humility is that there's good evidence from social psychology and other disciplines that our brains are systematically biased against people we disagree with. We create caricatures of them. For example, Republicans on average estimate that almost half of Democrats are Black, about twice the actual share. Meanwhile, Democrats estimate that almost half of Republicans earn at least $250,000 a year, when the actual share is 2 percent. Perceiving our own biases is much more difficult than recognizing the prejudice of the other side. A little self-doubt, and a little less self-righteousness, would do us all some good. We should listen as well as shout.

MOST OF THE TIME, I'm in step with the liberal multitude. I tend to be skeptical of military interventions and focused on human rights abroad. I believe in empowering women at home and abroad, and I have been a passionate critic of the criminal justice system and the war on drugs. I wrote an eight-part series on racism in the United States, entitled "When Whites Just Don't Get It," that was used in many school curriculums. Yet I also often annoyed my liberal readers by, as they saw it, poking them in the eye. Increasingly columnists have segmented audiences—liberals read liberal columnists, and conservatives read conservative columnists—so I felt some obligation to speak up and use my political capital when I felt that many of my fellow liberals were marching in the wrong direction.

When three white members of the Duke lacrosse team were accused in 2006 of raping a Black woman, liberals tended to react with outrage and calls for harsh punishment, and Duke suspended the lacrosse team's season. One of my more conservative colleagues wrote a column warning that it was difficult to know what had happened, but liberals dismissed him: *Of course a conservative would stand with privileged white jocks.* But I wrote a similar column warning against a rush to judgment, and that surprised readers who assumed that I would be repeating denunciations of racism and sexual violence. My hesitancy was given more credibility because of my liberalism, and it was vindicated when the lacrosse players were later exonerated. That experience made me think that fellow liberals are at least willing to hear me out when I take an unconventional view, and that we thus have a special responsibility to try to speak disagreeable truths to our base.

Likewise, I've regularly written columns denouncing anti-conservative bias on university campuses. Too often we are willing to embrace people who don't look like us, but only if they think like us. I've written columns arguing that just as it's reprehensible for conservative Christians to stereotype gay people, it's wrong of liberals to stereotype or mock people of faith. And every evangelical at a university will tell you that this is a real problem.

"Outside of academia, I faced more problems as a Black man," George Yancey, a Black evangelical professor of sociology, told me. "But inside academia I face more problems as a Christian, and it is not even close."

WHAT FRUSTRATED ME as much as the news media's complicity in Trump's rise was the enthusiasm he generated among some of my old friends in Yamhill. Working-class people were desperate and justifiably felt neglected by both parties—and finally they sensed someone was speaking to them and acknowledging their suffering. Trump was a fraud, scapegoating refugees and vilifying Muslims while claiming that he was going to bring back factories, but desperate people reached for any reed of hope. I blamed Trump for his scapegoating, but I also held Democrats and Republicans alike responsible for not having done more to address the pain in working-class towns like Yamhill.

Well-educated liberals mocked Trump for speaking at a fourth-grade level, according to analyses of his speech patterns; that turned out to be the lowest grade level of speech of any recent president.* But

* Jimmy Carter spoke at an eleventh-grade level, and Barack Obama at a high ninth-grade level; Truman was the lowest aside from Trump, at a sixth-grade level.

this kind of mockery rings hollow. The median American reads at a fifth- or sixth-grade level. If a president aims to communicate with the public, then that may require using direct, straightforward sentences—and disdain for the less educated reinforces the sense among working-class voters that they are being looked down on. It's very difficult for Democrats to win the hearts of people they condescend to.

Trump took the opposite approach. "I love the poorly educated," he declared in February 2016. Pundits smirked at that, and it seemed patronizing, but it went over better with working-class Americans than snooty liberal hostility.

When I won my Rhodes Scholarship, Michael Sandel, a newly arrived faculty member at Harvard who had recently completed a Rhodes, reached out to me, and we had coffee together. We chatted about my plans for Oxford and how I could get the most out of it. I've watched his career soar since then, as he became one of the world's most eminent political philosophers. He is best known for his video courses and for his book *Justice*, but I particularly admired his reproach of intellectuals for disdaining the less educated.

Sandel cites surveys showing that educated people are just as prejudiced as anyone else, but the people they are biased against aren't people of color or the obese or other traditionally stigmatized groups. Rather, they scorn the less educated. Sandel calls this "the last acceptable prejudice." Liberals often puzzle about why working-class people so often vote against their economic interest, but Sandel argues that what they seek is not so much redistributive justice as "a greater measure of contributive justice—an opportunity to win the social recognition and esteem that goes with producing what others need and value."

That rang true to me. So did the words of Arlie Russell Hochschild, a sociologist at the University of California at Berkeley, who is as liberal as I am but wrote warmly and sympathetically about working-class people in the South and their struggles. Arlie described their feelings: "You are a stranger in your own land. You do not recognize yourself in how others see you. It is a struggle to feel seen and honored." That described many of my old friends.

Sometimes my working-class friends exasperated me. After reporting in Iraq, I came back and spoke to one of them about it. He was completely unsympathetic to Iraqi suffering.

"The problem with those Iraqis is they don't value human life," he told me. "We should just nuke them."

Yet it was equally true that educated liberals often stereotyped white working-class voters as racists and bigots, in ways that were as fallacious as any other sweeping stereotype. People are complicated. Sure, there are some racists in the pro-Trump voting bloc, but there were many factors that led people to follow him. My friend Mary Mayor turned to Trump after she lost four people in her family to suicide and was herself homeless for seven years; that kind of suffering fosters desperation. The scholar Joan C. Williams castigated progressives for "class cluelessness" and wrote that while racism among some Trump supporters is real, "to write off white working-class anger as nothing more than racism is intellectual comfort food, and it is dangerous."

One manifestation of this class divide is the urban-rural chasm, and increasingly I found myself straddling it. Sheryl and I had spent more time in Yamhill since my dad died, partly to be with my mom, and then in 2018 we faced a crisis. Our farm had been producing Montmorency pie cherries since the 1940s, but not enough people were eating cherry pies. (The average American eats cherry pie only 1.2 times a year; I barely restrained myself from writing columns urging people to eat more cherry pie.) The only company buying cherries in the Yamhill area was winding down and could no longer take our fruit, so we had to find a new business model. This came just as Sheryl and I were reporting our book *Tightrope* and seeing the need in Yamhill for higher-value products, so after much family discussion we decided to pull out twenty acres of cherry trees and plant a cider apple orchard and a vineyard. This was painful, for those cherry trees were practically family friends, and the new vineyard and orchard would require a huge investment and lots of work. We saw it as a multigenerational project, so we made sure we had buy-in from our children. The kids were enthusiastic, so we planted grapevines and apple trees and launched Kristof Farms, our KristofFarms.com website and multiple social media accounts.

Nothing went smoothly. We have deer and elk in the area, so at great expense we erected a seven-foot deer fence to protect our grapes and apples from the wildlife. When it was completed, we discovered that we had managed to imprison several deer *inside* our impregnable deer fence, with little to eat except our apple trees and grapevines. After we managed to evict the deer, by inviting friends to herd the deer out through the gate, we had a bit of calm. Then the apples attracted four large bears, and we discovered that when a bear wants to go through a fence, it does.

These crises meant even more time spent on the farm. The kids were all adults now—each went to Harvard College and thrived there and found a niche in the adult world—and they loved spending time in Yamhill. Then came the pandemic, and what better place to socially isolate than a farm?

During the pandemic, many of the local problems got worse. People who had been in recovery fell off the wagon, because they no longer had to submit urine samples for drug tests and no longer had in-person group meetings. There was neither support nor accountability, plus social isolation increased.

My neighbor Mike Stepp—exuberant, cheerful little Mike—grew steadily more addicted to alcohol and meth. His wife had forced him to leave, and she was left to care for their two kids on her own; he was now $70,000 behind in child support. Mike was homeless, living first in a parking structure and then in the park near the library. He loved spending time with Sheryl and my kids and talking about the old days, and he proudly carried our books in his shopping cart. Sometimes he

With Mike Stepp when he was homeless in McMinnville.

would show up at a church breakfast for homeless people where my mom volunteered, his health failing, and he would pass messages to me through her. In 2020 he died on the street. I had to tell his brother Bobby the circumstances of Mike's death.

Then there was Chris Lawson, my old friend on the No. 6 school bus who had once used me as a punching bag. He became a homeless alcoholic. "He won't ever change," his sister, Darlene, told me. "The family has all tried to help. He just doesn't want to help himself." Darlene last heard from Chris in November 2021. She has reported him missing and guesses that he is gone. His two brothers preceded him in death; if Chris is dead, then all three Lawson boys on the No. 6 bus with me have passed.

When Sheryl and I wrote our book *Tightrope*, four of the five Knapp children were gone: Farlan died of liver failure from drug and alcohol abuse, Zealan died in a house fire when he was drunk and passed out, Rogina died of hepatitis from IV drug use and Nathan blew himself up while cooking meth. The youngest, Keylan, had survived in part because he had spent years in prison for drug offenses, and he was eager to tell his family story himself. He was planning to join us for an event on our book tour in the spring of 2020. But the pandemic led to cancellation of that event and also to the loss of his job, and then his mom called us: Keylan had died of an overdose. I don't have an exact count, but more than one-third of the children on my old No. 6 school bus are now dead from drugs, alcohol, suicide and reckless accidents.

The suffering of my old friends was a window into an America that was left behind and never seemed to get much attention in the media. More Americans were dying from drugs, alcohol and suicide every two weeks than had perished in twenty years of war in Afghanistan and Iraq, yet these deaths at home received little attention. One study found that the words most used by suicidal men were "worthless" or "useless," and it was wrenching to see friends consider themselves worthless. The loss of so many friends made me aware at a gut level of the distress around America—a distress that neither journalists nor politicians seemed sufficiently focused on resolving.

IN SOME WAYS, it seems absurd to compare the humanitarian crisis at home with those I covered abroad. Most people I interviewed in

Ethiopia or India thought of life even at the American poverty line as one of enormous luxury. The median American household living below the poverty line has a car, air-conditioning and either cable or satellite television. A median American below the poverty line has more living space than the average, non-poor European. Yet this can be misleading, for while low-income Americans may enjoy space and some material possessions, they struggle in other ways.

In Arkansas, I visited a boy with three televisions in his bedroom, two of them gargantuan large-screen models. But the home was chaotic, reeked of marijuana, had a broken front door and was used as a crash pad for people buying drugs and getting high. There was no food in the house, gangs were recruiting the boy, and the electricity company was trying to shut off power for non-payment (the boy's mom deployed a pit bull to keep the utility worker at bay). In material terms, the boy was doing fine; in every other dimension, he was living a horror show.

The work of a brilliant friend, Esther Duflo, a French economist at MIT who won a Nobel Prize for her research on global poverty, influenced me in this area. Esther is a numbers person, all data and equations, but what her research illuminated was something more squishy: the importance of hope. When people were mired in poverty in India and saw no way out, they gave up. They didn't try as hard and sometimes they wouldn't even accept a gift of a free cow because they were so sure that nothing could make a difference. On the other hand, if they accepted a cow, that sometimes broke the cycle of despair, and led them to try harder—so that the hope became self-fulfilling.

"The mental health part is absolutely critical," Esther told me. "Poverty causes stress and depression and lack of hope, and stress and depression and lack of hope, in turn, cause poverty."

Sir Fazle Abed, a Bangladeshi pioneer in the war on global poverty, agreed. "Poverty is not just poverty of money or income," he said. "We also see poverty of self-esteem, hope, opportunity and freedom. People trapped in a cycle of destitution often don't realize that their lives can be changed for the better through their own activities."

Some of my old friends in Oregon and people I interviewed in, say, the slums of Nairobi had hopelessness in common. My neighbors may have had cars and air-conditioning, but they didn't have hope for themselves or their children. Their children or grandchildren were being arrested on drug charges, families were unraveling, and young children were being neglected and struggling in school. All this led in turn to another parallel with humanitarian crises I had covered abroad: the rising menace of violence.

This was nurtured by Trump and the right-wing media and was sometimes directed at mainstream journalists. At the Republican National Convention in 2016, vendors sold a T-shirt showing a noose and the words: "Rope. Tree. Journalist. Some assembly required." It was popular enough that Walmart sold it as well, until being called out for promoting the lynching of reporters. Considering the venom, few in the journalism world were surprised when a gunman entered the *Capital Gazette* newsroom in Annapolis, Maryland, and shot five employees dead while wounding others.

Conspiracy theories merged and took off in bizarre new directions. Nearly one in five Americans said they believed that "a group of Satan-worshipping elites who run a child sex ring are trying to control our politics and media," and many more weren't sure, according to an NPR/Ipsos poll. Incredibly, a majority of Americans either believed that QAnon tale or thought it might be true.

In the summer of 2020, Fox News was full of panicked warnings about Antifa, the small band of self-proclaimed anti-fascists in Portland and other cities. Fox News warned that Antifa were taking over Black Lives Matter protests, which was absurd, yet some rural Oregonians responded with real fear. In the beautiful Oregon coastal town of Coquille, a sleepy logging community of 3,800 residents some 250 miles from Portland, a handful of BLM supporters decided to hold a demonstration. Rumors then spread that three busloads of Antifa rioters were coming from Portland to bust up the town. So the sheriff and his deputies put on bulletproof vests, prepared an MRAP (mine-resistant ambush protected) armored vehicle and took up defensive positions. Some two hundred local people turned out with rifles to protect their town from the invaders. No Antifa ever showed up, so people then prided themselves on how they had scared off the invaders.

I saw this hysteria near our farm. Sheryl, the kids and I parked on a logging access road to visit a property with the permission of the owner. A homeowner nearby saw our vehicle and somehow came to the conclusion that we were Antifa planning to set forest fires. He put a log behind our vehicle to keep us from leaving and called the sheriff.

This was ridiculous but offered a window into the dangerous alienation of rural America and working-class America.

Even before Trump, many rural people felt neglected and condescended to. They were poor, but what they wanted most of all wasn't a redistribution of wealth but a redistribution of respect. They didn't see why elite lawyers, investment bankers, professors and senators—or *New York Times* columnists, for that matter—should be looked up to, while farmers, truck drivers and factory workers who actually did tangible and important work should occupy a lower social tier. The coronavirus pandemic magnified that perception: It became clear that many people deemed "essential workers"—grocery store employees, farm workers, gas station attendants, hospital cleaners and garbage collectors—were paid and treated poorly.

It doesn't help that the United States, for all its claims to be a classless society, is intensely hierarchical and marked by a tendency to confuse economic failure with moral failure. "Loser" is a distinctly American insult, little employed in other countries. Nor does it help that many of society's "losers" were people of faith who felt that their religious views were being mocked by those who had succeeded in life. The upshot of all this was clouds of resentment in a working-class demographic that is often well armed.

In other countries—Sudan, Fiji, Sri Lanka, Syria and Iraq—I had observed how societies could spiral into unimaginable violence. It was difficult for me to imagine such an unraveling at home, but it was not impossible. In a way I had never imagined at the beginning of my career, I now felt that reporting on international crises helped me better understand my own country and the risks it faced.

36

Politics? "Don't Do It"

Portland had once been a model of urban planning, and in 1992 *The Atlantic* had published a story extolling the city with the headline "How Portland Does It." But it now seemed a model of how not to run a city. When officials couldn't figure out what to do, they announced ten-year plans meant to make a problem disappear. In 2004, for example, Portland adopted one such plan to eliminate homelessness; it sounded good, but ten years later the problem was worse than ever—and then it truly deteriorated. Tents were everywhere in Portland: on sidewalks, on grassy medians between highway lanes, under bridges.

Some 22,000 Oregon schoolchildren lacked homes, the Education Department reported. Crime surged as well, so the homicide rate in Portland in 2022 was fifteen per 100,000 inhabitants, compared to less than five in New York City. Criminals in Portland sometimes operated with impunity, raiding stores and walking out with merchandise. Friends had cars stolen, and we grew wary of parking at the Portland airport for fear that our car's catalytic converter would be stolen, a common problem.

This wasn't just a Portland issue, or just an Oregon problem. Up and down the West Coast, from San Diego to Seattle, homelessness had become worse, despite vast sums allocated to address it. All three West Coast states seemed to be bungling housing policy and public safety, in ways that undermined living standards and the quality of life for everyone.

Oregon ranked near last in the country for access to mental health services and addiction treatment, and this in turn affected children. I believe that education is the best metric for where a society will be in a quarter century, and we were struggling. Oregon had the third-lowest high school graduation rate in the country, and one study found it had worse K–12 outcomes than Mississippi.

Governor Kate Brown was stepping down, and there was no obvious successor. A small group of Democratic leaders and business leaders, desperate for improved governance, suggested I run.

In the journalism world, that idea is almost heretical. The Society of Professional Journalists offers this advice for journalists considering involvement in politics: "Don't do it. Don't get involved. Don't contribute money, don't work in a campaign, don't lobby, and especially, don't run for office yourself."

Then again, I had committed multiple heresies in my career. Some—such as my annual giving guide—had become orthodoxy. I didn't have any hankering to engage in politics, but I did admire some journalists who had taken the plunge into activism or politics. My old *Crimson* pal Bill McKibben left journalism to lead a movement to address climate change, and I applauded his passion and determination to make a difference. Between journalistic work, Michael Gerson worked in President George W. Bush's White House and helped nudge into existence the PEPFAR program on AIDS that has saved millions of lives. Samantha Power, a co-conspirator in the journalistic battle against genocide in Darfur, went to work for Barack Obama and later Joe Biden, keeping a focus on humanitarian issues.

I consulted former Democratic governors and others active in Oregon politics. This was a new world for me. I thought about the politicians I had come to know, and it was a smaller group than you might think. I didn't spend all that much time in Washington, which was already full of newspaper columnists, and I never attended the White House Correspondents' Dinner. I figured I was needed more in other places.

As a class, with many exceptions, politicians did not particularly impress me, but there was tremendous variability. The best example of a politician whose impact I saw in a tangible way was Franklin Roosevelt, even though he died fourteen years before I was born. Not only did his New Deal build my high school as a public works project, his rural electrification program transformed rural America by bringing power to farms like ours. And of course Social Security meant that poverty and hunger were no longer common for elderly Americans. People in Yamhill, including us, were significantly better off because of his presidency.

I often interviewed foreign leaders, and the conversations were sometimes just bizarre. Turkish president Recep Tayyip Erdoğan tried repeatedly to persuade me, an Armenian, that there had been no genocide against the Armenians—and he kept coming back to it. Aung San Suu Kyi of Myanmar tried to tell me that the Rohingya minority didn't exist. Hamid Karzai boasted in his Kabul office how safe Afghanistan was, after I had gone through more security checks than to enter the White House. Wang Qishan of China offered an "interview" and then gave introductory remarks that took up the entire forty-five-minute session, so I didn't have a chance to ask a single question.

In my foreign travels, the people who impressed me the most were often the social entrepreneurs who had started organizations to tackle problems in creative ways. Bangladesh produced two great ones, Muhammad Yunus of Grameen Bank and Fazle Abed of a poverty-fighting group called BRAC. Pakistan produced Malala Yousafzai, who campaigned for education and was braver and more inspiring than any Pakistani president I met. Indian politicians were often corrupt and demagogic, but a man named Bunker Roy started "Barefoot College" to train illiterate villagers. Ela Bhatt founded India's Self-Employed Women's Association to mobilize more than 1 million impoverished women. Haiti has had a series of forgettable presidents, but Father Joseph Philippe is a priest there who founded the country's largest microcredit organization, Fonkoze, lifting huge numbers of villagers out of poverty.

In the United States, there were politicians I sought out and admired. I periodically met with Senators Dick Durbin and Chris Coons, whom I considered policy wonks, and I knew and admired Oregon's senators, Ron Wyden and Jeff Merkley. An Oregon congressman, Earl Blumenauer, spoke at Oregon Boys State when I attended at age sixteen, impressed me ever since with his mastery of policy, and used his position to call attention to a range of neglected issues—sometimes by nudging me to write about them. (He now provided excellent advice about running for office.) Bill Clinton had a canny sense of how policy and politics interacted, and Barack Obama was smart and a deeply honorable president. I particularly admired Jimmy Carter for his work that I've described.

Some of the political leaders who had impressed me the most had been British. Former prime minister Gordon Brown wasn't as suave or articulate as Tony Blair, but he was deeply committed to creating a more just society—and world. After he was deposed, he worked tirelessly to advance female literacy in South Sudan and other remote parts of the world. Two other British politicians who never became prime minister—Chris Patten, the last governor of Hong Kong, and David Miliband, the foreign minister—represented the gold standard of leadership. Both were brilliant, pragmatic and committed to using their oratorical skills to give voice to those who lacked their platform. China denounced Patten as a "prostitute" and "villain for 1,000 generations," but he held firm in standing for democracy and restored British honor in Hong Kong. Miliband was edged out for Labour Party leader because his own brother ran against him, but he went on to lead the International Rescue Committee and become one of the world's most eloquent spokesmen for refugees.

What I learned from these leaders was the importance of being proactive rather than always reacting to events. I noted in them a strong moral compass; they consulted widely but navigated their own course. They also used the bully pulpit that comes with public office not just to address issues already being debated but, more important, to elevate their concerns onto the agenda. Often these were not particularly controversial issues, and this made them easier to achieve. Finally, they dug deeply into the evidence about the best policies to achieve their goals, listening to critics as well as advocates. They were pragmatic about finding practical steps to build a coalition of support. I had absorbed these lessons in crafting my columns and, ex officio, in my own efforts to tackle genocide, human trafficking, denial of women's rights and other issues. That was how I had met several of them, and I listened carefully to their strategic analyses of how to build public will for change.

One lesson from watching American politics was that the greatest innovation and creativity were often at the state and local level. The federal government was so polarized and constrained by checks and balances that it was usually difficult to conduct bold experiments. In contrast, states were the laboratories of democracy: Blue states rolled out liberal projects (like all-mail voting and relaxed drug laws), and red states tried conservative approaches (like loosening gun laws and tightening access to abortion). If one wanted to tackle national problems, the proving ground was now at the state level.

That's why another leader who shaped my thinking was closer to home: Tom McCall, a former journalist who served as the liberal Republican governor of Oregon when I was in grade school and high school. McCall may be among the greatest Oregonians ever, as *The Oregonian* once concluded, for he cleaned up the Willamette River and was a pioneer in his concern for protecting beaches and the environment more broadly. There were a couple of lessons that I took from McCall.

First, McCall grew up in rural Oregon, and his familiarity with both rural and urban areas helped him understand and lead the state. He helped bridge the urban-rural divide in a way that is desperately needed today. I wondered if my farm background might also be an asset in governing, or if I would be dismissed by rural voters as an elitist and globalist. I was frustrated that the Democratic Party was losing rural voters; this started with white working-class voters and was now spreading to Black and brown communities, especially Latino voters. I thought Democrats too often came across as condescending to such voters, disrespectful of their faith, and too quick to preach to them rather than listen to them. I hoped that in Oregon we might provide a model for how to reach some of those voters, many of them culturally conservative, and work with them on improving our collective well-being.

Second, McCall used his journalistic background and formidable communications skills to rally the public behind his goals. He had never been elected to the legislature and didn't see his role as tinkering with legislation, but rather he framed a vision for the state and then won people's support for that vision in a way that created a more durable path for change. Could I do something similar with my communications background?

Still, as I looked at McCall's career, the lessons were mixed. Much of his impact was achieved in his earlier role as a journalist when he highlighted the filth in the Willamette River, and his time as governor was consequential but not always pleasant. He was mortified when he suffered prostate cancer and newspaper readers were given details about the treatment, including amputation of his right testicle. "One ball McCall," he ruefully called himself. Coverage of his son Sam's bouts with addiction were also wrenching for him to endure. Then when he ran for a third term, this great man was soundly defeated in the Republican primary—a final humiliation. Did I want to invite such scrutiny and humiliation on myself and my family?

There were other good reasons not to run. I loved my job in journalism, and I felt I was effective at using it to place issues on the national agenda. President Biden phoned me about a column I had written while I was mulling all this (I didn't tell Biden that I was thinking of diving into politics), and I reflected that I might have less influence on the White House as a governor than as a columnist. Larry Summers, whom I had known since he was an economics tutor at my house at Harvard, was also skeptical of a run, saying, "There are lots of governors, but you have a platform that is really unusual and significant."

William Safire, a former columnist with a sharp wit, once was asked if he would take the job of secretary of state. Safire responded with puzzlement: "Why step down?"

Then again, others I consulted were enthusiastic. There was a yearning for new ideas and new leaders who might shake up the establishment and bring fresh blood and new ideas.

I had two threshold questions: First, could I win? Second, if I won, could I govern effectively and make a difference on issues I cared about? I worried about this second question because I didn't have political experience. I didn't know the legislators and county commissioners around Oregon. I wasn't steeped in state policy. I was an outsider, and while this might have political advantages, I worried that it might impair my effectiveness if I became governor.

The political insiders I consulted took different views of that. Some agreed that it was a minus not to have political experience and a network. Others thought it would be easier to start with fresh eyes. But whatever their views, they mostly thought that Oregon could benefit from someone outside the political class to shake things up.

"A governor isn't the ninety-first legislator," one business leader told me. "What a governor needs to bring to the table is vision and leadership."

The backdrop was Trump's assaults on the democratic system. I had been urging young people to get involved in the political system and work for change, and now I wondered if it wasn't my turn to walk the walk. For all my love of journalism, I had always thought there was something to Teddy Roosevelt's "Man in the Arena" speech: "It is not the critic who counts; not the man who points out how the strong man stumbles, or where the doer of deeds could have done them better. The credit belongs to the man who is actually in the arena, whose face is marred by dust and sweat and blood; who strives valiantly; who errs, who comes up short again and again."

But what if I quit my job, ran and lost? I figured that even with an all-out effort, there was only about a 50/50 chance that I would become governor. Teddy Roosevelt had some advice on that score as well, saying of people seeking public office: "If he fails, at least [he] fails while daring greatly, so that his place shall never be with those cold and timid souls who neither know victory nor defeat."

37

My Hat in the Ring

O ne question I immediately faced was whether I was even eligible to run for governor. The Oregon constitution stipulated that a governor had to have been a resident for three years prior to the election. The phrase in the constitution had never been defined. I had had a home on the farm in Yamhill since we built an extension on the house in 1994, and I had been managing the farm and paying taxes in Oregon. We had been spending more time on the farm since 2010, when my dad died, and especially since 2018, when we pulled out our cherry orchard and began Kristof Farms as a new cider and wine business. During the pandemic, we socially isolated on the farm. Yet I also had lived in the house in Scarsdale and had the job at the *Times.* I had paid taxes in New York for years. Unhelpfully, I had registered to vote in New York and had voted there as recently as 2020 (I switched at the end of 2020). In practical terms, I was a dual resident of both states, qualified to vote in either. So was I eligible to be governor?

We consulted ten leading Oregon lawyers, including several who had served on the state supreme court, and the consensus was that there was some ambiguity but that on balance I qualified. "Residency" clearly didn't require physical presence in Oregon, they noted: A senator may have a home in Washington, an ambassador or soldier may live abroad, an astronaut might be in the International Space Station—yet they could still be Oregon residents and eligible to run. So residency meant something like having a home, paying taxes and operating a business, and I met all three tests.

Lawyers also said that courts and secretaries of state preferred not to exclude candidates but to leave any uncertainties for voters to resolve at the ballot box. Indeed, Oregon's secretary of state, Shemia Fagan, allowed a Republican candidate to run for governor in 2022 even though he had testified in court the previous year that he lived mostly in California, and even though as late as March 2022 he was still apparently using a California address while making political donations. Likewise, Fagan's office did not even investigate a complaint that a Democratic legislative candidate did not reside in the district and was thus ineligible to run.

Legal experts did warn us that Democratic insiders might try to have me tossed off the ballot by going through Fagan, because she was part of a network backing a rival candidate. But they were confident that ultimately we would prevail.

Sheryl and I talked it over, and I discussed the idea with Gregory, Geoffrey and Caroline. "Go for it," Geoffrey urged. After weeks of discussion, that's what we decided to do. I had told just two people at the paper that I was thinking of running: A. G. Sulzberger, the publisher, and Katie Kingsbury, the opinion editor. To avoid any conflicts, I had stopped writing columns. Now I called A.G. and Katie and told them that I was going ahead—quitting a job I loved for a very uncertain political campaign. If I failed, I had no idea whether the *Times* would take me back or whether I'd be regarded in the news industry as politically tainted. I felt as if I was stepping off a gangplank into the unknown. But it also felt like something I should do. So after thirty-seven years as a *Times* journalist, I took the leap.

MY GUARDIAN ANGEL in Oregon politics was Carol Butler, a longtime political strategist in Portland who knew everyone and became my campaign chair. Our first challenge was to develop strategy and assemble a top team. James Carville, whom I knew from appearing with him on Bill Maher's show, peppered me with astute advice ("Keep saying 'Oregon can do better. This is not the best we can be'"), and veterans from the Obama and Clinton campaigns helped with staffing.

For consultants, we brought in Anson Kaye and Danny Franklin, both eminent figures in national campaigns, as well as Robert Gibbs, who had worked in the Obama White House.

You'd think that after interviewing presidents and senators for decades, I might have figured interviews out, but I was quite incompetent with the tables turned. In one of my first interviews, with the *Willamette Week* newspaper, the first question was a softball: Who are some of the people giving you advice? I didn't want to give their names without getting their permission, so I hemmed and hawed and struggled. I was awful.

One problem was that I tried to answer tricky questions, instead of sidestepping them. Carol and the team coached me on dodging questions: I had been frustrated for decades by politicians evading my questions, and now I was advised to mimic them.

The team also had to rein in my tendency to be a policy nerd. I had spent years studying how to tackle problems like education and homelessness. Keynes had written in 1924, "All the political parties alike have their origins in past ideas and not in new ideas." I agreed and was full of new ideas and evidence of what works to address problems, so I was eager to throw in references to randomized controlled trials, plus the experience of jurisdictions around the country from Houston to New York City.

"No!" Carol ordered. "Not New York City! Never use a New York example." Right: If you're accused of being a New York carpetbagger, that's not the best city to cite.

"Tell stories," Carol urged. "Talk about people you know who have been homeless. You have friends who are struggling in a way that is not true of other candidates. So tell those stories."

Carol was so aghast at my proclivity to bumble questions, and sometimes even answer them, that she brought in Kristen Grainger, a former communications director for Governor Kate Brown. Kristen in turn reeled in Melissa Navas, a former first-rate journalist who had served as press secretary to both Governor Brown and her predecessor, John Kitzhaber. The campaign manager was Margaret Jarosz, who had managed campaigns around the country, and her deputy was Michaela Kurinsky-Malos, a twenty-four-year-old prodigy who had already managed two statewide races in Oregon.

The team thought I was so awful at answering media questions that we went through hours of "media prep," which consisted of the group grilling me with questions like "You say you love Oregon—so why did you live in New York?" "You point to problems around the state, so you think that Governor Brown has failed?" "You say you're going to release your taxes, so why not just hand them over right now?" "Why not start by running for county commissioner and getting some experience?" "You've written enthusiastically about private sector labor unions, so you hate public sector unions?" "How can you manage a state when you've never managed anything?"

After each answer, the team would dissect my response and suggest a better one. Sometimes we would argue over just how evasive I could plausibly be, or what was witty versus what was insulting. When we workshopped questions about management experience, I wanted to say rather pompously that I had been weekend editor of *The New York Times* and had served on the boards of Harvard University and the American Association of Rhodes Scholars. From my point of view, all this had given me more management experience in world-class organizations than my rivals.

"You can't mention the word 'Harvard,'" one of the team emphasized. "Too elitist."

"Never say 'Rhodes Scholar,'" counseled another.

Anson Kaye and Danny Franklin, both fine writers, crafted an alternative answer that was much better than my own:

> It's true: I've never run for elected office in my life. I'm not a lawyer, a lobbyist or CEO. Of course, these are the kinds of people who have been running our state for decades. If you like where we have ended up, you should vote for someone else.
>
> I don't offer any of those things. What I offer is a lifetime spent standing with people who have been elbowed aside by their governments the world over, and doing everything I can to help make their lives better, no matter who might stand in the way. That's who I am, and it's something I've dedicated my life to . . .

In some ways, the craft of connecting to voters turned out to be not so different from the challenge of connecting to readers. "Tell stories," Carol kept advising, and I began doing that. I told of my old No. 6 school bus in Yamhill, and how one-third of the kids who rode the bus with me were now dead from drugs, alcohol, suicide and other "deaths of despair." I told of Mike Stepp and how he had just passed away on the streets of McMinnville. And I repeated Carville's mantra that this was not the best that Oregon could be.

Since I didn't want to be accused of being an elitist carpetbagger, I had to be careful about my wardrobe. Caroline's boyfriend had given me a Harvard rugby sweatshirt that I used on my morning runs, but now I stowed it in the closet. For a laptop bag, I had used a World Economic Forum shoulder bag from Davos. But carrying a Davos bag did not make me a man of the people.

I rarely mentioned my international reporting and tried to focus on Oregon. But I was peeved when I got questions suggesting I was too polite and might have trouble wrangling legislators and lobbyists. "Look, I've negotiated with warlords holding me at gunpoint," I replied, exasperated. "I've held my own with a mob carrying heads on pikes. If I can deal with warlords, a legislator will be a piece of cake." That went over well. Exasperation breeds authenticity.

So in my talks around the state, I reverted to my comfort zone of storytelling. I talked about a friend of mine who had relapsed during the pandemic and had overdosed seventeen times and been revived each time with Narcan. Once she overdosed in the morning and was rushed to the hospital emergency room. On being discharged in the afternoon, she immediately shot up in the hospital parking lot and had to be bustled right back into the ER.

Then one evening at home, I browsed Facebook and saw that this friend had just posted: "Well everybody, I tried. And I failed. So I'm pretty sure there's only one way out. My family deserves better than what I can do for them. So I'm checking out."

I put aside policy and politics to scramble to help a desperate friend. In the end, she was okay. She had written that message as a cry for help, and then gone to sleep. A thought nagged me: Was I exploiting my friends' suffering for selfish political purposes? I wrestled with that.

I also worried about the political ramifications of some of my friendships. What if people learned that I had sent money to the prison account of Bobby Stepp as he served a life sentence for raping a child? What if another friend, who can be violent when high, killed someone and it came out that we were buddies? Explaining that I was trying to help him into recovery would have sounded lame.

In the end, I concluded that campaign storytelling wasn't any more exploitative than journalistic storytelling. Rather, it was a chance to lift issues onto the agenda and generate political will for better policies. Putting a human face on these issues might help well-heeled Oregonians understand the dysfunction and desperation in working-class communities. So I spoke on the campaign trail about my school friend Stacy, who froze to death while homeless, about the woman working in a supermarket in Lincoln City who lived in her car because she couldn't afford housing, about a friend who was pregnant and using drugs because treatment wasn't sufficiently available.

On the trail, I came across a story that devastated me, and I shared it. An immigrant single mom was trying to give her two children, a girl in elementary school and a boy in middle school, opportunity in life. The mom left home at 4:30 a.m. daily to work as a maid and didn't return until 6:30 p.m., but she couldn't afford to rent an apartment. She lived in Beaverton, where 99 percent of rents are more than $1,000 a month, and the only housing she could afford to rent was a closet-sized garden shed for which she paid $650 a month. The shed had no plumbing, heating or electricity, but the owner ran an extension cord from the adjacent three-bedroom house (which was rented out to twenty-one immigrants each paying $250 a month) and allowed the family to get water from a garden hose. The toilet was a bucket.

The children couldn't bathe, developed lice and smelled. Other children teased them, and the daughter attempted suicide. Child welfare authorities were summoned and removed the children from this mom who loved her children. It's easy to blame the landlords, but it seemed to me the fundamental problem was our collective policy failure that led to a shortage of 110,000 housing units in Oregon, and consequently to stratospheric rents. In many other states, the mom would have been able to rent a studio apartment for $650 a month, but not in Oregon. We failed her and her children. That's the human face of policies that are grounded on good intentions but not on evidence.

I talked often about the lack of hope. I talked about the loneliness in rural areas, about the dysfunction that has led one in seven prime age men to drop out of the labor force. These are difficult pathologies to talk about honestly, but I've seen throughout my career how often we bungle policies toward problems that are difficult to discuss. Domestic violence. Mental illness. Drugs. Anything to do with sex.

After a talk, people would come up and shake hands. Very often someone would lower his or her voice and say something like *My sister is addicted. She's on the streets.* Or *My son died last year of an overdose. Our family will never recover.* At one talk, a woman came up to me and told me that she had been on my No. 6 bus in Yamhill a few years after me. She was doing fine, but her brother was addicted and homeless.

It was staggering how many families were touched by substance use and mental health issues, but stigma kept people from talking about it. I think if we could speak more openly about these issues, we'd have smarter and more compassionate policies. Anti-gay hostility began to melt once people came out of the closet and straight Americans realized that they had close friends who were gay, though this process is far from complete. If people came out of the mental health and addiction closet, maybe we could similarly achieve wiser and more compassionate policies.

Maybe one reason politicians are prone to scandal is that politics nurtures narcissism. I discovered, to my horror, that suddenly it really was all about me. When your circle is incessantly talking about you, and about how great you would be for the state, it helps to have people around you who will deflate you when necessary. Sheryl and the kids took on this responsibility.

ONE SURPRISE TO ME was that the campaign professionals had little regard for journalism as a driver of votes. I had assumed that my contacts in journalism and my large social media following would be a huge help. But the professionals said that the real driver was "paid media" (advertising) rather than "earned media" (interviews). "It's all about paid media," one said. "That swamps everything else. A good article can help a little bit, but the real impact of news coverage is when you say something dumb. Then there's a huge downside."

If I wasn't great at interviews to get earned media, I was also quite incompetent at paid media. We filmed several ads with Anson Kaye, one of America's best makers of political ads, and I figured it would be easy to look into the teleprompter and read. But instead of looking sincere, I looked like a deer in the headlights. When I was doing approximately the fortieth take of one script for an ad, I asked Anson about his work with President Obama. How many takes did Obama require for an ad?

"Oh, he sometimes needed a second take," Anson said. "Now, can you do this one more time, Nick? And with real feeling?"

Paid media, of course, required fundraising. Lots of it. That's the most humiliating part of running for office. I never yearned to be rich until I ran for office; then I dreamed of being a zillionaire and forgoing all this begging. We did have an edge, though, because I had many readers across Oregon and the country who had read my columns and books for decades and trusted me. We soon had a torrent of small donors, and Elizabeth Wilson, our experienced finance director, put me to work calling larger potential donors in my network.

"Hi, Bob, how are you? This is Nick Kristof. I haven't seen you since the last reunion. . . . Yeah, I'm running for governor here in Oregon. . . . You saw that in the paper, great! . . . Yes, as a Democrat! You didn't think I was a Trumper, did you? . . . Oh, you back President Trump? I didn't know that. . . . No, Bob, Democrats aren't Communists. . . . Bob, you know I'm not a Marxist. . . . If you could spare a contribution for old time's sake. . . . Two bits? You mean $2,000? . . . Oh, you mean 25 cents? . . . Well, Bob, never mind. See you at the next reunion."

I was incredibly lucky that I had generous friends and classmates who not only donated large sums, but also brought in their friends to donate as well. Boy, was I grateful. Even so, it's awkward to ask people for money. One of the most unpleasant parts of running for office is seeing a three-hour chunk on the day's calendar for "call time"— meaning that Elizabeth would give me a long list of names and numbers and I'd hound them for donations. What's worse, the names had amounts of suggested asks.

"You can't just ask for a donation in general," Elizabeth explained. "You have to ask for a specific amount. So if you think you can get $2,500, you ask for $5,000." That felt presumptuous, telling people not only that the best use of their money was a donation to my campaign but also that it should be $5,000. Yet when I asked other political professionals, they said that Elizabeth was exactly right. They also said Elizabeth was right when she tried to limit me to only six minutes a call. "The quicker the call, the more calls you make, the more money you raise."

Lots of calls went nowhere. But to an astonishing degree, people came through. Some *Times* readers had been relying on my philanthropic suggestions, and they trusted me even though I didn't know them.

"I'll donate," said one. "I've already put in hundreds of thousands of dollars to causes like obstetric fistula that you recommended."

I quickly became the state's first Democratic candidate to raise $1 million, in just a month. In Oregon, where there aren't many big donors, that fundraising won political credibility. So did some of the donors. Bill and Melinda Gates each donated $50,000, and Angelina Jolie put in $10,000. The Rhodes Scholar community contributed significantly, as did my Harvard class.

There was a certain awkwardness in a campaign that championed programs for left-behind Oregonians getting large donations from out-of-state financiers and technology zillionaires, so I was grateful that my single biggest donation was $75,000 from the United Food and Commercial Workers, the largest private sector union in Oregon.

I was deeply moved by some of the support. Liu Xiang, the Chinese student we had helped escape, now is an American citizen and donated $5,000. Sheryl gently discouraged him, noting that this was a lot of money for his budget. "I want to donate," he said. "Nick saved my life." John Thornton, chair emeritus of the Brookings Institution, donated $50,000, urged his network to help, and flew out to Oregon to cheer us on. My old traveling buddy Michael Gisser, a retired Skadden, Arps lawyer, provided a vast amount of free legal help. My former Oregon congressman, Les AuCoin, pledged monthly contributions. And so it went, with endless numbers of people writing checks or helping in some other way.

To raise money from small donors, we needed to hire a fundraising company that would hit people up with emails and direct mail. "You're going to have to do some soul searching," an experienced politician explained to me. "The most effective fundraising emails are the yuckiest. They're full of capital letters and demands to SEND MONEY NOW!!! or the world will end. Those emails sound like crazy people shouting from the street corner, but they do actually raise more money. So you can send nice, sober emails that you're proud of, or you can send trash and raise money. Up to you."

We compromised. We hired a firm that sent out two fundraising emails a week, which seemed too many to me ("I don't want to spam my followers!") but seemed woefully inefficient to the experts. ("You should send out emails at least daily!") The firm pillaged my own writings to craft the emails, and I reviewed any that went out over my signature, sometimes toning them down. OR WHEN MY MESSAGE WAS ALL CAPS, I made it lowercase.

The emails worked. Much of the money was from out-of-state, but there was also a huge response from within Oregon from people tired of the status quo. We almost immediately had more Oregon donors than the other Democratic candidates put together.

The money was rolling in. But now I had to prepare for another kind of incoming: the attacks from all directions.

38

Navigating a Campaign

I was used to verbal attacks. When I wrote about abortion rights, I'd be accused of being a baby-killer. If I criticized Israel, I was an antisemite. Even so, I was taken aback by the savagery of the discourse once I leaped into politics. Particularly on Twitter, the insults reached new levels of excoriation.

The hostility toward politicians felt relatively new. As a kid, I had admired many politicians: Bobby Kennedy symbolized something grand about America, something larger than ourselves. Some of my Oregon childhood heroes were politicians, including Senator Wayne Morse and Governor Tom McCall.

Much of that respect seems to have evaporated. Political leadership in America has become divorced from moral leadership, so we turn now for inspiration to sports figures or movie stars or Instagram celebrities. As I felt gusts of angry invective—including from swarms of young people disenchanted with all of politics—I reflected that we journalists helped nurture that disillusionment; as H. L. Mencken wrote, "Journalism is to politician as dog is to lamp-post."

When *The Oregonian* listed the one hundred greatest Oregonians of all time, not a single politician elected statewide from the last quarter century made the list. Instead, the contemporary figures were sports figures, business tycoons and pop culture celebrities (including one *New York Times* columnist, whose public approval may have plummeted when he ran for governor). I dreamed of reversing that disenchantment a wee bit, using my communications experience to provide some vision that could unite a core of voters and make politics seem more honorable. Alas, when I saw my Twitter feed become a cesspool, I wondered if that was naïve.

A vicious circle is at work. With politics less appealing, fewer good people want to seek elective office. I saw acutely the sacrifices that public officials make, and I became particularly impressed by those serving as state legislators—a thankless task that paid poorly yet attracted people deeply committed to forging a better state. I now feel like hugging every state legislator and county commissioner I meet.

Beyond the venom on Twitter, my campaign faced resistance at various levels. Some public officials were resentful: *We've been working in the trenches at low pay for years, and now you come vaulting in and want to run for governor?* While my outsider status helped overall, many voters were suspicious of my ties to Oregon: *Yes, you grew up here, but that was decades ago. You sent your kids to school in Scarsdale, New York. What do you know about fixing Oregon's problems?* A retired reporter at *The Oregonian* warned that I sounded like "a cocky know-it-all."

I also faced skepticism from those in the progressive left in Portland who were hostile to business. I believed in holding businesses accountable, but I didn't see capitalism as inherently evil and wanted companies to be part of the solution. I argued that Oregon should try harder to attract investments in semiconductors, clean energy and other sectors.

Frankly, I was also fed up with some elements of the woke left in Portland and their excuses for leftist violence. One day anarchists from Antifa and rightists from the Proud Boys had a shoot-out in Portland, reminding me of Yemen. Antifa and Black Lives Matter protesters periodically smashed windows of businesses and also of the Boys and Girls Club and other service organizations that primarily helped people of color. The violent protesters for racial justice were overwhelmingly white; one young man arrested for smashing windows at the Oregon Historical Society (which had a display about Black history) was a white Reed College senior from New York.

"I've always considered myself a good liberal," a woman who had helped start a shelter for troubled youth in Portland told me. "But those protesters smashed our windows and we had to close. I'm furious at them."

"Defund the police" gained currency with Portland's left, and in

June 2020 the Portland City Council chopped $15 million from the police budget (the city council restored the money the next year). This meant the disbanding of police units working in schools, investigating gun violence and patrolling public transit. While Portland homicides set a record, the number of sworn police officers fell to a three-decade low. Black neighborhoods were caught in a vise, for Portland police had an unmistakable history of virulent racism. But efforts to create accountability led Portland officers to retire or resign, often moving to suburban departments, and there were indications that some officers engaged in work slowdowns. Black neighborhoods suffered disproportionately from both racist policing and from cutbacks in policing.

Liberals and progressives need to face the blunt fact that in the places we govern, Portland included, there is a gap between our values and our outcomes. The number of Black homicide victims rose from eleven in 2019, the year before the police budget cuts, to thirty-nine the year after. These were hard issues that weren't easily addressed by ideological slogans. At an evening meeting with a large group of Portland leftists, I tried to make the point that the metric of progressivism should be progress—higher reading scores, more kids going to college, lower homicide rates, less racial inequity, fewer homeless people. Slogans are fine, but shouting "Housing Is a Human Right" does not actually put a roof over anyone's head. What's needed is more housing, better mental health and addiction services, and a thousand other interventions.

I argued that we needed to restore public safety in Portland to bring back tourists and shoppers, and I said that protesters who smashed windows, however great the cause, were simply making matters worse and helping to elect Republicans. Afterward one woman scolded me.

"I just wish you could show more compassion," she said, "for the people who are smashing the windows."

Sigh.

I am also skeptical of the progressive impulse to address problems by revising terminology. There are times when it makes strategic sense to change our wording. I avoid the term "gun control," because it's an instant turnoff for millions of Americans, and instead employ "gun safety." I likewise find it easier to win over centrists by talking less about "inequality" and more about "opportunity" (one poll found that 97 percent of Americans favor policies to boost opportunity). Yet in recent years the impulse on the left has been to offer an explosion of new terms. In Portland, some officials suggested that "homeless" was an insensitive term and that people should use "houseless." My homeless friends didn't get that; what they wanted was housing, not exhausting new terminology.

LGBT to *LGBTQIA2S+*. *Pro-choice* to *freedom to decide*. *Women* to *people with uteruses*. *Latinos* to *Latinx*. *Ex-felon* to *returning citizen*. *Mothers* to *birthing people*. I inhabit the world of words, and I grew dizzy. While the aim of changes in terminology is to become more inclusive, the result is often to be more exclusive. The linguistic tinkering works for some educated elites but bewilders working-class voters. It also sets up more hurdles to feeling part of a cause; people must know the right code words or they may feel unwelcome. Educated white people use the word "Latinx," but only 3 percent of Latinos prefer the term. Ritchie Torres, an Afro-Latino Democratic member of Congress, put it to me this way: "It's worth asking if the widespread use of the term 'Latinx' in both government and corporate America reflects the agenda-setting power of white leftists rather than the actual preferences of working-class Latinos."

I also worried that the linguistic contortions embraced by highly educated liberals antagonized the 62 percent majority of the country that lacked a college degree and that resented being told to change their nomenclature. When *The Lancet* medical journal tried to avoid dehumanizing trans people by referring to "bodies with vaginas," many women felt dehumanized. I heard from an ICU nurse in Idaho who was told to ask each patient for their identity: male, female, both or neither. Some patients were bewildered, others offended or hurt. The nurse told of the unintended effect on one patient: "One woman, post hysterectomy with complications, burst into tears and said, 'I hope I'm still a woman.'" The concern about stigmatizing trans people is legitimate, but overreach seems to me a gift to hard-right Republicans who campaign against wokeness; it's a self-inflicted error by Democrats.

The use of this language also sometimes seemed to me performative more than substantive, not so much a spur to action as a substitute for it. When the American Medical Association put out a fifty-four-page recommendation for "equity-focused" language, all I could think of was that if the AMA really cared about equity, it would stop opposing single-payer health care. Meanwhile, West Coast cities like Portland had some of the most sensitive terminology for people who were homeless, and yet some of the country's highest rates of unsheltered homelessness. I wished we put less effort into renaming problems and more into solving them.

Race has become a crucial prism through which to see the world for liberal whites (more than for African Americans, polling shows), and there's some logic to that. Today's inequities are deeply rooted in historical ones, and social science research shows that many people who believe in racial equality perpetuate racism. The sociologist Eduardo Bonilla-Silva has called this "racism without racists," and it reflects unconscious racism all around us. It's easy to denounce white supremacists, but what's more complicated is overcoming the attitudes that lead a white male executive to favor a white male junior executive, or a first-grade teacher to punish a Black child more severely than a similarly disruptive white child. Well-meaning liberals may endorse greater racial equality while still favoring local school financing, minimum lot zoning laws and legacy admission for universities—policies that benefit affluent whites and hurt low-income Black people.

The prism of race is useful if it starts difficult conversations, for you simply can't discuss inequality in America without considering race. Yet you also can't think deeply about inequality in America without looking at class. You likewise can't have a serious conversation about poverty without contemplating family structure: Isabel Sawhill of the Brookings Institution calculates that the rise of single-parent households since 1970 has increased the child poverty rate in America by 25 percent, yet liberals have often been reluctant to talk about family structure for fear of seeming racist or appearing to blame the victim. Even worse, some progressives oppose using the word "poverty" and recommend "oppressed" or "systematically divested." But how do you chip away at a problem if you can't talk about it openly?

One reason for liberals to talk more about class and opportunity is that there's abundant research showing that arguments win less public support when they are based on race. Even priming people to think about race makes them less empathetic overall: Telling Americans about racial inequity in the criminal justice system leaves them less supportive of reform. This is deeply frustrating, but we have to learn from it.

"Precisely because America is a racist society," Barack Obama wrote when he was in law school, "we cannot realistically expect white America to make special concessions towards Blacks over the long haul." A more effective strategy, he urged, is to "use class as a proxy for race."

One of the passions of the left, drawing partly on Ibram X. Kendi's book *How to Be an Antiracist*, has been the primacy of outcomes, not intentions. The idea is that if a policy leads to racial inequity, then it doesn't matter if the policy wasn't meant to be racist. By that standard, West Coast progressivism has done poorly. We made cities unaffordable, especially for people of color. We let increasing numbers of people struggle with homelessness, particularly Black and brown people. By 2021, Black people in Portland were being murdered at the rate of one per thousand per year, a higher rate than in other major cities notorious for violence. We reallocated education dollars to teaching about racism, but only 26 percent of Black third graders in Oregon are proficient at reading, compared to 53 percent of whites.

I don't fully agree with Kendi. I think intentions and framing can matter, but it's absolutely true that good intentions are not enough. What matters is improving opportunities and quality of life, and that's achieved not by waving fists and shouting slogans but by a painstaking process of following evidence, building coalitions and solving problems.

I HAD APPROACHED politics believing it was dysfunctional. I found that it's worse than I had thought. Oscar Wilde reportedly quipped that "God, in creating man, somewhat overestimated his ability"—and that seems particularly true of *Homo politicus*. The dependence on money gives great weight to large donors and means that candidates spend time with the people who least need help.

I hadn't appreciated the degree to which the political system also amplifies the power of older people. The median age of a primary voter in the United States is fifty-nine. The median dollar comes from a political donor who is sixty-six years old. This helped me, a sixty-two-year-old candidate, but it's bad for America. When I met groups of potential donors or voters, they mostly were too old to have children in the school system and their concerns were naturally those of retirees and soon-to-be-retirees. If you want to understand why America systematically underinvests in children, it has a good deal to do with a political system that magnifies the power of the elderly.

Richard Hofstadter wrote in his famous essay "The Paranoid Style in American Politics" that "American politics has often been an arena for angry minds." That is far more true now than when he wrote it: The fuel in partisan races is rancor for the other side. In Democratic gatherings, there was a simmering anger at Republicans that I was expected to stoke. But I don't despise *all* Republicans. I have Republican friends, and I think Democrats need to reach out more to win over those voters in the middle who sometimes decide elections. If Lincoln, near the end of the Civil War, could aim for "malice toward none," surely we can do the same today. It's not easy to get there from here, just as it wasn't in 1865, but it helps to dial down the rhetoric and to distinguish between leaders and voters. Leaders who deny election results should be held accountable, but we should avoid demonizing voters who fall for charlatans.

People are complicated. It would be difficult to think of anyone I have disagreed with more than Sam Brownback, the former Republican senator and governor from Kansas. Sam fought abortion rights, and he cut taxes and education so much as governor that even Kansas Republicans rebelled and helped elect a Democrat. Kansans suffered deeply for his mistakes. Yet on international human rights issues, he could be heroic. He was an ally in ending the genocide in Darfur, and he did everything he could to ease the suffering of people being bombed in the Nuba Mountains and of Muslim Uyghurs facing persecution in China. There were no votes in any of that, but he had a moral compass, even if, from my vantage point, he regularly misread it.

Covering societies that have tumbled into civil war left me with a sense of foreboding about the forces that cleave us. When we think of polarization, we mostly mean the fissure between right and left, but we're also fragmented within the left, and within the right. Internal disagreement became heresy, then treachery. Republicans denounced RINOs and cuckservatives, and Trump supporters invading the Capitol during the January 6 insurrection chanted "Hang Mike Pence!" People on the left didn't propose executing each other, but rifts and cancellations were still damaging.

It is the Balkanization of everything: Institutions have been tarnished, leaders disparaged, communities and even families divided. Social capital is dissolving. Partly this is because we all have toolboxes to express anger, and because scorn and fury go viral in a way that nuance does not. Jonathan Haidt, the social psychologist, wrote: "The past ten years of American life have become uniquely stupid."

I felt this acutely as I spent the pandemic living on the farm. Many of my friends on the right refused vaccines and believed conspiracy theories that COVID-19 was created by Bill Gates or Anthony Fauci for self-enrichment. I reported from hospital COVID wards, and it was tragic to see people dying unnecessarily because they believed Fox News pundits. The left responded with indefinite school closures that were also irrational. This was particularly true of West Coast Democrats; East Coast Democrats were more inclined to follow the abundant evidence that there was no significant risk of increased infection from keeping schools open. Then-Governor Gina Raimondo of Rhode Island, a Democrat, helped lead the way.

The prolonged school closures, especially on the West Coast, were a catastrophe for students, especially low-income and Black students. Reading and math scores plunged, 3 million children didn't show up for virtual classes and were lost in the system, and McKinsey estimated that some 1 million additional students would drop out of school. The San Francisco Federal Reserve estimated that this would cast a shadow over the American economy for the next seventy years.

All this of course exacerbated the polarization in America and inspired more of the toxic debates and name-calling that make governance so hard. On Twitter we all became cutthroats. I try very hard on social media not to be mean, but it's so easy online to wield a rapier and disembowel some right-wing loudmouth to thunderous applause. Sometimes it felt as if we were all becoming sociopaths.

We in journalism have become instruments of this fury, and also victims of it, for we lost the public trust. It became much easier to be defined by what you opposed than by what you stood for, and to see every issue as an opportunity to wage a moral crusade. I was uncomfortable with that. I want to solve problems, not thunder against evil. I want to build social capital and restore trust, not dissolve it.

The failures of states to address homelessness, housing prices, crime, drugs, mental health and educational failure seemed to me to create a larger risk. Some share of voters were so fed up that they were ready to abandon the idea of liberal democracy and accept demagogic authoritarianism. That explained the appeal of Trump, but it also explained the rise of the far right in Hungary, Poland and elsewhere—even the emergence of a neo-fascist prime minister in Italy. If mainstream politics didn't make progress on the daily challenges that ordinary people face, then those people would give up on mainstream politics. What's at stake isn't just housing policy, it's potentially our democratic system.

POLITICALLY, I'M HARD TO PEG. In some areas, I'm well to the left. I deeply believe in more investments in early childhood. Similarly, I'm strongly in favor of a much broader push to improve education outcomes and high school graduation rates, plus college access. For the last six years, I haven't eaten meat, because of the cruelty often associated with factory farming. I'd like to see greater regulation on chemical safety, for companies are using us as guinea pigs as they expose us to endocrine-disrupting chemicals that may have long-term consequences, possibly including epigenetic effects in the next generation.

On the other hand, I'm a pragmatist. I want evidence—ideally a randomized controlled trial—as well as the chance to kick tires and talk to people at the grassroots before I back a policy. I'm something of a skeptic of grand plans launched at conference tables, because the real world is invariably more complex than we anticipate. Sir Isaiah Berlin taught me that. Berlin quoted Kant: "Out of the crooked timber of humanity, no straight thing was ever made." That feels so true to me. We are complicated, conflicted organisms, and solving one problem creates new ones. We're not easily reduced to race or class, and we have many ends that we aim to advance, some of them conflicting or incommensurate. That's the challenge of all who aim to build a better world.

I recognize that we have fiscal constraints and can't pay for every admirable policy. As I was preparing to run for governor, a pair of old friends were starting over after a long period of addiction. A married couple with kids, they got clean and entered recovery programs. Although they didn't have jobs, social services helped them rent a nice apartment with the rent paid for six months, and they promptly went out and bought furniture on installment plans. I visited them in their apartment to celebrate their effort to start over, and I was taken aback by the beautiful apartment and furniture.

"How are you going to keep up the payments?" I asked the husband. "Are you going to get a job?"

"We keep getting these COVID checks," he answered. "Not sure what they're for, but we keep getting them so I keep spending them."

This felt as if it wasn't going to end well, and it didn't. My friends relapsed and were unable to pay the rent. The landlord started the eviction process, but instead of leaving, they invited others to move in with them until it was an overcrowded center for drug use. One of their friends died of an overdose in the apartment. They were soon homeless, and I figured the landlord would never again take a risk on a tenant.

This kind of abuse of the system is hard to talk about. But we have to wrestle with it if we want to get policy right. My belief is that self-destructive bad choices are real (my friends agree), but that the behavior is often rooted in early childhood trauma or other problems. The husband in this case was exposed to drugs and alcohol in utero and grew up in a chaotic and sometimes violent home. Yes, my friends had agency, and some people (disproportionately girls, for reasons we don't entirely understand) can escape a traumatic past. But we need to understand that people like my friends are prone to relapse and to abuse trust. Liberal policy has to catch up with that reality—without further dehumanizing those already struggling with histories of addiction and crime.

AS PROGRESSIVISM BECAME an ideology of the educated, it distanced itself from the disadvantaged people it nominally championed. One reason is the liberal tendency to scorn people of faith, particularly evangelicals or conservative Catholics.

I disagree profoundly with evangelicals on abortion, same-sex marriage and many other issues, but I also recognize that they have been leaders on prison reform, on tackling sex trafficking and on fighting the global AIDS pandemic. I knew Chuck Colson and, despite his Watergate involvement, deeply admired his pioneering work on prison reform. The best single government policy in my lifetime was perhaps President George W. Bush's pathbreaking initiative against AIDS, called PEPFAR, which has saved 25 million lives and turned the tide of the pandemic. So if we believe in being inclusive, let's be inclusive.

In my meetings with Democratic primary voters, people wanted to talk primarily about what boneheads Republicans are. Fair enough.

But Portland was a mess, and we couldn't blame Republicans for that, because there are barely any Republicans in Portland. It was a Democratic mess.

Yet despite the mixed bag my views represent, I have no doubt about my grounding as a Democrat and as a liberal. Democratic states have a life expectancy three years longer than Republican states. Household income in Democratic states is 25 percent higher than in GOP states, and child poverty is lower. Education is generally better in blue states, with more kids graduating from high school and college. The gulf between higher incomes and better outcomes in blue states and lower incomes and worse well-being in red states is growing wider, not narrower.

All this is correlation rather than causation, but I believe one factor among many is that governance has generally been better in Democratic jurisdictions, and that's one reason I vote Democratic. But I also think we have to be relentless empiricists and acknowledge our own mistakes. Too often we embrace policies that seem more performative than evidence-based solutions to difficult problems. Oregon desperately needs to address its pathetic high school graduation rate, and instead it took $2.8 million from the education budget to invest each year in putting tampons and sanitary pads in each restroom in every school in the state—including *boys'* restrooms in elementary schools, even boys' kindergarten bathrooms.

When you're taking desperately needed funds from the education budget to supply tampons in kindergarten boys' restrooms, you're veering into self-caricature.

DESPITE THE STRENGTH of the woke left in Portland, and despite the doubts about whether I was sufficiently Oregonian, our campaign was thriving. Oregonians, including those in Portland, were desperate for fresh blood and pragmatic problem solving. However progressive you are, you get sick of finding hypodermic needles on your sidewalk. You don't want your catalytic converter stolen.

We led in the polls, and Democratic powerbrokers began to tell our team that we were likely to win the governor's race.

Our allies in state government reported that Democratic insiders backing another candidate, Tina Kotek, were putting great pressure on

Shemia Fagan, the Oregon secretary of state, to declare me ineligible on the basis of residency. Fagan had a reputation as an entirely political animal, ferociously ambitious, and my removal would reward her political allies and eliminate a potential rival in statewide races. Fortunately, three former Democratic secretaries of state stepped up and publicly asserted that I was eligible, and so did a former state supreme court justice. Fagan herself had listed me twice as a leading Oregonian in the Oregon Blue Book that she published. With her three predecessors all saying I was eligible, we hoped it would be too nakedly political for Fagan to toss me from the ballot. We were wrong.

Without asking for my taxes or other residency information, Fagan ruled that I did not meet the residency requirement. We felt the law was on my side, but Fagan certainly wasn't. Political insiders were protecting their own.

We appealed to the Oregon Supreme Court. The ruling was scheduled for the morning of February 17, so Sheryl and I were driving into Portland to give a press conference on the court ruling, feeling pretty good, having been encouraged by local experts. My phone rang. It was Misha Isaak, our top lawyer. He had previously been legal counsel to Governor Brown and had been confident that we would win, but now his voice was heavy.

"We lost," he said. The court had declined to review whether I was a resident or not. It simply said it was the secretary of state's call. Our political campaign was over.*

As I walked into our campaign headquarters, I saw homeless people camped on the sidewalk. *I'm going to be fine*, I thought, *but what about them?* The campaign staff was there, some in tears. We hugged, and I thanked everyone for giving their all. We called a press conference, and I announced that I was ending my campaign. Sheryl, beside me, looked mournful; she had served as campaign finance chair and had pulled together one of the best donor networks in Oregon history. For my part, I truly was okay. The upside of a career covering war and genocide and human trafficking is that it provides perspective on life's periodic disappointments.

---

* Fagan's career was soon over as well. In 2023, she was caught up in an influence-peddling scandal and forced to resign. Federal authorities soon launched a criminal investigation into her conduct in office, and state officials mounted a separate inquiry into allegations that she had misused her position and cheated on expense reporting. Fagan denied any misconduct. Some news coverage noted that one element of her legacy was ousting me from the ballot.

With Sheryl at my side, announcing the end of my race for governor.
Photo by Kristen Grainger.

Running for governor, however unsuccessfully, was an education and a privilege. Campaigning for votes in small towns was exhilarating and left me with renewed appreciation for grassroots democracy. I learned about politics in ways that I never could have in other ways, and I gained a deeper understanding of the messy kitchen in which the policy sausage is made. It was the adventure of a lifetime, and while most of my professional adventures involved plane crashes or gunmen, this was less scary and no less thrilling. One of the things I've loved about journalism is the constant opportunity to learn new things and develop new muscles, and running for governor was the most invigorating of workouts, building sinews that I hadn't known existed.

What to do with our campaign war chest, which still had about $1 million in it? My initial impulse was to return the sums pro rata to donors, but it turned out that this would be too complex and expensive to do. So we spent some time exploring how I might use my funds to address the challenges I had campaigned on. We looked for programs with strong evidence of impact where our funds could catalyze a much larger sum. For example, Tracy Palandjian, head of Social Finance, a nonprofit that has pioneered creative ways to address social problems, recommended a pay-it-forward job training fund in collaboration with

Oregon's jobs program. We thought we could train seven thousand people at a time for better jobs, helping them become electricians, behavioral health specialists, health technicians and more. Sheryl and I began working with businesses, unions, community colleges and foundations to see if we could set this up. Sheryl and I also worked to bring an outstanding nonprofit, Vision to Learn, to Oregon to provide free glasses to the 20 percent of schoolchildren who need them but often don't get them. Vision to Learn began to work in Oregon during the 2023–24 school year, giving children with vision problems a fighting chance of success. Glasses can make all the difference. One little boy in a Vision to Learn school who had been failing suddenly improved his scores by 81 points and was suspected of cheating. The principal interviewed him, but the little boy pointed to his glasses and explained: "I could actually read the test this time." It was an honor to use my leftover campaign funds to help children like this, and I think my donors would welcome that use of their money.

My campaign flopped in the end, so I've been asked if I am embarrassed about it. Embarrassed? Not at all. I believe in big swings, and my life has been about taking calculated risks: As a result, I've tried and failed at lots of things. In this case, I saw problems and did my best to tackle them. I'm sorry I wasted the time of volunteers and the money of donors, but I think we did elevate issues like addiction and mental health that needed to be addressed—and I would still strongly encourage all kinds of people to take a risk and run for office.

I may be the first candidate for governor in Oregon who never had a single ballot cast in his favor. But Sheryl puts it more gently. She says that this side of North Korea, I'm the only person to have had a political career and never had a single voter cast a ballot against him.

39

"To Fill a Person's Heart"

Minutes after the secretary of state booted me off the ballot, my phone buzzed. A. G. Sulzberger texted me, "If you find yourself at a dead end, please make me your first call."

I did. I love the *Times*. When Abe Rosenthal had anointed me as a *Times*man in 1984, I had never imagined I would leave except perhaps on a stretcher. My fundamental identity is as a journalist.

People did reach out to me with interesting alternative proposals. Many suggested that I run for other political office, in particular the Oregon Sixth Congressional District, my district in Yamhill. There's no residency requirement for a congressional seat, and it was an open seat weighted toward Democrats. But I worried that a junior congressman can't accomplish much, and I thought I'd have a better platform as a writer. Some reached out about university presidencies—probably because I had proven myself a good fundraiser—and foundation presidencies. One news organization was looking for a top editor and another for a columnist, and Substack also came courting.

During the campaign, I had started an infrequent Substack newsletter that I enjoyed writing, and this kind of independent journalism can be extremely lucrative for a writer with a brand. I have 2.7 million followers on Twitter, Facebook and Instagram, and if I managed over time to lure one-half of 1 percent of them to subscribe to my Substack newsletter at $7 a month, that would generate more than $1 million a year. But that wouldn't be nearly as easy as it sounds, and it would mean that I would be preaching to a self-selected choir that largely agreed with me.

I thought about these options as I worked on the farm, tending our grapes and cider apples, pondering what I wanted to do next. There's something cathartic about farmwork. I write about war or genocide, and the war and genocide continue. But if a young grapevine is dying for want of water, then I water it and it revives. Coddling moths started chewing our apples, so we released tiny parasitic trichogramma wasps that are natural predators of coddling moths, and the apples were saved. The scale may be small but the impact of one's work on a farm is visible and satisfying.

Plus, the hard cider was delicious. We entered two of our Kristof Farms ciders in Glintcap, one of the largest international cider competitions, and they both won gold medals. One was the top-ranked American cider out of more than 150 entries. Another of our ciders won a double-gold at *Sip* magazine's Northwest Cider Competition. This wasn't going to make us rich—it's still not clear if the apples will subsidize our lifestyle, or if we will subsidize theirs—and it wasn't going to solve the world's problems, but it was a chance to make a high-quality

Sheryl and me with Connie, chief security officer at Kristof Farms. The cider apple orchard is behind us. *Photo by David Hume Kennerly.*

product that we were proud of. Just as I love the artistry of good writing, I love the craftsmanship of cider-making and wine-making. With Caroline in the lead on the family business, we experimented with a co-ferment of our cider with our Pinot Noir grape skins—delicious. Caroline and her boyfriend built our cider and wine website, Kristof Farms.com, and had fun honoring my mom as matriarch and appointing our farm dog, Connie, to be chief security officer.

In the vineyard, we had two kinds of wine grapes: Pinot Noir and Chardonnay. Both kinds of grapes can be fussy and temperamental, but local soils produce some of the finest Pinot and Chardonnay around the globe—and it was thrilling to aim to produce world-class wines with our family name on the label. A Yamhill winemaker, Adam Campbell, took us under his wing, and we had our first grape harvest in 2022; we began making careful plans to release the wines in early 2024. We tasted the juice as it fermented in the barrels and marveled at the changes. All this was building new muscles but also humbling. A severe frost came along and we watched it kill some of our Chardonnay buds, and there was nothing we could do. I had never heard of spider mites, but they turn out to be microscopic eight-legged creatures that essentially suck the chlorophyll out of grape leaves so that the plants can't photosynthesize well. It was refreshing in a strange way to fret not just about national health or education metrics but also about bugs in our grapes. And as a liberal columnist, I rarely met a regulation I didn't like, but as a farmer and small business owner, I found myself outraged by regulations that seemed ridiculous and limited what we could do. That was a useful lesson in the complexity of the world, and it made me love our wine and cider initiative even more.

Still, ink runs in my blood. I wanted to tackle larger problems. The war in Ukraine was underway, and I yearned to be there, uncovering atrocities and adding to the pressure on Russia to back off. I wanted to be reporting on the growing hunger around the world, in Somalia, Ethiopia and other countries. And I was impatient to report again on people left behind in America: I wanted to visit homeless encampments and job training programs and schools and understand more deeply America's problems and how to fix them. If I couldn't tackle those problems as governor, I could do so as a journalist.

Perhaps the grass is invariably greener on the other side of the fence. In journalism, I longed for the political levers to actually do things. In the political world, I longed for the journalistic freedom to tell stories, confront my followers with difficult truths, explore policy nuances, nag people about issues they don't much care about, set the agenda and change minds.

It has been half a century since I wrote my first professional news article, as an eighth grader contributing to the *Carlton-Yamhill Review*, and journalism has given me purpose. I've come to believe that we in the news business should focus not just on problems but also more on how to fix things. I'm a backer of what's called "solutions journalism," which aims not just to highlight problems but also to illuminate paths forward. I want to empower readers to act and solve problems, and the *Times* op-ed page or homepage is the best real estate in journalism coupled with the best editors. So I called A. G. Sulzberger and said I wanted back in.

IN JOURNALISM AND POLITICS ALIKE, I've talked a good deal about my childhood friends who struggled, but I also want to note how many others are thriving. My dairyman buddy, Bob Bansen, converted the family dairy into a successful organic farm. Now Bob has passed the dairy on to a son, Kyle, and is "retired" and taking it easy—milking only twice a day, five days a week. A group of us from high school get together periodically for lunch or a walk in the hills.

There have been some wonderful rebounds. My old classmate Mary Mayor is off the streets and making beautiful birdhouses that she sells to make a living (you can find them on her Instagram page, Cheep RentBirdhouses). After years of addiction, she is now a valued member of the community. Mary looks younger every day and is a reminder that people can sometimes clamber out of their difficulties if they get love and support.

In looking at friends' trajectories, I've come to believe that we often see poverty too technically and mechanistically. Yes, of course it's about lack of income and wealth, but it's also about a deficit of purpose, of self-esteem, of belonging, of love. What may matter above all is hope.

I have hope. But there's sometimes a misperception that hope is myopic or Panglossian, a naïve faith that things will somehow work out. No, hope is a strategy to follow evidence and achieve the better outcomes that are possible if you work at it. "Hope is more like a muscle than an emotion," wrote Amanda Ripley in *The Washington Post*. "It's a cognitive skill, one that helps people reject the status quo and visualize a better way." That's the hope that led my dad through Romania, Yugoslavia, Italy and France to a new life in America. That's the hope that Desmond Tutu showed. And researchers find that people can be trained in hope to better manage problems, and that this in turn can be infectious. Just as my dad infected me with hope, I try to infect others—not with a simpleminded hope that we're all going to sing "Kumbaya" together, but a hope based on evidence and tempered by disappointment and pragmatism.

True, there are risks. We may destroy our planet through climate change, and democracy is under attack in the United States and a number of foreign countries. Yet I've seen that we can solve problems when we work at it. Teen pregnancy seemed an intractable problem, for what can one do about adolescent hormones? But comprehensive sex education and long-acting contraceptives reduced teen births in America by 75 percent. Homelessness is a difficult challenge, but President Obama cut veteran homelessness by almost half. All this is a reminder that we have solutions, however imperfect, and we have the resources; what we lack is the will.

Journalism can help muster that will. I believe with all my heart that we *can* summon will and change the landscape.

How can someone who for decades has been immersed in genocide, poverty and disease believe in progress? Because I've seen that progress. When I was a child, a majority of all humans had always been illiterate. Now we're approaching 90 percent literacy. I remember when more than 35,000 children died each day around the world from hunger, diarrhea and other causes. Now we're down to 13,000 dying daily—still horrible, but so much better.

When historians look back, I think they will identify surging well-being, health and education as the most important trend underway in the early twenty-first century. So many people now live better lives, and also get a chance to contribute to the world.

One of my friends is Sultana, an Afghan woman whom I originally met by email when she was a teenager confined to her family compound in Kandahar. The Taliban had closed schools for girls, so she had no chance to get a formal education, and she was living in one of the poorest countries in the world. She might have been destined to be one more illiterate and impoverished Afghan woman.

Yet Sultana's compound had Internet, and relatives gave her a laptop and books. She devoured them and on the Internet taught herself English. She moved on to math and science, teaching herself calculus and struggling with string theory and quantum mechanics. She reached out by email to an American professor of astrophysics, who was intrigued to get cogent questions about advanced mathematics from a teenage girl in Afghanistan who had never graduated from elementary school. He introduced her to me, and I helped her get a visa to study at university in America. That's how the world is changing, how opportunity is being created, how more people are getting a chance to make this a better world. It's the kind of thing that fills me with hope.

Hope may also have been protective in my career. Researchers have found that military combat veterans who are optimists are much less likely to suffer PTSD than those who are pessimists. Martin Seligman, the social psychologist, has estimated that pessimism is as bad for cardiovascular health as smoking two or three packs of cigarettes a day. Optimists live at least six years longer than pessimists on average. So even having seen and reported on some of the worst that the world has to offer, I commend optimism to you.

We are an amazing species. That's my foremost takeaway from a career reporting on the edge. I wrote about my plane crash in Congo, about the warlord who was massacring Hutu and detained me, but the Congolese person who has left the deepest impression on me is my old friend Denis Mukwege, a doctor who started the Panzi Hospital in Bukavu.

Denis was sickened by the rape of women and girls around him in eastern Congo. He saw so many young girls with fistulas caused by rape and grew outraged at the wounds that he was stitching up. While Denis healed the patients in his hospital, he also wanted to heal the violence, so he began to speak up against war and sexual violence. That made him an enemy of the country's warlords and president. Gunmen invaded his home and would have assassinated him except for the heroic intervention of one of his staff members, who tackled a gunman and was shot dead. The gunmen then fled. Denis eventually won the Nobel Peace Prize for his courage. Then he went back to Bukavu to stitch girls up, speak out, risk his life and make this a better world. When you think of Congo, please don't conjure warlords or corrupt officials—think of Dr. Denis Mukwege.

Denis is a magnificent human being. But he isn't as much of an exception as you might think.

Nauseating evil is often escorted by incomparable courage. Extreme challenges produce extreme strength, decency and humanism. The cruelty of apartheid produced saints like Nelson Mandela and Desmond Tutu. Tutu stood against white South Africa, of course, but in later years he also denounced genocide in Darfur and stood resolutely against fellow Black South Africans who vilified gay people. Tutu said he did not worship a "homophobic God." It was painful for him to challenge his own people, but he did so unflinchingly.

Tutu once said something profoundly simple and wise that has guided my journalism, and it applies as well to addiction in the United States as to poverty in southern Africa: "There comes a point where we need to stop just pulling people out of the river. We need to go upstream and find out why they're falling in." Yes. Tutu taught me to do more hiking upstream.

One of the things I loved about Tutu was his self-deprecating jokes, his ability to erupt spontaneously in infectious laughter that warmed hearts yet also constituted a battle cry against injustice. Somehow for a man who had endured so much, he was buoyant and optimistic. "Hope is being able to see that there is light despite all of the darkness," he said. Like so many of my role models, Mandela and Tutu lived lives braided with humility and purpose, sprinkled with hope.

WE JOURNALISTS WRITE while hunched over laptops on deadline with incomplete information while battered by salvos of lies. We must be comfortable with imperfection, because our work is full of it.

Myriad mistakes punctuate my career. I stumbled badly in my column by writing about the FBI "person of interest" whom some agents suspected of involvement in the anthrax attacks; he was later declared innocent. Likewise, I wrote about a Cambodian woman, Somaly Mam, whose claims of having been a sex slave are now suspect. In other columns, I was too credulous, or too glib, or too simplistic. I always tried never to be mean-spirited, but I regularly fell short at that. I took too many risks, putting not only myself in harm's way but those around me as well, and risking the well-being of my family if something had gone terribly wrong.

To my great shame, I've occasionally got sources in trouble. Once in a Tibetan area of China, I slipped out of a conference to do some reporting on my own, and a local man gave me a motorcycle ride. I later heard that State Security agents, when they realized that I had escaped my minders, found witnesses who had seen him give me a ride—and the police then confiscated his motorcycle. He was a good man who simply did me a favor, and he suffered for it, yet I didn't even have a way of visiting him again or paying for his motorcycle.

On another occasion during Myanmar's genocidal cruelty to the Rohingya, I sneaked past checkpoints into a Rohingya village where I interviewed a woman who had lost her child because she couldn't get medical care. I thought I had protected her, but I later heard indirectly that the authorities had tracked her down. I haven't been able to verify that and I don't know if she was punished, but I'm haunted by the fear that I inflicted suffering rather than alleviated it.

My metrics of success and failure have evolved over the years. I was deeply ambitious in school and early in my career. I worked hard to get A's, to get fellowships and prizes, to get bylines, to get to the *Times* and then get promoted to foreign correspondent and columnist. I built a résumé I was proud of. But my colleague David Brooks makes a useful distinction between "résumé virtues"—gaining a Rhodes or winning a Pulitzer—and "eulogy virtues," the deeper qualities for which a person is missed when they are gone. And as my career progressed, I became more attentive to those eulogy virtues.

What mattered to me increasingly wasn't prizes but purpose. One of the recognitions that meant the most to me wasn't a prize but Archbishop Tutu declaring me an "honorary African." When *The Washington Post* wrote that I "reshaped opinion journalism" to become more focused on human rights and social justice, that cheered me on. When I see my former assistants succeed in the profession, that's thrilling. I'm proud that one, Natalie Kitroeff, is now Mexico City bureau chief of the *Times*.

Conversely, the doubts that arise are about eulogy virtues. Am I supportive enough of Sheryl, my mom and the kids? Did I do enough to mentor young journalists as I was once mentored? Was I responsive enough to the people who reached out to me and asked for help, including those writing from prison? Was I there for friends in Yamhill who needed me? I wrote about them, but did I do enough to help them get off drugs or help their children get an education? I helped pay for funerals, but could I have done more to keep people alive?

When I was growing up, we sometimes talked in our family about the qualities we most admired. My dad and I admired people who were smart; my mom admired people who were nice. I still respect intelligence, but I've seen how education and a facility with words is often mistakenly conflated with intelligence. I've also seen "the best and the brightest" drag us into war in Iraq and display indifference to misery in working-class America, so I've come to believe that what counts isn't just IQ but also a larger intelligence encompassing empathy and the humility to recognize that one may be wrong. This was a tension that Sir Isaiah Berlin wrestled with: Humility should check our hubris without producing moral paralysis. Tutu and Mandela both achieved that, for they stood unequivocally against apartheid while retaining their appreciation of complexity and of the humanity of their oppressors.

I've served on many Rhodes Scholar selection committees, and sometimes we see applicants of dazzling intellectual wattage who are focused entirely on résumé qualities. I sometimes compare these people's perspective to a brilliant scholar's myopic analysis of a great painting—studying it only in terms of the pigments, the measurements of the canvas, its physical characteristics. There is a role for genius in the chemical analysis of a Rembrandt, but that material analysis misses the aesthetic dimension that is the essence of the painting; it neglects art, it obscures the intent of the painting, it forgets its beauty.

The parallel in the canvas of our daily lives is the need for purpose. The aesthetic of humanity revolves around purpose. That's the moral dimension to our existence. There's growing evidence from neuroscience and social psychology that finding purpose makes us happier and healthier. It even lengthens our lives. So I still admire intelligence, but I now define it as intellect that is harnessed to a larger cause—and this somewhat blurs the line into niceness.

Many of us went into journalism because it seemed to have purpose embedded in it, but I can testify that there is nothing intrinsically noble about those who go into this field. I've watched national television hosts who are always warm on camera brutally mistreat crew members. And it was said of one of my *Times* colleagues that he loved humanity and hated humans.

Margaret Bourke-White, the legendary twentieth-century photographer for *Life* magazine, showed extraordinary bravery as she documented the horrors of India's partition in 1947. One of her famous photos was of parents burying their four-year-old son after he starved to death. Yet she reportedly made the parents bury the child, unearth him, and rebury him—again and again—to get the shot just right.

That's not the norm, of course. In the television world, so many people who are radiant on camera—Ann Curry, Katie Couric, Oprah Winfrey, Judy Woodruff and innumerable others—are just as genuine, warm and decent when the lights go down. And in the print world, my entire career has benefited from great journalists looking out for me, and periodically rescuing me from myself.

Journalism is wildly inconsistent: Good journalism has never been better, yet much of punditry has rarely been so reckless. Many people who call themselves journalists—especially in the opinion world— seem to have no standards whatsoever. They hear it and they broadcast it, write it or tweet it, without any serious effort to verify the information or to be fair. Journalists have power, and some simply enjoy wielding it as a weapon. Bullying shames our profession, and so does the rush to judgment and excoriation that often characterizes opinion journalism. Readers and listeners, you deserve better.

Before I write a column criticizing someone, I call up the person. "I'm going to take a whack at you," I explain, "and I'd like to hear you out." That's a print reporter's instinct, but in the digital world that sometimes doesn't happen, and the unfairness damages the credibility of all journalism. And while I deeply believe that journalism should be infused with values, I worry that some journalists don't appreciate how risky this can be and don't fully understand that journalistic passion must also be tethered to a commitment to accuracy, decency and respect for others. That's how we build trust with an audience. My colleague Tom Friedman once told me that columnists can be in the lighting business or the heating business, offering illumination or ramping up emotions. I think we do best when shedding light. Journalism functions better as a flashlight than as a bludgeon.

THE *TIMES* HAS CHANGED more in the last half-dozen years than in the previous thirty, and this is for the better. The old communications room, with its humming telexes, is no more, and the recording room that took dictation is gone as well. Our ranks have become filled by better-educated and better-trained reporters, roughly half of whom are now women. Reporters are far more racially and ethnically diverse so that we tap a broader range of experiences (although the ranks are perhaps less class-diverse, for there are few journalists from working-class origins and few with military or conservative faith backgrounds).

We now have our own James Bond–style Q, who hands out the latest satellite phones or personal trackers or other gear. If we're going to a country like China or North Korea, we're given a dummy laptop and phone that won't give away our secrets. We may be given the latest in microphones and recording devices for a podcast, or perhaps we'll travel with a video journalist carrying drones.

I felt the degree of change after rejoining the *Times* in the fall of 2022 and traveling to Ukraine to cover the war there. In the old days, I would have just booked my ticket. Now there were several editors to coordinate with, security advisors to consult, supplies of flak jackets and helmets to borrow from. When I was traveling in eastern Ukraine near the front, the *Times* sent along a security specialist to help keep me safe along with my interpreter and driver. These were changes for the better, meant to keep journalists alive, and I welcome them; I've lost too many friends in this line of work. The curmudgeon in me can't help rolling my eyes a little, but this is one bureaucracy I welcome.

Yet for all the changes, at the end of the day our basic craft remains the same as when I began at the *Times* in 1984, or as in the time of Homer almost three millenniums ago. It's storytelling.

On that trip to Ukraine, I traveled to an area recently liberated from Russian rule. I visited several Russian torture chambers that reminded me of the human capacity for evil, but I also spent many hours with a woman who left me inspired. Alla was a manager at the gas bureau who secretly spied on the Russians during the occupation, reporting by cell phone to the Ukrainians on Russian military locations and then deleting her texts. If she had been caught, she would have been executed. In the end, the Russians imprisoned Alla but for a different reason: She was overheard making disparaging remarks about Russia, and she refused to collaborate with the occupiers. Russian interrogators stripped Alla naked and beat her with a cable, and subjected her to electrical shocks as well. For good measure, they did the same to her husband, so she could hear him scream. They raped her daily and subjected her to sexual humiliations.

Yet they broke before she did: They discovered they needed Alla to run the gas bureau, so they freed her. "I will not leave without my husband," she told them, so they agreed to free her husband as well. Once free, Alla and her husband escaped in the only direction available—into Russia. They slipped through checkpoints and finally made it out to Estonia and back through Poland to Ukraine. Alla had endured torture that would be humiliating to disclose to anyone, let alone to a foreign journalist writing for millions, yet she did so—to use the truth to hold the Russians accountable.

Alla reminded me of a truism of conflict reporting: As I've already said, shoulder to shoulder with the worst people, you find the best. The Russian interrogators reflected the human capacity for barbarity, but Alla showed the even greater human capacity for resilience, strength, courage and decency. Yes, we are an amazing species.

I verified Alla's story and published it, and I'd like to think that the power of her story helped raise the costs of Russian brutality just a little bit. This kind of storytelling—it feels like what I was made to do.

For all journalism's faults, I'd still argue that a journalist's toolbox is an ideal one with which to find purpose. Journalism is an act of faith. It is an act of hope. It is a belief that truth can be a powerful force for justice. It rests on the confidence that information and ideas can change the world. This isn't new: It's what I admired in Anthony Lewis's columns in the 1970s. It takes new forms today, for I get emails or Facebook messages from people all over the world asking me to write about some outrage—"or at least tweet about it"—because that may free someone from prison or stop the torture of a political prisoner.

Regularly I get desperate letters from prisoners serving long sentences who claim to be innocent, who beg me to investigate and give them their lives back. That's because of articles I've written about people who are unjustly imprisoned, but I don't have the resources to take on the cases of all who write. Their letters stack up, nagging at me—but also reminding me that journalism at its best offers a lifeline to the forgotten.

The reporting toolbox can feel inadequate, and I've felt painfully frustrated when writing about the Darfur genocide or even about addiction at home. But uncovering truth is a long struggle, and there is meaning simply in the effort, even if it feels like a Sisyphean project. *"La lutte elle-même vers les sommets suffit à remplir un coeur d'homme,"* wrote Camus. *"Il faut imaginer Sisyphe heureux." The struggle to the heights is itself enough to fill a person's heart; one must imagine Sisyphus happy.*

This struggle to uncover truth strikes me as more essential than ever because of America's polarization and recent efforts to undermine democracy. I've seen how countries can drift toward authoritarianism, using populist measures. Poland and Hungary have done that in recent years, and Venezuela did something similar under Hugo Chávez. In the United States, I believe the risk is not so much that people like me will be arrested and sent to Guantánamo. It would be far more subtle.

The danger is of a creeping, populist authoritarianism. It would take the form of "tightening election security" in ways that reduced voting. We would see the politicization of the civil service and United States military—imagine Michael Flynn as secretary of defense. The IRS could be weaponized to intimidate critics and judges. The broader federal regulatory apparatus would be used to punish or intimidate news organizations, unions and nonprofits that tried to blow the whistle. We might see assassinations and intimidation, along with some toleration of the use of violent groups like the Proud Boys to intimidate opponents. In a highly polarized country, it could become difficult to achieve unanimous juries needed for convictions of violent offenders— and this in turn would incentivize more violence.

None of this would turn the United States into North Korea, but democracy is a sliding scale and we could end up less like Canada and more like Hungary. We could even end up with fissures so severe, especially in the aftermath of a disputed presidential election, that they would lead to serious efforts at secession. What I've seen repeatedly in my career is that history evolves slowly for a time and then lurches. Lenin is said to have observed (it's a dubious attribution): "There are decades when nothing happens, and there are weeks when decades happen."

So much is at stake, and that's one reason journalists must not settle for being dispassionate stenographers, quoting first one side and then the other. Our foremost obligation is to report the truth, wherever it lies and whomever this offends. This is tricky to navigate in practice, but today once again—as in McCarthyism, the civil rights movement and the Vietnam War—truth must be paramount. We journalists shouldn't dispassionately observe our way to authoritarianism; we shouldn't be neutral about upholding democracy.

The hope that I've built up over a career covering war and dictatorship, genocide and poverty, spurs me on. This isn't a naïve optimism, but one modulated by seeing how much can go wrong and how horrific the consequences are when events tumble out of control. This is a scarred hope, an echo of Mandela's or Tutu's, one that acknowledges human frailty and also believes in self-efficacy and in our capacity to right wrongs and fix problems. It's a hope nurtured by seeing the defeat of apartheid and Jim Crow and the decline of illiteracy and extreme poverty, by celebrating the gains from environmental protection, civil rights movements and the empowerment of women. It's a hope that is the opposite of complacency or resignation but instead spurs action and can be self-fulfilling—if we first recognize and confront the challenges squarely, and that's where journalists come in.

I SOMETIMES LEAF through my old passports. I have two or three passports at a time, which the State Department allows with a good reason; mine was that I needed a second to collect visas before my frequent trips, and sometimes a third that was specially authorized to permit travel to North Korea. But juggling passports gets complicated. One time as I was leaving Australia, a puzzled immigration officer stared at her computer and found no record of me entering. "Oops," I said, "try this passport instead."

My passports are huge, like paperback books, for I get extension after extension stapled in at overseas embassies. My last passport had 170 pages. Browsing through old passports, I smile at the Kiribati visa stamp, for it is almost as big as the entire country. The same is true of the Cape Verde visa. An Afghan visa is a pasted photocopy because the embassy ran out of visa stamps. In contrast, Somalia is nerve-racking to visit and may barely cohere as a country, but its visa is a technological marvel with a hologram, bar code and photo of the holder. Some of my passport stamps are from countries that no longer exist, like Zaire, Upper Volta, East Germany and the USSR. And some border officers I've met didn't even have stamps.

"Vu à la sortie," seen at the departure, scrawled a customs officer on the Guinea–Sierra Leone border, followed by some illegible scribble. Or perhaps that was the Burundi-Congo border, or the Gabon–Republic of Congo border. At a remote corner of the India-Nepal border, an immigration officer named R. K. Singh dutifully recorded the location and added: "Arrival 9:20 hours, departure 9:50 hours."

These passports are incomplete records. North Korea and Transnistria don't stamp passports, and Northern Cyprus stamped a separate slip of paper. I slipped into countries like Sudan and Syria without permission to cover conflicts, and I once accidentally wandered from rural Somaliland across an unmarked border into Ethiopia. I try to avoid exit stamps from Gaza into Israel because some Arab countries bar entry if they see some indication that you've been to Israel. I cover up anything that looks as if I've been to Israel with Egyptian visa stamps that I buy at the Cairo airport. (Always buy a few extra in case you have a passport problem you need to cover up.)

After sneaking into Sudan from South Sudan, interviewing rebels in the Nuba Mountains.

Knocking on the door of a grand ayatollah in Mashhad, Iran. He granted me an interview.

All the passport stamps trigger memories. In Myanmar of canoeing into a Rohingya village to evade checkpoints and report on genocide; in Pakistan of trying to sneak *into* a prison to meet a professor falsely charged with blasphemy; in Greece of trying to identify the island that was Odysseus's ancient Ithaca; in the Marshall Islands of interviewing the country's president while he was drunk at a bar. A reformist Iranian ambassador, Mohammad Javed Zarif, gave me an Iranian visa stamp once, and then hardline security officials detained and searched me—to find evidence against me that they could use to discredit Zarif. "You are with the CIA?" the interrogator asked. "Or with Mossad? We can keep you as long as we need to find out."

Yet the threats are the exception. The security officials in Iran may have threatened me, but an Iranian family on a Caspian Sea beach took my kids and me under their wing and invited us to their nearby home, behind high walls. Then they served mojitos from their stash of illegal liquor, enveloping us with hospitality.

Friends worry for me when I travel to war zones or to places like South Sudan or Somalia. But what friends don't realize is how many local people are always looking out for me. They're people like Professor Benda in Congo, persuading a warlord to let me go. Or Magboula, the genocide survivor in Darfur who offered me her scarce water. Or the bush taxi driver in Ghana who risked his own safety to wait for me as the two soldiers robbed me.

I think of the time I was on a bus in the Algerian desert and a family invited me to get off with them at their home. We stepped off the bus in the middle of nowhere—no houses to be seen—and I worried that I had been set up. But then they led me into their burrow: They lived underground in a cave to protect from the heat, and they offered me a room and food and water to freshen up. There turned out to be an underground village of burrows, and the people were kind and hospitable as I stayed two days with them. Ever since, I've tried not to use "troglodyte" in a pejorative way.

Along with the passports I have piles of money left over from trips. Most of it is worthless: Venezuelan inflation was so great that I had stacks of bills and wondered if I could make money buying Venezuelan currency and selling it for paper recycling. The same was true of stacks of Bolivian currency in 1985 at the beginning of my career. Then there are the Iraqi dinars with Saddam Hussein's picture on them—don't try spending those in Iraq today. I have $70 worth of Tonga currency, the pa'anga, because the only currency exchange at the airport was closed when I left the country, and I haven't found any place outside of Tonga willing to trade pa'anga. If you're planning to visit Tonga, I'll give you a good rate.

In interviewing people from enormously different cultures, I learned something of the universality of the human condition. On the surface, so much appears different, especially in traditional Muslim societies where I reported. In Chad, I saw women who walked about topless but were careful to cover their hair. Yet the commonalities are even more striking. The Chadian woman is modest and would be embarrassed to be seen naked—that is, with her hair uncovered. Perhaps I overstate the "universality" of the human condition, for I've certainly come across sociopaths and sadists. But broadly speaking, I've found that whatever our gender, pigment, ethnicity, faith or culture, we're all siblings.

Some of those passports and bills remind me of lonely, jet-lagged nights in remote places, sick with diarrhea or malaria, worrying about bedbugs or scorpions or the *j'ba fofi* Congolese tarantula, and of course missing Sheryl and the kids. I telephoned or Skyped them and we caught up—for a few moments it was almost as if we were together—and then we hung up and I was still jet-lagged, feverish and lonely.

Yet that's how it is. You go, you try to get people to care, and you try not to get killed doing it.

So we talk our way through checkpoints, charm murderous soldiers, rush injured children to the hospital, and work to get readers at home to feel compassion for desperate fellow humans. Inconsistently, often ineffectively, we try to fight war, poverty and disease with our fragile tools—a laptop, a phone, a camera—and we chase hope.

me. At Harvard, my classmates at *The Harvard Crimson* taught me so much about journalism; I still remember Tom Blanton coaching me on how to write a feature profile. A Rhodes Scholar selection committee similarly upended my life by then awarding me the chance to study at Oxford. I studied law and was in some danger of becoming an attorney, so perhaps I should also thank stodgy British judges in property cases for making land law so dull that I was able to pull myself away.

American University in Cairo welcomed me as an escaped lawyer to study Arabic, and then, as recounted here, the *Washington Post* metro desk did me the favor of not hiring me so that I had to go to *The New York Times* to get a journalism job. I still don't entirely know why Abe Rosenthal hired me as a reporter in 1984, but thank God he did. John Lee, Warren Hoge and Fred Andrews gave me a series of opportunities at the *Times*, and Joe Lelyveld was a longtime coach in my years as foreign correspondent, political writer and editor. Joe set a standard as editor that has rarely been met and never surpassed.

I hope it's clear in this memoir how much I benefited from colleagues not only at the *Times* but also at competing publications, for foreign correspondents have each other's backs (when they're not knifing each other in the back). Then there are the stringers, interpreters and drivers without whom we couldn't do our work in dangerous places. I probably wouldn't be alive today if it weren't for the help of people like Professor Benda, who extricated me from gunmen in Congo. Interpreters and stringers take all of the risks and get none of the credit, but when you read stories from some war zone, remember that they make possible the stories and bylines you read.

During Howell Raines's era as editor of the *Times*, I was evicted from my role as weekend editor. I was a lost puppy, rescued by the publisher, Arthur O. Sulzberger Jr., and the editorial page editor, Gail Collins. Arthur then made me a permanent columnist, and subsequent opinion editors—Andy Rosenthal, James Bennet and Katie Kingsbury—put up with my periodic whining, experimentation and insubordination. When my political career ended ingloriously, after what seemed like ten minutes, it was the new publisher, A. G. Sulzberger, who with Katie took me back to my *Times* home. I've now worked for three Sulzbergers as publishers of the *Times*, and not only is the newspaper lucky to have had them as stewards but so is America. The *Times* is a pillar of American democracy and a public good for the world.

Acknowledgments

Perhaps the first person to thank in this journalistic memoir is Anna Bourgina, a Russian refugee and friend of my parents who for my sixth birthday gave me a toy printing press called the John Bull Printing System. My friend Thomas and I used the press to start a little newspaper, and my journalism career was born.

There were so many others who encouraged me in school and got me addicted to reading, which of course is halfway to writing. Those include librarians, teachers (Juanita Trantina, Betty Krier) and extraordinary authors like Walter Brooks, a *New Yorker* writer who in his spare time penned the Freddy the Pig series. I thought those were the best kids' books ever.

In high school, I was a journalistic troublemaker, so I owe special gratitude to the journalism teachers in Yamhill to whom I gave gray hairs, Olga Petrovich and Sue Smith. The local newspaper editor, Jeb Bladine of the *News-Register*, hired me as a part-time writer when I was sixteen and opened my eyes to the world of professional journalism. I'd thank the *News-Register* photographer Tom Ballard, but he made photography so alluring that I came perilously close to becoming a news photographer instead of a writer. Oh, to heck with it; I'll thank him anyway.

Then the admissions committee at Harvard took a chance on a farm kid from Oregon attending a small, rural high school that had never had an Ivy League applicant before. That was transformative for

At the opposite end of the power dynamic from the *Times* publisher are the news assistants, but they were just as important to my career and to making me look good. I tried to hire the very best assistants when I became a columnist and did all I could to nurture their careers—and they in turn served as editors, telling me when a column idea didn't work or when a phrase might be offensive. They also browbeat visa officers, checked facts and did their best to keep me safe. My columnist assistants have been Christina Lem, Winter Miller, Natasha Yefimov, Hilary Howard, Natalie Kitroeff, Liriel Higa, Zoe Greenberg, Gina Cherelus and Spencer Cohen. Remember those names: They will be some of journalism's brightest lights.

My hometown, Yamhill, is where my heart is. Yes, we have issues of addiction and dysfunction that I sometimes explore, but we're also a wonderful community. Check it out. Try the local produce (including Kristof Farms Cider and Kristof Pinot Noir) at Source Farms shop, or have lunch at the Larson House in Yamhill or Park & Main in nearby Carlton. Friends in the area, including Bob Bansen, Joni Marten, Lisa Jernstedt and Susan Baumgartner, remain treasured companions.

I consider myself lucky to be associated with two great institutions—*The New York Times* and Knopf publishing house—that have maintained the highest editorial standards while also finding a strong business model for quality work. For more than two decades, Knopf has been my publisher of book after book, and it is simply the best publishing company in the world today. I'm particularly indebted to my longtime editor there, Jonathan Segal, who still wields a pencil and improves every page. And then, after I file a later draft, he does it again. That just doesn't happen much in publishing today outside of Knopf. The legendary editor in chief of Knopf, Sonny Mehta, died in 2019, but the company continues gloriously under Reagan Arthur and Jordan Pavlin.

So many others at Knopf and its parent, Penguin Random House, make books like this come together by managing translation rights, audio books, marketing, art, legal rights and more. As at the *Times*, the idea is to empower writers, not rein them in. Special credit to Ellen Feldman, who oversees copy editing, and Jessica Purcell and the publicity team at Knopf. Sarah Perrin and Isabel Frey Ribeiro helped the process go smoothly. Our lecture agents at American Program Bureau have also sent Sheryl and me on the road all across America to talk about our books—and I'm sure they'll dispatch me again to speak about this one. Several of our books were made into PBS documentaries by a team at Show of Force led by Maro Chermayeff, and I'm so grateful for the exposure those documentaries brought; *Half the Sky* reached No. 1 on the *New York Times* best-seller list not when it was published but after the documentary aired.

Ever since I was a correspondent in Beijing, my literary agents have been Mort Janklow and Anne Sibbald. Mort died as I was writing this memoir, but Anne is a dear friend as well as an advisor. She and her colleagues at Janklow & Nesbit have counseled me on which books to write and how to find the best editor; it was she who led me to Jon Segal.

My friends Jayne Riew, Lisa Belkin and David Sanger read this manuscript and offered excellent advice; thanks to Lisa's prudent edits, you're not reading more about old girlfriends. Glenn Kramon read the entire manuscript and offered the kind of careful edit that made him a legendary figure at the *Times*. Rukmini Callimachi helped me get records from Romanian security agency archives about my family, and Gelu Marian Trandafir translated them. Steve Crowley turned out to have a folder relating to the plane crash we were in together in Congo and graciously shared it; he's also a great person to have next to you when your plane is about to crash.

Kudos to an Oregon State University graduate student, Katey McIntosh, who did an outstanding job as a fact-checker, constantly rescuing me from myself. Katey also provided sage recommendations on sharpening my arguments throughout.

For helping dig up photos for this book or providing permissions, I owe thanks to Robert DeGiulio, Gerry Lewin, David Hume Kennerly, Paul Andrew, Dan Esty, Tom Patterson, Naka Nathaniel, Barney Scout Mann, the American Academy of Achievement, Du Bin, Giles Clarke, Kristen Grainger, Jeff Roth, Walt Baranger and Craig Smith.

In the end, everything comes down to my family—in writing this book, and in living this life. It's tough at times to be a family member of a foreign correspondent who dashes off to distant wars or writes provocations that lead to death threats. When my children were young, there were things they had trouble understanding. When Caroline was six years old and I purchased two teenage girls from their brothels in Cambodia, a stranger stopped us on the street. "Thank you for buying those two girls," the woman told me. We walked on, but Caroline was flummoxed. "Dad," she said hesitantly, "you bought two girls?"

So a special thanks to Gregory, Geoffrey and Caroline for their patience, for accompanying me on foreign trips when they were young, for not minding when we were arrested together in China or South Sudan, for backpacking with me in the Cascades when I needed to work off my traumas, for facilitating the healing by working on the farm together to make great hard cider and Pinot Noir, and for sharing in the joint adventure of starting our Kristof Farms brand. Caroline also read a draft of the manuscript and, as a devotee of memoirs, offered excellent feedback.

I owe so much to my parents, and I hope that comes through. My dad died in 2010, but he would have loved to read this and recount his family stories. If I am at times a rogue reporter, it's in part because of the power of his life journey and the way it shaped me. I was eager to locate relatives of Robert Morisset, the French diplomat who saved my dad's life. The French Embassy in Washington and the diplomatic archives in Paris tried to help me track down his family, as did Elliot Thoral, a very talented and diligent high school student in France. Morisset and his wife died childless, and I was unable to locate any living relative. If some distant Morisset cousin is reading this, know that the Kristofs will always owe the Morissets—and will pay it forward.

As for my mom, she was always a shining example of how women hold up half the sky or more: I'm sure she's one reason I've advocated so strongly for empowering women and unleashing their ability to make the world a better place. My mom, now in her nineties, had a severe stroke as I was completing this book, but before that she read the chapters about our family.

It must be evident to anyone reading this far how much I owe the other half of my own sky, Sheryl WuDunn. Our previous books were written together, so it was strange to write one by myself. Sheryl did edit the whole book, of course, but more than that, she has edited my life and made me a better person and dad. The twists and turns of our married life have taken us in many directions—running toward gunfire in China, crawling through tunnels in Vietnam, backpacking through snow in Oregon, my running for governor—and all that is a tribute to Sheryl's tolerance for her husband. Other than a White House state dinner together with the Obamas, she hasn't necessarily relished all of our journalistic thrills together and might have preferred instead the calm of a vacation villa in Tuscany. I owe her more than I can say.

Sheryl and I ended the acknowledgments in each of our past books by disavowing the customary piety that any errors are solely the fault of the author. "Any errors," we wrote, "are entirely the fault of our spouse." This time that doesn't work. I'm on my own. Mea culpa.

Index

Page numbers in *italics* refer to photo captions.

A NOTE ABOUT THE AUTHOR

Nicholas D. Kristof grew up on a farm outside Yamhill, Oregon, raising sheep in 4-H and FFA and attending a small country school. When he turned sixteen and could drive, he began working after school as a reporter for the local paper. He graduated Phi Beta Kappa from Harvard in three years and then studied law at Oxford on a Rhodes Scholarship, winning first-class honors. He joined *The New York Times* in 1984 and spent many years as a foreign correspondent. He has lived on four continents, visited 170 countries and forgotten a number of languages.

He won his first Pulitzer Prize with his wife, Sheryl WuDunn, for coverage of the Tiananmen democracy movement in China; they were the first couple to win a Pulitzer for journalism. He became a columnist for the *Times* in 2001 and won a second Pulitzer for coverage of the Darfur genocide. He has also won an Emmy and various humanitarian prizes, backpacked from Mexico to Canada, been arrested in more countries than he can count, run for governor of Oregon, broken three hours in a marathon and produced prize-winning Kristof Farms hard cider. He continues to travel the world for his *Times* column, and *The Washington Post* said he has "reshaped opinion journalism." Kristof and WuDunn have three children who help them grow cider apples and Pinot Noir grapes on the Oregon farm, watched by elk, bear and eagles.

A NOTE ON THE TYPE

This book was set in Janson, a typeface long thought to have been made by the Dutchman Anton Janson, who was a practicing type-founder in Leipzig during the years 1668–1687. However, it has been conclusively demonstrated that these types are actually the work of Nicholas Kis (1650–1702), a Hungarian, who most probably learned his trade from the master Dutch typefounder Dirk Voskens. The type is an excellent example of the influential and sturdy Dutch types that prevailed in England up to the time William Caslon (1692–1766) developed his own incomparable designs from them.

Composed by North Market Street Graphics,
Lancaster, Pennsylvania

Printed and bound by Berryville Graphics,
Berryville, Virginia

Designed by Cassandra J. Pappas